The Health of Adults in the Developing World

A World Bank Book

The Health of Adults in the Developing World

EDITORS
Richard G. A. Feachem
Tord Kjellstrom
Christopher J. L. Murray
Mead Over
Margaret A. Phillips

Published for the World Bank
Oxford University Press

Oxford University Press

OXFORD NEW YORK TORONTO
DELHI BOMBAY CALCUTTA MADRAS KARACHI
KUALA LUMPUR SINGAPORE HONG KONG TOKYO
NAIROBI DAR ES SALAAM CAPE TOWN
MELBOURNE AUCKLAND

and associated companies in

BERLIN IBADAN

Published by Oxford University Press, Inc.
200 Madison Avenue, New York, N.Y. 10016

Manufactured in the United States of America
First printing April 1992

Library of Congress Cataloging-in-Publication Data

The Health of adults in the developing world / edited by Richard G.A.
Feachem . . . [et al.].
p. cm.
Includes bibliographical references.
ISBN 0-19-520879-X
1. Public health—Developing countries. I. Feachem, Richard G.,
1947–
RA441.5.H454 1992 92-7246
613'.0434'091724—dc20 CIP

Contents

Foreword

ALTHOUGH THE CONTROL of infectious diseases during infancy and childhood is of undoubted importance, it will not, on its own, lead to a lifetime of good health. This volume draws attention to the causes and consequences of disease and ill health in adults in developing countries and to the burden they impose not only on individuals themselves but on their families and on society at large.

The adult population is the productive sector of society. Any impairment of its capacity through disease or disability will inevitably lead to a decline in national productivity and a slowdown in overall national development. This in turn will adversely affect the health of persons of all ages within the population.

Researchers and policymakers will find that this book contains useful data on adult mortality and morbidity. However, it also draws attention to the need for more and better information on problems and risk factors.

By focusing more attention on this age group, we can hope to improve its health status and productivity and ultimately the quality of life of the entire population.

Hiroshi Nakajima
Director-General
World Health Organization

Preface

THE ORIGINS OF THIS BOOK lie in events and discussions at the World Bank in Washington in the autumn of 1988.

First, Dean Jamison, previously chief of the Population, Health, and Nutrition Division at the World Bank, had moved to the University of California at Los Angeles (UCLA) and was leading a major review of priorities for disease control in developing countries. This review already indicated that certain health conditions were being neglected in the research and policy undertaken by the World Bank and the international public health community. These conditions included some that are important now (such as cardiovascular disease and injuries) and others that are certain to become so (such as lung cancer).

Second, I had arrived in Washington to take up a post in the Population, Health, and Nutrition Division and was looking for a substantial piece of research or policy work. My original intention had been to work on a new initiative in the field of health information that would assist health sector policy formulation and resource allocation in developing countries. However, it was decided that the health information initiative was not appropriately led from the World Bank, although the task remains of the utmost importance, as this book emphasizes repeatedly. I therefore turned my attention to the neglected issues of adults and the things that kill them.

Third, and of greatest importance, elsewhere in the Bank two operations divisions dealing with the health sector in specific countries had realized that adult health, noncommunicable diseases, and injuries were important in the countries of their domain. Richard Bumgarner, working with colleagues in China, and John Briscoe and Nancy Birdsall, working with colleagues in Brazil, were already well advanced in producing substantial analyses of the health agenda emerging in those countries. It was their work that clinched the decision in the Population, Health, and Nutrition Division to undertake such an analysis with a worldwide perspective. This book is the result.

The decision to press ahead with a substantial effort rested with

Ann Hamilton (director of the Population and Human Resources Department) and Anthony Measham (chief of the Population, Health, and Nutrition Division). Their support and commitment to this subject and to this book have been total. To complete the task a team was gathered at the World Bank in Washington. It included some staff members: Kamal Ahmad, Randy Bulatao, Mead Over, and myself; and some consultants: Carlos Dora, Margaret Phillips, and Carla Willis. Also enlisted into the project from the outset were Christopher Murray from Harvard and Tord Kjellstrom from the World Health Organization (WHO), Geneva. Later on, we were fortunate to be joined by Jeffrey Koplan and Richard Rothenberg of the Centers for Disease Control (CDC), Atlanta, by Randy Ellis and Joyce Huber from Boston University, by Orville Solon from the University of the Philippines, by Gonghuan Yang from the Chinese Academy of Preventive Medicine, and by Xinjian Qiao from Harvard. This team was assisted by a number of scientists around the world who made substantial specific contributions. These contributions are all noted at appropriate points in the book, but special mention must go to Alan Lopez at WHO, Ian Timaeus at the London School of Hygiene and Tropical Medicine, and Dean Jamison at UCLA.

The team worked on this book for more than two years. It has been a stimulating and educational experience. The team had three particular features. It was international, with persons from Australia, Bangladesh, Brazil, New Zealand, the Philippines, Sweden, the United Kingdom, and the United States. It was multidisciplinary, with specialists in economics, epidemiology, demography, environmental health, and medicine. Above all, most members had no prior track record of work on this particular subject. If the reader feels that there is any merit or originality in the analysis and interpretations contained here, it is to this last feature of the team that I would draw his or her attention.

A number of specialists reviewed parts or all of the manuscript, some on several occasions, or made other specific contributions. We are most grateful for their assistance. These specialists include the four anonymous reviewers commissioned by the World Bank's Publications Department, together with Peter Barss, Alan Berg, Nancy Birdsall, Jose-Luis Bobadilla, John Briscoe, Richard Bumgarner, David Dunlop, Willy de Geyndt, Julio Frenk, Fred Golladay, Davidson Gwatkin, Jacques van der Gaag, Jeff Hammer, Ralph Harbison, Gail Harrison, Ishrat Husain, Ann Kern, Timothy King, Jo Martins, Tom Matte, Henry Mosley, Philip Musgrove, Charlotte Neumann, Gretel Pelto, Helena Restrepo, Gordon Smith, Michael Strong, Stephen Thacker, Anne Tinker, and Frederick Trowbridge. Review meetings were held in Atlanta, Geneva, and Washington, and we are grateful to CDC, WHO, and the World Bank for organizing these and to all the participants for their comments.

Particular mention should be made of the role of WHO in this subject and in support of this book. In the past two decades, only WHO has been working consistently on chronic diseases, smoking, and injuries in the developing world. The programs may have been underfunded, but the subjects were kept alive in international forums, and useful work was done. Individual WHO staff have assisted in the production of this book; among them, Tord Kjellstrom was a member of the authorship team, Alan Lopez provided substantial support to the mortality analyses, and valuable assistance was received from E. Chigan, R. Henderson, M. Jancloes, C. Romer, and K. Stanley. The successful implementation of the recommendations contained in this book will depend to a considerable extent on the leadership that WHO is able to provide.

A special note of appreciation is due to Rebecca Schilling of Corporate Science, Inc., Atlanta, Georgia, whose editorial hand has guided the production of this book throughout its gestation. Additional editorial, administrative, and secretarial assistance in the production of this book were most ably provided by Helene Shovlar and Paula Stanley in London and by Zarine Vania in Washington.

Contributors

Rodolfo A. Bulatao	*World Bank, Washington, D.C.*
Randall P. Ellis	*Department of Economics, Boston University*
Richard G. A. Feachem	*London School of Hygiene and Tropical Medicine*
Joyce H. Huber	*Health Economics Research, Waltham, Massachusetts*
Tord Kjellstrom	*World Health Organization, Geneva*
Jeffrey P. Koplan	*Centers for Disease Control, Atlanta, Georgia*
Christopher J. L. Murray	*Harvard School of Public Health*
Mead Over	*World Bank, Washington, D.C.*
Margaret Phillips	*Health economist, Mexico*
Xinjian Qiao	*Harvard School of Public Health*
Richard B. Rothenberg	*Centers for Disease Control, Atlanta, Georgia*
Orville Solon	*School of Economics, University of the Philippines*
Carla Willis	*Abt Associates, Cambridge, Massachusetts*
Gonghuan Yang	*Institute of Epidemiology and Microbiology, Chinese Academy of Preventive Medicine, Beijing*

1. *Introducing Adult Health*

Richard G. A. Feachem, Margaret A. Phillips, and
Rodolfo A. Bulatao

THE OBJECTIVE of this book is to stimulate discussion, research, and action on the topic of adult health in developing countries. Nearly 90 percent of children in developing countries survive to be adults, even in some of the poorest countries of Sub-Saharan Africa (Feachem and Jamison 1991), due to substantial reductions in child mortality. Too many of these adults still die relatively young. In Africa, 38 percent of fifteen year olds do not survive to see their sixtieth birthdays. Among the survivors, many suffer from chronic impairments, frequent illnesses, and injuries. The ill-health of adults imposes a major burden on health services as well as large, negative consequences on families, communities, and societies. Demographic trends have had the effect of increasing the absolute and relative importance of adults and their health problems. Nevertheless, policy development in the area of adult health is weak, and the research necessary to support sound policy decisions has been neglected. This book seeks to place adult health firmly on the agenda of health policymakers and researchers.

The need for this book, and for the heightened analytical attention to adult health that it advocates, derives from the current imbalance between resource allocation in the health sector and understanding of health needs and solutions. Sick adults consume a very substantial proportion (often more than half) of health sector resources in developing countries. Yet the nature of their health problems remains poorly understood, and policy in both the curative and preventive subsectors is rudimentary. Throughout the developing world, tuberculosis, cardiovascular diseases, cancers, and injuries are major causes of adult ill-health. Yet each is, in various ways and for different reasons, seriously neglected in research and policy. In the absence of improved understanding and policy in the area of adult health, expenditure on the treatment of sick adults can be expected to grow rapidly, as it has in the developed world. Much of this expenditure may be inappropriate in the sense that there may be alternative investments that would produce greater benefits to public health.

These alternative investments may lie in alternative adult treatment, in the prevention of adult disease, and in child health. More efficient resource allocation may also arise from better targeting on particularly disadvantaged groups within society. The efficiency and equity of the allocation of health sector resources, concerns which permeate this book, demand better understanding and improved policy formulation. It is necessary to get an intellectual grip on adult health to redirect and control the runaway juggernaut of expenditure on adult health.

The chapters of this book document the nature and extent of adult ill-health in developing countries. No new data were collected. Existing mortality data were reworked extensively to provide a new picture of the levels, trends, and cause structure of adult deaths. Several unpublished sources of data were brought together to reveal that the current understanding of adult morbidity is poor. Disparate strands of evidence on the consequences of adult ill-health were compiled to help quantify the burden adult ill-health places on families, communities, and societies. Any treatment of a new topic that relies on data collected largely for other purposes requires sound judgment in the interpretation of such data. One objective of this book is to encourage specific research on adult health, and the authors acknowledge that the results of such research may modify some of their conclusions.

This book is intended for a broad readership, including researchers (in health policy, health economics, demography, epidemiology, and public health) and health policymakers in developing country governments and in development agencies. To serve this wide readership, the authors have tried to keep the use of technical jargon to a minimum and to explain methodological complexities fully. Material about underlying relationships and patterns—which will be of most interest to the research community—is presented together with practical guidance about future directions and priorities for action for all developing country governments to consider. This book stops short, however, of a comprehensive analysis of options for improving adult health, and readers should not expect fully justified prescriptions for action. The aim is to document the problem, to suggest priority areas for research, and to point to some hopeful avenues for policy and action. Subsequent research and programmatic experience will allow the formulation of comprehensive adult health policies.

The Scope

Much of this book documents the burden of adult ill-health in the developing world. Chapter 2 analyzes the overall level and specific causes of adult mortality, chapter 3 presents data on adult morbidity, and chapter 4 explores the social and economic consequences of adult morbidity and mortality. Chapter 5 moves beyond measuring the burden to identifying some of the key determinants of adult ill-health in the developing world and the types of intervention strategies that could modify these determinants and improve adult health. Chapter 6 summarizes the conclusions of the book, identifies areas for future research, and proposes a set of cost-effective options in primary and secondary prevention, case management, and palliation for developing country decision makers to consider.

This book uses a broad definition of adult ill-health that includes all major adult health problems, be they communicable, noncommunicable or injuries. Productive discussions about adult health and ill-health have been slowed by divergent views about what *adult health* means. For some, adult health means controlling chronic diseases. For others, adult health is mainly a concern of relatively wealthy countries. For still others, adult health implies a focus on urban elites rather than rural masses. For some, adult health suggests prevention, whereas for others it implies sophisticated curative technology in secondary or tertiary hospitals. Adult health, as used in this book, embraces all major health problems of adults. It includes the poor and the wealthy, the urban and the rural, the employed and the unemployed, men and women. It concerns not only diseases experienced by adults, but also childhood exposures to risk factors for adult disease. This embracing view helps to identify adult health priorities and appropriate corresponding policies.

The Age Focus

This book defines *adults* as those aged fifteen through fifty-nine years, *children* as those younger than fifteen years—either preschool (nought through four years) or school-aged (five through fourteen years), and the *elderly* as those aged sixty years and older.[1] The categories we have chosen are, like any others, somewhat arbitrary, but have several advantages. Adults, aged fifteen through fifty-nine years, include nearly all those in society who are economically productive, biologically reproductive, and responsible for the support of children and elderly dependents. Preschool children continue to receive substantial attention from the international public health community. School-aged children are a distinct group in terms of their health problems and the opportunities to reach them with preventive programs.[2] The elderly, sixty years and older, have their own distinct health problems, are more likely to be dependent than to have dependents, and are a group for which premature death becomes increasingly difficult to define and for which health goals are concerned more with the quality of life than its prolongation (Fries, Green, and Levine 1989). Adults are not a homogeneous group, and some of the analyses in this book distinguish younger (fifteen to thirty-nine years) from older (forty to fifty-nine years) adults. Younger adults are more at risk from maternal ill-health, injuries, and alcohol and drug use. Older adults are more likely to suffer from cardiovascular diseases and cancers.

The danger in using any set of age categories is that of forgetting that all adults were once children, that most will become elderly, and that the concern should be for the health of individuals throughout their lifetimes. Where current understanding permits, this book addresses the lifetime nature of health status. For example, the causes of adult ill-health that originate during childhood are discussed. Several interventions to improve adult health target children. Such interventions include hepatitis B immunization and education about sexual behavior, tobacco use, and dietary habits. Just as experiences in childhood can affect adult health, what happens during the adult years can have important repercussions for the elderly. The classic example is tobacco. Data presented in chapters 5 and 6 demonstrate that although tobacco is an important cause of adult ill-health, it is of even greater importance for the elderly, and the recommendations made in chapter 6 for reducing tobacco use among adults have important implications for the elderly. A separate but related intergenerational dimension of adult health is the effect that adult ill-health or death has on the health of younger and older family members (chapter 4).

The age-based analysis in this book has the potential to generate an unproductive debate about the equity of investment in adult versus child health. Such a debate is unproductive because the policy decisions that need to be made are not a matter of choosing between different groups of people—they are the same people at different ages. Poor children, who suffer excessive morbidity and mortality rates, become poor adults, who also suffer excessive morbidity and mortality rates. Given that cost-effective interventions exist to improve adult health, it is equitable to seek to preserve the health of disadvantaged adults who were once disadvantaged children.

The Disease and Mortality Focus

Much of this book deals with specific causes of illness and death.[3] Most adult mortality is due to fewer than ten major causes, and in some countries half of all adult mortality is attributable to only three causes—cancers, cardiovascular diseases, and injuries (see chapter 2). A detailed understanding of what is known and not known about these major causes of death is essential to formulating appropriate prevention and case management policies.[4]

However, focusing on diseases and injuries, and more specifically on mortality from specific diseases and injuries, has limitations. It falls short of addressing the World Health Organization's concept of positive health—a state of complete mental, physical, and social well-being. It underplays the significance of diseases whose morbidity and disability effects are disproportionately high with respect to their mortality effects, such as mental illness, osteoarthritis, guinea worm, and onchocerciasis (chapter 3). It may misrepresent the importance of several underlying causes of death, such as diabetes and malnutrition. Outcomes not related to death, but which nonetheless increase welfare, such as attentive health staff and comfortable health service surroundings, also are minimized implicitly in importance. Furthermore, the choice of disease groupings, which are to some extent arbitrary, may influence the conclusions about priority diseases.

Available data, however, present a vague and incomplete picture of morbidity problems and fail to provide any solid information on several important causes of adult morbidity (for example, mental illness). While mortality data misrepresent the importance of several health conditions, the reality is that mortality statistics represent the only continuous source of information on an unequivocal manifestation of health status (Shapiro 1977).[5]

The need to go beyond a disease-specific approach is most acute when analyzing determinants and consequences and when making recommendations for policy. Many diseases share common determinants and children become orphans when their parents die from whatever cause. To overcome the danger that a partial health picture, drawn from cause-specific mortality data, may influence recommendations for priority action inappropriately, chapter 5 pays particular attention to determinants that are likely to have major effects on morbidity and whose effects are broader than a single disease. The prominent example is tobacco use, which is a major risk factor for three groups of important adult diseases—cancers, cardiovascular disease, and chronic obstructive lung disease (chapter 5). Chapter 6 identifies prevention of tobacco use as being, partly for this reason, especially cost-effective.

This book does not emphasize health services issues such as financing, training, decentralization, or the balance between primary, secondary, and tertiary facilities. These substantial topics, which concern the whole population and not just adults, have received considerable attention elsewhere. In addition, many of the solutions to adult ill-health lie outside traditional health services. Nor does this book attempt more than a superficial analysis of socioeconomic determinants of adult ill-health and the macroeconomic solutions they imply. The authors believe that there are substantial improvements to be made in adult health through relatively focused interventions. Such interventions can be financed through reallocating, in a manner that increases equity and efficiency, the resources already expended on adult health.

The Need

There is a lack of policy explicitly addressing the major health problems of adults in developing countries, except for those caused by tropical diseases (for example, malaria) and those associated with pregnancy. This lack of policy is as acute in the World Bank and other development assistance agencies as it is in developing country governments themselves. For example, except for the World Health Organization, few agencies or governments have, or are even thinking of, policies for reducing tobacco use and traffic accidents, even though these issues may be as important for the health of developing country populations as diarrhea or leprosy.

The Adult Health Policy Vacuum

Over the past thirty years, the focus of intellectual and research activity in international public health has been in two distinct areas—tropical diseases and the health of children. Tropical diseases are not a precisely defined group, but they are all communicable and they are caused mostly by protozoan or helminthic parasites with complex life cycles. Malaria, onchocerciasis, schistosomiasis and the trypanosomiases are examples of tropical diseases that have received much attention. Some microbial infections, notably cholera and leprosy, have also been studied. The more recent emphasis on children's health in general, and on the communicable diseases of childhood in particular, has led to major advances in the case management and prevention of diarrhea, measles, polio and tetanus in childhood. Increasing efforts are now being directed to the treatment and prevention of acute respiratory infections in childhood, which are responsible for a substantial proportion of deaths in childhood throughout the developing world. In the last few years, interest has broadened to include risk factors for perinatal and maternal death, and maternal health has become a major separate focus of concern.

The origins of the interest in tropical diseases and children's health are quite different (Warren 1990). The focus on tropical diseases came from the association made in colonial times between tropical medicine and the study and treatment of parasitic diseases. The colonial powers found that the health of their expatriate civil servants and their military personnel was threatened by a group of parasitic diseases that were either of limited importance in Europe (for example, malaria) or non-existent (for example, African sleeping sickness). The private sector, influential throughout colonization, found these same diseases threatened the health of their expatriate managers and their indigenous workforce. In addition, missionary doctors became involved with caring for people with selected endemic diseases, especially leprosy. The discoveries in the late nineteenth century of the basic biology and life cycles of the important parasites of people living in the tropics created a tradition of equating tropical medicine with a particular group of diseases, mainly parasitic, which continues to this day.

The focus on children's health has a more analytic pedigree. In the 1950s and 1960s, demographers showed the horrifying magnitude of death rates in childhood in less developed countries. At the same time, epidemiologists showed that the majority of these deaths were attributable to a short list of communicable diseases superimposed upon a background of low birth weight, malnutrition, and environmental squalor. This led to strategies for improving children's health by immunizing against selected diseases, reducing exposure to environmental and behavioral risk factors, and promoting selected cost-effective approaches to case management. More recently, better documentation of the magnitude and nature of maternal illness and death has stimulated a parallel concern for the health status of mothers. With the exception of malaria, the diseases principally responsible for the high sickness and death rates of children and their mothers are not those traditionally equated with tropical medicine.

Tropical diseases and children's health have not only dominated thinking in the academic and research community over the past thirty years, they have also influenced the strategies of development agencies and developing country governments profoundly. Development agencies, particularly bilateral and non-governmental agencies, have concentrated their efforts on tropical diseases, children's health, and maternal health. Developing country governments, while emphasizing the overall development of health services, have tended to target these same areas through special programs. This strong focus has been both appropriate and effective. As a result, the incidence of some tropical diseases and the rates of child death in developing countries have been reduced greatly.

However, a large and obvious gap remains—namely, adult health problems that are not caused by tropical diseases and that include the following:

- Cancers
- Cardiovascular diseases

- Chronic obstructive lung disease
- Diabetes
- Injuries
- Sexually transmitted diseases (including AIDS)
- Tuberculosis.

For some of these health problems, especially tuberculosis, the epidemiology is well known and agencies have had considerable experience in case management and prevention. For others, such as injuries, little is known about their epidemiology and many developing countries have yet to initiate specific preventive measures. In general, the health problems of adults in developing countries are not understood well. Knowledge of the levels, causes, distribution, and determinants of sickness and death among adults is extremely deficient compared with the detailed information available for children. In many poorer countries even the overall level of adult mortality is not known with any certainty. Partly because of this lack of knowledge, and partly because attention has been focused on tropical diseases and child health, a policy vacuum on adult health exists within governments and agencies—a vacuum that has serious consequences, as outlined in the following paragraphs.

The Importance of Adult Health

Adults comprise more than half of the population of the developing world, numbering about 2.05 billion in 1985, or 56 percent of the population (table 1-1), and this adult population is growing (figure 1-1).[6] Even in Sub-Saharan Africa, the region with the lowest proportion, 49 percent of the population is adult. The majority of adults live in Asia and the Pacific (1.41 billion). China alone has more adults than the three non-Asian regions combined, and India has twice as many as any non-Asian region (figure 1-2).

Adult death rates are higher than generally recognized. Boys who reach fifteen years of age in developing countries have about a 25 percent chance of dying before age sixty, and in some countries this risk is over 50 percent, compared with the average in developed countries of about 12 percent. More than ten million adults die in developing countries each year. This mortality and the morbidity that inevitably accompanies it place considerable demands on health services: adults are major consumers of health sector resources.

Health risks that adults take may have deleterious effects on the health of other age groups. This can happen directly, as in the effects of maternal smoking on the fetus and the effects of other passive smoke exposures, or indirectly as a result of the important role adults play in their families. Adults form the majority of the productive

Table 1-1. Population by Broad Age Groups, World and Major Regions, 1970–2015

Region and year	Percent of population aged (years)			Population aged 15–59 years (millions)		
	0–14	15–59	60+	Men	Women	Total
World						
1970	37.5	54.2	8.3	1004	1000	2004
1985	33.7	57.5	8.8	1414	1371	2784
2000	31.2	59.2	9.6	1866	1805	3672
2015	27.5	61.3	11.2	2350	2280	4630
Industrialized Countries						
1970	26.6	59.2	14.2	299	322	621
1985	22.1	61.9	16.0	364	366	730
2000	19.9	61.7	18.4	392	388	780
2015	18.7	59.8	21.4	398	391	789
Developing Countries						
1970	41.8	52.2	6.0	704	679	1383
1985	37.5	56.0	6.5	1050	1005	2054
2000	34.1	58.6	7.4	1476	1415	2891
2015	29.3	61.7	9.1	1953	1887	3840
Industrial Market Economies[a]						
1970	26.0	59.0	15.0	196	205	401
1985	20.7	62.0	17.3	236	235	471
2000	18.6	62.4	19.0	255	250	505
2015	17.4	59.4	23.2	251	245	496
Industrial Nonmarket Economies[a]						
1970	27.7	59.6	12.6	103	117	220
1985	24.5	61.5	13.7	127	130	257
2000	22.4	60.4	17.2	137	137	273
2015	21.0	60.7	18.3	147	146	292
Latin America and the Caribbean						
1970	42.5	51.5	6.0	74	73	147
1985	37.6	55.7	6.8	112	112	224
2000	31.9	60.5	7.6	160	160	320
2015	25.5	64.3	10.2	206	206	412
Sub-Saharan Africa						
1970	44.8	50.5	4.7	73	75	148
1985	46.0	49.4	4.6	111	114	226
2000	45.1	50.4	4.5	180	183	363
2015	41.0	54.2	4.8	292	295	587
Middle East and North Africa						
1970	44.6	49.6	5.7	63	61	124
1985	42.7	52.1	5.2	101	95	196
2000	41.3	53.4	5.3	158	148	306
2015	35.4	58.5	6.1	241	229	471

(Table continues on the following page.)

Table 1-1 (continued)

Region and year	Percent of population aged (years)			Population aged 15–59 years (millions)		
	0–14	15–59	60+	Men	Women	Total
Asia and the Pacific						
1970	40.9	52.8	6.2	492	469	961
1985	35.0	58.0	7.0	727	684	1411
2000	30.6	61.1	8.4	980	925	1905
2015	25.1	64.1	10.8	1214	1158	2373
India						
1970	40.4	53.6	6.0	154	144	297
1985	39.2	54.6	6.3	217	201	417
2000	33.4	59.4	7.2	309	291	600
2015	27.4	63.8	8.7	405	383	788
China, Hong Kong, and Taiwan						
1970	39.7	53.5	6.8	237	217	447
1985	29.6	62.2	8.2	345	317	662
2000	26.4	63.3	10.2	426	396	823
2015	21.6	64.5	14.0	485	461	946
Other Asia and Pacific						
1970	44.0	50.5	5.5	109	108	217
1985	39.0	55.1	5.8	165	167	332
2000	33.4	59.7	6.9	244	237	481
2015	27.2	64.0	8.8	24	314	638

a. Throughout this book, the developed countries (or industrialized countries) are divided into those with market economies and those with nonmarket economies (the former communist countries), as listed in appendix tables A-1e and A-1f. No account is taken of recent political and economic changes in central Europe, because the data analyzed predate these changes.

Source: Bulatao and others (1990).

work force and the majority of those on whom others depend. When adults become ill or die, dependents may suffer from lack of care or from a deterioration in the family food supply or income. The effect is likely to be greater in developing countries where the dependency burden per capita is higher (0.78 dependents per adult) than in developed countries (0.61 dependents per adult).[7] Among developing countries, the dependency burden is lowest in Asia, at 0.73, and highest in Sub-Saharan Africa, at 1.02. Finally, ill-health during the adult years is probably an important determinant of subsequent ill-health as adults age and become elderly.

Not only does adult ill-health impose a substantial burden on society, but the nature of this ill-health differs in several important respects from childhood illness. Adult ill-health involves more non-communicable disease, more long-term morbidity and more disabil-

Figure 1-1. Growth in the Adult Population by World Region, 1970–2015

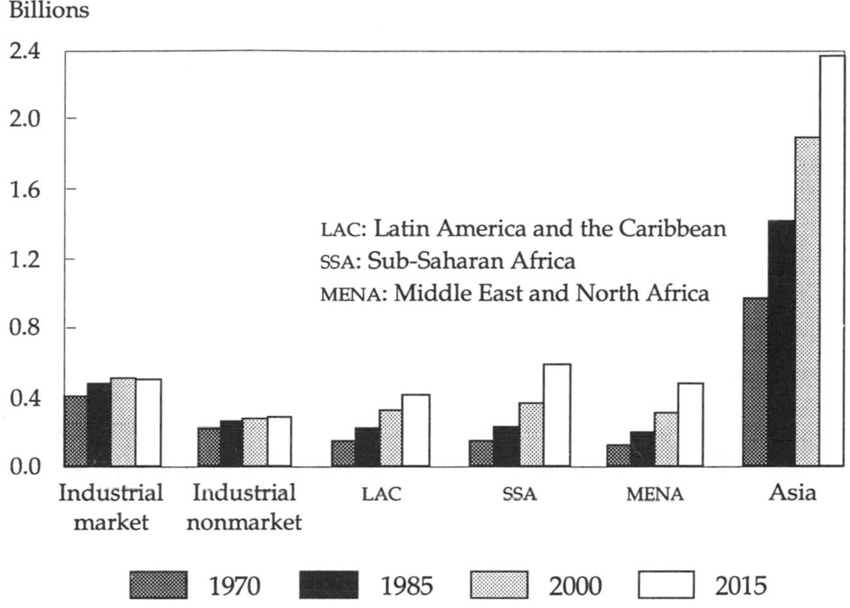

Source: Bulatao and others (1990).

ity, and is more strongly related to life-style risk factors. Because of these differences, policymakers cannot reduce adult ill-health simply by expanding policies that have been effective in improving child health.

Despite the importance of adult health, some readers may worry that this book possibly heralds a shift of attention away from the health of children. They may point out that infectious diseases and malnutrition in childhood still constitute unfinished business and that many of the factors that made it imperative to improve child health still exist: the difference in mortality rates for children in developed and developing countries remains high (and higher than that for adults as a whole); the control of several important childhood diseases is cost-effective in terms of cost per death averted and even more so when years of life saved is the measure used to assess effectiveness; adults are capable of caring for themselves and making their own choices, while children are not; and adults receive a sizeable share of health budgets already. Some may argue that the elderly rather than children or adults are the proper new concern of developing countries. The elderly are at greater risk of ill-health and often are

Figure 1-2. Distribution of Adult Population by Developing Regions, 1985

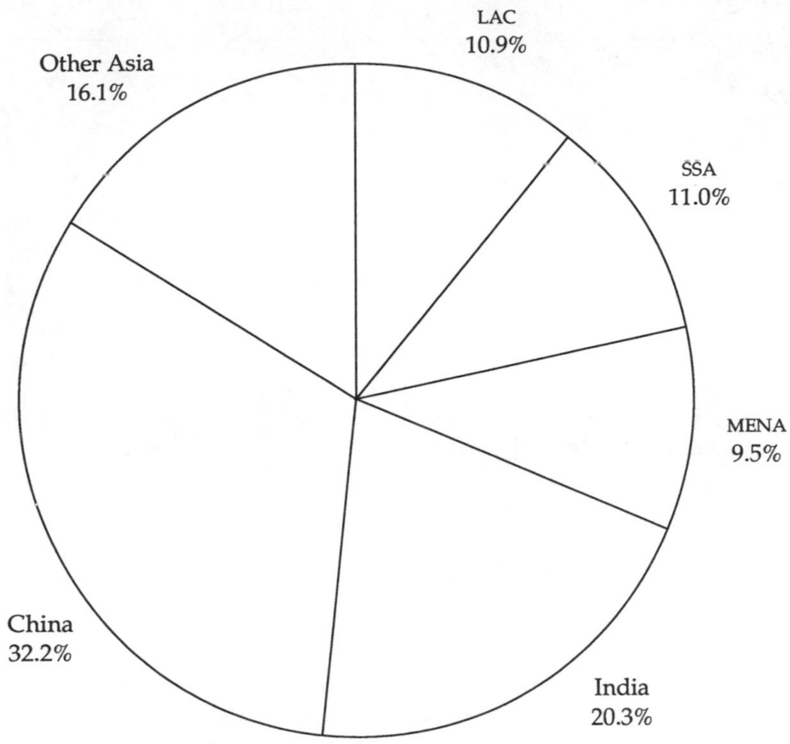

LAC: Latin America and the Caribbean
SSA: Sub-Saharan Africa
MENA: Middle East and North Africa

Source: Bulatao and others (1990).

less well served than adults by current health care systems. Furthermore, they are, as a group, growing at a faster rate than the adult population (table 1-1). The authors of this book agree with many of these observations, with certain caveats.[8] Proposing that more attention be devoted to the issue of adult health does not mean that resources should be shifted away from children or the elderly, but rather that policymakers and researchers should examine what is known and not known about adult health and decide whether current practices and resource allocations are appropriate for the health needs of this large and growing segment of the population. What is required is some careful thinking about how best to deploy the considerable resources currently devoted to adults. Indeed, the first recommendation for action (chapter 6) concerns the need to reduce investment in inefficient and inequitable treatments provided to adults.

The Changing Picture of Adult Health—The Health Transition

The health picture in developing countries is changing. Generalizing broadly, there is a shift toward a greater prominence of diseases suffered by adults and the elderly—particularly noncommunicable diseases and injuries—sometimes called the epidemiologic transition (Omran 1971). Paradoxically, this is being accompanied by a fall in age-specific death rates from some of these diseases (as shown in chapter 2). Because the picture is complex and the terminology used to explain it is not always consistent, and because an understanding of the nature of these changes in disease patterns is essential for designing effective adult health policy, this book offers a new characterization and a new terminology for these phenomena.

The phrase *health transition* is used to refer to all those changes in the levels and causes of illness and death that are occurring in developing countries and have taken place to a large extent already in developed countries. The term *epidemiologic transition* is sometimes used to describe this, but because it refers also to the more limited phenomenon of shifts in the relative importance of different diseases, it is not used in this book. The health transition is the net result of the operation of three components, not all working in the same direction: the demographic component, the risk factor component, and the therapeutic component.

THE DEMOGRAPHIC COMPONENT. The age structures of populations are changing throughout the developing world. As a result of declining fertility and mortality rates, populations are becoming older and the median age is rising. The growth in the adult population in developing countries is more rapid than the growth in the population as a whole. For example, between 1970 and 1985, the adult population grew at an annual rate of 2.6 percent, whereas the total population grew only at 2.2 percent. While these growth rates are expected to slow, adult growth rates will still be larger than for the whole of the population over the next few decades. As a result, adults will continue to increase as a proportion of the total population, reaching 62 percent by 2015, and almost doubling in number between 1985 and 2015 (table 1-1). The elderly will increase even more rapidly. Children will decline in relative importance, from 38 percent in 1970 to 29 percent in 2015. The adult population will grow fastest in Sub-Saharan Africa, at an annual rate of 3.2 percent between 1985 and 2000, with the Middle East and North Africa next (3.0 percent), followed by Latin America and the Caribbean (2.4 percent) and Asia and the Pacific (2.0 percent). Between 1985 and 2015, the number of adults will increase 160 percent in Sub-Saharan Africa, 140 percent in the Middle East, 80 percent in Latin America and 70 percent in Asia.

This aging of the population—the faster growth of the adult population compared with that of children or of the population as a whole—results in adult illness (notably from noncommunicable disease) and adult deaths becoming relatively more common. In the absence of commensurate declines in morbidity and mortality rates, the rapid increase in the number of adults will lead to rapid increases in the number of adults who become sick and who die.

THE RISK FACTOR COMPONENT. Changes in the prevalence of exposure to risk factors, and in the magnitude of the risks, alter age-specific morbidity and mortality rates. The risk factor component of the health transition influences the demographic component through changes in age-specific mortality rates, but is completely unaffected by the demographic component. It takes the form of changes in exposure to the underlying causes of specific diseases in specific age groups, such as those that accompany the development process—urbanization, industrialization, and changing life styles—as well as particular risk-averting interventions, such as vaccination and environmental sanitation. Risk factor effects are manifest in both absolute and relative terms. In absolute terms, rates of adult communicable and reproductive ill-health are declining overall (although the rates of some specific diseases are increasing, notably AIDS and tuberculosis) because of declining exposure to certain, fairly well understood risk factors. Somewhat counterintuitively, adult death rates from many noncommunicable diseases are declining also (chapter 2), although for reasons not clearly understood. Some suspected risk factors for noncommunicable disease in adults are difficult to measure (for example, certain social and psychological factors) and others remain unidentified (for example, putative viral etiologies for certain cancers). In relative terms, because disease and death rates are declining faster among children than adults, and because rates of communicable and reproductive ill-health are declining faster than rates of noncommunicable disease, the risk factor component works to increase the relative importance of noncommunicable disease and adult ill-health.

THE THERAPEUTIC COMPONENT. The therapeutic component refers to changes in the probability that an ill or infected individual will become chronically ill or die (the case-fatality rate) as a result of changes in access to, use of, and effectiveness of curative health services. As with the demographic and risk factor components, the therapeutic component of the health transition causes changes in both absolute and relative rates of chronic impairment and death. In absolute terms, improvements in modern chemotherapy reduce the rates of adult death and chronic impairment from several causes, such as tuberculosis and onchocerciasis. In relative terms, there has been generally more progress (due largely to antibiotics) in reducing communicable disease case-fatality rates than the case-fatality rates from injuries, cardiovascular diseases, or cancers. The result is that these latter causes of death become relatively more important in the absence of other changes.

The increase in the absolute number of sick and dead adults is due to the demographic component, the effects of the risk factor and therapeutic components being in the opposite direction (appendix 1-A). The relative increase in adult deaths compared to childhood deaths is caused by the demographic and risk factor components, although mainly by the former (appendix 1-A). The relative increase in certain causes of adult ill-health (notably many noncommunicable diseases) compared to other causes is due to the risk factor and therapeutic components.

Vague statements about the rising importance of noncommunicable diseases and injuries—statements that fail to clarify whether they refer to the number of deaths, proportions of deaths, or crude, age-standardized, or age-specific rates of death—have created much confusion. The analyses in chapter 2 substantiate the fact that, despite a widespread belief to the contrary, age-specific rates for many particular noncommunicable diseases and for noncommunicable diseases as a whole are declining in developing countries, while their numbers, both absolutely and relative to communicable diseases, are increasing. There is little evidence that age-specific rates of most noncommunicable diseases have risen, despite urbanization and industrialization, and the dominant cause of the increased importance of noncommunicable disease during the health transition is demographic change, combined with declining rates of communicable diseases due to changes in risk factors and therapeutic services.

Current health sector and development policies affect the health transition in several ways: they have an impact on the demographic component, accelerating the aging of the population by reducing mortality and fertility rates and increasing life expectancy; they have a complex influence on risk factors, tending to reduce exposure to many risk factors and increase exposure to others; and they lower case-fatality rates by improving health services. The relationship between development and the health transition has yet to be fully elucidated.

For policymakers, the central adult health problem is the rising absolute number of adults who are sick and dying due to noncommunicable diseases and injuries. The demands of this politically vocal group will inevitably lead to rapidly growing expenditures unless preventive action is taken. The main cause of this central adult health problem is the growth in the adult population, much of which is unavoidable during the next few decades. The main solution lies in reducing exposure to risks (thereby reducing age-specific disease rates) and lowering case-fatality rates by increasing the use of effective curative services.

The Book

This book explores the largely uncharted subject of adult health in developing countries. The authors hope it will be a provocation: a provocation to debate, to research, and to action. The chapters that follow challenge readers to accept that rates of noncommunicable diseases are falling with development (chapter 2); that adult morbidity is poorly understood and very difficult to measure (chapter 3); that adult ill-health has major consequences for children, the family and society (chapter 4); that a few specific determinants of adult ill-health—such as the global epidemic of tobacco use—are worthy of serious attention (chapter 5); and that immediate action should be taken by governments, aid agencies, and development banks to increase understanding, to develop policy, and to intervene in certain specific areas (chapter 6). The authors of this book hope it will stimulate research, analysis and policy development and lead ultimately to a strategic package of cost-effective measures for improving adult health—a strategic package analogous to that which has achieved so much for children's health in the past decade.

Appendix 1-A: Projected Changes in Adult Deaths and Their Relation to Population and Mortality Changes

The number of adult deaths in developing countries will increase substantially in coming decades. Three countries illustrate the prospects: in Burkina Faso and Pakistan, adult deaths will rise 60 percent in thirty years (from 1985–90 to 2015–20); in Zimbabwe, adult deaths will rise 20 percent in the same span (see figure 1-A1). These increases will occur despite falling mortality rates. The risk of dying between the ages of fifteen and sixty, for instance, should fall 25 percent in Burkina Faso and Pakistan and almost 50 percent in Zimbabwe. The increases in deaths will be due simply to increases in the number of adults as a result of past (and in some cases continuing) high fertility.

The exact contribution that population growth will make to increases in adult deaths can be estimated by dividing the difference between current deaths and deaths thirty years in the future into components due to changes in population and changes in mortality rates. There are two ways to perform this decomposition. The effect of different populations (and age structures) can be assessed at initial

Figure 1-A1. Percentage Change in Number of Adult Deaths (1985–90 = 100 percent)

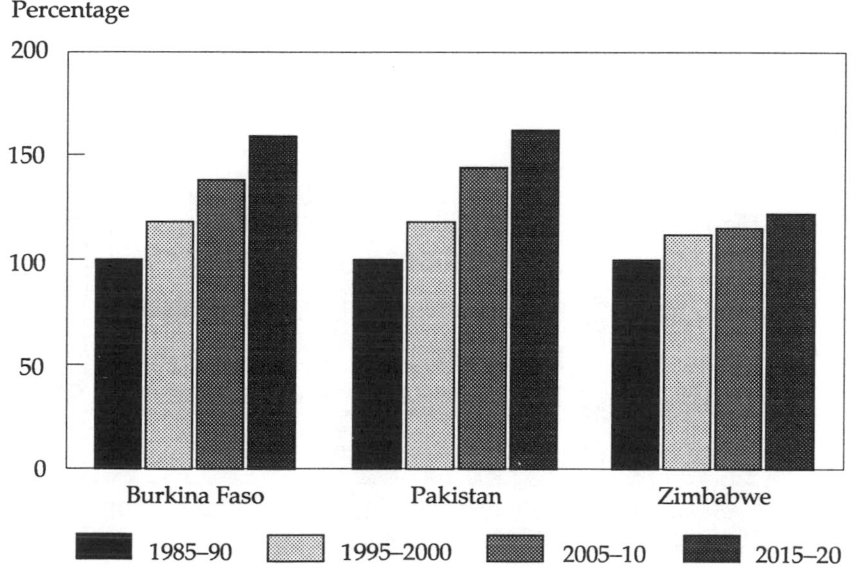

Source: Authors' calculations.

Figure 1-A2. Effects of Population Change and Mortality Change on Percentage Change in Adult Deaths, 1985–90 to 2015–20

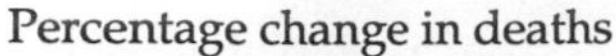

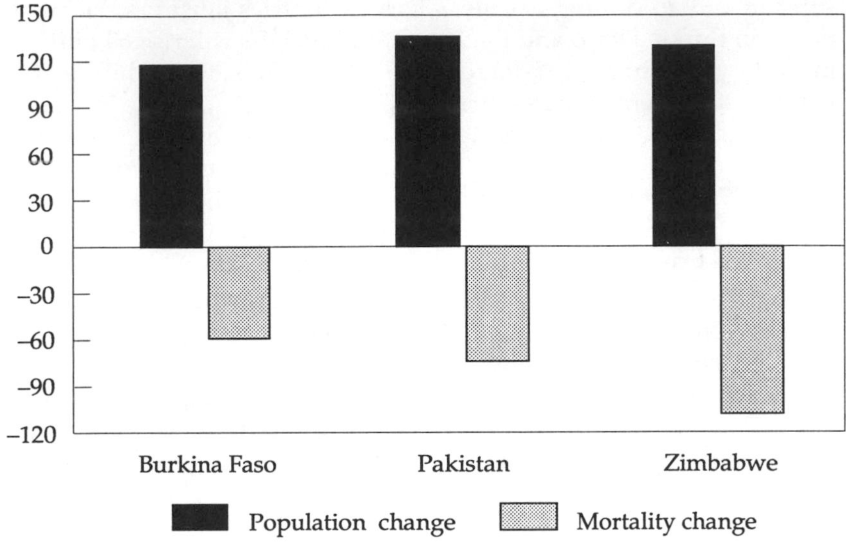

Source: Authors' calculations.

Figure 1-A3. Distribution of Deaths by Broad Age Group, 1985–90 and 2015–20

Percentage

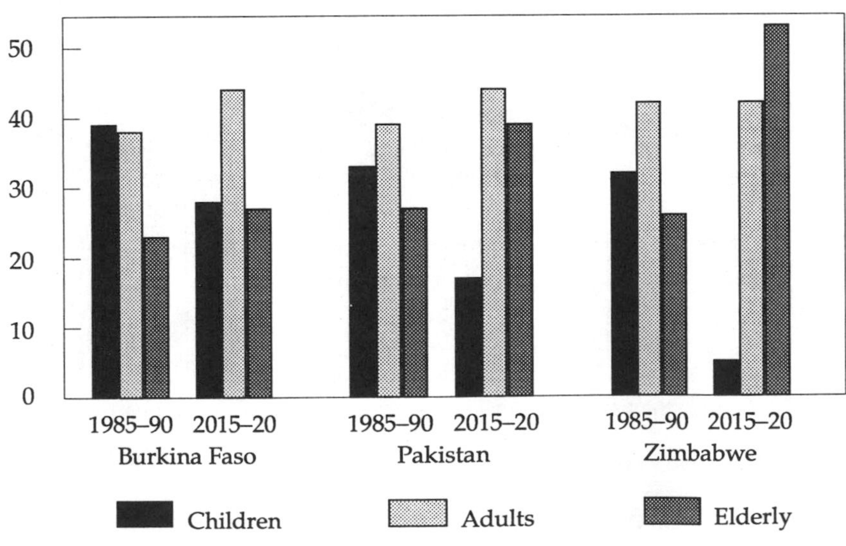

Source: Authors' calculations.

mortality levels, while the effect of different mortality levels is assessed at final population levels. Alternatively, the effect of different populations can be assessed at final mortality levels, while the effect of different mortality levels is assessed at initial population levels (Das Gupta 1978). The following paragraphs in this appendix present simple averages across the two approaches.

Population growth by itself is projected to more than double the number of adult deaths in each of the three countries after thirty years (see figure 1-A2). The effect of changing mortality rates is projected to be roughly half as large as the effect of population change in Burkina Faso and Pakistan, and five-sixths as large in Zimbabwe. In each country, this change is in the opposite direction from the effect of population growth.

As a proportion of all deaths, adult deaths should rise from 38–39 percent to 44 percent in Burkina Faso and Pakistan over thirty years, while remaining essentially unchanged at 42 percent in Zimbabwe (see figure 1-A3). With continuing declines in fertility, each of these countries should see a declining number of child deaths over this period. In Zimbabwe, this will be offset by an increasing number of deaths among the elderly: elderly deaths, 40 percent fewer than adult deaths in 1985–90, are projected to become 25 percent more numer-

Figure 1-A4. Effects of Population Change and Mortality Change on Change in Proportion of Deaths Among Adults, 1985–90 to 2015–20

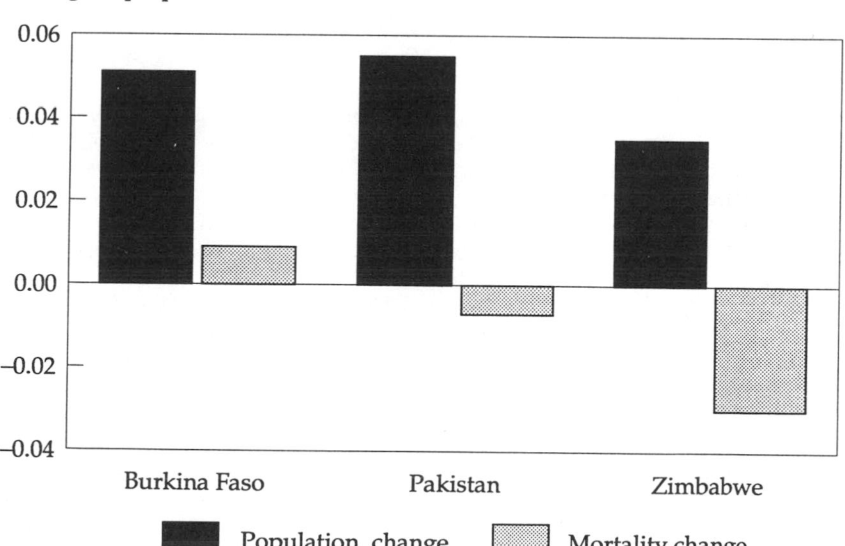

Source: Authors' calculations.

ous than adult deaths by 2015–20. Burkina Faso, with a minimal increase in the proportion of deaths among the elderly, is almost at the other end of the developing country spectrum from Zimbabwe, and Pakistan is roughly intermediate between these two countries.

Decomposition shows that the effect of changing age structure is to raise the proportion of adult deaths by 3.6 to 5.5 percentage points in the three countries (see figure 1-A4). The effect of changing mortality rates among age groups is variable, raising the proportion of adult deaths by 1 percentage point in Burkina Faso but reducing the proportion by 3 percentage points in Zimbabwe.

Notes

1. No consistent international nomenclature exists for age groups. The World Health Organization uses *adolescents* (ten to nineteen years) and *youth* (fifteen to twenty-four years). The demarcation between adults and the elderly is controversial, but of little importance. The World Health Organization's Health of the Elderly Programme defines the elderly as people aged sixty years and older, while the United States Bureau of the Census in its report on *Aging in the Third World* variously defines the elderly as people aged fifty-five, sixty or sixty-five years and older (Kinsella 1988).

2. The health of school-aged children, its importance, and the opportunities for intervention in the classroom have attracted increased attention recently (Halloran, Bundy, and Pollit 1989; Jamison and Leslie 1990; Leslie and Jamison 1990; Pollitt 1990).

3. This book excludes detailed analysis of some causes of adult ill-health because their importance for children has made them a target for intervention and research already. Malaria is a good example. That this book does not discuss malaria in detail does not imply that malaria is unimportant for adults in the developing world. On the contrary, the authors hope that focusing attention on adult health will strengthen the attention malaria and other parasitic diseases receive.

4. A companion volume to this book, entitled *Disease Control Priorities in Developing Countries* (Jamison and Mosley, forthcoming) will be published in 1993. It comprises disease-specific analyses of epidemiologic and economic data on the important causes of illness in the developing world. It includes chapters on all of the major causes of adult morbidity and mortality referred to in this book. The authors have drawn on this material heavily, especially in chapter 6. Readers should refer to Jamison and Mosley (forthcoming) for supporting details on specific diseases. The table of contents and advanced drafts of individual chapters can be obtained from the Population, Health, and Nutrition Division, The World Bank, Washington, D.C. 20433, USA. For an overview of some of the main conclusions of this work, readers may consult Mosley, Jamison, and Henderson (1990) and Jamison and Mosley (1991).

5. If developing countries develop their health policies using available cause-specific mortality data, they will be doing no more or less than the developed countries. With the exception of cancer incidence and a few specific reportable diseases, developed countries lack reliable morbidity data and

base their health objectives and policies on trends and differentials in age-specific and cause-specific mortality rates.

6. An early paper on world population growth (Notestein 1945) predicted a world population of 3.3 billion by 2000. Current estimates indicate that by 2000 the world probably will have 3.7 billion adults and a total population of over 6 billion (table 1-1).

7. Both of these ratios count all children and the elderly as dependents and are higher than conventional dependency ratios which typically do not classify those aged between sixty and sixty-four years as dependents.

8. For certain important adult groups, and for certain diseases, the mortality differentials are higher for adults than for children. The risk of maternal mortality can be one hundred times greater in developing countries than in developed countries (Walsh and others forthcoming), while the risk of death in childhood is only six to twenty times greater in developing countries (chapter 2, table 2-3). The cost-effectiveness of providing certain important health services for children (notably vaccinations and oral rehydration therapy) has been favorable, but this does not necessarily imply that increasing the levels of resources to these interventions is efficient: once the most receptive and accessible targets have been reached, costs per unit of effectiveness are likely to rise substantially. As for the greater autonomy of adults, their limited access to information about health, the existence of externalities and imperfections in the market for health care, and the already substantial involvement of government in the provision of adult health services all make a strong argument for not neglecting adults in health policy.

References

Bulatao, R. A., E. Bos, P. W. Stephens, and M. T. Vu. 1990. *World Population Projections: 1989–90.* Baltimore: Johns Hopkins University Press.

Das Gupta, P. 1978. "A General Method of Decomposing a Difference Between Two Rates into Several Components." *Demography* 15(1):99–112.

Feachem, R. G. A., and D. T. Jamison, eds. 1991. *Disease and Mortality in Sub-Saharan Africa.* New York: Oxford University Press for the World Bank.

Fries, J. F., L. W. Green, and S. Levine. 1989. "Health Promotion and the Compression of Morbidity." *Lancet* i:481–83.

Halloran, M. E., D. A. P. Bundy, and E. Pollitt. 1989. "Infectious Disease and the Unesco Basic Education Initiative." *Parasitology Today* 5(11):359–62.

Jamison, D. T., and J. Leslie. 1990. "Health and Nutrition Considerations in Educational Planning: II The Cost and Effectiveness of School-Based Interventions." *Food and Nutrition Bulletin* 12(3):204–14.

Jamison, D. T., and W. H. Mosley. 1991. "Disease Control Priorities in Developing Countries: Health Policy Responses to Epidemiological Change." *American Journal of Public Health* 81(1):15–22.

Jamison, D. T., and W. H. Mosley, eds. Forthcoming. *Disease Control Priorities in Developing Countries.* New York: Oxford University Press for the World Bank.

Kinsella, K. 1988. "Aging in the third world." *International Population Reports Series* P–95, No. 79. Washington, D.C.: United States Department of Commerce Bureau of the Census.

Leslie, J., and D. T. Jamison. 1990. ''Health and Nutrition Considerations in Educational Planning: I Educational Consequences of Health Problems among School-Age Children.'' *Food and Nutrition Bulletin* 12(3):191–203.

Mosley, W. H., D. T. Jamison, and D. A. Henderson. 1990. ''The Health Sector in Developing Countries: Problems for the 1990s and Beyond.'' *Annual Reviews of Public Health* 11:335–58.

Notestein, F. 1945. ''Population: The Long View.'' In: Schultz, T. W., ed., *Food for the World.* Chicago: University of Chicago Press.

Omran, A. R. 1971. ''The Epidemiologic Transition: A Theory of the Epidemiology of Population Change.'' *Millbank Memorial Fund Quarterly* 49:509–38.

Pollitt, E. 1990. *Malnutrition and Infection in the Classroom.* Paris: Unesco.

Shapiro, S. 1977. ''A Tool for Health Planners.'' *American Journal of Public Health* 67:816–17.

Walsh, J., C. N. Feifer, A. R. Measham, and P. J. Gertler. Forthcoming. ''Maternal and Perinatal Health Problems.'' In: Jamison, D. T., and W. H. Mosley, eds., *Disease Control Priorities in Developing Countries.* New York: Oxford University Press for the World Bank.

Warren, K. S. 1990. ''Tropical Medicine or Tropical Health: The Heath Clark Lectures, 1988.'' *Reviews of Infectious Diseases* 12(1):142–56.

2. *Adult Mortality: Levels, Patterns and Causes*

Christopher J. L. Murray, Gonghuan Yang, and Xinjian Qiao

THIS CHAPTER EXPLORES the levels, patterns, and causes of adult mortality in the developing world and challenges a number of misconceptions about adult mortality. Some of the more striking conclusions of the chapter are summarized below.

- There are substantially higher rates of adult mortality in developing countries than in industrialized countries with market economies.
- Adult mortality is a matter for concern for populations in all stages of the health transition, not just for post-transition populations.
- Child and adult mortality can vary independently so that single indicators of mortality, such as the infant mortality rate or life expectancy, are not sufficient to monitor changes in both adult and child mortality.
- In nearly all developing countries, men's mortality is higher than women's, despite the extra risks associated with childbearing and cancers of the cervix and breast; however, avoidable mortality is generally higher for women.
- The pattern of mortality by cause is not a simple function of the overall level of mortality or life expectancy and therefore cannot be estimated or predicted reliably from such information.
- As overall adult mortality rates decline, both the aggregate communicable and aggregate noncommunicable disease mortality rates of adults decline. With very few exceptions (for example, breast cancer), cause-specific adult mortality rates have declined during the past decades in developing countries for which such information is available.

The beginning of this chapter discusses the sources of information on adult mortality, uses model-based estimates to give an overview of adult mortality in the developing world, and examines historical and contemporary patterns of overall adult mortality in industrialized and developing countries using empirical data.[1] The last part of the chapter focuses on specific causes of adult death, presenting a framework for cause-of-death analysis and the results of using this framework to analyze empirical data.[2]

Measuring Adult Mortality

When using existing data to analyze a new topic like adult mortality in developing countries, it is important to pay close attention to the quality of information. Estimates of adult mortality can be divided into two broad groups: empirical and model-based. Because both types have assumptions and limitations that affect the analyses in this chapter, this section focuses on the origins and nature of these data.

Empirical estimates are measurements of mortality based on vital registration systems, censuses, or surveys. Sources of empirical data on adult mortality can be divided into three groups: vital registration systems, direct questions posed in surveys and censuses, and the application of indirect techniques to survey or census data for mortality measurement.

A vital registration system that records 100 percent of vital events is the best empirical source for measuring adult mortality. Good empirical data are available for a number of Latin American and Caribbean countries, a few nations in Asia, but no countries in continental Sub-Saharan Africa.[3] Sample registration systems, which record vital events in a subset of the population, provide good information for a few additional countries, most notably China and India.

Empirical estimates also may be derived from direct and indirect questions asked during censuses and surveys. Accuracy varies widely depending on the exact details of the census or survey, the questions that are asked, who asks and answers the questions, and even the manner and circumstances in which the questions are asked. Direct questions about deaths in the household during the last twelve months tend to yield unreliable results (Blacker 1984), with a few exceptions such as the 1982 census in China. Indirect techniques based on questions about the survival of spouses, parents, or other kin have been developed to estimate adult mortality (Timaeus 1990; Timaeus and Graham 1988; United Nations 1983). These analyses provide rare empirical information on adult mortality in Sub-Saharan Africa. Another indirect method of estimating adult mortality is to compare cohorts in two successive censuses. Variance in census coverage, however, and the lack of age-specific information on migration in most countries limit the usefulness of this method (United Nations

1984). Regardless of the limitations of the different ways to measure adult mortality, each method that uses data from a vital registration system, survey or census reflects some real measurement of adult mortality.

Because many countries do not have vital registration systems and because censuses or surveys are infrequent and expensive undertakings, there are many gaps in the knowledge about mortality in the developing world. Nevertheless, the United Nations Population Division (United Nations 1989b), the World Bank (Bulatao and others 1990) and the United States Bureau of the Census (1988) have taken the responsibility for making population estimates and projections by five-year age groups for nearly every country. These population projections require input data on mortality levels in every age group. The gaps in the empirical data base on mortality are filled by these agencies using model-based estimates. These model-based estimates of mortality are also disseminated widely in publications and used in conducting research and guiding policy choices (Murray 1987).

The term *model-based* applies to the use of two distinct sets of models in producing mortality estimates: a) models for updating empirical estimates, and b) model life tables. First, when vital registration data, censuses or surveys are used to make an empirical estimate of mortality in any country, such an estimate will be at least three years out of date because of the inevitable delays in collecting and publishing vital registration data or because indirect techniques are capable only of producing estimates of mortality as it was several years before the survey. For some Sub-Saharan African countries with infrequent surveys, such empirical estimates can be twenty-five years or more out of date. A model of assumed decline in mortality is used to generate current and future estimates from these old empirical figures. The actual rate of decline is assumed to be similar for countries with very different health policies, and these estimates do not reflect the likely effect of specific socioeconomic changes. Second, model life tables are employed to estimate and project age-specific mortality rates from information on a single indicator, such as life expectancy, which is the output from a model of assumed mortality decline.[4] The Coale and Demeny model life tables are the most frequently used for this task. For some countries, there are no empirical mortality data available; in these cases, both the level and age pattern of mortality are assumed by choosing a particular family and level of Coale and Demeny model life tables.

Censuses and multicountry survey programs, most notably the World Fertility Survey (Cleland and Scott 1987) and more recently the USAID-sponsored Demographic and Health Surveys, have provided a substantial empirical base for estimating child mortality (Hill and Pebley 1989).[5] As a consequence, the model-based child mortality estimates have a strong empirical component (United Nations 1988). The empirical sources for measuring adult mortality in developing countries, particularly in Sub-Saharan Africa and Asia, are much less extensive. In many cases, the level and the entire age pattern of adult mortality are based solely on child mortality estimates and the use of model life tables. For these countries, therefore, model-based estimates of adult mortality are not based on any empirical measurements.

The World Bank's estimates of adult mortality in Nigeria illustrate the complex interplay of empirical data and assumptions leading to a model-based estimate. The World Bank does not begin with an empirical estimate but obtains from the United Nations their model-based estimates of the infant mortality rate and life expectancy for each sex. There were no sources of nationwide mortality data in Nigeria (a nationwide Demographic and Health Survey was conducted in 1990). The United Nations was forced to base their estimate on several small-scale surveys of child mortality in one or two states conducted in the 1970s and on mortality levels of neighboring countries. The United Nations describes their estimation process as based on a qualitative review of these data and not a quantitative analysis. Using these limited data for children, the United Nations generated a hypothetical age pattern of mortality at all other ages using the model life table North. These estimates for overall mortality in the mid–1970s were used to generate current estimates by assuming that life expectancy improved by two years every five chronological years. In turn, the World Bank used the United Nations results for the infant mortality rate and life expectancy and model life table North to regenerate the age pattern of adult mortality used in their projection model. For many of the world's poorer countries, the empirical basis for estimates of mortality, especially adult mortality, is tenuous, and estimates produced by various agencies may disagree substantially.

Because of the gaps in empirical mortality data, this chapter uses model-based estimates, despite their limitations, to provide an overview of adult mortality in the developing world. Doing so is justified on three grounds:

- Model-based estimates are more robust the larger the population is; here the population is all adults in the developing world.
- Model-based estimates provide the only way to characterize overall adult mortality in developing countries.
- The rough confidence intervals for these model-based estimates are not unacceptably wide (see note 6).

For all other purposes (for example, for providing country-specific measurements and for exploring the relationships between the mortality of children and adults, men and women, and younger and older adults), this chapter uses empirical data exclusively. Consequently, the conclusions reached from these analyses are free from the systematic biases introduced by model assumptions and differ from some previous work that has relied on model-based estimates. The major drawback, however, is that these analyses can be done only for countries having adequate empirical data (table 2-4). No country in continental Sub-Saharan Africa is within this group, and more generally, the situation in the world's poorer countries is inadequately represented in the empirical analyses. Extending the analysis contained in this chapter to the countries of Sub-Saharan Africa and other poorer countries—as empirical data become available for these countries—is an important research task.

Overview of Adult Mortality in the Developing World

To provide an overview of adult mortality in the developing world, 1988 age-specific mortality has been calculated using model-based World Bank estimates of the infant mortality rate and life expectancy at birth and the Coale and Demeny model life table North (table 2-1).

The Age Pattern of Mortality

The classic age pattern of mortality in developing countries is that up to half of all deaths may occur in children younger than five years. Child mortality risks in excess of a hundred per thousand live births are common. After age five, mortality rates are substantially lower until about ages sixty-five or seventy.[6] Although the cumulative probability of dying rises sharply in the first five years of life in developing countries, it also continues to rise at a steady rate throughout the adult years. The net effect is that while the mortality risk during each five-year period of the adult years is relatively low compared to the mortality risks of the very young and the very old, the cumulative risk of dying as an adult (between ages fifteen and sixty) is large. Although more than one third of all deaths in the developing world are deaths of children, 27 percent are deaths of adults (table 2-1). This contrasts with Japan (the country with the longest life expectancy) where, in 1987, 1.2 percent of all deaths were deaths of children and 19 percent were deaths of adults.

Table 2-1. Distribution by Age of Deaths, Avoidable Deaths, and Avoidable Years of Potential Life Lost in the Developing World, 1988

		Avoidable				
				Discounted YPLL[b]		
Age group (years)	*Deaths*	*Deaths*	*YPLL*[a]	*3 percent*	*8 percent*	*15 percent*
Numbers (thousands)						
0–4	15,000	14,500	1,215,000	442,000	180,000	96,000
5–14	2,200	2,000	154,000	61,000	25,000	13,500
15–59	10,600	7,600	370,000	188,000	91,000	50,000
60+	12,200	5,600	61,000	48,000	34,000	23,000
Total	40,000	29,700	1,800,000	739,000	330,000	182,500
Percentage distribution						
0–4	37.5	48.8	67.5	59.8	54.5	52.6
5–14	5.5	6.7	8.6	8.3	7.6	7.4
15–59	26.5	25.6	20.6	25.4	27.6	27.4
60+	30.5	18.9	3.4	6.5	10.3	12.6
Total	100.0	100.0	100.0	100.0	100.0	100.0

Note: YPLL were calculated using an age-weight of eighty-five years minus the age at death. The computation of the age distribution of deaths was based on World Bank estimates of the infant mortality rate (IMR) and the expectation of life at birth (e_0); see text for details. Avoidable deaths, avoidable YPLL, and avoidable discounted YPLL were calculated using Japanese mortality rates as a reference.

a. Years of potential life lost

b. Percentages refer to different discount rates used to calculate discounted YPLL

Source: Authors' calculations.

Avoidable Mortality

Researchers have used two approaches to assess the degree of avoidable or preventable mortality (Uemura 1989). One approach focuses on specific diseases considered to be preventable with current knowledge. The second approach focuses on a reference population with low mortality and uses the mortality pattern of this population as a reasonable goal for all populations. In this approach, avoidable deaths are those that would not occur if the rates of the reference population applied.[7] Because this second approach is based on a mortality rate that has been achieved, it is more realistic than the approach based on diseases considered to be preventable. Accordingly, this chapter uses the second approach to evaluate avoidable adult mortality in the developing world. In doing so, it is acknowledged that this approach makes no allowance for genetic factors that may affect mortality differently in different communities. This approach also uses *avoidable* to mean what is avoidable biologically and technically but not necessarily economically; it does not take into consideration the cost of avoiding each type of death. Thus when this chapter states, for example, that 70 percent of deaths in a community are avoidable, it does not imply that the community can afford to prevent all of these deaths.

In calculating avoidable deaths, the choice of reference mortality rates can alter the number of avoidable deaths substantially. A variety of reference rates have been proposed (Waaler 1980; Woolsey 1981). Most recently, Uemura (1989) calculated the lowest mortality rate for each five-year age group reported by any country to the World Health Organization. These rates have been proposed as a synthetic set of reference rates for calculating avoidable mortality. Using a real population as a reference avoids the potential for unidentified interactions and tradeoffs among age-specific mortality rates. Japan, the country with the world's highest life expectancy, serves as our reference for calculating avoidable mortality. None of the basic findings presented in this chapter, however, would change if Sweden or Switzerland served instead as the reference population. Likewise, if the higher socioeconomic groups in any western nation, all of which have low adult mortality rates, were used as the reference population, the results would be similar to those found when Japan is used as the reference population. Using the Japanese mortality standard, 97 percent of deaths in childhood in the developing world are avoidable. Perhaps more surprisingly, 72 percent of adult deaths are avoidable also. In total, an estimated 14.5 million deaths of children and 7.6 million deaths of adults are avoidable (table 2-1). Nearly one half of all avoidable deaths are in children, but more than a quarter of avoidable deaths occur during the adult years.

Years of Potential Life Lost

Deaths of children involve a greater loss of life span than deaths of adults, especially when adult deaths occur at the end of the adult age range. To account for these differences in loss of potential life, each avoidable death was weighted by eighty-five minus the age at death to estimate the avoidable years of potential life lost.

Even using this type of measure that heavily weights the importance of childhood death, adult deaths account for more than 20 percent of avoidable years of potential life lost in developing countries (table 2-1). Avoidable adult deaths are fairly evenly distributed throughout the adult age group, with a slight excess between ages twenty and twenty-nine (figure 2-1a). As a consequence, avoidable adult years of potential life lost are concentrated in the younger adult age groups (figure 2-1b).

Some authors (Barnum 1987; Evans and Murray 1987; Prost and Prescott 1984) use discounted years of potential life lost. The rationale for discounting is that society prefers benefits, such as life gained, now rather than in the future. The discount rate captures the extent of this time preference. Table 2-1 provides estimates of avoidable years of potential life lost computed with various discount rates. As the discount rate rises, adult deaths become relatively more important in comparison to deaths in childhood. Prost and Prescott (1984) and Barnum (1987) have proposed the use of productivity-weighted discounted years of potential life lost. This measure weights each year of life by the likely contribution to total social production. While detailed indicators specific to local wages and markets can be derived, table 2-2 lists aggregate productivity-weighted avoidable years of potential life lost in developing countries. Each year from age nought to age fourteen and for ages sixty and older is given a productivity weight of zero, and each year for the ages fifteen through fifty-nine is given a productivity weight of one.[8] Thus a death at one year of age represents a stream of forty-five productive years of life lost that would have begun in fourteen years. Because childhood deaths have this stream of nonproductive years followed by productive years, the age distribution of productivity-weighted avoidable years of potential life lost is highly sensitive to the discount rate (table 2-2). The assumption that years of life past age sixty have productivity weights of zero is arbitrary and used for illustrative purposes only. It should not imply that the elderly are unproductive.[9] The share of productivity-weighted years of potential life lost due to adult deaths ranges from

Figure 2-1a. The Distribution of Adult Avoidable Deaths in the Developing World by Age for Both Sexes Combined, 1988

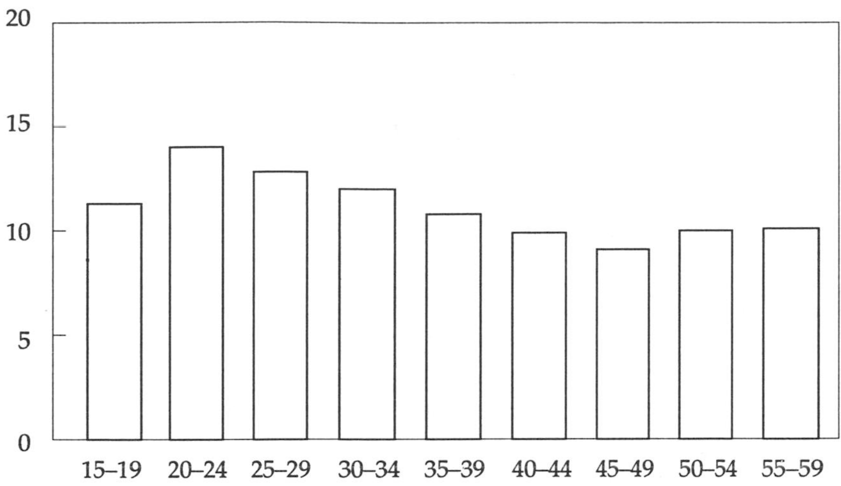

Source: Authors' calculations.

Figure 2-1b. The Distribution of Adult Avoidable Potential Years of Life Lost by Age for Both Sexes Combined, 1988

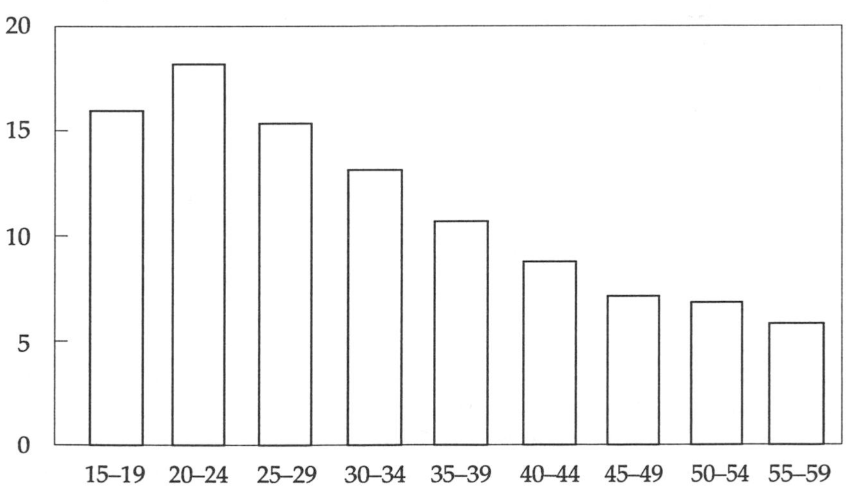

Source: Authors' calculations.

Table 2-2. Distribution by Age of Productivity-Weighted, Discounted, Avoidable Years of Potential Life Lost in the Developing World, 1988

	Productivity-weighted discounted avoidable years of life lost[a]		
Age group (years)	*3 percent*	*8 percent*	*15 percent*
Numbers (thousands)			
0–4	234,500	60,000	14,000
5–14	42,000	16,000	6,500
15–59	118,000	70,000	43,000
60+	0	0	0
Total	395,000	146,000	63,500
Percentage distribution			
0–4	59.4	40.8	21.4
5–14	10.7	11.1	10.2
15–59	29.9	48.1	68.3
60+	0.0	0.0	0.0
Total	100.0	100.0	100.0

Note: Productivity-weighted avoidable years of potential life lost were calculated by giving a weight of 1 to each year of life between ages fifteen and sixty and a weight of zero to years of life at all other ages. This is based on the assumption that the productive age group in most countries is fifteen to fifty-nine year olds, which is subject to considerable cultural variation. There are many societies in which people older than sixty years play vital economic and social roles. This indicator does not take into account consumption during those years during which individuals are not producing.

a. Percentages refer to different discount rates

Source: Authors' calculations.

30 to 68 percent as the discount rate increases from 3 to 15 percent. A higher discount rate reduces the importance of childhood deaths and increases the importance of adult deaths.

45Q15 and Other Probabilities of Death

Another way to quantify adult mortality is to express it as the analog of the child mortality measure 5Q0. The first number in this notation refers to the number of years in the probability interval and the second number refers to the age at which the interval starts. 5Q0 is the probability of death from birth to age five. 45Q15 is the probability of death between age fifteen and age sixty—in other words, the percent of fifteen year olds who will die before their sixtieth birthday. For the developing world as a whole, the 45Q15 is 25 percent for men and 22 percent for women, indicating that about one out of every four fifteen year olds in the developing world dies before age sixty (table 2-3). For comparison, the 45Q15 in Japan is 11 percent for men and 6 percent for women. In the developing world, the risk of dying before age five is considerably lower than the risk of dying between the ages of fifteen and sixty; the 5Q0 is 12 percent for boys and 10 percent for girls (table 2-3). Subtracting the Japanese 45Q15 and 5Q0 from those of the developing world yields avoidable risks of death of 11 and 9 percent for boys and girls, respectively, and 13 and 16 percent for men and women.

Because 45Q15 communicates the burden of adult mortality risk in an intuitively clear fashion, it is used throughout this book as the preferred indicator of adult mortality. One limitation, however, of 45Q15 as an indicator of adult mortality is that it does not take into consideration the ages at which adults die. At various points in this chapter, years of potential life lost are used to convey information on the age distribution of adult deaths. In addition, the adult age group is divided into younger and older adults, making use of 25Q15 (the percent of fifteen year olds who will die before reaching age forty) and 20Q40 (the percent of forty year olds who will die before reaching age sixty).[10]

To calculate 45Q15 for the six major regions of the world (table 2-3), World Bank model-based life expectancy estimates and Coale and Demeny model life tables were used. Because the estimates are model generated, the sex differences in 45Q15 among different regions may be spurious (see the following section in this chapter). Nevertheless,

Table 2-3. Model-Based Estimates of Adult and Child Mortality Risk by Region, 1988

	45Q15		*5Q0*	
Region	*Male*	*Female*	*Male*	*Female*
Developing World				
Asia	23.5	20.0	9.7	8.2
Latin America/Caribbean	22.5	14.8	7.5	6.3
Middle East/North Africa	27.3	23.4	13.0	11.1
Sub-Saharan Africa	37.9	31.8	18.1	16.1
Total	24.9	22.1	11.6	9.9
Industrialized				
Market	11.8	5.1	1.2	0.8
Nonmarket	20.9	10.8	1.7	0.9

Note: Estimates were based on life expectancy at birth reported by the World Bank and the model most used by the World Bank in the estimates for that region. These estimates are not robust, especially the reported sex differences, which do not correspond well with empirically based estimates available for some countries. The estimate for the industrialized market region females (5 percent) is clearly too low, even lower than the lowest adult female mortality population known (Switzerland—see table 2-4).

Source: Authors' calculations.

these values indicate that adult mortality varies widely, from 38 percent for men in Sub-Saharan Africa to 5 percent for women in industrialized market countries. The region with the highest adult mortality is Sub-Saharan Africa, followed by the Middle East/North Africa, Asia, and Latin America/Caribbean. According to these model-based estimates, adult male mortality levels in Latin America and the Caribbean are only slightly higher than those of industrialized nonmarket countries.[11] In both, the mortality of men is high relative to the mortality of women.

Empirical Patterns of Overall Adult Mortality

This section examines the empirical data on adult mortality, starting with the historical record of adult mortality during the last century in industrialized and developing countries. Current levels of adult mortality recorded in vital registration data are discussed next, followed by consideration of other data sources for Africa, India, China, and Nauru. Finally, all these sources are used to examine the relationships between child and adult mortality, mortality in men compared to women, and younger versus older adult mortality.

Historical Changes in Overall Adult Mortality

The historical records of vital registration data in industrialized countries make it possible to characterize trends in adult mortality and compare these trends to the overall reduction in mortality. Industrialized countries were developing countries in the nineteenth century and the early part of the twentieth century. Their historical records illustrate the evolution of adult mortality in populations that have experienced the health transition. In England and Japan, the 45Q15 has declined during the past 100 years from more than 40 percent to less than 15 percent for men and to less than 10 percent for women (figures 2-2a through 2-3b). Both adult and child mortality have declined during the last century in these two countries and in Italy and Sweden (figures 2-4a through 2-5b), but at different paces, possibly because of different sets of socioeconomic determinants. Whether the recent reductions in adult mortality in some of these countries are due to improved access to more effective medical interventions, or to changes in life style and environment, is unknown.[12]

Changes in adult and child mortality have not paralleled each other in these countries. For example, child mortality has decreased faster than adult mortality for males in Italy, while the opposite is true in Sweden. Differences in the rate of change in adult mortality among countries are particularly noticeable during the last quarter century.

(Text continues on p. 39.)

Figure 2-2a. Male Mortality in England and Wales, 1860–1987

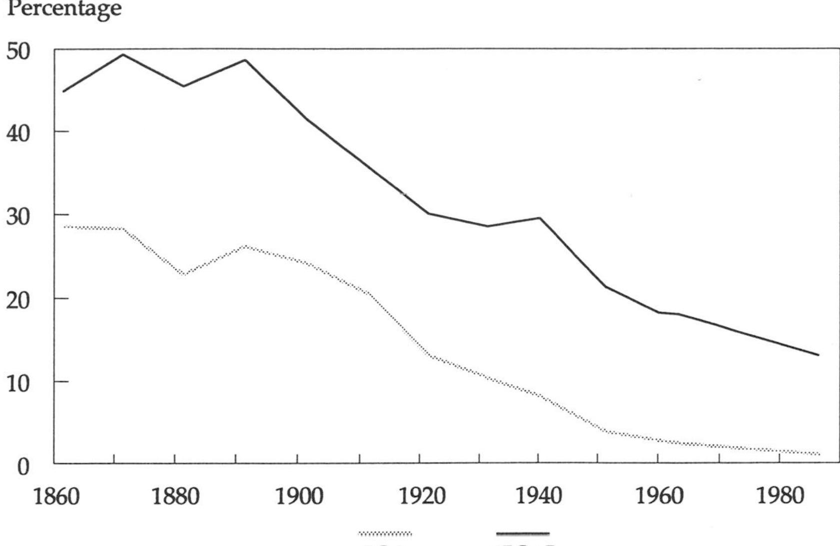

Source: Authors' calculations.

Figure 2-2b. Female Mortality in England and Wales, 1860–1987

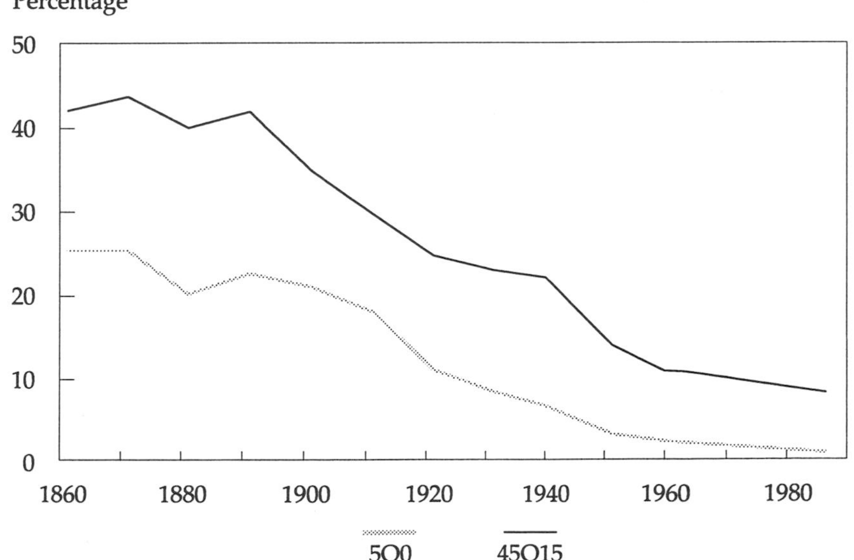

Source: Authors' calculations.

Figure 2-3a. Male Mortality in Japan, 1899–1987

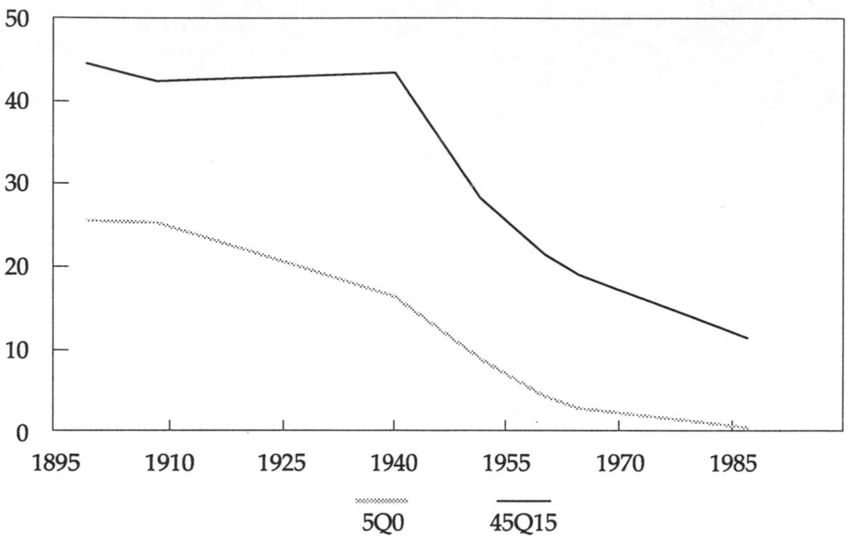

Source: Authors' calculations.

Figure 2-3b. Female Mortality in Japan, 1899–1987

Percentage

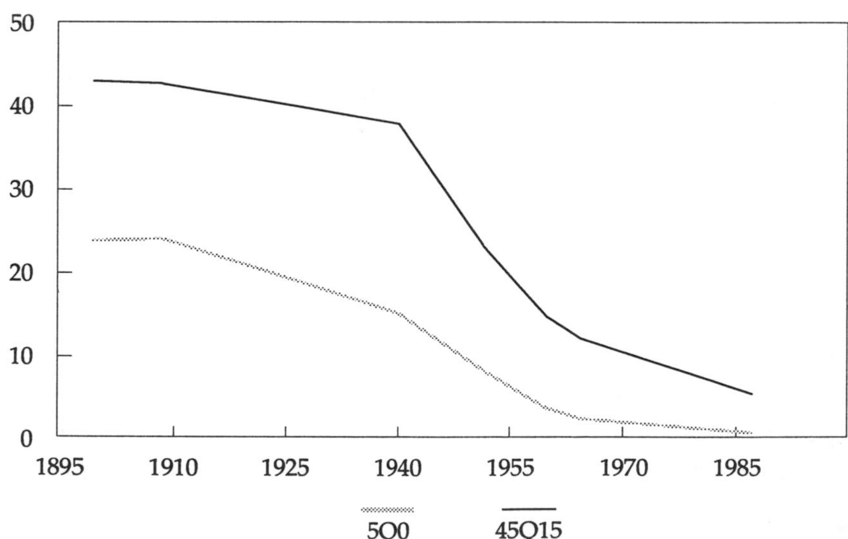

Source: Authors' calculations.

Figure 2-4a. Male Mortality in Italy, 1880–1985

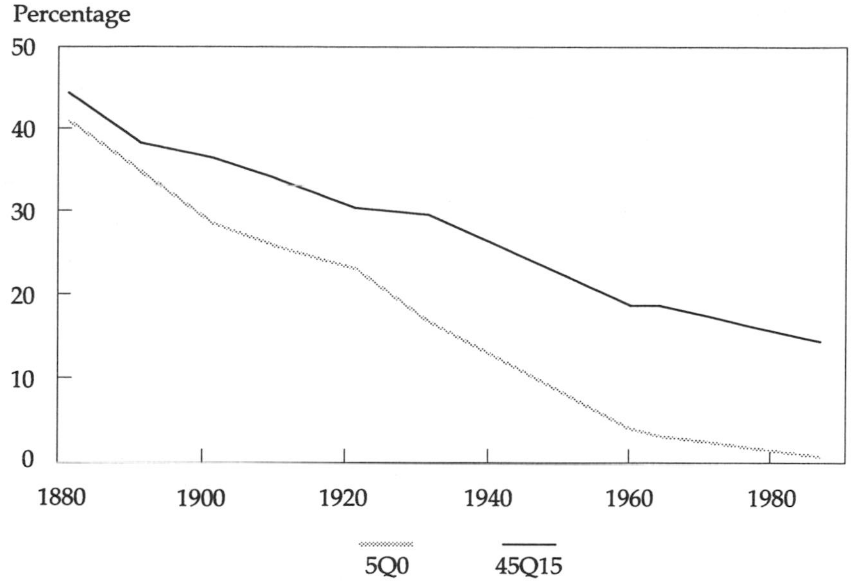

Source: Authors' calculations.

Figure 2-4b. Female Mortality in Italy, 1880–1985

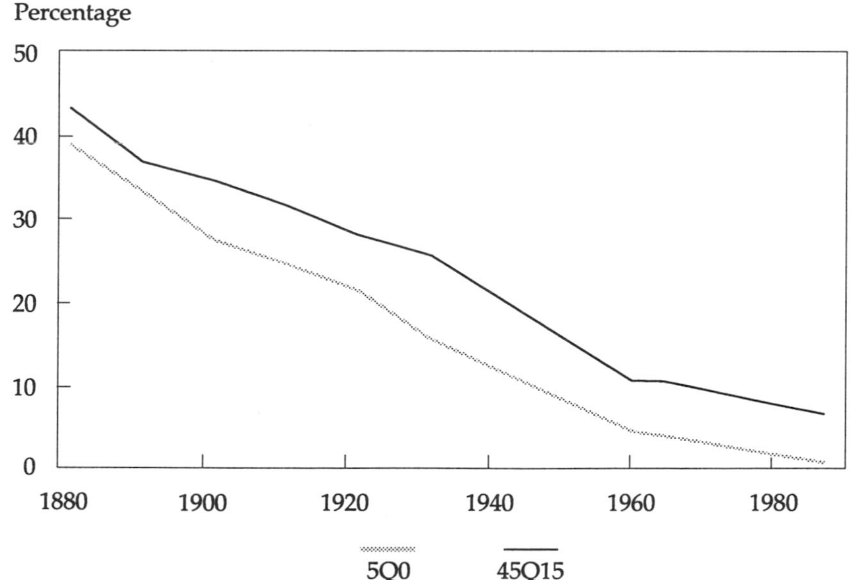

Source: Authors' calculations.

Figure 2-5a. Male Mortality in Sweden, 1910–86

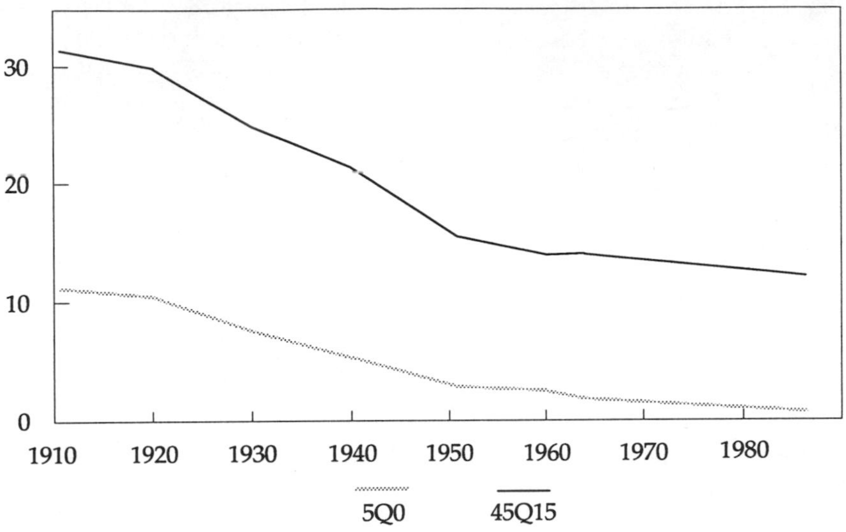

Source: Authors' calculations.

Figure 2-5b. Female Mortality in Sweden, 1910–86

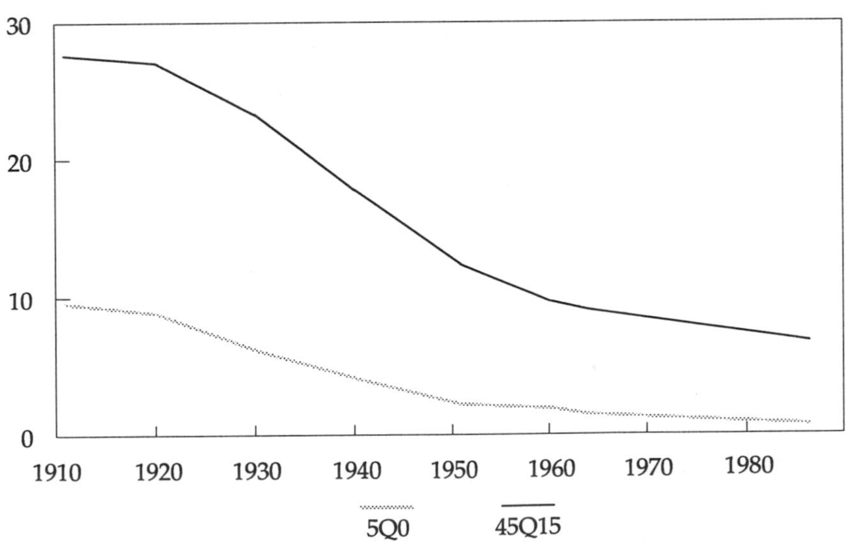

Source: Authors' calculations.

Some countries, such as Italy and Japan, have continued to experience substantial reductions while others, such as Sweden, have not.

Long sequences of vital registration data are unavailable for most developing countries, making it difficult to characterize the trends in adult mortality in the developing world. Notable exceptions are some Latin American countries, such as Chile, and a number of smaller Caribbean states. Adult male mortality in Chile has declined from a 45Q15 of 63 percent in 1909 to less than 19 percent in 1986 (figure 2-6a). Adult female mortality in Chile has declined also (figure 2-6b).

Excellent vital registration data for five countries (Chile, Costa Rica, Cuba, Singapore, and Sri Lanka) make it possible to analyze trends in adult mortality since 1950 (figures 2-7a and 2-7b). These five countries are used extensively in the cause-of-death analysis presented in the last part of this chapter. During the last thirty-five years, adult male mortality has declined in Chile, Costa Rica, and Singapore, while remaining the same in Cuba and Sri Lanka (figure 2-7a). Despite the widely acclaimed overall decline in mortality in Sri Lanka (Marga Institute 1984), Sri Lankan men have not experienced a decline in mortality during the last three decades. Adult female mortality has declined in all five countries, although the decrease in Cuba has been small (figure 2-7b).

Despite a few important exceptions, such as Sri Lanka, that illustrate the heterogeneity of adult mortality patterns, the historical record shows that both adult male and female mortality have declined along with overall mortality in most countries. The extent of the decline in the mortality rates of men and women in most industrialized countries has not been widely appreciated. For example, in describing the epidemiological transition, Omran (1971) mistakenly thought reductions in mortality affected mostly children and women rather than men.

Current Overall Levels of Adult Mortality

The following sections examine current adult mortality levels first in countries having vital registration systems and then in countries where incomplete but useful mortality data have been collected.

VITAL REGISTRATION SYSTEM DATA. This section examines empirical data for all countries known to have complete vital registration systems, defined as systems that capture 90 percent or more of deaths occurring in the community (United Nations 1989a). Complete vital registration data are available for most industrialized countries and the majority of Latin American states. In Asia, Africa, and the Middle East, only a few countries have complete vital registration systems.

Figure 2-6a. Male Mortality in Chile, 1909–86

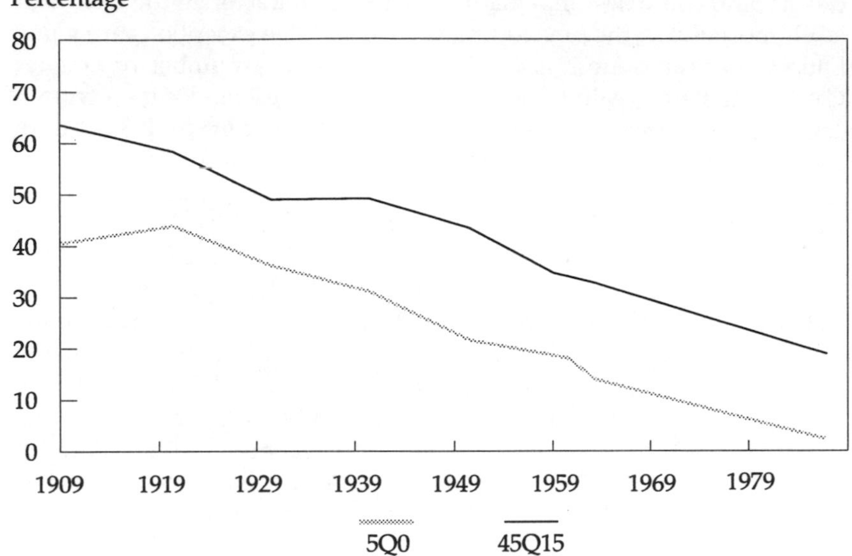

Source: Authors' calculations.

Figure 2-6b. Female Mortality in Chile, 1909–86

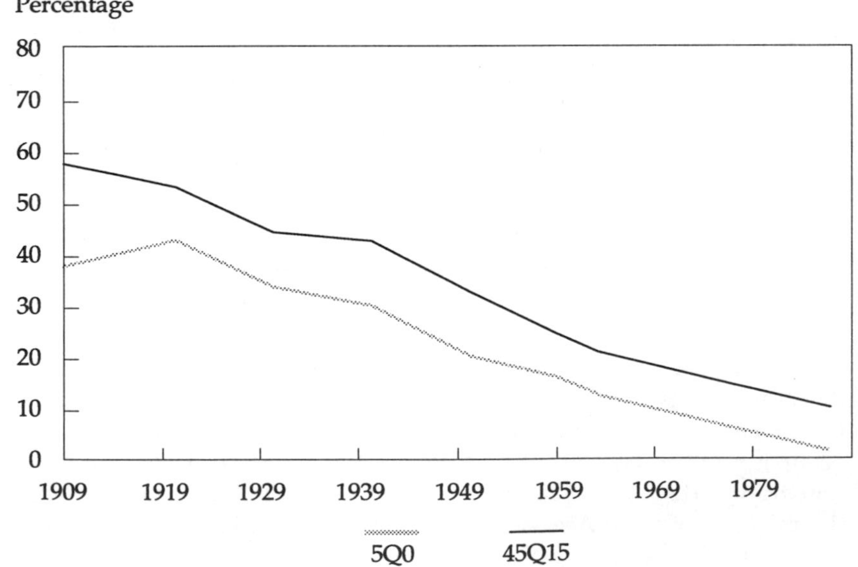

Source: Authors' calculations.

Figure 2-7a. Male 45Q15 for Chile, Costa Rica, Cuba, Singapore, and Sri Lanka Since 1950

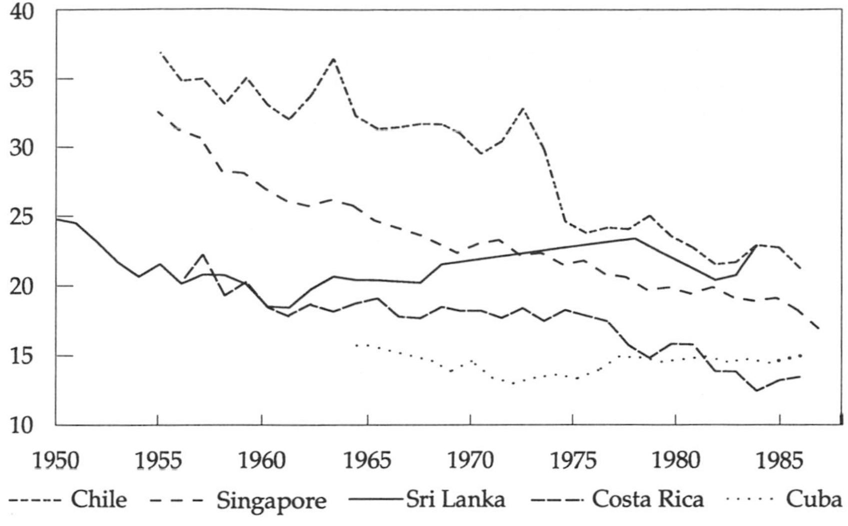

Source: Authors' calculations.

Figure 2-7b. Female 45Q15 for Chile, Costa Rica, Cuba, Singapore, and Sri Lanka Since 1950

45Q15/percentage

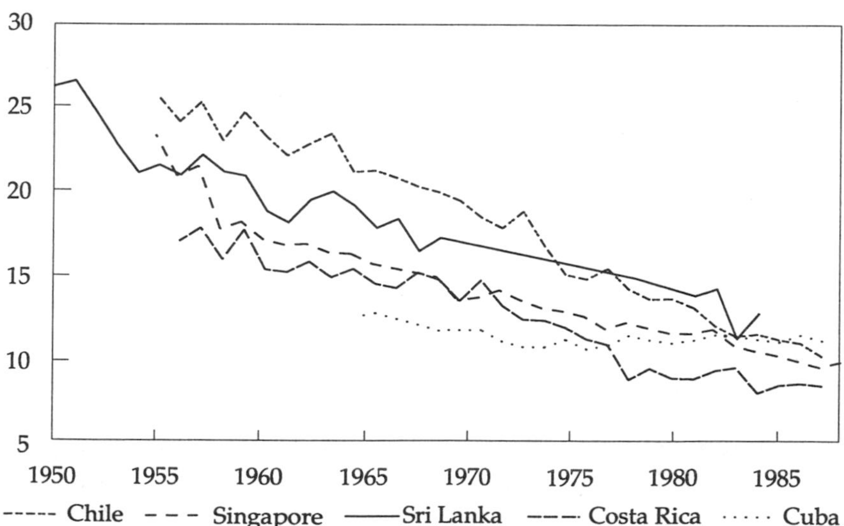

Source: Authors' calculations.

45Q15 and 5Q0 have been computed for all countries that report complete vital registration data to the World Health Organization (table 2-4). This sample of countries covers only a narrow range of 45Q15 (5 to 19 percent for women and 11 to 31 percent for men) and is not representative of the developing world. Not surprisingly, countries with good vital statistics tend to have low mortality. Seychelles, Suriname, and Mauritius—which have variable annual rates because of the small sizes of their populations—raise the upper bound of mortality in this sample considerably. For these same countries, table 2-4 provides estimates of young adult mortality (25Q15) and old adult mortality (20Q40) as well. Appendix tables A-1a to A-1f provide best estimates of 45Q15 and 5Q0 for all countries—calculated when possible from empirical data, otherwise from model-based data.

Adult mortality is not uniformly low in industrialized market countries. Countries with low risks include Japan, Greece, Iceland, Malta, Netherlands, Sweden, and Switzerland. Switzerland reports the world's lowest mortality risk for women, a 45Q15 of 5.4 percent. Countries with higher adult mortality risk include Denmark, Ireland, Luxembourg, New Zealand, Portugal, and the United States. The remainder have relatively low mortality risk for women but high mortality risk for men when compared to Japan. Male-female differences in 45Q15 range from 5 percentage points in Iceland to 12 percentage points in Finland. In industrialized nonmarket countries, the mortality risks of men are 10 to 15 percentage points higher than the risks of industrialized market countries, whereas the mortality risks of women are only 1 to 2 percentage points higher. Consequently, male-female differences in 45Q15 in industrialized nonmarket countries exceed 10 to 15 percentage points. The mortality risks of women in some Latin American countries (Argentina, Chile, Costa Rica, and Puerto Rico) have reached industrialized market country levels. In Costa Rica, the mortality risks of women are lower than in the United States. The mortality risks of men in most Latin American countries, however, are high, ranging from 13 percent in Costa Rica to 31 percent in Suriname.

Vital registration data provide an opportunity to characterize the relationship between 45Q15 and GDP (Gross Domestic Product) per capita. In general, 45Q15 for low income countries is higher than for high income countries, but the relationship is weak for the forty-six countries with vital registration and GDP per capita data ($R^2 = 0.32$ for men and 0.34 for women). In the same set of countries, the relationship between 5Q0 and GDP per capita is slightly stronger ($R^2 = 0.50$ for boys and 0.46 for girls). For both men and women, Costa Rica, Greece, Hong Kong, Malta, and Spain have much lower levels of adult mortality risk than expected for their income; they may be con-

Table 2-4. Mortality Risks of Adults (45Q15), Children (5Q0), and Young Adults (25Q15) and Old Adults (20Q40) for the Fifty-Seven Countries Reporting Vital Registration Data for the Most Recent Year Available, 1983-1987

	45Q15		5Q0		25Q15		20Q40	
Region/Country	*Male*	*Female*	*Male*	*Female*	*Male*	*Female*	*Male*	*Female*
Developing								
Africa								
Mauritius	26.8	13.5	3.4	2.3	4.9	3.1	23.0	10.7
Seychelles	33.3	16.1	2.3	2.3	7.5	2.7	27.9	13.8
Asia								
Hong Kong	12.5	5.7	0.8	0.7	1.7	1.0	10.9	4.7
Singapore	16.3	9.9	1.1	0.8	2.7	1.6	13.9	8.5
Sri Lanka	22.9	12.8	4.3	3.9	6.6	4.0	17.5	9.2
Latin America/Caribbean								
Antigua and Barbuda[a]	14.2	8.8	0.9	0.3	1.8	1.4	12.7	7.5
Argentina	19.8	10.8	3.1	2.5	3.8	2.3	16.7	8.6
Bahamas	23.5	12.4	3.4	2.3	6.9	3.5	17.8	9.3
Barbados	13.6	10.8	2.3	1.7	3.2	2.4	10.7	8.6
Chile	19.3	10.3	2.6	2.1	4.4	1.9	15.6	8.5
Costa Rica	13.4	8.5	2.5	2.1	3.3	1.6	10.4	7.1
Cuba	15.0	11.2	1.9	1.5	4.1	2.9	11.3	8.5
Dominica[a]	14.3	15.0	1.7	2.1	2.4	1.2	12.2	14.0
Guatemala[a]	22.9	16.9	13.0	12.4	8.4	5.7	15.9	11.8
Guyana	24.2	14.7	3.1	2.5	5.8	2.9	19.6	12.1
Martinique	17.1	11.2	1.0	1.1	4.6	2.6	13.1	8.8
Mexico	25.3	14.5	3.9	3.2	8.0	3.5	18.8	11.4
Panama	13.4	8.3	2.7	3.2	3.8	2.3	9.9	6.1
Puerto Rico	20.6	8.6	1.6	1.3	5.8	1.8	15.7	7.0
St. Vincent	22.2	14.6	2.9	3.0	3.9	1.9	19.1	12.9

(Table continues on the following page.)

Table 2-4 (continued)

Region/Country	*45Q15* Male	*45Q15* Female	*5Q0* Male	*5Q0* Female	*25Q15* Male	*25Q15* Female	*20Q40* Male	*20Q40* Female
Suriname	31.5	18.5	4.3	3.2	9.8	4.4	24.1	14.7
Trinidad and Tobago	22.1	14.8	2.5	2.0	5.6	2.8	17.5	12.4
Uruguay	18.3	10.2	3.3	2.7	3.5	2.2	15.4	8.1
Venezuela	20.0	11.7	3.9	3.1	6.0	2.6	14.9	9.3
Middle East								
Bahrain	14.4	11.4	2.9	0.7	2.4	1.8	12.3	9.8
Israel	13.0	7.7	1.5	1.3	2.2	1.2	11.1	6.6
Kuwait	11.7	7.9	2.1	1.7	2.0	1.0	9.9	6.9
Industrialized Market								
Australia	13.7	7.5	1.2	0.9	3.3	1.4	10.8	6.2
Austria	16.8	7.6	1.2	1.0	3.7	1.4	13.6	6.3
Belgium	15.5	8.3	2.0	1.6	3.4	1.6	12.5	6.8
Canada	14.3	7.7	1.1	0.9	3.3	1.3	11.5	6.4
Denmark	15.8	10.2	1.1	0.9	3.2	1.4	13.0	8.9
Finland	19.0	7.1	0.8	0.5	3.9	1.4	15.7	5.8
France	17.6	7.3	1.1	0.9	3.9	1.6	14.3	5.8
Greece	12.0	6.0	1.4	1.1	2.7	1.2	9.6	4.8
Iceland	12.1	7.3	0.8	0.9	3.0	1.2	9.4	6.2
Ireland	14.9	8.8	1.1	0.9	2.7	1.1	12.5	7.8
Italy	14.5	6.7	1.3	1.1	2.6	1.1	12.2	5.6

Japan	11.5	5.6	0.6	0.6	2.2	1.1	9.5	4.6
Luxembourg	17.9	8.9	1.2	1.2	4.1	1.4	14.3	7.6
Malta	12.2	6.5	1.0	0.8	2.1	1.0	10.3	5.6
Netherlands	12.7	7.2	1.1	0.9	2.1	1.2	10.8	6.0
New Zealand	15.7	9.4	1.6	1.3	4.1	1.7	12.2	7.8
Norway	14.0	6.9	1.2	0.9	2.9	1.1	11.4	5.9
Portugal	17.7	8.1	1.8	1.5	4.5	1.7	13.7	6.4
Spain	14.2	6.1	1.1	0.9	3.0	1.2	11.5	5.0
Sweden	12.6	6.7	0.8	0.7	2.7	1.2	10.1	5.5
Switzerland	13.0	5.4	0.9	0.6	3.4	1.1	10.0	4.3
United Kingdom	13.7	8.4	1.3	1.0	2.4	1.2	11.6	7.1
United States	17.7	9.4	1.4	1.1	4.6	1.8	13.7	7.7
West Germany	15.2	7.5	1.2	0.9	2.8	1.3	12.8	6.2
Nonmarket								
Bulgaria	20.7	9.5	2.0	1.6	4.0	1.8	17.3	7.9
Czechoslovakia	23.0	10.1	1.7	1.3	3.7	1.5	20.0	8.7
Hungary	28.1	12.8	2.2	1.7	5.4	2.2	24.0	10.8
Poland	25.0	10.4	2.1	1.6	4.7	1.6	21.3	8.7
Romania	22.4	11.5	2.3	2.7	4.6	2.3	18.6	9.2
Yugoslavia	20.0	9.8	3.0	2.7	3.6	1.6	17.0	8.2

Note: The analyses of overall mortality presented in this chapter used data from fifty-seven countries and territories that report complete vital registration data to the World Health Organization. The analyses of causes of death exclude three countries (Antigua and Barbuda, Dominica, and Guatemala) for which registration data may be less than 80 percent complete (Lopez 1989). Also in the cause-of-death analyses, data from the United Kingdom were entered separately for each of three divisions (England and Wales, Northern Ireland, and Scotland). Therefore, the sample sizes for the overall mortality analyses and the cause-of-death analyses were fifty-seven and fifty-six countries and territories, respectively.

a. Not included in cause-of-death analyses

Source: Authors' calculations.

sidered examples of adult good health at low cost (see Halstead, Walsh, and Warren 1985). Conversely, Hungary, Seychelles, Suriname, and the United States have higher levels of both male and female 45Q15 than would be predicted from their GDP. Some caution is needed in interpreting this relationship, however, because most high mortality countries have not been included in the analysis because they do not have complete vital registration data. A comparison of the regressions of 45Q15 on GDP per capita and 5Q0 on GDP per capita shows whether countries with lower-than-expected child mortality for their income also have lower adult mortality, or whether those with higher-than-expected child mortality also have higher adult mortality. In this sample of forty-six populations, the males in fourteen populations (30 percent of the sample) have lower-than-expected child mortality and higher-than-expected adult mortality for their income or vice-versa, and the same is true for females in nine populations (20 percent of the sample). Thus, if a country has lower 5Q0 than expected for its income, it does not follow necessarily that adult mortality is relatively low also.

DATA SOURCES FOR SUB-SAHARAN AFRICA. Adult mortality estimates for Sub-Saharan Africa have been prepared by Timaeus (1991) based on an analysis of survey and census data on orphanhood, widowhood, and the population age structure. Timaeus reported his results as expectation of life at age fifteen; these have been converted to 45Q15. His estimates were derived using logit life tables of the Brass General Standard (Brass and others 1968) for which there is a linear relationship between expectation of life at age fifteen and 45Q15. The estimates in table 2-5 are, therefore, less robust than estimates based on vital registration data, but they provide much needed information about adult mortality levels in Sub-Saharan Africa. Male 45Q15 ranges from 18 percent in northern Sudan to 58 percent in Sierra Leone. Female 45Q15 ranges from 15 percent in Congo to 54 percent in Sierra Leone. Male mortality is notably high in Botswana, Lesotho, and Swaziland, which some have attributed to migrant work in South African mines (Packard 1989). Differences between male and female 45Q15 range from 22 percent in Lesotho to -7 percent in Malawi. To put these levels of adult mortality in perspective, men in Sierra Leone have higher mortality rates than men in England and Wales did in the middle of the nineteenth century (figure 2-2a).

THE INDIAN SAMPLE REGISTRATION SYSTEM. The Indian Sample Registration System has been collecting vital statistics on a sample of the Indian population since the 1960s and provides age-specific mortality data for each state in India. Using state-specific life tables based on

Table 2-5. Adult Mortality Risk in Sub-Saharan Africa Ranked by Male 45Q15, 1965–81

Country	Year to which estimate applies	45Q15 Male	45Q15 Female	45Q15 Male-female difference
Sierra Leone	1970	57.9	54.1	3.8
Swaziland	1972	49.4	32.8	16.6
Lesotho	1976	48.3	25.9	22.4
Burundi	1970–1	46.5	39.7	6.9
Liberia	1971	43.9	38.1	5.8
Botswana	1981	42.6	28.1	14.4
Ghana	1968–9	41.2	36.8	4.4
Benin	1970	39.7	35.0	4.7
Côte d'Ivoire	1978–9	35.5	33.5	2.0
Malawi	1971	34.8	41.4	−6.7
Senegal	1978	33.7	27.9	5.8
Kenya	1974	32.4	18.2	14.2
Mauritania	1975	32.1	23.9	8.2
Cameroon	1975	30.1	21.9	8.2
The Gambia	1978	28.4	23.7	4.7
Zimbabwe	1975	26.2	15.7	10.4
Tanzania	1965	25.0	21.5	3.5
Congo	1967	24.6	15.5	9.1
Uganda	1965	23.7	22.8	0.9
Northern Sudan	1975	18.2	18.8	−0.7

Note: 45Q15 were estimated from life expectancies at age 15 (e_{15}), published by Timaeus (1991), which were based on the Brass General Standard, using the equation 45Q15 = 1420 − 22.17(e_{15}).

Source: Timaeus (1991).

data from the Indian sample registration system (Roy and Lahiri 1988), the 45Q15 was calculated for each state for the period 1970 to 1983 (table 2-6). Male 45Q15 ranges from 21 percent in Punjab to 39 percent in Orissa. Female 45Q15 is lowest in Kerala (16 percent) and highest in Orissa (37 percent). While Kerala has the lowest child and female adult mortality in India, its male 45Q15 is nearly 4 percentage points higher than in Punjab. The well-publicized good health status in Kerala, as assessed using the infant mortality rate and life expectancy as indicators (Nag 1985; Panikar and Soman 1984) and as compared to other states such as the Punjab, may need to be reinterpreted when focusing on adults. The aggregate figures for India show that the 45Q15 is 3.4 percentage points higher for men than for women.

The notion that female mortality is higher than male mortality in India is widely held. Dyson (1984, 1987), however, has analyzed

Table 2-6. Estimates of Adult and Child Mortality Risk in Selected Indian States, Ranked by Male 45Q15

	45Q15		5Q0	
	Male	*Female*	*Male*	*Female*
Orissa	39.0	37.4	20.8	21.9
Andra Pradesh	36.6	30.9	19.1	18.7
Gujarat	34.7	26.5	21.1	22.9
Tamil Nadu	33.8	33.4	17.6	17.3
Uttar Pradesh	33.2	31.5	26.8	33.6
Rajasthan	33.0	26.9	21.9	24.7
Madhya Pradesh	32.9	30.5	23.0	24.8
Karnataka	31.8	28.5	13.7	14.3
Maharashtra	30.9	24.5	15.0	15.7
Kerala	24.4	16.4	8.9	8.9
Punjab	20.7	16.8	14.2	17.7
All India	32.8	29.4	19.9	22.0

Note: Estimates based on sample registration system data for 1970–1983.
Source: Calculated from all-India and state life tables in Roy and Lahiri (1988).

available data on mortality in India and concluded that at present male mortality rates are higher than female mortality rates after about ages thirty to thirty-five. This crossover point has been declining in recent decades. In the all-India life table based on sample registration system data for 1970–1983 (Roy and Lahiri 1988), the crossover point occurs between the ages of thirty-five and thirty-nine. For India as a whole, 25Q15 is 8 percent for men and 10 percent for women; 20Q40 is 27 percent for men and 21 percent for women. If past trends have been maintained, the mortality crossover point may be at a younger age by now.

CHINA. More than 32 percent of adults in developing countries live in China (chapter 1, figure 1-2). Data from a 1982 Chinese census provide reliable detailed information on deaths in the preceding twelve months. Housheng, Arriaga, and Banister (1988) have used the 1982 census results to calculate life tables for each province. Table 2-7 shows the 45Q15 and 5Q0 computed from these life tables and ranked by level of female 45Q15. Women's mortality risk is highest in some of the poor provinces (20 percent in Qinghai) and lowest in the major cities (9 percent in Shanghai). Some wealthier provinces, however, such as Jilin, have high adult mortality risk even when they have low child mortality. Sex differences by province in 45Q15 ranged from 6.1 to -0.8 percentage points. For China as a whole in 1981, male 45Q15 was 18 percent (only about 1 percentage point more than in the United States), and female 45Q15 was 15 percent.

Table 2-7. Estimates of Adult and Child Mortality Risk in Chinese Provinces, Ranked by Female 45Q15, 1981, and Comparison of Totals for 1981 and 1986
(percentage)

	45Q15		*5Q0*	
	Male	*Female*	*Male*	*Female*
Qinghai	20.7	20.1	12.6	11.7
Guizhou	18.7	18.3	14.2	15.0
Yunan	19.3	18.2	14.6	13.9
Jilin	18.8	18.0	3.0	2.8
Sichuan	21.2	18.0	9.4	9.8
Xinjiang	17.2	18.0	20.2	18.5
Shaanxi	19.4	17.8	6.4	6.3
Gansu	19.3	17.7	6.1	6.0
Heilongjiang	18.4	17.6	4.7	4.0
Hubei	21.6	17.6	6.0	5.5
Inner Mongolia	18.0	16.8	5.7	5.2
Hunan	19.5	16.7	7.7	7.4
Ningxia	16.5	15.1	10.0	8.7
Shanxi	17.9	15.1	4.4	4.3
Jiangxi	19.4	15.0	7.3	8.2
Fujian	21.2	14.8	3.8	3.9
Liaoning	15.8	13.7	3.7	2.9
Anhui	17.9	13.7	4.5	4.7
Henan	18.2	13.1	3.3	3.3
Guangxi	16.7	12.9	6.2	6.4
Shandong	16.8	12.8	3.0	2.9
Tianjin	14.1	12.5	2.6	2.3
Hebei	15.8	12.5	3.1	2.8
Xhejiang	17.0	11.9	4.7	5.2
Jiangsu	17.7	11.9	5.1	5.2
Guangdong	17.6	11.4	3.8	3.8
Beijing	13.4	10.9	2.1	1.9
Shanghai	12.7	8.7	3.2	2.4
Total 1981	18.3	14.6	6.0	6.0
Total 1986	16.0	12.3	3.0	3.0

Note: These probabilities were calculated from provincial life tables computed from 1982 census results by the United States Bureau of the Census. The life tables were based on a question in the 1982 census that asked about deaths in the last twelve months. The total figures for 1986 were based on a similar question asked in a survey of one percent of households in 1987.
Source: Authors' calculations.

A 1987 survey of a one percent sample of the Chinese population provides more recent data on age-specific mortality. According to the 1987 data, adult mortality risk declined to 16 percent for men and 12 percent for women (table 2-7). Whether these declines are real or artifactual is difficult to determine (Zhou Youshang 1989). Another source of information on mortality in China is the disease surveillance points system operated by the Chinese Academy of Preventive Medicine. Adult mortality risks reported by this system and adjusted appropriately (see the part of this chapter called "Causes of Adult Death") were 15 and 11 percent for men and women, respectively, in 1987, and 14 and 12 percent for men and women in 1988. These levels are lower than those measured by the 1982 census and those estimated by the 1987 one percent sample. Differences from 1987 to 1988 may be due to variation in the set of communities reporting. Yet another source of information for assessing the level of adult mortality in China is the vital registration system that covers a population of 98 million. Data from this system yield a total 45Q15 of 16 percent for men and 12 percent for women in 1987.

The 1982 census in China also collected data on a variety of socioeconomic variables at the provincial level. Relationships between 45Q15 (and, for comparison, 5Q0) and the following variables were examined: per capita output, peasant expenditure per capita, population having primary education or more, population having high school education or more, population living in urban areas, female participation in labor force, hospital beds per thousand, medical personnel per thousand, highway kilometers per thousand, and the percent of non-Han ethnic minorities. These relationships were explored using univariate, multivariate linear and stepwise linear regressions. In the univariate regressions, statistically significant relationships ($p<0.05$) were found between adult and child mortality in both sexes and the income and education variables—more income and more education were associated with lower mortality.

Because of substantial multicollinearity between the independent socioeconomic variables, the results of the multivariate analysis are difficult to interpret. The adjusted R^2 was 0.66 for men, 0.63 for women, 0.84 for boys and 0.82 for girls. Because of multicollinearity, no independent variable coefficients for adult mortality were statistically significant ($p<0.05$), except for the percent of non-Han ethnic minorities (larger ethnic minorities were associated with higher mortality of men). Lower child mortality was related significantly ($p<0.05$) to more high school education, fewer health services per capita, and a lower percent of ethnic minorities. Together these socioeconomic variables explain a considerable portion of the variance in adult mortality between provinces, but the data do not allow more precise identification of explanatory factors. The same variables explain more of the variance in child mortality than they explain of the variance in adult mortality. The implication is that other variables may be needed to explain the pattern of adult mortality.

NAURU. The pacific island nation of Nauru (not included in table 2-4) has a high per capita income from phosphate mining and has had a rapid change in diet and personal behaviors during the last three decades, including an enormous increase in caloric intake, alcohol consumption, and motorcycle riding (Schooneveldt and others 1988; Taylor and Thoma 1985). Mortality data compiled by Taylor and Thoma (1985) for 1976–1981 provide an opportunity to calculate the 45Q15 for Nauruans.[13] The 45Q15 was 62 percent for men, which is probably the highest male 45Q15 recorded in any population in recent time, and 25 percent for women. For adults aged fifteen to sixty-four, injuries accounted for 28 percent of men's deaths and 20 percent of women's deaths, and diabetes complications caused 9 percent of men's deaths and 15 percent of women's deaths.

Relationships Between Probabilities of Death for Various Ages and Sexes

The following sections examine certain assumptions about these relationships and the data that support them.

Child and Adult Mortality

There is a popular notion that child and adult mortality rates are associated very closely—an example is the widespread use of the infant mortality rate as an indicator of total mortality. Another example is the use of model life tables for estimating adult mortality; implicit in any family of model life tables is a one-to-one mapping of child mortality to adult mortality. The relationship between 5Q0 and 45Q15 in Chile, Costa Rica, Cuba, Singapore, and Sri Lanka during the thirty-five-year period 1950–1985 is closer for females than for males (R^2 = 0.77 versus 0.32). By combining the vital registration estimates of 45Q15 and 5Q0 for the countries in table 2-4 with the estimates for Indian states and Chinese provinces, the association can be tested across all populations for which recent mortality estimates are available. A similar pattern emerges; the R^2 is 0.77 for females and 0.50 for males. Perhaps the mortality of women is associated more closely with child mortality because of various social, economic, and environmental factors shared by mothers and children, possibly including direct interactions between maternal and child death.

Gender Differentials in Adult Mortality

The popular notion that adult female mortality is higher than adult male mortality in developing countries may have been reinforced by the recent safe motherhood initiative (Herz and Measham 1987). Preston (1976) and Heligman (1982) presented data to suggest that excess female mortality in the reproductive age groups is more common in high mortality populations. The highest mortality developing country populations for which data are available for analysis are historical ones from Chile, Costa Rica, Cuba, Singapore, and Sri Lanka (figures 2-7a and 2-7b). For four countries—Chile, Costa Rica, Cuba, and Singapore—adult male mortality risk has been higher than adult female mortality since 1950. For Sri Lanka, 45Q15 was greater for women than for men in the 1950s and 1960s. With the decline in Sri Lankan female 45Q15 and the stagnation in male 45Q15 in the 1970s and 1980s, adult mortality risk in Sri Lanka is higher now for men than for women. The vital registration data in table 2-4 illustrate that excess male mortality risk is the rule rather than the exception, even for young adults. In Latin America and central Europe, absolute differences in 45Q15 of more than 10 percentage points are common. This pattern is also true in Africa (table 2-5). The extraordinarily high mortality of men in Botswana, Lesotho, and Swaziland may be related to migrant laborers who work in South African mines and suffer high rates of tuberculosis (Packard 1989). In both India and China, nearly all states or provinces have excess male mortality (tables 2-6 and 2-7).

The debate about the age at which female and male adult mortality rates cross over in India calls attention to sex differences in the mortality of younger adults (aged fifteen to thirty-nine years). If maternal mortality were to make female mortality higher than male mortality, it should be evident in the reproductive years. The relationship between male and female 25Q15 for all the countries in table 2-4 and the longitudinal data for Chile, Costa Rica, Cuba, Singapore, and Sri Lanka for 1950–85 was examined. For all populations male 25Q15 is greater than female 25Q15 except for Sri Lanka in the 1950s and 1960s. As noted above, young adult mortality is higher for women than for men in India as well. There is virtually no population with excess female mortality risk among older adults.

Mortality in Younger and Older Adults

By combining the vital registration data from countries with complete systems (table 2-4) with longitudinal data from Chile, Costa Rica, Cuba, Singapore, and Sri Lanka for 1950–85, the relationship between younger and older adult mortality risk can be explored. For females, a 25Q15 of 6 percent is associated with a 20Q40 of approximately 14 percent. For males, a 25Q15 of 6 percent is associated with a 20Q40 of about 18 percent. Mortality risk of younger adults can vary independently of the mortality risk of older adults. The R^2 for the relationship between 25Q15 and 20Q40 is 0.54 for males and 0.64 for females. Some countries with high 25Q15 have low 20Q40 and vice versa.

Reference Tables

Appendix tables A-1a to A-1f, at the end of the book, provide a compilation of estimates of 45Q15 for all countries. Where empirical data are not available, World Bank model-based estimates are presented.

Causes of Adult Death

The preceding sections have described the range of adult mortality levels in the developing and industrialized worlds and the substantial declines that some countries have experienced. In this section, causes of adult mortality in developing and industrialized countries are examined. Understanding these causes is essential to designing and implementing interventions to reduce adult mortality. This section begins with a selective review of previous studies on adult mortality, followed by an explanation of this chapter's framework for analyzing several cause-of-death data sets. The results of this analysis, presented in the second part of this section, seek to answer three questions:

- What are the major causes of adult mortality?
- Which causes explain the difference in adult mortality levels between countries with low and high adult mortality?
- Which, if any, causes appear to be rising as overall adult mortality declines?

Review of Previous Studies

Several researchers have addressed patterns of causes of death in the developing world and globally (see Hayes and others 1989, for a review). Preston (1976) analyzed life tables for forty-three national populations, including long historical sequences for developed countries such as the United States and England and Wales compiled by Preston, Keyfitz, and Schoen (1972). Included in Preston's 1976 analysis were life tables for nine developing countries: Chile, Colombia, Costa Rica, Guatemala, Mexico, Panama, Taiwan, Trinidad and Tobago, and Venezuela. Cause-specific age-standardized death rates were related to the overall age-standardized death rate. Diseases were classified according to eleven categories: respiratory tuberculosis, other infectious and parasitic diseases, neoplasms, cardiovascular disease, influenza/pneumonia/bronchitis, diarrhea, certain chronic diseases, maternal diseases, diseases of infancy, violence, and other/unknown.

Preston explored the relationship between cause-specific mortality and total mortality to characterize the cause-of-death structure at different levels of overall mortality. Linear regressions of age-standardized cause-specific death rates on the total age-standardized death rate all had significant positive slopes except for neoplasms in men and women and cardiovascular diseases in men. A positive slope for a cause means that as the total mortality rate decreases, the mortality rate from that particular cause decreases also. A larger slope implies that a larger percentage of the decrease in total mortality is due to changes in that cause. Some causes with large slopes explained much of the differences between low and high mortality populations; such causes included respiratory tuberculosis, other infectious and parasitic diseases, influenza/pneumonia/bronchitis, diarrheal diseases, and "other/unknown" diseases for both men and women (slopes >0.1). The large category of "other/unknown" diseases (slope >0.3) was closely and inversely related to cardiovascular diseases and neoplasms. Using a variety of indirect evidence, Preston (1976) argued that the slope for cardiovascular disease was positive after accounting for cardiovascular cases that probably were misclassified as "other/unknown."

Hakulinen and others (1986) took Preston's approach farther and estimated the relationship between cause-specific mortality and overall mortality for specific age groups. Using Preston's data base and 1980 vital registration data from the World Health Organization, they made estimates of the total number of deaths from each of these causes for major regions in the world. More recently, the World Bank (Bulatao and Stevens, forthcoming) has been estimating the number of deaths due to particular causes in different regions using relationships between cause-specific and total mortality. The World Bank has taken the Hakulinen equations for the eleven Preston groups of causes and re-estimated the parameters relating cause-specific, age-specific mortality rates to total age-specific mortality rates, using additional vital registration data for 1985. To provide a breakdown for more specific causes within each of these eleven groups, the World Bank has generated equations using just the 1985 registration data. In many cases, these age-specific, cause-specific regression equations are not statistically significant and have poor explanatory power. Both Hakulinen and others (1980) and Bulatao and Stevens (forthcoming) use Preston's original 1976 equation for cardiovascular diseases without using his adjustments for misclassified cardiovascular diseases in the category "other/unknown." Therefore, they project rising rather than declining cardiovascular disease mortality rates.

Framework Used in This Analysis

While previous studies provide estimates of the causes of death in the developing world, the approach used here for studying the causes of adult death is fundamentally different. The historical cause-of-death data for European populations at the end of the nineteenth century and first half of the twentieth century (which dominate the Preston analysis) may not be good predictors of causes of death in Sub-Saharan Africa and Asia today. This chapter examines directly the available empirical data on adult mortality and tests the relationships between cause-specific mortality and total mortality. A variety of indicators of adult mortality (cause-specific 45Q15, age-standardized years of potential life lost and avoidable mortality rates) are used, and, perhaps most importantly, an alternative framework for organizing the causes of death is presented.

CAUSE-OF-DEATH CLASSIFICATION. The International Classification of Diseases (ICD) includes codes for more than one thousand different causes of death (WHO 1978). This complex array of causes is organized into seventeen chapters (table 2-8). Much simpler analytical frameworks have often been used to highlight general patterns in these thousand causes of death. The seventeen chapters of the ICD have been divided traditionally into three categories—infectious and parasitic diseases, chronic diseases, and ill-defined causes—and this may have led to the popular belief that as mortality falls, deaths from infectious and parasitic diseases decline rapidly while deaths from chronic diseases increase. To understand trends of specific causes of death requires more detail than these traditional broad categories can provide, but not as much detail as the individual ICD codes provide. The appropriate framework for analysis also must balance the need for detail on specific causes to which interventions can be tailored against the inevitable decline in reliability and comparability inherent in more detailed cause-of-death data. The framework used here divides the causes of death into three groups—communicable and reproductive diseases (Group I), noncommunicable diseases (Group II) and injuries (Group III)—and then subdivides each group into a limited set of major causes.

Group I includes the subdivisions of diarrhea, helminthic diseases, malaria, venereal diseases, tuberculosis, and maternal causes, perinatal causes, and respiratory infections. The unusual aspect of this clas-

Table 2-8. Chapters in the International Classification of Diseases, Ninth Revision

Chapter	*Causes*
I	Infectious and parasitic diseases
II	Neoplasms
III	Endocrine, nutritional and metabolic diseases and immunity disorders
IV	Diseases of the blood and blood-forming organs
V	Mental disorders
VI	Diseases of the nervous system and sense organs
VII	Diseases of the circulatory system
VIII	Diseases of the respiratory system
IX	Diseases of the digestive system
X	Diseases of the genitourinary system
XI	Complications of pregnancy, childbirth and the puerperium
XII	Diseases of the skin and subcutaneous tissue
XIII	Diseases of the musculoskeletal system and connective tissue
XIV	Congenital anomalies
XV	Certain conditions originating in the perinatal period
XVI	Symptoms, signs and ill-defined conditions
XVII	Injury and poisoning

Source: WHO (1978).

sification is that it includes maternal causes, diseases of early infancy, nutritional deficiencies, and the acute respiratory infections together with traditional infectious and parasitic diseases. All these causes decline at much faster rates than overall mortality as socioeconomic conditions improve. In addition, these causes now account for a relatively small share of deaths in industrialized countries. This classification involves separating the ICD chapter of respiratory diseases into acute and chronic components, which, depending on the country and ICD revision in use, can be difficult. Nevertheless, such a division of respiratory diseases is critical if any policy-relevant statements about respiratory diseases are to be made, because infectious and chronic respiratory diseases have different sets of determinants and potential interventions.

Group II (the noncommunicable diseases) includes neoplasms, endocrine disorders, blood diseases, cardiovascular diseases, chronic respiratory diseases, skin and subcutaneous diseases, nervous system disorders, musculoskeletal diseases, congenital anomalies, and symptoms and signs of senile and ill-defined conditions. Two aspects distinguish this categorization from others: the exclusion of injuries and the inclusion of senile and ill-defined conditions. For many countries, mortality caused by senile and ill-defined conditions has declined as overall mortality has declined. The hypothesis is that, at least for adults, deaths coded as senile or ill-defined are much more likely to have been caused by noncommunicable diseases than by communicable and reproductive diseases or by injuries. Preston (1976) found that cardiovascular diseases, neoplasms, and conditions classified as ''other/unknown'' were highly correlated. He also found that countries with higher than expected cardiovascular mortality for their level of total mortality had lower than expected mortality from conditions classified as ''other/unknown,'' and that the reverse was true also. This close inverse relationship with the category ''other/unknown'' was not true for other groups of causes, with the exception of neoplasms. Finally, interviewers who work with relatives to ascertain causes of death report that people remember deaths due to acute infectious processes, maternal mortality, and injuries better than deaths due to other causes, making it unlikely that senile and ill-defined deaths include miscoded deaths due to these causes. One caveat is that including deaths caused by senile and ill-defined conditions with deaths caused by noncommunicable diseases may markedly affect the overall interpretation of historical trends in causes of death. If much of the change in noncommunicable mortality is due to changes in the category ''senile and ill-defined,'' the conclusion that noncommunicable diseases are increasing or decreasing would depend on the validity of including senile and ill-defined conditions in Group II.

Deaths caused by injuries, including both intentional (suicide and homicide) and unintentional injuries, constitute Group III. Injury death rates are the most variable across countries and across communities within countries; they are affected by a distinct set of social, cultural, political, and economic factors; and they are the most unaffected by changes in other death rates. For these reasons, and because adult injuries in the developing world are common and poorly understood, injuries are separated from the other noncommunicable causes of death in this classification system.

ANALYSIS CAVEATS. Certain caveats apply to using coded cause-of-death data. A spectrum of data quality exists, extending from autopsy-confirmed causes of death to responses by the general public to survey questions. The gold standard is an autopsy combined with a detailed clinical history of a patient's course of illness before death. At the other extreme, the cause of death may be reported by a non-health professional who has no firsthand information about the dead person. Between these extremes are deaths coded by qualified physicians familiar with the patient and deaths coded as the result of using a standard protocol to interpret what relatives or friends say about the circumstances of death. Such verbal autopsies may be surprisingly accurate for some causes of death (Garenne and Fontaine 1986; Darkaoui and others 1989).

Not only does the quality of cause-of-death data vary from community to community but it also varies by cause. Some causes such as childhood infectious diseases, injuries and maternal mortality are easier to diagnose than site-specific cancers, cardiovascular diseases, or digestive diseases. Styles and trends in coding deaths also vary over time. For example, virtually no deaths were coded as marasmus and kwashiorkor in the Caribbean until the University of the West Indies became active in public health and nutrition research (Murray 1988). Not only do styles of coding change, but the ICD codes themselves have been revised nine times. Any comparison over time necessitates bridge coding between various ICD revisions (Faust and Dolman 1963 and 1965; Klebba and Dolman 1975). Appendix table A-2 provides the ICD codes from the sixth, seventh, eighth, and ninth ICD Revisions (WHO 1948, 1957, 1967, 1978) that were used in this cause-of-death classification system. Although the codes may not be directly comparable between revisions, enough similarity exists to identify trends over time.

Additional caveats apply to comparing ICD coded deaths to deaths coded by other systems. ICD codes identify the underlying cause of death; the codes of many lay reporting systems, however, identify the direct cause of death. In routine cause-of-death data, some diseases may be underreported because the final cause of death appears unrelated to the true pathogenesis. Diseases such as malaria (Giglioli 1972), schistosomiasis, Chagas disease (Maguire and others 1987), hepatitis B (Beasley, Lin, and Hwang 1981), diabetes (Fuller 1985), tuberculosis (Goldman 1980) and others may be underrepresented in cause-of-death data because the final cause of death may be different. Examples of elevated cause-specific death rates include renal diseases in hyperendemic malaria areas, cor pulmonale from schistosomiasis, and sudden death from Chagas disease.

The optimal approach for analyzing mortality rates of diseases that may be misrepresented in cause-of-death data is debatable. One strategy (Walsh 1988) is to make disease-specific estimates of mortality based on informed estimates of incidence rates and case-fatality rates. The major limitations of this epidemiologic approach are twofold. First the confidence intervals are tremendously wide for both the incidence and case-fatality rates of many causes, and, second, there is insufficient detail on how each cause varies with total mortality. Here, only cause-of-death data are used, an approach that is likely to misrepresent the burden of some diseases.

Several measurements are useful in assessing cause-specific adult mortality, and all are analogous to the measurements of overall mortality used in the first part of this chapter. The preferred measure is the cause-specific 45Q15, which does not change necessarily as overall mortality changes. As death risks from other causes change, however, the cause-specific 45Q15 may change even if the age-specific mortality rates from this cause do not change. To adjust for this effect, a mortality-standardized cause-specific 45Q15 could have been used. Usually cause-specific 45Q15 and mortality-standardized cause-specific 45Q15 are similar, and so only 45Q15, and not mortality-standardized 45Q15, is reported. Age-standardized cause-specific adult years of potential life lost incorporates information on the age distribution of deaths in adulthood. Age-specific avoidable mortality risk is used also for each broad group of causes of death (Groups I, II, and III), calculated by using 1987 Japanese cause-specific mortality risks as references.

None of these measures includes the number or proportion of deaths due to specific causes. The focus of the analysis in this chapter is on rates and risks and not numbers or proportions. Distinguishing between rates and proportions is important in correcting the common misperception that Group II disease rates rise with declines in total mortality. The percentage of deaths due to Group II diseases rises but the rates and risks do not. Concentrating on rates and risks allows a distinction between the effects of the demographic component and the effects of the risk factor and therapeutic components in the health transition (see chapter 1). A change in age structure towards a relatively older population (the demographic component) tends to decrease the proportion of Group I deaths and increase the proportion of Group II deaths, even if age-specific rates and risks stay constant.

Analysis of Empirical Data on Causes of Adult Death

In this section, the cause-of-death framework is used to analyze longitudinal data for selected developing countries and cross-sectional data for a variety of developing and industrialized countries. An objective assessment of the quality of these data is hampered by the lack of validated measures of the accuracy and reliability of cause-of-death coding. Possible measures that may correlate with quality include the percentage of deaths coded as senile or ill-defined or the percentage of deaths that have been medically certified. Lopez (1989) made one of the few attempts to classify international data by quality of coding. He grouped data into two categories: those with 100 percent medical certification, including data from thirty-three industrialized countries and seven developing countries or territories (Argentina, Chile, Costa Rica, Cuba, Hong Kong, Singapore, and

Uruguay); and those with less than 100 percent or an unknown percent of medical certification. The limitation of this classification system is that medical certification does not guarantee high quality coding nor does lay reporting make data useless—some verbal autopsies correlate well with hospital data.

This section uses data from all countries that have complete vital registration systems and report cause-of-death data to the World Health Organization. The section includes data that are less than 100 percent medically certified. All statistical relationships, however, were tested independently for both types of data (100 percent medically certified deaths and less than 100 percent medically certified deaths). With one exception (breast cancer; see the section *Cross-Sectional Data Analysis* later in this chapter), there was no difference in the results when countries with less than 100 percent medical certification of deaths were included. Using the broader data set makes it possible to include more developing countries in the analysis and examine a wider range of mortality levels. To supplement these national registration data, this section also discusses various small-scale studies from India and Sub-Saharan Africa and presents a detailed examination of physician-confirmed causes of death in China.

CAUSE-OF-DEATH TRANSITION IN FIVE DEVELOPING COUNTRIES. To examine historical changes in the adult cause-of-death structure, data from five countries that have experienced substantial improvements in life expectancy during the last thirty-five years were analyzed. All five countries (Chile, Costa Rica, Cuba, Singapore, and Sri Lanka) have complete vital registration systems, and all but Sri Lanka have medical certification of all deaths.[14] Overall changes in adult male and female mortality risk for these five countries were outlined in the first part of this chapter (figures 2-7a and 2-7b).

Figures 2-8a through 2-12b show the overall trends in each of these countries for male and female adult mortality risk from communicable and reproductive diseases (Group I), noncommunicable diseases (Group II), and injuries (Group III). The overall patterns are consistent. For men, noncommunicable causes account for most deaths, followed by injuries and communicable diseases. For women, noncommunicable diseases also cause most deaths, but communicable and reproductive diseases have until recently caused more deaths than injuries. This difference between the sexes is attributable more to lower injury rates than to higher communicable disease rates in women.

In all of the countries except Cuba, the 45Q15 from noncommunicable causes declined substantially during the last thirty-five years for

(Text continues on p. 66.)

Figure 2-8a. Adult Male Mortality by Group of Mortality Causes, Chile, 1955–86

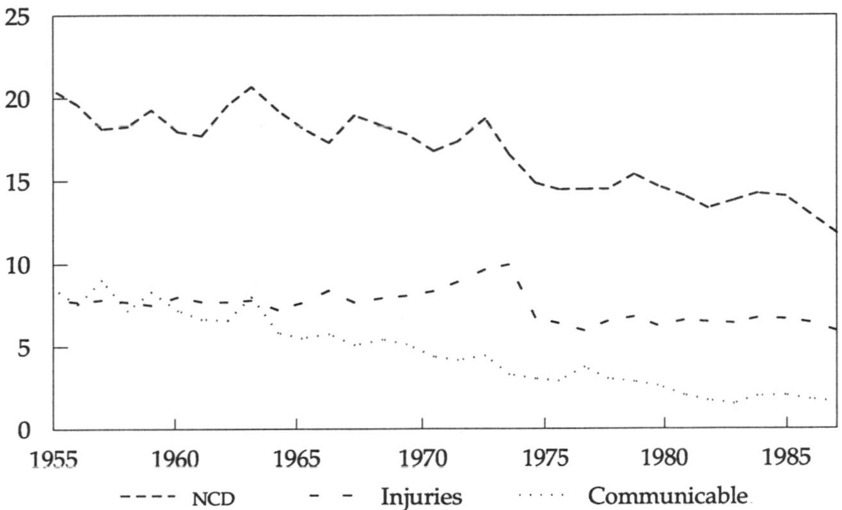

Source: Authors' calculations.

Figure 2-8b. Adult Female Mortality by Group of Mortality Causes, Chile, 1955–86

45Q15/percentage

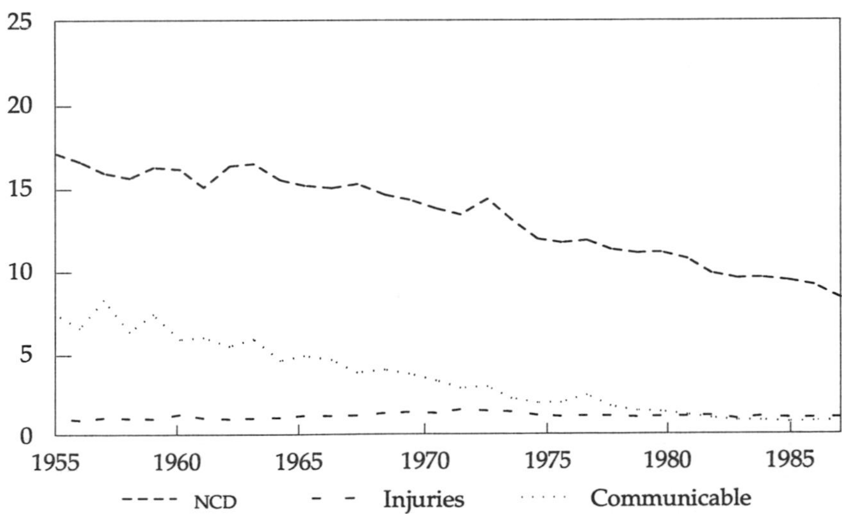

Source: Authors' calculations.

Figure 2-9a. Adult Male Mortality by Group of Mortality Causes, Costa Rica, 1956–86

45Q15/percentage

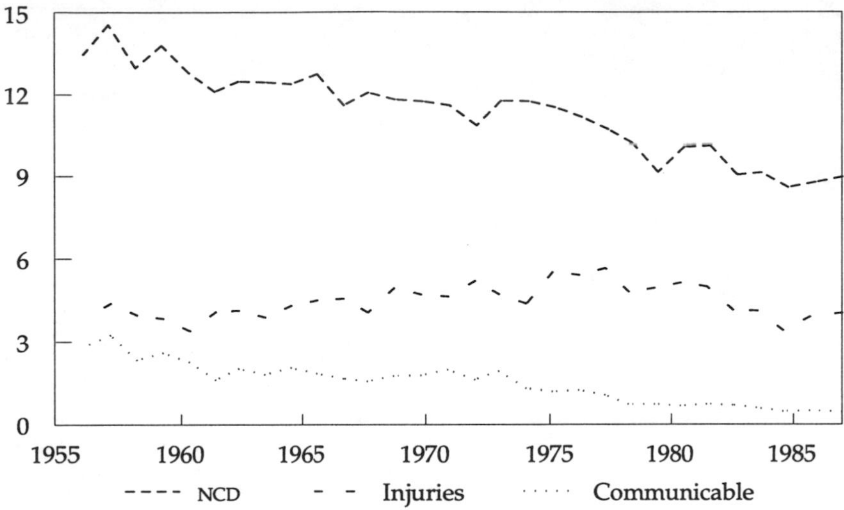

Source: Authors' calculations.

Figure 2-9b. Adult Female Mortality by Group of Mortality Causes, Costa Rica, 1955–86

45Q15/percentage

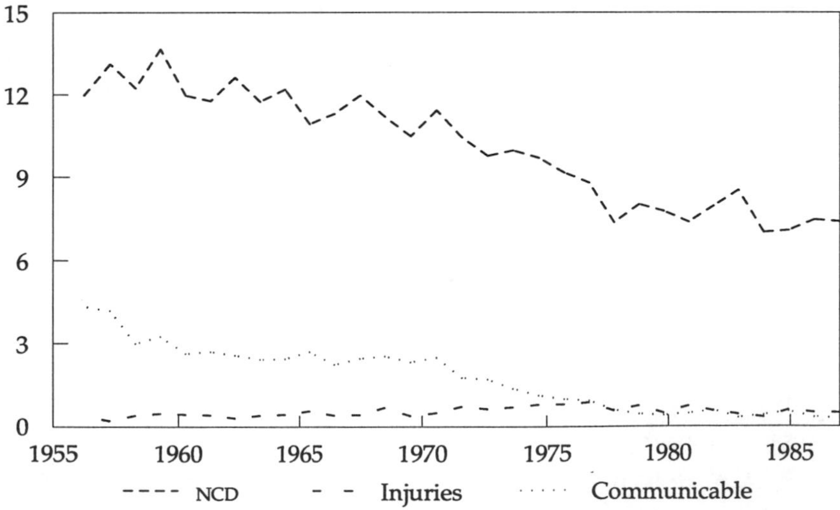

Source: Authors' calculations.

Figure 2-10a. Adult Male Mortality by Group of Mortality Causes, Cuba, 1964–86

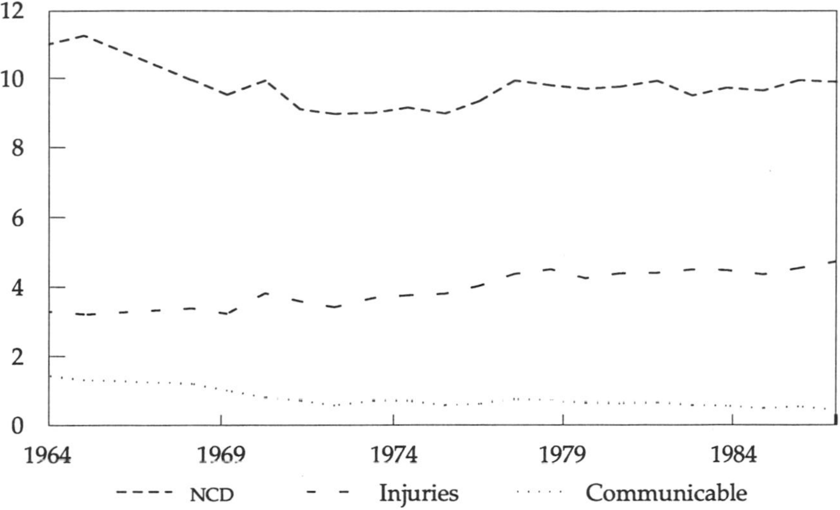

Source: Authors' calculations.

Figure 2-10b. Adult Female Mortality by Group of Mortality Causes, Cuba, 1964–86

45Q15/percentage

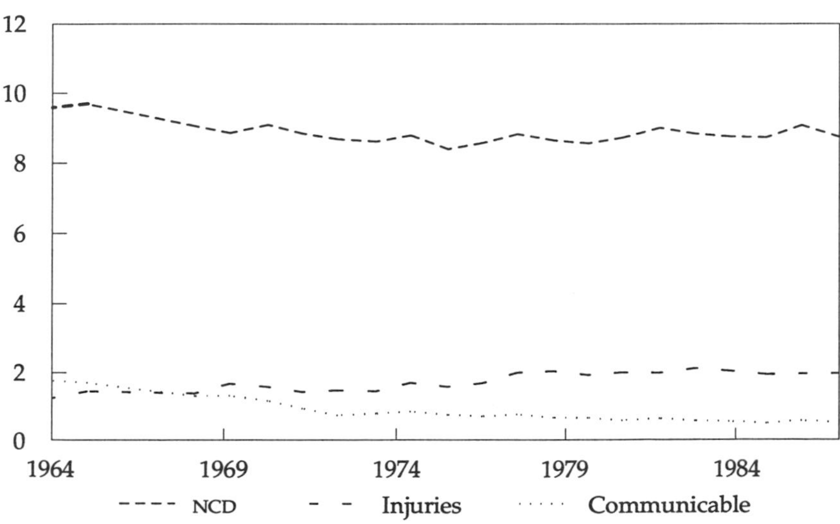

Source: Authors' calculations.

Figure 2-11a. Adult Male Mortality by Group of Mortality Causes, Singapore, 1955–87

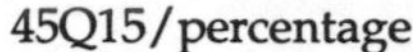

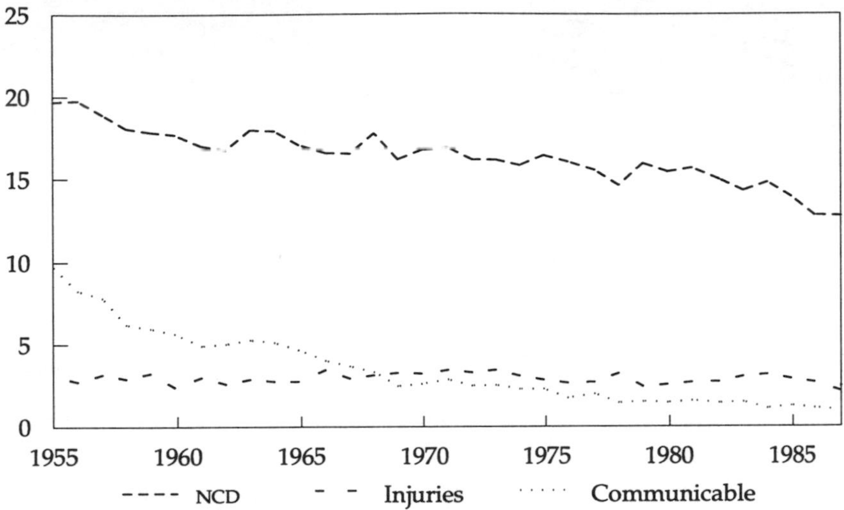

Source: Authors' calculations.

Figure 2-11b. Adult Female Mortality by Group of Mortality Causes, Singapore, 1955–87

45Q15/percentage

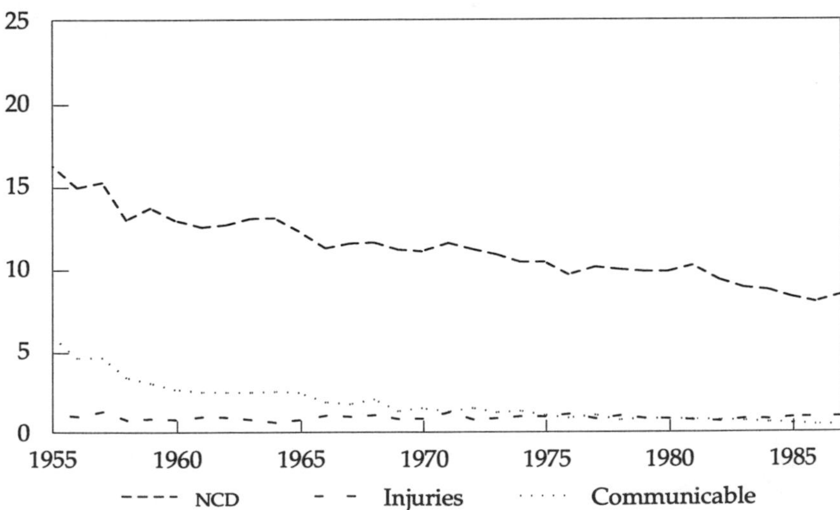

Source: Authors' calculations.

Figure 2-12a. Adult Male Mortality by Group of Mortality Causes, Sri Lanka, 1950–83

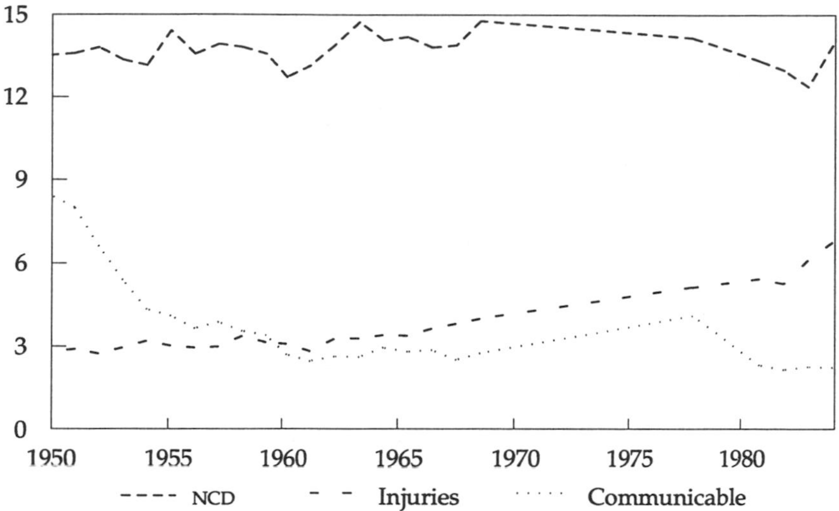

Source: Authors' calculations.

Figure 2-12b. Adult Female Mortality by Group of Mortality Causes, Sri Lanka, 1950–83

45Q15/percentage

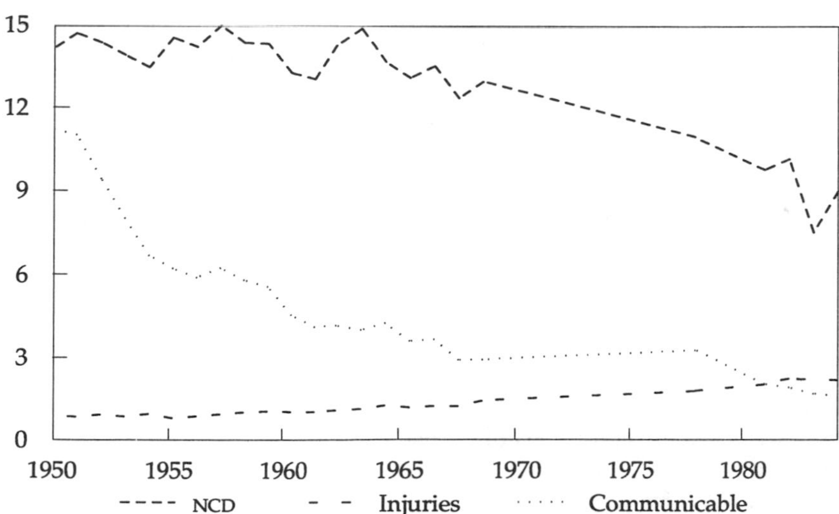

Source: Authors' calculations.

women. Similarly, the 45Q15 for women from communicable and reproductive causes dropped in all five countries, the decrease in Sri Lanka being particularly remarkable. The 45Q15 from injuries tends to be low for women, but has been increasing in Cuba and Sri Lanka. For men, the decline in risk from noncommunicable causes has been consistent, but in Cuba and Sri Lanka it has not been as large as the decline for women. Injuries have increased as causes of death for men in Cuba and Sri Lanka while decreasing in Chile. At some point in time, declining communicable and reproductive disease mortality risks become less than the relatively constant injury mortality risks (figures 2-8a through 2-12b). The year when injury mortality risk became greater varies for men in different countries, from before 1955 in Costa Rica to 1968 in Singapore. A similar crossover between Group I and Group III occurs in women's mortality risks also, but at later dates and at lower levels of risk.

The causes of death that account for the decline in adult mortality risk in these five countries might also be the causes that should be targets for action in other developing countries. Table 2-9a shows, for women, the absolute change in each cause-specific 45Q15. In Chile, Costa Rica, and Singapore, 40 to 50 percent of the total decline in women's mortality risk has been due to the decline in communicable and reproductive diseases. Tuberculosis accounts for 20 percent of the total decline. Maternal and respiratory infections explain the rest of the communicable disease reduction. Perhaps more surprisingly, half of the decline in the mortality risk of women in these countries is due to reductions in noncommunicable disease death risks. Most of this reduction is explained by changes in cardiovascular diseases, digestive diseases, senile and ill-defined causes of death, and, in some countries, neoplasms. Finally, injuries have accounted for little or none of the overall decline in women's mortality risk. In Sri Lanka, the 45Q15 from injuries has increased by more than 100 percent from 1950 to 1983 from levels that were already high enough to be studied intensively in the 1950s (Straus and Straus 1953).

The picture for men is similar (table 2-9b), although the mortality of men in Cuba and Sri Lanka has changed little. In the other countries, the decline in communicable diseases explains 30 to 50 percent of the overall decline, most of which is explained by reductions in tuberculosis (18 to 31 percent) and respiratory infections. Half of the decline in the mortality risk of men is due also to reductions in noncommunicable disease death risks. While most of this reduction can be attributed to cardiovascular diseases, neoplasms, and digestive diseases, the pattern of decline for men is less consistent across countries than it is for women.

Table 2-9a. Declines in Cause-Specific 45Q15 since the 1950s and 1960s for Women in Five Developing Countries with Vital Registration Data: Chile, Costa Rica, Cuba, Singapore, and Sri Lanka

Cause of death	*Chile (1955–86)*	*Costa Rica (1956–86)*	*Cuba*[a] *(1964–86)*	*Singapore (1955–87)*	*Sri Lanka (1950–83)*
I. Communicable and reproductive	6.5	4.1	1.2	5.4	9.6
Diarrhea	0.1	0.2	0.0	0.1	0.2
Tuberculosis	2.9	1.3	0.6	3.3	2.6
Malaria	0.0	0.2	0.0	0.1	0.8
Venereal diseases	0.1	0.0	0.0	0.1	0.0
Respiratory infections	2.1	0.4	0.0	1.2	2.3
Maternal	1.4	1.4	0.4	0.7	2.7
II. Noncommunicable	8.8	4.5	0.9	7.7	5.1
Neoplasms	1.0	0.6	0.4	−0.2	−0.7
Endocrine	0.0	−0.4	−0.1	−0.5	0.0
Cardiovascular	3.1	0.9	0.1	1.6	0.6
Respiratory	0.0	−0.4	−0.3	−0.3	0.2
Digestive	1.6	0.3	0.2	1.3	1.0
Senile and ill-defined	2.1	1.4	0.1	1.9	1.6
III. Injuries	0.0	−0.1	−0.7	0.3	−1.3
Unintentional	0.6	−0.1		0.2	−0.2
Motor vehicle transport	0.0	−0.3		−0.1	−0.1
Intentional	0.0	0.0		0.0	−1.0
Suicide	0.0	0.0		0.1	−1.0
Homicide	0.0	0.0		0.0	0.0
Undetermined	−0.6	0.0		−0.1	−0.2
Total	15.3	8.5	1.3	13.3	13.3

Note: Numbers are the absolute declines in 45Q15 due to specific causes of death. Negative numbers indicate a rise. For each group of causes, the component declines do not necessarily sum to the total decline because not all component causes have been included.

a. For later years, complete injury codes were not reported for Cuba.

Source: Authors' calculations.

Table 2-9b. Declines in Cause-Specific 45Q15 since the 1950s and 1960s for Men in Five Developing Countries with Vital Registration Data: Chile, Costa Rica, Cuba, Singapore, and Sri Lanka

Cause of death	*Chile (1955–86)*	*Costa Rica (1956–86)*	*Cuba*[a] *(1964–86)*	*Singapore (1955–87)*	*Sri Lanka (1950–83)*
I. Communicable and reproductive	6.9	2.4	1.0	8.8	6.2
Diarrhea	0.1	0.1	0.0	0.2	0.1
Tuberculosis	4.3	1.3	0.8	6.1	3.2
Malaria	0.0	0.1	0.0	0.1	0.7
Venereal diseases	0.2	0.2	0.1	0.6	0.0
Respiratory infections	2.3	0.3	0.0	1.8	1.7
II. Noncommunicable	8.7	4.5	1.1	6.6	−0.4
Neoplasms	0.6	0.8	0.5	−0.9	−0.6
Endocrine	−0.1	−0.4	0.0	−0.4	0.1
Cardiovascular	3.7	0.4	0.0	1.3	−1.3
Respiratory	0.1	−0.4	−0.1	−0.5	0.1
Digestive	0.6	0.1	0.5	1.3	0.8
Senile and ill-defined	2.1	1.7	0.0	2.2	−0.5
III. Injuries	1.9	0.0	−1.4	1.0	−3.9
Unintentional	5.1	0.2		1.1	−0.7
Motor vehicle transport	−0.3	−0.9		0.0	−0.4
Intentional	0.1	−0.1		−0.1	−2.6
Suicide	0.0	−0.3		0.3	−2.3
Homicide	0.1	0.2		0.0	−0.3
Undetermined	−3.2	−0.1		−0.4	−0.6
Total	17.6	6.9	0.7	16.3	1.9

Note: These numbers are the absolute declines in 45Q15 due to specific causes of death. Negative numbers indicate a rise. For each group of causes the component declines do not necessarily sum to the total decline because not all component causes have been included.

a. For later years, complete injury codes were not reported for Cuba.

Source: Authors' calculations.

Trends in the causes of adult death in these five countries suggest several conclusions. First, most of the declines in adult mortality risk in these countries can be attributed to reductions in tuberculosis, respiratory infections, maternal mortality, digestive diseases, and, possibly, some reduction in cardiovascular diseases. Second, injury mortality accounts for a significant but highly variable component of adult male mortality risk and has declined little in the five countries analyzed.[15] Third, when overall mortality risks are constant, as in Cuba and Sri Lanka, the cause-of-death structure may be undergoing substantial change. In both of these countries, reductions in the communicable disease mortality of men were matched by increases in injury mortality. If this pattern were to apply to other countries, it would supply further evidence that the overall mortality risk is not a good predictor of the cause-of-death structure.

CROSS-SECTIONAL VITAL REGISTRATION DATA. An alternative strategy to examining the historical experience of selected developing countries is to analyze all those countries with vital registration systems that capture nearly all deaths and report deaths by cause. The fifty-six countries or territories with complete vital registration data and detailed cause-of-death data include most industrialized market and nonmarket economies, most of Latin America, and a few countries from Asia (table 2-4). This sample includes forty populations in which all deaths are medically certified and sixteen populations in which the percentage of medically certified deaths is less than 100 percent or unknown (Lopez 1989). Unfortunately, the sample is not representative of developing countries with moderate to high adult mortality. Its main advantage, however, is the data it provides about specific causes of death, such as site-specific cancers, although with this finer detail, differences in coding practices between countries are more likely to confound the data. Some developing countries, most notably Sri Lanka, appear to underreport cancer deaths; nevertheless, they are included here. A more serious coding problem (an extraordinarily high level of adult mortality from diarrhea) excluded the data from Guatemala from this analysis.

Table 2-10 provides the means and standard deviations for cause-specific 45Q15 for men and women in the fifty-six populations with complete vital registration and cause-of-death reporting. For men, the mean 45Q15 was 0.8 percent for Group I, 13 percent for Group II, and 4 percent for Group III causes of mortality. Specific causes with a 45Q15 greater than 0.5 percent included lung cancer, ischemic heart disease, cerebrovascular accidents, chronic liver disease/cirrhosis, senile and ill-defined, motor vehicle injuries, and suicide. For women, the mean 45Q15 was 0.5 percent for Group I, 8 percent for

Table 2-10. The Means and Standard Deviations of Cause-Specific 45Q15 by Gender in Fifty-Six Countries with Complete Vital Registration Data
(percentage)

	Men		*Women*	
Cause of death	*Mean*	*Standard deviation*	*Mean*	*Standard deviation*
I. Communicable and reproductive	0.79	0.83	0.49	0.49
Diarrhea	0.06	0.17	0.03	0.01
Tuberculosis	0.14	0.17	0.06	0.09
Malaria	0.00	0.00	0.00	0.00
Venereal diseases	0.00	0.00	0.00	0.00
Helminths	0.01	0.02	0.01	0.02
Respiratory infections	0.35	0.35	0.16	0.13
Maternal & perinatal	0.00	0.00	0.07	0.10
II. Noncommunicable	12.92	3.45	8.04	2.31
Neoplasms	3.64	1.24	3.34	0.74
Esophagus	0.14	0.15	0.03	0.03
Stomach	0.34	0.20	0.18	0.15
Colon/rectum	0.27	0.16	0.27	0.13
Liver	0.10	0.18	0.04	0.05
Lung	1.00	0.56	0.28	0.21
Breast	0.00	0.00	0.78	0.34
Cervix	0.00	0.00	0.31	0.27
Lymphatic/hematopoietic	0.33	0.11	0.24	0.07
Lip, oral cavity, pharynx	0.19	0.18	0.04	0.05
Endocrine	0.43	0.43	0.42	0.52
Diabetes mellitus	0.33	0.39	0.35	0.48
Cardiovascular	5.53	2.13	2.54	1.26
Hypertensive disease	0.28	0.35	0.23	0.36

Ischemic heart disease	2.94	1.36	0.82	0.47
Cerebrovascular	1.03	0.69	0.74	0.43
Atherosclerosis	0.10	0.22	0.04	0.08
Respiratory	0.41	0.27	0.22	0.14
COPD[a]	0.33	0.24	0.18	0.13
Digestive	1.32	0.98	0.52	0.34
Chronic liver disease/cirrhosis	0.81	0.67	0.27	0.23
Ulcers stomach/duodenum	0.10	0.13	0.02	0.03
Senile and ill-defined	0.57	0.66	0.32	0.49
III. Injuries	4.07	1.67	1.11	0.42
Unintentional	2.41	1.08	0.62	0.31
Transport	1.25	0.71	0.33	0.19
Motor vehicle	1.03	0.56	0.29	0.15
Water	0.03	0.08	0.00	0.00
Poisoning	0.11	0.16	0.03	0.04
Falls	0.21	0.12	0.05	0.05
Fires	0.05	0.05	0.04	0.11
Drowning	0.24	0.38	0.03	0.04
Intentional	1.26	0.81	0.40	0.29
Suicide	0.89	0.73	0.33	0.28
Homicide	0.35	0.50	0.07	0.07
War	0.02	0.12	0.00	0.03
Undetermined	0.39	0.67	0.08	0.10
Total	17.78	5.13	9.63	2.87

Note: See table 2-4 for the list of these fifty-six countries and territories; see appendix table A-1 for the years for which the most recent data were available from them; see appendix table A-3 for the country-specific data from which these means and standard deviations are derived. Causes within the three major categories of this table are ordered according to the International Classification of Diseases, 9th Revision. For each group of causes the component mean values do not necessarily sum to the total mean because not all component causes have been included.

a. Chronic obstructive lung disease

Source: Authors' calculations.

Group II, and 1 percent for Group III causes of mortality. Specific causes with a 45Q15 greater than 0.5 percent included breast cancer, ischemic heart disease, and cerebrovascular accidents. Causes of mortality that had higher 45Q15 values for women than for men included maternal causes, breast cancer, cervical cancer, and diabetes mellitus. For reference, appendix tables A-3a and A-3b give the cause-specific 45Q15 for women and men in each of the fifty-six populations in this sample.

AVOIDABLE MORTALITY. To identify the age pattern of excess mortality from communicable and reproductive causes, noncommunicable causes, and injuries in Australia, Costa Rica, Ecuador, and Sri Lanka, avoidable mortality rates by age group were calculated using Japanese rates as references. Noncommunicable diseases contributed largely to avoidable deaths at older ages, injuries to avoidable deaths at younger ages. These four countries exhibit tremendous heterogeneity in the age pattern of avoidable mortality. Not only is the cause and age pattern entirely different between countries, it is also different for women and men in the same country. In Costa Rica most of the avoidable deaths among men involve injuries between ages twenty-five and forty-five, while most of the avoidable deaths among women involve noncommunicable diseases at older ages.[16] None of these countries has significant levels of avoidable communicable and reproductive mortality. This finding probably reflects the inadequacy of the sample rather than the true pattern in other developing countries, where avoidable mortality most likely involves communicable and reproductive diseases.

YEARS OF POTENTIAL LIFE LOST. Using age-standardized years of potential life lost per thousand adults to examine the age-distribution of specific causes of death gives more importance to causes that affect younger adults. For example, the injury mortality of men in this sample accounts for 24 percent of 45Q15 (table 2-10) but 37 percent of age-standardized adult years of potential life lost. Almost all specific injuries affect younger adults particularly. For example, motor vehicle injuries account for 5 percent of male 45Q15 in the cross-sectional sample (table 2-10) and 11 percent of age-standardized adult years of potential life lost. Other causes that have a relatively greater effect on young adults include tuberculosis, diarrhea, maternal mortality, and lymphatic/hematopoietic cancers. In contrast, most neoplasms, endocrine disorders, cardiovascular diseases and digestive diseases have a greater effect on older adults.

The Relationship Between Cause-Specific Adult Mortality and Total Adult Mortality

The relationship between cause-specific adult mortality and total adult mortality is important for two reasons. First, if there is a close relationship between specific causes and total mortality, then cause-specific mortality can be predicted from the level of mortality. This is the assumption underlying predictions by Hakulinen and others (1986) and the World Bank (Bulatao and Stevens, forthcoming). The idea that each level of mortality has a characteristic cause-of-death structure is also the basis of much previous writing on the epidemiologic transition (Omran 1971). Second, an understanding of the relationship between specific causes and total mortality may help identify those causes that are most responsible for explaining the difference between high and low mortality populations. The relationship between cause-specific and total adult mortality was examined in the two data sets described in preceding sections of this chapter (the longitudinal data for Chile, Costa Rica, Cuba, Singapore, and Sri Lanka, and the cross-sectional data from fifty-six countries and territories). The longitudinal data provide information on cause of death over a wide range of total 45Q15. The cross-sectional data make it possible to assess relationships between total mortality and more detailed causes such as ischemic heart disease and site-specific neoplasms. The two data sets combined form the basis for generating the best predictions of the cause-of-death structure for hypothetical populations in which the total 45Q15 ranges from 10 to 50 percent.

LONGITUDINAL DATA ANALYSIS. Table 2-11 gives the results for women in Chile, Costa Rica, Cuba, and Singapore of regressing each cause-specific 45Q15 on total 45Q15 minus that cause.[17] The statistically significant linear relationships were positive, except for those of endocrine disorders, respiratory diseases, motor vehicle injuries, and intentional injuries.[18] The strength of the associations was highly variable (R^2 = 0.1 percent for unintentional injuries, 86 percent for tuberculosis). Strong associations (R^2 > 30 percent) included tuberculosis, venereal diseases, respiratory infections, and maternal mortality (Group I); and neoplasms, cardiovascular diseases, digestive disorders, and senile and ill-defined conditions (Group II). Regressions of each cause versus total 45Q15 were used to estimate how much change in 45Q15 was due to changes in each cause; 40 percent of such change involved Group I causes, 60 percent involved Group II, and 1 percent involved Group III. Specific causes that were major determinants of mortality risk change were tuberculosis (17 percent),

Table 2-11. The Relationship between Cause-Specific 45Q15 and Total 45Q15 Minus that Cause for Women and Men, Longitudinal Data from Chile, Costa Rica, Cuba, and Singapore

	Women		Men	
Cause of death	R^2	*Slope*	R^2	*Slope*
I. Communicable and reproductive	82.5	0.629[a]	73.3	0.451[a]
Diarrhea	29.5	0.006[a]	37.0	0.005[a]
Tuberculosis	85.6	0.205[a]	70.9	0.239[a]
Malaria	4.5	0.002	3.3	0.001
Venereal diseases	37.5	0.003[a]	21.9	0.008[a]
Respiratory infections	72.3	0.132[a]	81.3	0.118[a]
Maternal	58.3	0.090[a]		
II. Noncommunicable	82.7	1.331[a]	53.7	0.741[a]
Neoplasms	47.7	0.099[a]	8.9	0.039[a]
Endocrine	26.2	−0.021[a]	4.4	−0.004
Cardiovascular	45.7	0.142[a]	7.3	0.065[a]
Respiratory	26.5	−0.018[a]	0.1	0.000
Digestive	38.8	0.150[a]	42.1	0.187[a]
Senile and ill-defined	54.9	0.131[a]	46.8	0.084[a]
III. Injuries	1.7	−0.012	11.4	0.110[a]
Unintentional	0.1	−0.003	5.0	0.058
Motor vehicle transport	6.7	−0.006[a]	0.2	−0.003
Intentional	5.7	−0.015[a]	0.5	0.005
Suicide	2.6	−0.009	2.5	0.006
Homicide	3.9	−0.002	2.0	0.004
Undetermined	0.9	−0.005	0.0	−0.001

Note: The R^2 is a measure of the strength of the relationship between cause-specific 45Q15 and total 45Q15 minus that cause. It is the proportion of the variation in the latter explained by changes in the former. The slope measures the direction and importance of each cause in explaining changes in total 45Q15 minus that cause. A negative sign means that the cause increases as total 45Q15 decreases, and a positive sign means that the cause declines as total 45Q15 decreases. A larger slope means that a larger component of a unit change in 45Q15 is due to the cause.

a. Significantly different ($p < 0.01$) from zero

Source: Authors' calculations.

respiratory infections (12 percent), maternal mortality (9 percent), neoplasms (10 percent), cardiovascular diseases (14 percent), digestive diseases (15 percent), and senile and ill-defined conditions (12 percent).

In similar regressions for men (table 2-11), no group of causes increased as total mortality declined. Strong associations were fewer than for women. Diarrhea, tuberculosis, and respiratory infections (Group I) and digestive diseases and senile and ill-defined conditions (Group II) had R^2 values of more than 30 percent. Several large causes of mortality (motor vehicle injuries, suicides, homicides) had no statistically significant ($p < 0.01$) relationship with total mortality. Change in 45Q15 was due to various causes: 33 percent involved Group I causes, 50 percent involved Group II causes, and 17 percent involved Group III causes. Specific causes that were major determinants of mortality risk change include tuberculosis (20 percent), respiratory infections (11 percent), cardiovascular diseases (10 percent), digestive diseases (18 percent), senile and ill-defined conditions (8 percent) and unintentional injuries (11 percent).

CROSS-SECTIONAL DATA ANALYSIS. In the preceding analysis of the longitudinal data, the inclusion of older data coded according to the ICD sixth and seventh revisions precluded the analysis of more detailed causes, such as site-specific neoplasms. The cross-sectional data, which were coded mostly according to the ICD ninth revision, permit a more detailed analysis of causes. As discussed above, national data are of two types, those with complete medical certification of deaths and those without. Independent analyses of these two types of data yielded only slight differences, and so this section presents the results of the combined analyses.[19] Regression results for the relationship between causes of adult death and total adult mortality risk in these cross-sectional data from fifty-six countries (table 2-12) show generally weaker relationships than the longitudinal analysis, probably due to the narrower range of the independent variable in this sample and possible autocorrelation in the longitudinal data. Despite lower R^2 values, the causes with the strongest relationships are nearly the same, despite possible changes in health service technology and socioeconomic factors during the last thirty-five years.

For women, the mortality risk from breast cancer rises and the mortality risk from cervical cancer declines as total mortality risk declines ($p < 0.01$ for both relationships). The decline in women's risk of cardiovascular disease mortality appears to be due both to reductions in ischemic heart disease and cerebrovascular accidents. Finally, detailed injury codes show that women's mortality risk from drowning and homicide declines with total mortality risk. As total mortality risk declines for men, mortality risk from lymphatic/hematopoietic neoplasms increases significantly ($p < 0.01$), and mortality risk from hypertensive heart disease and cerebrovascular accidents decreases. Declines in mortality risk from digestive diseases appear to be due to declines in risk of chronic liver diseases/cirrhosis and ulcers. Among specific causes of injuries, the mortality risk from drowning and homicide declines significantly with total mortality risk.

Table 2-12. The Relationship between Cause-Specific 45Q15 and Total 45Q15 Minus that Cause for Women and Men in Fifty-Six Populations with Recent Cause-of-Death Data

	Women		Men	
Cause of death	R^2	*Slope*	R^2	*Slope*
I. Communicable and reproductive	45.1	0.131[a]	45.1	0.123[a]
Diarrhea	15.4	0.014[a]	11.5	0.011
Tuberculosis	8.1	0.009	16.0	0.013
Malaria	2.5	0.000	1.1	0.000
Helminths	0.0	0.000	2.1	0.000
Venereal diseases	21.5	0.003[a]	17.0	0.002
Respiratory infections	32.8	0.027[a]	45.3	0.049[a]
Maternal	37.1	0.021[a]	0.0	
II. Noncommunicable	43.9	2.037[a]	32.7	0.853[a]
Neoplasms	1.7	−0.034	7.7	−0.064
Esophagus	0.2	0.001	7.5	0.008
Stomach	0.2	0.002	0.1	−0.001
Colon/rectum	1.7	−0.006	2.7	−0.005
Liver	0.1	0.000	0.7	−0.003
Lung	1.5	−0.009	2.4	−0.017
Breast	28.2	−0.060[a]	1.4	0.000
Cervix	46.5	0.069[a]	0.0	
Lymphatic/hematopoietic	0.6	−0.002	16.4	−0.008[a]
Lip, oral cavity, pharynx	1.1	−0.002	0.0	0.000
Endocrine	43.5	0.138[a]	11.9	0.030
Diabetes mellitus	40.6	0.121	14.1	0.029
Cardiovascular	37.5	0.405[a]	17.2	0.228[a]
Hypertensive disease	14.5	0.050[a]	38.8	0.044[a]
Ischemic heart disease	29.0	0.097[a]	0.1	0.007
Cerebrovascular	39.3	0.106[a]	30.0	0.080[a]
Atherosclerosis	4.0	0.006	17.1	0.018
Respiratory	8.4	0.014	22.3	0.025[a]
COPD[b]	13.8	0.017[a]	31.7	0.027[a]
Digestive	21.8	0.059[a]	44.3	0.148[a]
Chronic liver disease/cirrhosis	2.9	0.011	24.6	0.069[a]
Ulcers stomach/duodenum	10.6	0.003	50.6	0.019[a]
Senile and ill-defined	7.1	0.049	5.1	0.030
III. Injuries	18.1	0.067[a]	34.0	0.245[a]
Unintentional	35.3	0.053[a]	17.0	0.087[a]
Transport	3.2	0.009	0.2	0.004
Motor vehicle	1.5	0.006	0.14	−0.004
Water	0.1	0.000	7.3	−0.004
Poisoning	1.6	−0.002	1.1	0.003
Falls	3.9	0.002	8.9	0.007
Fires	13.6	0.000	7.6	0.003
Drowning	15.6	0.006[a]	26.3	0.040[a]

Table 2-12 (continued)

	Women		Men	
Cause of death	R^2	*Slope*	R^2	*Slope*
Intentional	1.5	0.012	25.5	0.083[a]
Suicide	0.2	−0.004	3.7	0.028
Homicide	21.8	0.012[a]	13.0	0.037[a]
War	1.9	0.005	6.9	0.037
Undetermined	6.3	0.003	2.8	0.004

Note: See table 2-11 for an explanation of R^2 and slope. The regression equations for detailed injury codes excluded countries such as Cuba and Romania that report no deaths from intentional injuries.

a. Significantly different ($p < 0.01$) from zero

b. Chronic obstructive lung disease

Source: Authors' calculations.

While most of the strong relationships are the same for both the longitudinal and cross-sectional data, subtle differences exist in the cause-of-death structures (compare table 2-11 with table 2-12). There is only one example of a contradictory statistically significant relationship: endocrine disorders in women has a negative slope in the longitudinal data and a positive slope in the cross-sectional data. In most cases, the differences are in statistical significance. For example, the strong relationship between tuberculosis and total adult mortality in the longitudinal data is absent in the cross-sectional data. Such discrepancies may be due to data deficiencies or perhaps to nonlinear relationships with total adult mortality. Tuberculosis may decrease to a low level at moderate mortality levels so that there is little or no relationship in low mortality countries with total mortality. In addition, some causes (such as endocrine disorders) may rise at first during the transition from high to moderate total mortality and then decline during the phase from moderate to low mortality. More intensive investigation of the patterns of change over time needs to be done for some of these causes before their relationship with total mortality can be characterized adequately.

PREDICTED CAUSE-OF-DEATH PATTERNS. One of the potential uses of these cause-specific mortality equations is to predict the adult cause-of-death structure for countries without cause-of-death information. To provide the best estimates, both the longitudinal and the cross-sectional data sets were combined to produce the predicted patterns of cause-specific 45Q15 for hypothetical populations having a range of total 45Q15s (tables 2-13a and 2-13b). For some causes of death, the

Table 2-13a. Predicted Values of Cause-Specific Female 45Q15 at Different Levels of Total Female 45Q15
(percentage)

	Total 45Q15			
Cause of death	*10*	*20*	*30*	*40*
I. Communicable and reproductive[a]	0.6	4.2	7.7	11.3
Diarrhea[a]	0.0	0.1	0.2	0.3
Tuberculosis[a]	0.1	1.5	3.0	4.4
Malaria[a]	0.0	0.0	0.0	0.1
Venereal diseases[a]	0.0	0.0	0.1	0.1
Respiratory infections[a]	0.2	1.2	2.3	3.3
Maternal[a]	0.1	0.9	1.6	2.4
II. Noncommunicable[a]	8.3	14.7	21.1	27.5
Neoplasms[a]	3.4	4.3	5.2	6.1
Endocrine	0.4	0.4	0.4	0.5
Cardiovascular[a]	2.6	4.4	6.3	8.1
Respiratory	0.3	0.2	0.2	0.2
Digestive[a]	0.5	1.9	3.2	4.5
Senile and ill-defined[a]	0.3	1.4	2.5	3.6
III. Injuries	1.1	1.1	1.2	1.3
Unintentional	0.6	0.7	0.8	1.0
Motor vehicle[a]	0.2	0.2	0.1	0.0
Intentional[a]	0.4	0.3	0.2	0.1
Suicide	0.3	0.2	0.1	0.1
Homicide	0.1	0.1	0.1	0.1
Undetermined	0.1	0.1	0.1	0.2
Total	10.0	20.0	30.0	40.0

Note: The figures given are the female 45Q15 values predicted for a country with a total female 45Q15 of 10, 20, 30, or 40 percent, based on regressions of cause-specific 45Q15 and total 45Q15, using longitudinal data from four developing countries and cross-sectional data from fifty-six populations.

Data from countries that report no deaths from intentional injuries (e.g. Cuba and Romania) were excluded from the regression analyses of detailed injury codes.

For each group of causes, the values of the component causes do not necessarily sum to the group value because not all component causes have been included.

a. Causes for which the relationship between the cause and total 45Q15 minus that cause were significant ($p < 0.01$) for the combination of the longitudinal and cross-sectional data sets.

Source: Authors' calculations.

predictions are based on statistically significant relationships (for example, tuberculosis and digestive diseases). There remains, however, a percentage of 45Q15 that cannot be attributed with much certainty to specific causes of death on the sole basis of total adult mortality.

One major caveat about the predicted Group I and Group II 45Q15

Table 2-13b. Predicted Values of Cause-Specific Male 45Q15 at Different Levels of Total Male 45Q15
(percent)

	Total 45Q15			
Cause of death	*20*	*30*	*40*	*50*
I. Communicable and reproductive[a]	2.0	5.1	8.2	11.2
Diarrhea[a]	0.1	0.1	0.2	0.3
Tuberculosis[a]	0.9	2.7	4.4	6.2
Malaria[a]	0.0	0.0	0.0	0.0
Venereal diseases[a]	0.0	0.1	0.2	0.2
Respiratory infections[a]	0.7	1.7	2.7	3.7
II. Noncommunicable[a]	13.5	18.6	23.7	28.8
Neoplasms	3.7	4.0	4.4	4.8
Endocrine	0.3	0.4	0.4	0.4
Cardiovascular[a]	4.8	6.0	7.1	8.2
Respiratory	0.4	0.5	0.6	0.7
Digestive[a]	1.7	3.5	5.3	7.1
Senile and ill-defined[a]	0.8	1.6	2.3	3.1
III. Injuries[a]	4.5	6.3	8.1	10.0
Unintentional[a]	2.9	4.0	5.1	6.2
Motor vehicle	0.9	0.9	0.9	0.9
Intentional	1.1	1.3	1.5	1.7
Suicide	0.7	0.8	0.9	0.9
Homicide	0.3	0.5	0.6	0.7
Undetermined	0.6	1.1	1.6	2.1
Total	20.0	30.0	40.0	50.0

Note: The figures given are the male cause-specific 45Q15 values predicted for a country with a total male 45Q15 of 20, 30, 40, or 50 percent, based on regressions of cause-specific 45Q15 and total 45Q15, using longitudinal data from four developing countries and cross-sectional data from fifty-six populations.

Data from countries that report no deaths from intentional injuries (e.g. Cuba and Romania) were excluded from the regression analyses of detailed injury codes.

For each group of causes, the values of the component causes do not necessarily sum to the group value because not all component causes have been included.

a. Causes for which the relationship between the cause and total 45Q15 minus that cause were significant ($p < 0.01$) for the combination of the longitudinal and cross-sectional data sets.

Source: Authors' calculations.

in high mortality populations is that although a straight line gives as good a fit (in terms of variance explained) as a logarithmic function does, the slope for Group I appears to rise at higher mortality levels. Plotting the regression residuals versus total adult mortality confirmed this change in slope. Consequently, in these estimates based on linear equations, the predicted Group I 45Q15 will be too low, and the Group II 45Q15 too high, for high mortality populations, a pattern that is confirmed by the small-scale data from India and Africa presented in the next section.

Other Sources of Cause-of-Death Data for Asia and Sub-Saharan Africa

India, with a population of about 850 million, is an important country not included in the cause-of-death data analyzed thus far. Unfortunately, India does not have a complete national vital registration system. Studies of selected populations provide some indications of the Indian pattern of causes of adult death. Eighteen percent of the deaths of men and women aged fifteen to sixty-four years in a group of Punjabi villages in 1957–59 were due to tuberculosis, and 5 percent were due to maternal causes (Gordon, Singh, and Wyon 1965). When these results were analyzed in terms of 45Q15, Group I and II causes accounted for equal shares of total 45Q15. A study of 8,457 deaths in health care facilities and other institutions in Madras (1975–76) found that 20 percent of men's deaths and 11 percent of women's deaths were due to tuberculosis, and, notably, 24 percent of women's deaths were due to suicides (Kachirayan and others 1983).

The Indian survey of rural causes of death collects information on a sample of the Indian population and uses lay reporters to assign causes of death. While the quality of this cause-of-death coding is questionable, these data do provide one of the few sources of information on the causes of death throughout rural India (India, Office of Registrar General 1988). Using these data on deaths by specific causes and ages, table 2-14 was generated for adults aged fifteen to fifty-four years. (Data for adults aged fifty-five to fifty-nine were not available.) Because denominators are not available, only the percent distribution of adult death is reported.

For Indian women, communicable and reproductive diseases accounted for 41 percent of deaths, noncommunicable diseases accounted for 43 percent, and injuries accounted for 16 percent. Total 45Q15 for females in India in 1970–83 was 29 percent (table 2-6), and the predicted distribution for a community with this level of female 45Q15 (calculated from table 2-13a) is 25 percent due to communicable and reproductive diseases (Group I), 70 percent due to noncommunicable diseases (Group II), and 5 percent due to injuries (Group III). The rural pattern of causes of death in India is considerably different and reflects either poor attribution of cause by lay reporters or an alternative cause-of-death structure with higher than expected mortality rates from communicable and reproductive diseases and injuries, a pattern also reported in Gordon, Singh, and Wyon (1965) and

Table 2-14. Distribution of Deaths of Indian Women and Men by Cause, 1986
(percentage)

	Women		Men	
Cause of death	*All ages*	*15–54 years*	*All ages*	*15–54 years*
I. Communicable and reproductive	39.4	40.6	37.8	35.0
Diarrhea	6.6	6.6	5.8	5.5
Typhoid	1.9	2.5	1.7	2.1
Other diarrhea	4.7	4.1	4.0	3.4
Tuberculosis	3.6	10.9	6.7	17.8
Malaria	1.5	1.4	1.7	2.1
Pneumonia/influenza	7.2	3.5	5.8	2.3
Pneumonia	5.9	1.8	4.8	1.7
Influenza	1.3	1.7	1.0	0.6
Unclassified fever	6.2	6.6	5.4	5.9
Pregnancy and childbirth	2.1	9.3	0.0	0.0
Perinatal	10.2	0.0	10.8	0.0
Other	2.0	2.2	1.6	1.4
Whooping cough	0.2	0.1	0.1	0.0
Other	1.8	2.2	1.5	1.4
II. Noncommunicable	54.6	43.3	54.5	45.2
Cancer	3.1	6.7	2.7	4.4
Circulatory	8.3	12.6	9.6	15.3
Bronchitis/asthma/unspecified cough	8.0	7.7	9.9	8.3
Bronchitis/asthma	7.6	7.1	9.3	7.5
Unspecified cough	0.5	0.6	0.5	0.9
Digestive disorders	4.5	8.9	5.2	9.1
Ulcer/acute abdomen	1.9	4.8	2.7	4.7
Digestive unspecified	1.2	1.8	1.0	1.5
Jaundice/cirrhosis	1.4	2.3	1.6	2.9
Nervous system	3.9	3.9	3.7	3.7
Senility	24.4	0.0	20.8	0.0
Other	2.4	3.5	2.6	4.5
III. Injuries	6.0	16.1	7.7	19.8
Unintentional	4.3	10.9	5.2	12.1
Drowning	0.9	2.1	0.9	1.6
Motor vehicle	0.7	1.6	2.2	6.5
Burns	1.4	4.9	0.4	1.0
Intentional	1.0	3.8	1.3	4.1
Suicide	0.8	3.1	0.8	2.7
Homicide	0.2	0.7	0.5	1.4
Undetermined	0.7	1.4	1.3	3.6

Note: The specific causes included in the category "Other" listed here under Group II were not specified.

Source: India, Office of Registrar General (1988).

Kachirayan and others (1983). The high percentage of injuries is in part attributable to burns, which may reflect a real and special aspect of the Indian cause-of-death structure.

For Indian men, communicable and reproductive diseases accounted for 35 percent of deaths, noncommunicable diseases for 45 percent, and injuries for 20 percent (table 2-14). For comparison, the predicted percentage distribution for a community with a male 45Q15 of 33 percent (table 2-6) is 18 percent due to Group I, 61 percent to Group II, and 21 percent to Group III causes of death (calculated from table 2-13b). The agreement between the survey results and these predictions is better for men than for women, although the survey attributes almost twice the percentage of deaths to communicable and reproductive diseases than predicted.

No continental Sub-Saharan African nation has a complete vital registration system. Data are available on hospital admissions and deaths (Olubuyide and Solanke 1990; Williams, Hayes, and Smith 1986), but have the major limitation of selection bias. A limited number of communities have been monitored intensively, most often for childhood deaths (Bradley and Gilles 1984; Feachem and Jamison 1991; Garenne and Fontaine 1986; Greenwood and others 1987; Omondi-Odhiambo, Van Ginneken, and Voorhoeve 1990), and cause-of-death data have been compiled for a few African cities (Ayeni 1980; Fargues and Nassour 1987). Only a limited number of studies have provided information about adult deaths, and this information is for broad groups of causes and wide age groups. The data for a rural area at Machakos, Kenya (Omondi-Odhiambo, Van Ginneken, and Voorhoeve 1990) illustrate the results of one of these studies (table 2-15). Neither the age groups nor the cause groups in that study are compatible with the framework used in this book, but the results are informative, nonetheless. As in India, communicable and reproductive (Group I) causes are more important than predicted for even the highest mortality countries (tables 2-13a and 2-13b). These small-scale studies highlight the urgent need for better data on causes of death in high mortality Sub-Saharan African and Asian populations. Such data also will serve to clarify the increasing contribution of AIDS to adult mortality in most countries (appendix 2-C).

Causes of Death in China

This section takes an in-depth view of the adult cause-of-death structure in China. As described in chapter 1, 32 percent of all developing world adults live in China, and a variety of sources offer fairly comprehensive information on the causes of adult death in China. China does not have a complete vital registration system; the ministry of

Table 2-15. Distribution of Adult (Fifteen to Sixty-Four Years) Deaths by Cause in a Rural Area of the Machakos District, Kenya, 1975–1978

Cause of death	*Percentage*
I. Communicable and reproductive	39.6
Intestinal infections	2.3
Tuberculosis	15.8
Malaria	1.7
Other infectious and parasitic	18.1
Nutritional and metabolic[a]	1.7
II. Noncommunicable	43.2
Neoplasms	8.2
Circulatory	2.9
Respiratory[a]	4.1
Digestive	9.9
Other	7.6
Unknown	10.5
III. Injuries	17.2

Note: The causes belonging to the category "Other" were not specified.

a. According to the classification system used in this book, deaths from these causes are divided between Group I (communicable and reproductive causes) and Group II (noncommunicable causes). Because of insufficient information, however, this type of separation could not be made for these data.

Source: Omondi-Odhiambo, Van Ginneken, and Voorhoeve (1990).

public health collects and collates registration data for a population of 98 million people living in selected cities and counties. Recently China has started to code deaths recorded in the vital registration system according to the International Classification of Diseases, Ninth Revision (WHO 1978) as well as to share summary data from this system internationally. Two other sources provide information on causes of death in China: the 1973–75 cancer mortality survey and the disease surveillance points system (DSP). The cancer survey was an ad hoc follow-up of one million deaths to determine their causes. The DSP system is an ongoing program of the Chinese Academy of Preventive Medicine for collecting information on causes of death. The data analyzed in this section are DSP data.

The DSP system comprises a series of Chinese communities where deaths are registered and causes attributed by physicians or other health workers. Nearly all causes of death in urban communities are determined by physicians, while in rural communities more causes of death are determined by other health workers. A characteristic that distinguishes the DSP system from the vital registration system is the active follow-up that the DSP team conducts for each death. The first "points" or data collection sites were established in 1978. By 1986 there were 58 disease surveillance sites, and by 1987 there were 71. A new expansion is underway, and by 1991 more than 100 sites were collecting data on causes of death.

Because the sample of disease surveillance points is neither random nor representative of the poorer rural areas of China, the DSP data have been adjusted to compensate for the bias towards wealthier communities.[20] DSP data were available for 1986, 1987, and 1988. Because the data for these years were not directly comparable,[21] the data for each year have been analyzed separately. In addition, combined estimates of 45Q15 for each cause of death were calculated using data from the forty-seven points reporting for both 1987 and 1988.

Table 2-16 provides the adjusted 45Q15 by cause for all of China based on the DSP data.[22] The 1987 and 1988 adjusted estimates differ markedly for some specific causes but agree for most. Chinese men and women have rates of esophageal, stomach and liver cancers that are much higher than the mean for all countries with vital registration data (table 2-10). Table 2-17 provides a comparison of 45Q15 for major groups of causes with the predicted cause-specific 45Q15 based on the equations implicit in table 2-13. From this comparison, Chinese women appear to have substantially higher death rates than predicted from tuberculosis, chronic respiratory diseases, unintentional injuries, and suicides. The higher than predicted cardiovascular disease mortality is largely attributable to pulmonary heart disease, which often is a consequence of chronic obstructive pulmonary disease. Chinese men have substantially higher mortality risks from tuberculosis and suicides; all other risks are within 50 percent of the predicted risks, except for low rates of respiratory infections and endocrine disorders.

The 1987 and 1988 DSP data show that the overall mortality risk of men and women in rural China is higher than in urban China (three percentage points difference in adjusted 45Q15). The rural excess involves all three categories of causes of death (communicable and reproductive, noncommunicable, and injuries). Men in rural China are more likely to die from tuberculosis, pulmonary heart disease, poisoning, falls, and suicides. Women in rural China are more likely to die from tuberculosis, maternal causes, pulmonary heart disease, poisoning and suicides.

AGE-STANDARDIZED ADULT YEARS OF POTENTIAL LIFE LOST. Age-standardized adult years of potential life lost were computed using the adjusted 1987 DSP data for China. Compared to women, men lost

Table 2-16. Adjusted Estimates of Cause-Specific 45Q15 for Chinese Women and Men, Disease Surveillance Points Data

	Women		Men	
Cause of death	*1987*	*1988*[c]	*1987*	*1988*[c]
I. Communicable and reproductive	1.24	1.05	1.05	1.11
Diarrhea	—	0.03	—	0.09
Tuberculosis	0.72	0.42	0.72	0.54
Malaria	0.00	0.00	0.00	0.00
Venereal diseases	0.00	0.00	0.00	0.00
Helminths	0.01	0.03	0.02	0.02
Respiratory infections	0.10	0.16	0.08	0.17
Maternal	0.23	0.21	0.00	0.00
II. Noncommunicable	7.71	8.35	10.28	10.30
Neoplasms	2.45	2.80	4.28	3.90
Esophagus	0.25	0.30	0.72	0.42
Stomach	0.53	0.57	0.93	0.72
Colon/rectum	0.15	0.17	0.14	0.22
Liver	0.37	0.52	1.22	1.19
Lung	0.23	0.39	0.59	0.56
Breast	0.19	0.21	0.00	0.00
Cervix	0.23	0.10	0.00	0.00
Leukemia	0.01	0.14	0.05	0.12
Nasopharynx	0.05	0.06	0.16	0.13
Endocrine	0.19	0.09	0.14	0.12
Diabetes mellitus	0.13	0.07	0.13	0.11
Cardiovascular	3.83	3.61	4.34	3.92
Hypertensive disease	0.19	0.24	0.22	0.33
Ischemic heart disease	0.39	0.50	0.69	0.51
Cerebrovascular	1.52	1.33	1.68	1.55
Pulmonary heart disease[a]	0.85	0.79	1.17	1.00
Rheumatic heart disease	0.60	0.51	0.35	0.31
Other heart diseases	—	0.03	—	0.03
Respiratory	0.52	0.39	0.48	0.48
COPD[b]	0.47	0.34	0.39	0.33
Digestive	0.65	0.67	1.29	1.07
Chronic liver disease/cirrhosis	0.32	0.31	0.76	0.61
Ulcers stomach/duodenum	0.09	0.15	0.25	0.18
Senile and ill-defined	0.05	0.08	0.05	0.08
III. Injuries	2.12	2.48	3.71	2.87
Unintentional	0.91	1.29	2.65	2.05
Transport	0.36		0.67	
Motor vehicle	0.24	0.26	0.58	0.57
Poisoning	0.25	0.56	0.39	0.43
Falls	0.09		0.57	

(Table continues on the following page.)

Table 2-16 (continued)

Cause of death	*Women* 1987	*Women* 1988[c]	*Men* 1987	*Men* 1988[c]
Fires	0.01		0.05	
Drowning	0.10		0.29	
Other unintentional	—	0.47	—	1.06
Intentional	1.22	1.19	1.26	0.82
Suicide	1.18	1.11	1.00	0.70
Homicide & war	0.03	0.08	0.26	0.12
Total	11.08	11.87	15.04	14.29

—Not available.

Notes: This analysis includes three more causes in the cardiovascular disease category because they are unusually important in China.

Blank entries occur because cause-specific injury codes were not reported in 1988.

For each group of causes the value of the component causes do not necessarily sum to the group value because not all component causes have been included.

a. Because pulmonary heart disease is often a consequence of chronic obstructive pulmonary disease, some analysts would include it with respiratory diseases.

b. Chronic obstructive pulmonary disease.

c. Because the set of Disease Surveillance Points reporting in 1987 was different from 1988, changes in the 45Q15 from 1987 to 1988 may be due to changes in the composition of the sample population.

Source: Authors' calculations.

62 percent more total years of potential life. The percentage distribution for women and men by group of causes (Groups I–III) is shown in figure 2-13. Women lose 16 percent more years of potential life from communicable and reproductive diseases than men do. Men lose 53 percent more years from noncommunicable diseases (Group II) and 63 percent more from injuries (Group III) than women do. It is an unusual aspect of the cause-of-death structure in China that women lose a third of their age-standardized years of potential life to deaths from injuries. The breakdown by cause (figure 2-14) shows that tuberculosis accounts for half or more of all years of potential life lost from Group I causes by both men and women. Women's greater numbers of years of potential life lost from Group I causes are due largely to maternal mortality. The distribution of age-standardized years of potential life lost to deaths from site-specific cancers (figure 2-15) is different for men and women. For men, esophageal, stomach, and liver cancer deaths account for two-thirds of the years of potential life lost due to cancer. The breakdown of cardiovascular disease mortality (figure 2-16) shows the importance of pulmonary lung disease as a cause of mortality in both sexes and high rates of rheumatic heart disease in women. Finally, the distribution of adult years of potential

(Text continues on p. 93.)

Table 2-17. Comparison of Cause-Specific 45Q15 Values Generated from Chinese Disease Surveillance Points (DSP) Data with Values Predicted by Regressions (Tables 2-13a and 2-13b) of Cause-Specific 45Q15 and Total 45Q15

	Women		*Men*	
Cause of death	*Ratio of DSP value to predicted value*	*DSP value minus predicted value*[a]	*Ratio of DSP value to predicted value*	*DSP value minus predicted value*[a]
I. Communicable and reproductive	1.2	−0.87	1.7	0.45
Tuberculosis	2.9	0.47	5.8	0.60
Respiratory infections	0.3	−0.21	0.3	−0.19
Maternal	1.2	0.03	n.a.	n.a.
II. Noncommunicable	0.9	−1.30	0.9	−0.85
Neoplasms	0.7	−1.03	1.2	0.80
Endocrine	0.5	−0.19	0.4	−0.19
Cardiovascular[b]	1.4	1.01	1.0	0.02
Respiratory	1.8	0.52	1.2	0.09
Digestive	1.0	−0.02	1.4	0.37
Senile and ill-defined	0.1	−0.38	0.1	−0.39
III. Injuries	2.0	1.05	1.0	0.08
Unintentional	1.5	0.31	1.1	0.31
Motor vehicle	1.1	0.01	0.6	−0.37
Intentional	3.3	0.85	1.3	0.28
Suicide	4.1	0.89	1.5	0.35
Homicide	0.5	−0.03	0.9	−0.02

n.a. = Not applicable

a. Absolute difference in 45Q15

b. In China, pulmonary heart disease contributes 0.85 percent to the cardiovascular 45Q15. If pulmonary heart disease is included in the category "Respiratory," then the cardiovascular 45Q15 would be only slightly more than predicted.

Source: Authors' calculations.

Figure 2-13. The Percentage Distribution of Age-Standardized Adult Years of Potential Life Lost for Groups I, II, and III for China in 1987, DSP Data

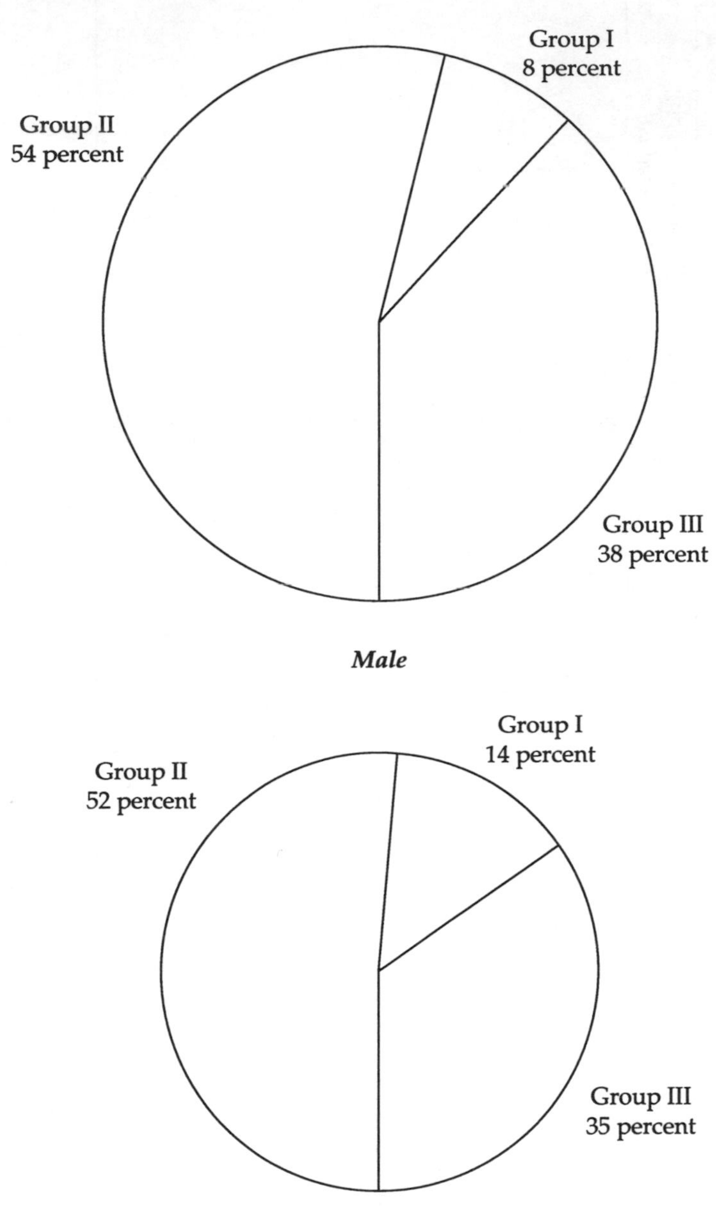

Source: Authors' calculations.

Figure 2-14. The Percentage Distribution of Age-Standardized Years of Potential Life Lost for Specific Group I Causes for China in 1987, DSP Data

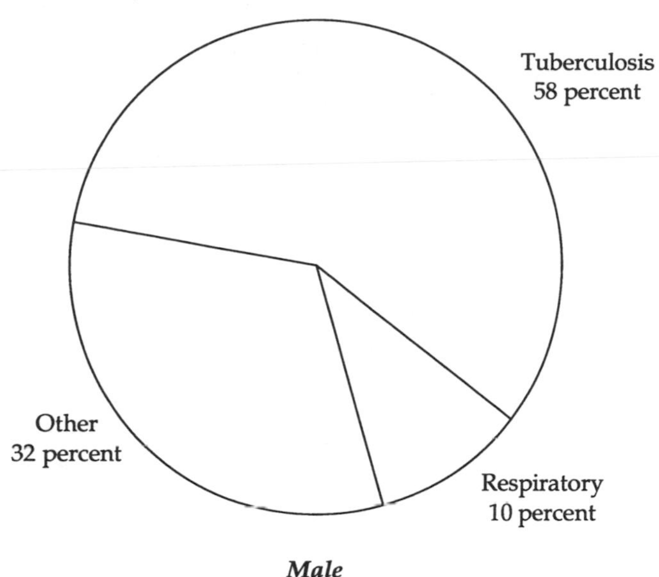

Male

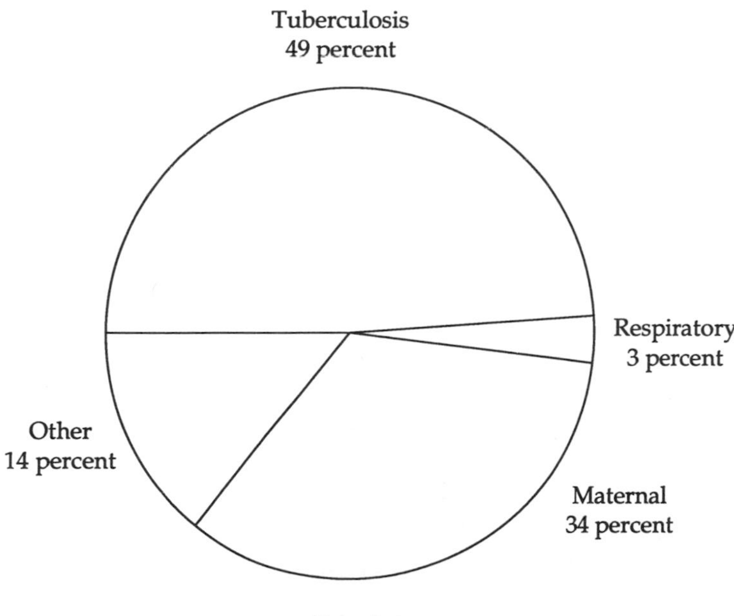

Female

Source: Authors' calculations.

Figure 2-15. The Percentage Distribution of Age-Standardized Adult Years of Potential Life Lost for Site-Specific Neoplasms for China in 1987, DSP Data

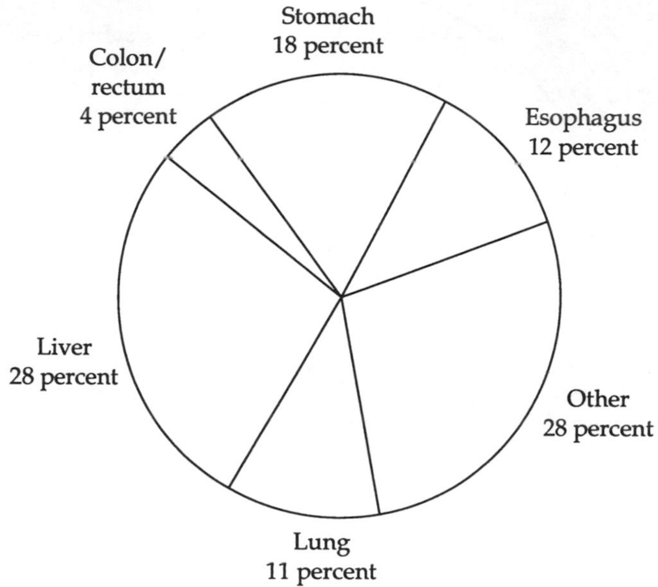

Male

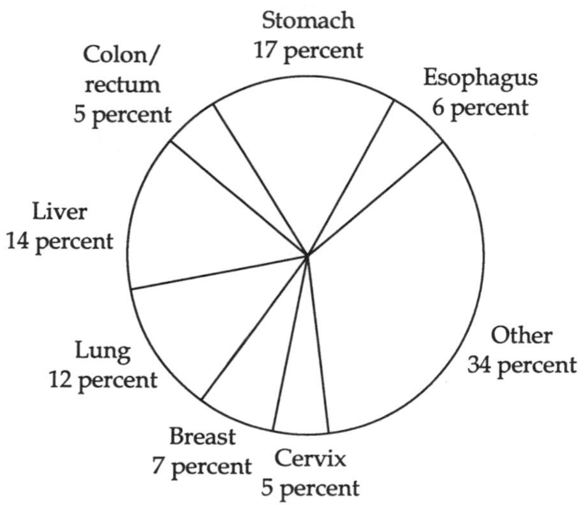

Female

Source: Authors' calculations.

Figure 2-16. The Percentage Distribution of Age-Standardized Adult Years of Potential Life Lost for Specific Cardiovascular Diseases for China in 1987, DSP Data

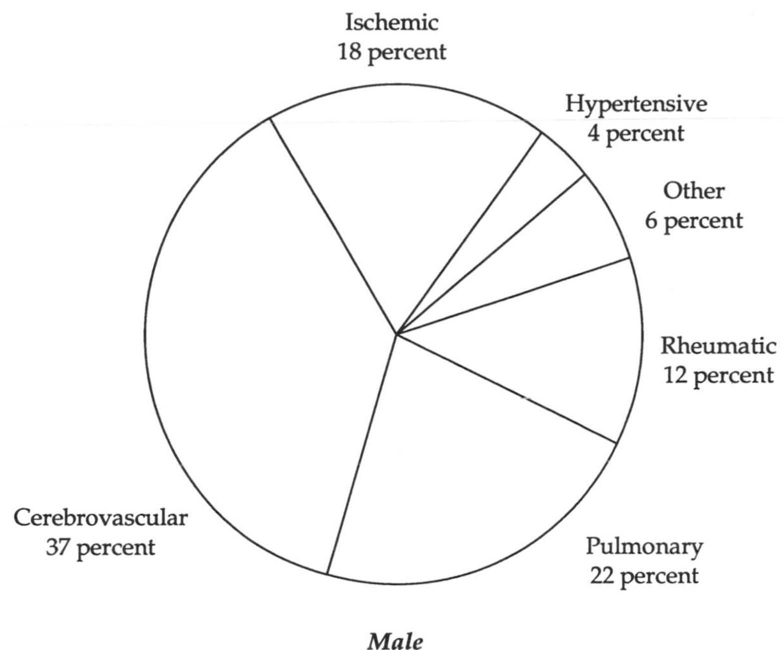

Male

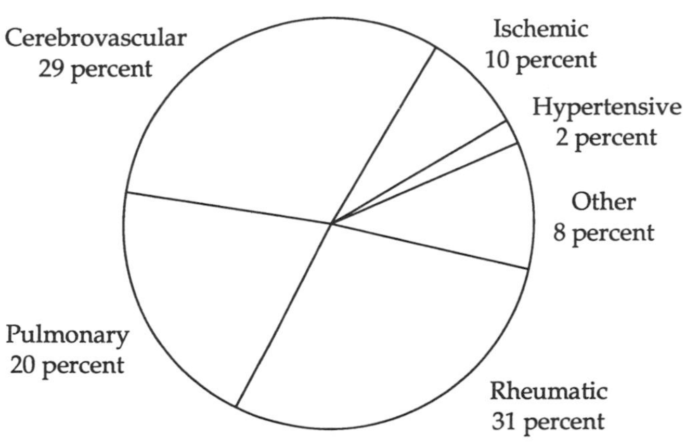

Female

Source: Authors' calculations.

Figure 2-17. The Percentage Distribution of Age-Standardized Adult Years of Potential Life Lost for Specific Group III Causes for China in 1987, DSP Data

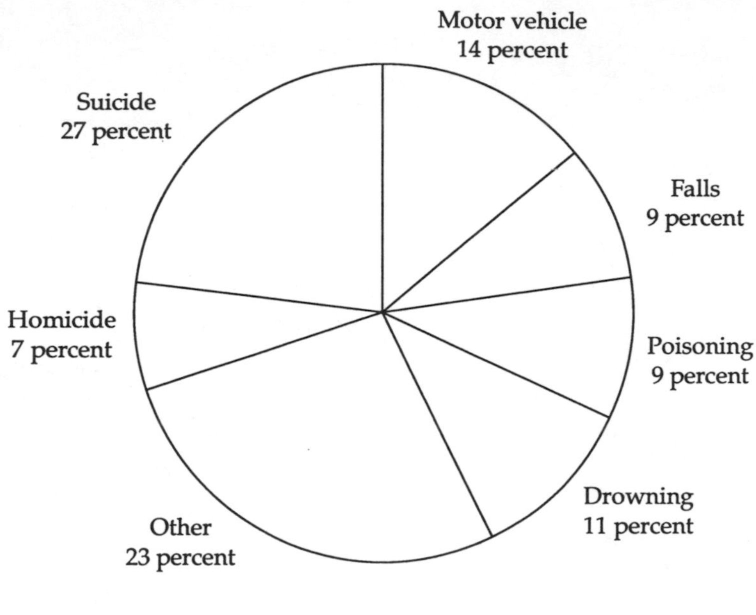

Male

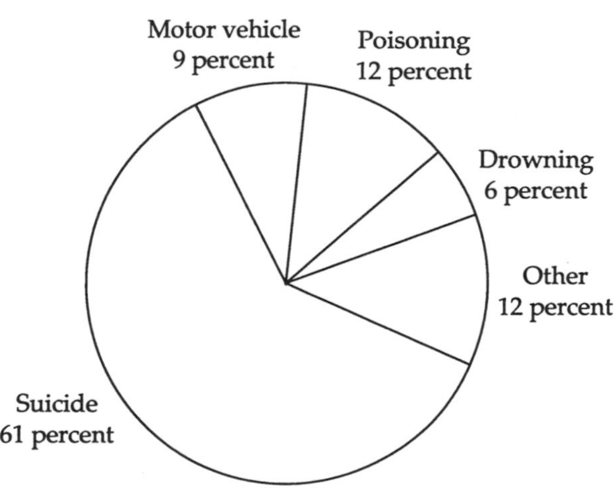

Female

Source: Authors' calculations.

life lost from injuries (Group III) (figure 2-17) shows the importance of suicide among Chinese women. Poisoning, which in some cases may be misidentified suicide, is also an important cause of lost life.

ANALYSIS OF CAUSE-SPECIFIC DSP DATA DISAGGREGATED BY DATA COLLECTION SITE. The DSP data from the forty-seven data collection sites that reported in both 1987 and 1988 make it possible to produce cause-specific estimates of 45Q15 for a range of communities with different overall levels of adult mortality risk. The relationship between each cause and total 45Q15 minus that cause was analyzed as in the previous sections for other data sets. All of the R^2 values were much lower than in the previous analyses, the highest value for any cause being only 29 percent (for tuberculosis among women). The pattern of associations with total mortality, however, was similar to that found in other countries. The generally weaker associations may be due to the small sample sizes at each data collection site when death data were disaggregated by cause and age group.

For Chinese women, the only statistically significant ($p < 0.01$) relationships between cause-specific and total 45Q15 minus that cause were for communicable and reproductive diseases as a group, tuberculosis, maternal mortality, and digestive diseases. These were also three of the causes with the strongest relationships to total 45Q15 in the analysis of the combined longitudinal and cross-sectional data. For Chinese men, statistically significant relationships ($p < 0.01$) were found for only tuberculosis and digestive diseases. In summary, there is large variation in cause-specific mortality rates among DSP data collection sites that bears little relationship to the total adult mortality risk. However, the results are similar to those of the longitudinal and cross-sectional analysis presented earlier.

Summary and Conclusions

Adult mortality levels vary widely across and within countries. The probability of death between ages fifteen and sixty ranges in order of magnitude from more than 50 percent for both women and men in parts of West Africa to about 5 percent for women in Switzerland and Japan. Among industrialized countries, adult mortality varies more than child mortality. Historical changes in adult mortality have varied widely also across and within countries. Many industrialized countries have had tremendous declines in adult mortality risk during the last 100 years. These declines, however, have not occurred in all industrialized countries. Some, like the countries of central Europe, have high risks of adult mortality, and some ethnic and cultural groups within countries, like black men in the United States, continue to have exceptionally high mortality risks (appendix 2-A).

Excess adult male mortality risk seems to be the rule rather than the exception in Latin America, industrialized nonmarket countries, and Africa. With few exceptions, excess male mortality involves both younger men (ages fifteen to thirty-nine years) and older men (ages forty to fifty-nine years). Furthermore, the cause-of-death data indicate that even in high mortality countries, maternal mortality accounts for less than 10 percent of female adult mortality (table 2-13a), while the chance of dying from tuberculosis is nearly twice as high. This argues against an exclusive focus on maternal causes of mortality among women of reproductive ages as advocated implicitly by the Safe Motherhood movement (Herz and Measham 1987).

Considerable evidence argues for the necessity of examining adult and child mortality separately. Close relationships between 5Q0 and 45Q15 cannot be assumed, and the relationship between 5Q0 and 45Q15 is weaker for males than for females. Estimates of adult mortality that are based exclusively on measurements of child mortality have wide confidence intervals. In addition, limited evidence from China (not presented) suggests that the socioeconomic determinants of adult and child mortality are different. Finally, the historical patterns of declines in adult and child mortality have been different in some countries, as in Sri Lanka, where child and adult female mortality declined substantially while adult male mortality stayed the same.

As overall adult mortality declines, some broad patterns are evident. Mortality from communicable, reproductive, and noncommunicable diseases declines for both women and men.

The finding that mortality from noncommunicable diseases declines as overall mortality declines is perhaps the most noteworthy of this analysis.

As overall mortality declines, injury mortality remains relatively constant for women but appears to decline for men, although more slowly than overall mortality declines. This relationship between overall mortality and injury mortality in men is highly variable across countries.

One of the purposes of studying the empirical record of causes of adult death is to identify those causes that are large, decreasing, increasing, or controllable. Determining which causes of adult death are the most important depends on the particular indicator used to measure cause-specific mortality. Rankings of cause-specific 45Q15 and age-standardized adult years of potential life lost give different results. The rank order of each cause also depends on the mortality level of the community examined. In high adult mortality countries, the largest causes for women (in decreasing order of 45Q15) are cardiovascular diseases, neoplasms, tuberculosis, digestive diseases, respiratory infections, and maternal mortality. For men, the ranking by 45Q15 in high mortality countries is quite different: cardiovascular diseases, digestive diseases, unintentional injuries, tuberculosis, neoplasms and respiratory infections. Using years of potential life lost, diseases that affect younger adults (i.e., almost all injuries, tuberculosis, causes of maternal mortality, and lymphatic/hematopoietic cancers) become more important. Cardiovascular diseases and neoplasms tend to have higher death rates among older adults and thus are less important when using age-standardized years of potential life lost.

Perhaps the most useful way to assign importance to causes of death is to find those that explain the difference between high and low mortality populations. Analysis of longitudinal data for the four developing countries of Chile, Costa Rica, Cuba, and Singapore (table 2-11) and cross-sectional data for fifty-six countries (table 2-12), reveals the most important causes explaining such differences in women's mortality. They are, in decreasing order, cardiovascular disease, tuberculosis, digestive diseases, senile and ill-defined causes, respiratory infections, maternal mortality, and neoplasms. Roughly one third of the differences between populations with high and low adult female mortality can be explained by tuberculosis, respiratory infections, and maternal mortality. For men, the most important causes are, in decreasing order of importance, tuberculosis, digestive diseases, unintentional injuries, respiratory infections, and senile and ill-defined conditions. Efforts to accelerate the decline in adult mortality in developing countries should focus on these causes that explain mortality declines in some countries and the differences between countries with high and low mortality. It is gratifying to note that, while Preston (1976) found that the category "other/unknown causes" accounted for one third of the difference between high and low mortality countries in his analysis of all age groups combined, the category "senile and ill-defined causes" in the analyses of this chapter explains less than 10 percent of the differences in 45Q15.

For women, there is evidence that mortality caused by breast cancer, motor vehicle injuries, and intentional injuries is increasing as overall adult mortality decreases. For men, there is evidence that mortality caused by lymphatic/hematopoietic cancers is increasing. Other causes may be expected to become more important in countries where the prevalence of known risk factors is rising. In particular, large rises in AIDS, lung cancer, and tuberculosis mortality may be expected in many developing countries, but the start of these pandemics is not captured by the historical data analyzed here (see appendixes 2-C and 2-D).

Mortality rates for some causes of death are neither decreasing nor increasing but are amenable to intervention. Such causes include liver cancer and cirrhosis caused by the hepatitis B virus and lung cancer mortality caused by smoking. It also appears to be technically feasible to reduce the mortality rates for a number of unintentional injuries, including those from motor vehicle collisions (see chapter 6).

The specific causes of adult death are not a simple function of the overall level of adult mortality. Statistical relationships between most cause-specific adult mortality risks and overall mortality risk were weak in all three independent data sets analyzed (the longitudinal data from four countries, the cross-sectional data from fifty-six countries and the DSP data from China). Some countries, like Cuba and Sri Lanka, have had major declines in mortality from communicable and reproductive diseases but concomitant increases in injury mortality so that overall mortality risks have remained the same. In general, overall mortality risk serves as a poor predictor of the specific causes of death.

As mentioned, major declines occur in noncommunicable diseases as a group, particularly digestive diseases in both sexes and cardiovascular diseases in women and possibly men. This observation runs counter to some widely held beliefs. Westernization and concomitant changes in diet, smoking, and life style—many of which are income elastic—are thought to increase noncommunicable disease rates, particularly cardiovascular diseases, often called the diseases of affluence. Because of this, the decline in cardiovascular and digestive disease mortality among adults in the developing world is perplexing. Perhaps as overall mortality declines, socioeconomic improvements decrease some unknown critical risk factors, possibly of an infectious nature. If so, the declines in these unknown risk factors must outweigh increases in smoking and other well-characterized risk factors. Or perhaps access to medical services postpones deaths from cardiovascular diseases and other noncommunicable diseases to after age sixty. While there is no basis for choosing between these hypotheses, they have different implications for policy. More detailed analysis of the cross-sectional data (table 2-12) indicated that, for men, hypertensive heart disease and cerebrovascular accidents were declining while ischemic heart disease was highly variable with no discernible relationship to total mortality. Most of the risk factor data implying rising risks of mortality apply largely to ischemic heart disease and not to the aggregate group of cardiovascular diseases. The epidemiology of cardiovascular diseases—and, even more so, of digestive diseases—in developing countries is poorly understood and deserves attention.

The analyses presented in this chapter are based almost exclusively on the empirical record to date. They have, therefore, three major limitations. First, some diseases may cause more mortality than recorded in the cause-of-death data. Some possibilities have already been discussed including malaria, Chagas disease, and diabetes.

There is no solution to this problem except to remind the reader of this limitation. Second, future patterns of causes of death may differ from the past or present. For example, the HIV epidemic in Central and East Africa promises to increase adult mortality rates and alter the cause-of-death pattern (appendix 2-C). Tuberculosis mortality rates, for instance, are expected to rise substantially. The future pattern of causes of death may also be different if specific risk factors are increasing whose impact is not well reflected in the empirical data to date. The strongest evidence for such a risk factor is cigarette consumption (appendix 2-D). Third, empirical data are unavailable for the high mortality countries, and therefore the experiences of countries in Sub-Saharan Africa and South Asia are seriously underrepresented in these findings.

Appendix 2-A. Black American Adult Mortality

Adult mortality not only varies widely from country to country but also among groups and communities within countries. Sub-national differences by ethnic group and socioeconomic variables are common in child mortality (United Nations 1985) but poorly documented for adult mortality. One striking example of a difference in adult mortality within a country is the difference between the mortality risks of blacks and whites in the United States. For blacks, the 45Q15 is 30 percent for men and 16 percent for women. For whites, the 45Q15 is 16 percent for men and 9 percent for women (See Murray [1990] for more detail). The mortality rate of black men in the United States is higher than that of black men in The Gambia. The United States is concerned about excess mortality among black children, for whom the 5Q0 is 2.3 percent for boys and 1.9 percent for girls compared to 1.2 percent for white boys and 0.8 percent for white girls. In absolute terms of human loss, however, these differentials are an order of magnitude smaller than the adult mortality differentials, which receive much less attention. Figure 2-A1 shows the historical changes in male adult mortality for whites and all other races between 1901 and 1985; minority adult male mortality has consistently lagged fifty years behind white mortality (NCHS 1988). The striking differences in mortality in the United States are partly (perhaps mainly) the result of differences in income and social class (Navarro 1990).

Figure 2-A1. Adult Male Mortality of Whites and all other Races Combined, United States, 1901–85

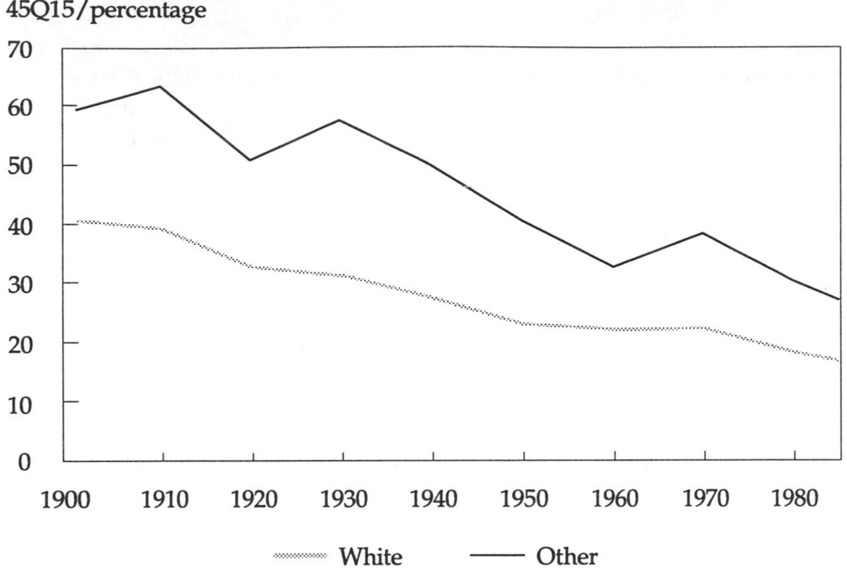

Source: Authors' calculations.

Appendix 2-B. Equity and Adult Mortality

Some analysts believe that adult disease is worse among the rich. The strongest evidence refuting this misconception has already been presented in this chapter in the sections on levels of adult mortality. The greatest burden of adult mortality is not in the industrialized world but in the least developed and poorest developing countries. More than half of the men in parts of West Africa die before reaching sixty while only one in ten die in Japan or Switzerland. In some countries, disadvantaged groups (for example blacks in the United States) have much higher adult mortality risks than the rest of the community. Other evidence demonstrates that lower social and economic groups within countries have higher mortality and higher exposures to risk factors for both noncommunicable and communicable diseases.

Three examples illustrate the important inequity of adult death. First, a recent World Bank study on adult health in Brazil showed that lower income and poorly educated groups have higher rates of risk factors such as hypertension, alcohol consumption, obesity, and smoking. These disadvantaged groups also have higher mortality rates from cancers, cardiovascular diseases, other noncommunicable

Table 2-B1. Female 45Q15 for the Three Major Groups of Causes of Death for Disease Surveillance Points (DSP) Ranked by Income (Industrial and Agricultural Output Per Capita), China, 1987–1988

Income quartile	*Group I*	*Group II*	*Group III*	*Total*
1 (Highest)	0.4	6.7	1.2	8.3
2	0.4	7.9	2.0	10.3
3	0.6	7.6	2.4	10.6
4 (Lowest)	1.4	8.9	2.7	13.0

Note: Computed using data for the forty-seven DSP points reporting for both 1986 and 1987 and industrial and agricultural output data from the 1982 census.

diseases, and injuries (World Bank 1989a). Second, the Whitehall study (Marmot, Shipley, and Rose 1984) followed civil servants in London over a ten-year period. Adult mortality was lower in each higher grade of the civil service, through all ten grades. The differences in mortality were not trivial: age-adjusted mortality rates over ten years were 4.7 percent for administrators, 8.0 percent for professionals and executives, 11.7 percent for clerical workers, and 15.6 percent for the workers in the lowest grades in the civil service. A final example comes from the analysis of the DSP data for China (see table 2-B1). On the basis of income per capita (the actual income variable measured was industrial and agricultural output per capita), communities with the highest incomes not only have the lowest total adult female mortality, but also the lowest adult female mortality in each of three groups of causes. Conversely, the lowest income communities have the highest adult female mortality due to all three groups of causes. The ratio comparing the 45Q15 in the lowest income group to that of the highest income group is 3.5 for Group I causes of death, 1.3 for Group II, and 2.3 for Group III. Clearly, poor women in China suffer greater health risks than do their richer counterparts.

Appendix 2-C. The Effect of the HIV Epidemic on Mortality in Sub-Saharan Africa

The human immunodeficiency virus (HIV) epidemic in West, Central, and East Africa already is a serious cause of morbidity and mortality. For example, in Abidjan, Côte d'Ivoire, HIV infection was found in 41 percent of adult male cadavers and 32 percent of adult female cadavers examined in two morgues in 1988 and 1989 (de Cock and others 1990). The full effect that the HIV epidemic will have on mortality in these regions is not known because the course of the epidemic is still evolving and there is a considerable time lag between HIV seroconversion and death. Because HIV is largely sexually transmitted in these regions, most of the infections involve young adults, as eventually most of the deaths will also.

A variety of models have been developed to project the demographic impact of the HIV epidemic in Africa (Anderson and May 1988; Anderson, May, and McLean 1988; Bongaarts and Way 1989; Bulatao and Bos 1990). While the focus of these models has been on the ultimate effect that the HIV epidemic will have on population growth, by necessity these models include estimates of increased mortality from HIV infection. The models vary both in their assumptions and their estimates of how much mortality may increase. The most alarming predictions from these models suggest mortality may increase to the point that population growth will become negative.

To illustrate the potential effect of the HIV epidemic on adult mortality, the conservative results from Bulatao and Bos (1990) were used to project the absolute increase in 45Q15 from the HIV epidemic in Zaire. Current HIV seropositive prevalences in Zaire are estimated to be 3.4 and 3.3 cases per thousand men and women, respectively. Three future scenarios were examined (see table 2-C1): a decreasing, moderate, or high risk of HIV infection. According to these scenarios, if the risk of HIV infection becomes moderate or high by 1995, the overall 45Q15 in parts of West, Central, and East Africa may rise to 55 to 75 percent in the next ten to fifteen years.

Appendix 2-D. Smoking-Attributable Mortality in the Developing World

Smoking has a delayed effect on mortality, such that a current increase in smoking rates is followed decades later by an increase in mortality rates. A tremendous body of epidemiologic evidence has been accumulated on the effect smoking has on mortality through increases in lung cancer, ischemic heart disease, and many other causes of death. The causes of death most closely associated with smoking in the United States include oral cancer, cancer of the larynx, lung cancer, and chronic obstructive pulmonary disease (see table 2-D1).

For developing countries, estimates of smoking-attributable mortality are based on applying the known patterns of the United States to developing country cause-of-death data. Using this method, the World Health Organization's Consultative Group on Smoking-Attributable Mortality (WHO 1990) estimated that one million deaths can be attributed to smoking in the developing world. This estimate has a very wide confidence interval (the true number of deaths may be as few as 0.5 million or as many as 1.5 million) because of the

Table 2-C1. Estimates of the Increases in 45Q15 from the HIV-Associated Mortality of Men and Women in Zaire, According to the Bulatao and Bos (1990) Projection Model

	Absolute increase in 45Q15 (percent)					
	Decreasing risk of HIV infection		*Moderate risk of HIV infection*		*High risk of HIV infection*	
Years	*Male*	*Female*	*Male*	*Female*	*Male*	*Female*
1990–1995	1.8	2.3	8.3	10.5	24.7	30.5
1995–2000	1.1	1.4	16.4	20.6	30.8	37.8
2000–2005	0.4	0.5	21.8	27.3	29.3	36.2

Note: Computation based on applying the incremental increase in adult mortality to the current levels of adult mortality estimated for Zaire by the World Bank. The risks of HIV infection represent hypothetical 1995 HIV seropositive prevalence rates among men and women, respectively, such that a decreasing risk represents hypothetical prevalence rates of 1.4 and 1.5 per thousand, a moderate risk 2.7 and 2.8 per thousand, and a high risk 7.5 and 5.5 per thousand. The higher increases in female 45Q15 from this analysis are a function of the seropositive prevalence data used by Bulatao and Bos (1990) in which women become HIV seropositive at younger ages than men and thus have a higher probability of dying between the ages of fifteen and fifty-nine years. This may only be a reflection of the limited data about the age distribution of seroconversion in this population.

Table 2-D1. The Percent of Mortality Due to Specific Causes of Death Attributable to Smoking, United States

	Percentage of deaths attributed to smoking	
Smoking-associated cause of death	*Female*	*Male*
Oral cancer	41.3	68.8
Esophageal cancer	53.6	58.9
Stomach cancer	25.4	17.2
Pancreatic cancer	14.2	30.0
Laryngeal cancer	41.3	80.6
Lung cancer	75.0	79.6
Cervical cancer	36.9	
Bladder cancer	27.4	37.1
Hypertensive heart disease	14.8	15.6
Ischemic heart disease (ages 20–64 years)	18.1	28.5
Ischemic heart disease (ages 65 years and older)	7.5	15.9
Cardiac dysrhythmias	34.4	39.9
Cerebrovascular disease	13.9	9.6
Other circulatory disease	31.5	23.8
Pneumonia/influenza	9.3	20.8
Bronchitis/emphysema/asthma	69.4	85.0
Other chronic obstructive lung disease (COPD)	69.4	85.0
Ulcers	44.5	47.9

Note: These estimates are based on epidemiologic data for the United States from various longitudinal surveys. (USDHHS, 1989). Therefore, they reflect the cumulative history of smoking patterns and local patterns of disease risk in the United States.

dearth of data on smoking rates and causes of death in many developing countries.

There are two reasons why the effect of smoking on lung cancer, ischemic heart disease, and other causes of death does not appear in this chapter's analyses. First, the epidemic of tobacco use is too recent in some countries to be reflected in historical mortality data. Second, smoking-attributable mortality mainly involves the elderly (see figure 2-D1). While 30 percent of smoking-attributable mortality in the developing world involves adults aged fifteen to fifty-nine years, 70 percent involves the elderly (i.e., men and women sixty years old and older). Only 9 percent of smoking-attributable mortality involves adults younger than fifty years.[23]

For some developing countries (for example, China), in which smoking rates are high, the total mortality of adults may increase solely because of smoking (World Bank 1989b). Making estimates and projections of smoking-attributable mortality in specific developing countries, however, requires accurate information on past, current, and predicted smoking rates. Acquiring this information on smoking patterns should be a priority for many developing countries.

Figure 2-D1. Estimated Distribution of Smoking-Attributable Mortality by Age in Developing Countries

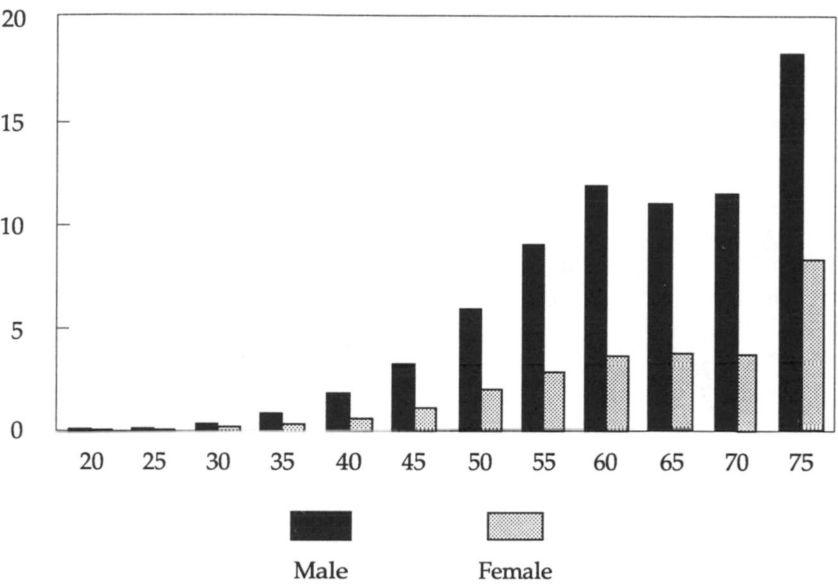

Source: Authors' calculations.

Notes

1. Much of the data analysis in this chapter is based on vital registration data provided by Dr. Alan Lopez of the World Health Organization, without whose generous support this work would not have been possible. The World Health Organization's vital registration databank is an essential resource for cause-of-death research. See Lopez (1989).

2. The analysis presented in this chapter has benefited greatly from comments, suggestions and data provided by Richard Bumgarner, Sunil Chacko, Lincoln Chen, Monica Das Gupta, Tim Dyson, Alan Lopez, Ian Timaeus, Steve Tollman, and John Wyon.

3. These countries are listed in table 2-4. According to United Nations convention, Sub-Saharan Africa includes the island countries of Mauritius and Seychelles.

4. Model life tables are based on assumed fixed patterns of age-specific mortality rates. The most widely used are the Coale and Demeny model life tables (Coale and Demeny 1983). By examining historical empirical life tables

for largely Western populations, Coale and Demeny defined five families of model life tables: North, East, South, West and General. Published life tables with a wide range of mortality levels are available for each family. To the extent these models represent the true age pattern of mortality in a population, any age-specific mortality rate defines the entire age pattern of mortality. Several other types of model life tables are available. Because of the perception that the Coale and Demeny model life tables were not entirely representative of developing country mortality patterns, the United Nations Population Division published a set of model life tables for developing countries (United Nations 1982). Unfortunately, they are not as widely used for demographic estimation as the Coale and Demeny life tables.

5. The DHS program is funded by the United States Agency for International Development and administered by the Institute for Resource Development, 8850 Stanford Boulevard, Suite 4000, Columbia, MD 21045, USA.

6. Model life table North was used because in the World Bank projection system, countries with the vast majority of the developing world population (China, India, and others) are modeled using the North family of models. A split-level procedure was used to choose the specific North mortality level for children and adults. The choice of model can influence the estimated level of adult mortality substantially. To provide the reader with a sense of the confidence interval for these estimates, the number of deaths in adult age groups was calculated using the other Coale and Demeny model life tables (East, South, and West). The percentage of deaths in the adult age groups varied from 21 to 32 percent, compared to 27 percent using North (table 2-1).

7. In notation: avoidable deaths = $P_x\ (m_x - m_x{}^*)$, summed from $x=0$ to $x=e$, where P_x is the population in age group x; m_x is the death rate in the population in age group x; $m_x{}^*$ is the death rate in that age group in the reference population; and e is the maximum age in the population.

8. Varying the productivity weights so that they reflect, for example, rising productivity with age during the adult years had only a minor effect on the age distribution of productivity-weighted avoidable years of potential life lost when compared to the effect of altering the discount rate by even one percentage point.

9. When productivity weights greater than one are given to years of life after age sixty, they tend to magnify the importance of adult deaths relative to deaths in childhood. More sophisticated productivity weighting functions could have been used; for example, $20x - 0.25x^2 + 100$, where x = age in years, would give a weight of 100 at birth, rising to 500 at age forty and declining to 0 at age eighty-five. This weighting function would not substantially change the results except to give a nonzero weight to deaths between the ages of sixty and eighty-five.

10. Because these are probabilities, 45Q15 is not the arithmetic sum of 25Q15 and 20Q40; 45Q15 = 25Q15 + (1-25Q15) 20Q40.

11. Throughout this book, the developed countries (or industrialized countries) are divided into those with market economies and those with nonmarket economies (the communist or ex-communist countries), as listed in statistical appendix tables A-1e and A-1f. No account is taken of recent political and economic changes in central and eastern Europe, because the data analyzed predate these changes.

12. The substantial literature on the roles of social and economic factors and health services in explaining mortality decline has not focused on adult

mortality directly (Halstead, Walsh, and Warren 1985; McKeown 1979; Preston 1975). The case for a substantial role for health service provision in mortality reduction may be different in adults than in children.

13. Taylor and Thoma (1985) reported only an abridged life table for adults (the age groups used included fifty-five to sixty-four years). In computing 45Q15 for Nauruans, the mortality of adults aged sixty to sixty-four years was assumed to be twice the mortality of adults aged fifty-five to fifty-nine years. If anything, this approach underestimates 45Q15.

14. Because many deaths in Sri Lanka are not medically certified, these data must be considered less reliable.

15. Yet, as described later in this chapter, injuries are a substantial cause of potentially avoidable mortality for some of these countries. Future reductions in adult male mortality risk in these countries will have to include reductions in injury mortality.

16. Using Japan as the reference population may underestimate avoidable deaths due to injuries in these countries; men in Malta and the Netherlands have injury 45Q15 values less than 50 percent of the Japanese risk.

17. Various functional forms of the regression equations were used. Log transformations did not significantly improve the R^2 but did improve the distribution of residuals for aggregate Group I and Group II. The log transformations, however, worsened the fit for the disaggregated causes. For this analysis and the subsequent cross-sectional analysis, only the linear relationships of the form

cause-specific 45Q15 = b (total 45Q15 − cause-specific 45Q15) + constant

are reported.

18. This data set is a combination of time series data for four countries. The regression statistics have not been adjusted for autocorrelation which may be present. Autocorrelation will not bias the parameter estimates but will lead to an underestimate of the variance in the estimates. The significance tests, therefore, must be interpreted with caution.

19. Regressions of the two types of data were notably different for one cause, breast cancer in women. The analysis of the 100 percent medically certified data showed no statistically significant relationship, while the analysis of the other data found a significant rise in breast cancer with lower total 45Q15. Developing countries with higher mortality were represented better in the latter analysis (in which total 45Q15 ranged from 7.8 to 18.5) than in the analysis of the 100 percent medically certified data (in which total 45Q15 ranged from 5.3 to 12.8). Breast cancer may rise at moderate levels of total mortality but stagnate at lower levels.

20. DSP data collection sites are distributed across China in every province. Sites are categorized as urban or rural. Rural sites are truly rural, unlike the category "county" used in many Chinese statistics, which includes small cities. Urban DSP data collection sites are subdivided into three groups (urban I–III) according to size. Rural sites are subdivided into four groups (rural I–IV) according to a composite socioeconomic indicator. Statistical appendix table A-4 compares the distribution of the DSP sample population in these three urban and four rural groups to the distribution of the Chinese population in these same groups based on the 1982 census. The DSP sample overrepresents urban areas and underrepresents the poorer rural areas. Rural groups III and IV, the least developed, which together make up only 5 percent of the DSP sample, constitute 32 percent of the Chinese population. The DSP sample also

underrepresents the rural group II by 50 percent. Where appropriate, this section reports adjusted totals that weight the DSP data by category according to the 1982 census distribution. As there are no DSP data for rural group IV, the rural III sample is weighted by the combined population of rural III and rural IV. In 1990, additional DSPs were added, and DSP data are becoming progressively more representative.

21. Data from these years are not directly comparable because 1) the specific set of causes of death has varied from year to year (for example, detailed injury codes are available only for 1987); 2) in some years, groups of causes had subtotals computed at each data collection site, which introduced substantial errors; and 3) the collection sites that report data vary from year to year. For these reasons, reported differences in cause-specific 45Q15 among the years 1986, 1987 and 1988 are unlikely to be real.

22. For validation, these DSP results were compared to the vital registration data. For urban areas, the adjusted DSP total 45Q15 was only slightly higher than the vital registration value. Although the category "county" in the vital registration data does not correspond well to the rural DSP category, the 1987 county vital registration 45Q15 was only 1.5 percentage points higher for men and 1.3 percentage points higher for women. County vital registration data yielded higher rates of tuberculosis and respiratory disease and lower rates of heart disease than rural DSP data. The quality of coding for causes of death in the vital registration system is unknown. The vital registration system relies solely on death certificates, while the DSP system actively investigates causes of death.

23. This age distribution was calculated by applying United States smoking-attributable mortality rates to the age structure of the developing world. It somewhat overestimates smoking-attributable mortality among men and women younger than sixty years because the cause-specific mortality data (table 2-10) are not age-specific. The likelihood that a death from lung cancer at age thirty is due to smoking is lower than the likelihood at age seventy-five, because of the lag between starting to smoke and developing lung cancer.

References

Anderson, R. M., R. M. May. 1988. "Epidemiological parameters of HIV transmission." *Nature* 333:514–19.

Anderson, R.M., R. M. May, and A. R. McLean. 1988. "Possible Demographic Consequences of AIDS in Developing Countries." *Nature* 332:228–33.

Ayeni, O. 1980. "Causes of Mortality in an African City." *African Journal of Medical Science* 9:139–49.

Barnum, H. 1987. "Evaluating health days of life gained from health projects." *Social Science and Medicine* 24:833–41.

Beasley, R. P., C. C. Lin, and L. Y. Hwang. 1981. "Hepatocellular Carcinoma and Hepatitis B Virus: A Prospective Study of 22,707 Men in Taiwan." *Lancet* ii:1129–33.

Blacker, J. G. C. 1984. "Experiences in the Use of Special Mortality Questions in Multi-Purpose Surveys: The Single Round Approach." In *Data Bases for*

Mortality Measurement. Population Studies No. 84 (ST/ESA/SER.A/84/10:79–89). New York: United Nations. Department of International Economic and Social Affairs.

Bongaarts, J., and P. Way. 1989. "Geographic Variation in the HIV Epidemic and the Mortality Impact of AIDS in Africa." *Population Council Working Papers* No. 1. New York: Population Council.

Bradley, A. K., and H. M. Gilles. 1984. "Malumfashi Endemic Diseases Research Project XXI. Pointers to Causes of Death in the Malumfashi Areas, Northern Nigeria." *Annals of Tropical Medicine and Parasitology* 78(3):265–71.

Brass, W., A. J. Coale, P. Demeny, D. F. Heisel, F. Lorimer, A. Romaniuk, and E. Van de Walle. 1968. *The Demography of Tropical Africa*. Princeton: Princeton University Press.

Bulatao, R. A., and E. Bos. 1990. *Projecting the Demographic Impact of* AIDS. Washington, D.C.: Population, Health, and Nutrition Division, World Bank.

Bulatao, R. A., E. Bos, P. W. Stephens, and M. T. Vu. 1990. *World Population Projections: 1989–90 Edition*. Baltimore: Johns Hopkins University Press.

Bulatao, R. A., and P. W. Stevens. Forthcoming. "Estimates and Projections of Mortality by Cause: A Global Overview, 1970-2015." In D. T. Jamison and W. H. Mosley, eds., *Disease Control Priorities in Developing Countries*. New York: Oxford University Press for the World Bank.

Cleland, J., and C. Scott. 1987. *The World Fertility Survey. An assessment*. Oxford: Oxford University Press.

Coale, A. J., and P. Demeny. 1983. *Regional Model Life Tables and Stable Populations*. 2d Ed. New York: Academic Press.

Darkaoui, N., M. Garenne, R. Bakkali, and R. Belwali. 1989. "Verbal Autopsies at a National Level. A Study in Morocco." Johns Hopkins Seminar on Verbal Autopsies, March 13–15, Baltimore, Maryland.

De Cock, K. M., B. Barrere, L. Diaby, M. F. Lafontaine, E. Gnaore, A. Porter, D. Pantobe, G. C. Lafontant, A. Dago-Akribi, M. Ette, K. Odehouri, and W. L. Heyward. 1990. "AIDS—The Leading Cause of Adult Death in the West African City of Abidjan, Ivory Coast." *Science* 249:793–96.

Dyson, T. 1984. "Excess Male Mortality in India." *Economic and Political Weekly* 19(10):422–26.

———. 1987. "Excess Female Mortality in India: Uncertain Evidence on a Narrowing Differential." Paper Presented to the Workshop on Differential Female Health Care and Mortality, January 1987, Dhaka.

Evans, T. G., and C. J. L. Murray. 1987. "A Critical Re-examination of the Economics of Blindness Prevention under the Onchocerciasis Control Programme." *Social Science and Medicine* 25(3):241–49.

Fargues, P., and O. Nassour. 1987. "Les saisons et la mortalité urbaine en Afrique: les décès à Bamako de 1974 à 1985." IUSSP Seminar on Mortality and Society in Sub-Saharan Africa, October 19–23, Yaoundé, Cameroon.

Faust, M. M., and A. B. Dolman. 1963. "Comparability of Mortality Statistics for the Fifth and Sixth Revisions: United States, 1950." *Vital Statistics - Special Reports* 51(2).

———. 1965. "Comparability of Mortality Statistics for the Sixth and Seventh Revisions: United States, 1958." *Vital Statistics - Special Reports* 51(4).

Feachem, R. G. A., and D. T. Jamison. eds. 1991. *Disease and Mortality in Sub-Saharan Africa*. New York: Oxford University Press for the World Bank.

Fuller, J. H. 1985. "Causes of Death in Diabetes Mellitus." *Hormone and Metabolic Research Supplement* 15:3–9.

Garenne, M., and O. Fontaine. 1986. "Assessing Probable Causes of Deaths using a Standardized Questionnaire: A Study in Rural Senegal." IUSSP Seminar on Comparative Studies of Morbidity and Mortality: Old and New Approaches to Measurement and Analysis, 7–12 July, Siena, Italy.

Giglioli, G. 1972. "Changes in the Pattern of Mortality Following the Eradication of Hyperendemic Malaria from a Highly Susceptible Community." *Bulletin of the World Health Organization* 46:181–202.

Goldman, N. 1980. "Far Eastern Patterns of Mortality." *Population Studies* 34(1):5–19.

Gordon, J. E., S. Singh, and J. B. Wyon. 1965. "Causes of Death at Different Ages, by Sex, and by Season, in a Rural Population of the Punjab, 1957–1959: A Field Study." *Indian Journal of Medical Research* 53(9):906–17.

Greenwood, B. M., A. K. Bradley, A. M. Greenwood, P. Byass, K. Jammeh, K. Marsh, S. Tulloch, F. S. J. Oldfield, and R. Hayes. 1987. "Mortality and Morbidity among Children in a Rural Area of the Gambia, West Africa." *Transactions of the Royal Society of Tropical Medicine and Hygiene* 81:478–86.

Hakulinen, T., H. Hansluwka, A. D. Lopez, and T. Nakada. 1986. "Estimation of Global Mortality Patterns by Cause of Death." In H. Hansluwka, A. D. Lopez, Y. Porapakkham, and P. Prasartkul., eds., *New Developments in the Analysis of Mortality and Causes of Death*. Bangkok: Mahidol University.

Halstead, S. B., J. A. Walsh, and K. S. Warren. 1985. *Good Health at Low Cost*. New York: Rockefeller Foundation.

Hayes, R., T. Mertens, G. Lockett, and L. Rodrigues. 1989. "Causes of Adult Death in Developing Countries; A Review of Data and Methods." *Population, Health and Nutrition Working Paper*, Series 246. Washington, D.C.: World Bank.

Heligman, L. 1982. "Patterns of Sex Differentials in Mortality in Less Developed Countries." In L. T. Ruzicka, A. D. Lopez, eds., *Sex Differentials in Mortality: Trends, Determinants and Consequences*. Canberra: Australian National University.

Herz, B., and A. R. Measham. 1987. *The Safe-Motherhood Initiative: Proposals for Action*. Washington, D.C.: World Bank.

Hill, K., and A. R. Pebley. 1989. "Child Mortality in the Developing World." *Population and Development Review* 15(4):657–87.

Housheng, H., E. Arriaga, and J. Banister. 1988. "China: Provincial Patterns of Mortality." Presentation at Seminar on Mortality and Morbidity in South and East Asia, Beijing, August 29–September 2.

India, Office of Registrar General. 1988. "Survey of Causes of Death (Rural)." *Annual Report 1986*. New Delhi: Ministry of Home Affairs.

Kachirayan, M., S. Radkakrishna, R. Ramakrishnan, A. M. Ramanathan, and V. Sreenivas. 1983. "Study of Registered Deaths in Madras City."*Indian Journal of Medical Research* 77:564–73.

Klebba, A. J., and A. B. Dolman. 1975. "Comparability of Mortality Statistics for the Seventh and Eighth Revisions of the International Classification of Diseases." *Vital and Health Statistics* Series 2, No. 66.

Lopez, A. 1989. *Causes of Death Among Adults Aged 15–59 Years*. Geneva: Division of Global Epidemiological Surveillance and Health Situation Assessment, World Health Organization.

McKeown, T. 1979. *The Role of Medicine: Dream, Mirage or Nemesis?* Oxford: Basil Blackwell.

Maguire, J. H., R. Hoff, I. Sherlock, A. C. Guimaraes, A. C. Sleigh, N. B. Ramos, K. E. Mott, and T. H. Weller. 1987. "Cardiac Morbidity and Mortality Due to Chagas' Disease: Prospective Electrocardiographic Study of a Brazilian Community." *Circulation* 75(7):1140–45.

Marga Institute. 1984. *Intersectoral action for health: Sri Lanka study*. Colombo.

Marmot, M. G., M. J. Shipley, and G. Rose. 1984. "Inequalities in Death—Specific Explanations of a General Pattern." *Lancet* i:1003–06.

Murray, C. J. L. 1987. "A Critical Review of International Mortality Data." *Social Science and Medicine* 25(7):773–81.

———. 1988. *The Determinants of Health Improvement in Developing Countries: Case-Studies of St. Lucia, Guyana, Paraguay, Kiribati, Swaziland, and Bolivia*. Oxford: Oxford University, D. Phil. thesis.

———. 1990. "Mortality among Black Men." *New England Journal of Medicine* 322(3):205–06.

Nag, M. 1985. "The Impact of Social and Economic Development on Mortality: Comparative Study of Kerala and West Bengal." In S. B. Halstead, J. A. Walsh, and K. S. Warren, eds., *Good Health at Low Cost*. New York: Rockefeller Foundation.

Navarro, V. 1990. "Race or Class Versus Race and Class: Mortality Differentials in the United States." *Lancet* 336:1238–40.

NCHS (National Center for Health Statistics). 1988. "Vital Statistics of the United States 1985." *Volume II - Mortality Part A*. Hyattsville, Maryland: National Center for Health Statistics.

Olubuyide, I. O., and T. F. Solanke. 1990. "The Causes of Death in an Elderly African Population." *Journal of Tropical Medicine and Hygiene* 93:270–74.

Omondi-Odhiambo, J. K. Van Ginneken, and A. M. Voorhoeve. 1990. "Mortality by Cause of Death in a Rural Area of Machakos District, Kenya in 1975–78." *Journal of Biosocial Science* 22:63–75.

Omran, A. R. 1971. "The Epidemiologic Transition: A Theory of the Epidemiology of Population Change." *Millbank Memorial Fund Quarterly* 49:509–38.

Packard, R. M. 1989. "White Plague, Black Labour." *Tuberculosis and the Political Economy of Health and Disease in South Africa*. Berkeley: University of California Press.

Panikar, P. G. K., and C. R. Soman. 1984. *Health Status of Kerala. The Paradox of Economic Backwardness and Health Development*. Trivandrum, Kerala: Center for Development Studies.

Preston, S. H. 1975. "The Changing Relation Between Mortality and Level of Economic Development." *Population Studies* 29(2):231–48.

———. 1976. *Mortality Patterns in National Populations: With Special Reference to Recorded Causes of Death*. New York: Academic Press.

Preston, S. H., N. Keyfitz, and R. Schoen. 1972. *Causes of Death: Life Tables for National Populations*. New York: Seminar Press.

Prost, A., and N. Prescott. 1984. "Cost-Effectiveness of Blindness Prevention by the Onchocerciasis Control Program in Upper Volta." *Bulletin of the World Health Organization* 62:795–802.

Roy, T. K., and S. Lahiri. 1988. "Recent Levels and Trends in Mortality in India and its Major States: An Analysis Based on SRS Data." In K. Srinivasan and S. Mukerji, eds., *Dynamics of Population and Family Welfare 1987*. New Delhi: Himalaya Publishing House.

Schooneveldt, M., T. Songer, P. Zimmet, and K. Thomas. 1988. "Changing Mortality Patterns in Nauruans: An Example of Epidemiological Transition." *Journal of Epidemiology and Community Health* 42:89–95.

Straus, J. H., and M. N. Straus. 1953. "Suicide, Homicide and Social Structure in Ceylon." *American Journal of Sociology* 58:461–69.

Taylor, R., and K. Thoma. 1985. "Mortality Patterns in the Modernized Pacific Island Nation of Nauru." *American Journal of Public Health* 75(2):149–55.

Timaeus, I. 1990. *Advances in the Measurement of Adult Mortality from Data on Orphanhood*. Research Paper 90-1. London: Center for Population Studies, London School of Hygiene & Tropical Medicine.

———. 1991. "Adult Mortality." In R. G. A. Feachem and D. T. Jamison, eds., *Disease and Mortality in Sub-Saharan Africa*. New York: Oxford University Press for the World Bank.

Timaeus, I., and W. Graham. 1988. *Measuring Adult Mortality in Developing Countries: A Review and Assessment of Methods.* Research Paper 88-4. London: Center for Population Studies, London School of Hygiene & Tropical Medicine.

Uemura, K. 1989. "Excess Mortality Ratio with Reference to the Lowest Age-Sex-Specific Death Rates Among Countries." *World Health Statistics Quarterly* 42(1):26–48.

United Nations. 1982. *Model Life Tables for Developing Countries.* Population Studies 77. New York: United Nations.

———. 1983. *Manual X: Indirect Techniques for Demographic Estimation*. New York: United Nations.

———. 1984. *Data Bases for Mortality Measurement*. New York: United Nations.

———. 1985. *Socio-Economic Differentials in Child Mortality in Developing Countries*. New York: United Nations.

———. 1988. "Mortality of Children under Age 5." *World Estimates and Projections, 1950–2025*. New York: United Nations.

———. 1989a. *Demographic Yearbook 1987*. New York: United Nations.

———. 1989b. *World Population Prospects 1988*. New York: United Nations.

United States Bureau of the Census. 1988. *World Population Profile: 1987.* Washington D.C.: United States Government Printing Office.

USDHHS (United States Department of Health and Human Services). 1989. *Reducing the Health Consequences of Smoking: 25 Years of Progress. A Report of the Surgeon General*. DHHS Publication No. (CDC) 89-8911. Rockville, Maryland: Centers for Disease Control, United States Department of Health and Human Services.

Waaler, H. 1980. "Inequalities in Health: An Economic Comment." In H. Smedby, ed., Inequality in Health Services in the Scandinavian Countries. The First Scandinavian Symposium on Health Services Research, 13–15

November, 1980, Tampere, Finland. *Scandinavian Journal of Social Medicine* Supplement 34:67–72.

Walsh, J. A. 1988. *Establishing Health Priorities in the Developing World*. New York: United Nations Development Program.

Williams, E. H., R. J. Hayes, and P. G. Smith. 1986. "Admissions to a Rural Hospital in the West Nile District of Uganda over a Twenty-Seven Year Period." *Journal of Tropical Medicine and Hygiene* 89:193–211.

Woolsey, T. 1981. "Toward an Index of Preventable Mortality." *Vital and Health Statistics*. Series 2, No. 85. Hyattsville, Maryland: United States Department of Health and Human Services.

World Bank. 1989a. *Adult Health in Brazil: Adjusting to New Challenges*. Report No. 7807-BR. Washington, D.C.: World Bank.

———. 1989b. *China: Long-Term Issues in Options for the Health Sector*. Report No. 7965-CHA. Washington, D.C.: World Bank.

World Health Organization. 1948. *Manual of the International Statistical Classification of Diseases, Injuries and Causes of Death. Sixth Revision*. Geneva: World Health Organization.

———. 1957. *Manual of the International Statistical Classification of Diseases, Injuries and Causes of Death. Seventh Revision*. Geneva: World Health Organization.

———. 1967. *Manual of the International Statistical Classification of Diseases, Injuries and Causes of Death. Eighth Revision*. Geneva: World Health Organization.

———. 1978. *Manual of the International Statistical Classification of Diseases, Injuries and Causes of Death. Ninth Revision*. Geneva: World Health Organization.

———. 1990. "Tobacco-Attributable Mortality: Global Estimates and Projections." *World Health Organization Tobacco Alert, December 1990*. Geneva: WHO Consultative Group on the Statistical Aspects of Tobacco-Attributable Mortality.

Zhou Youshang, Ras Kegin, and Zhang Deying. 1989. "An Analysis of Infant Mortality Rates in China." *Journal of Population Science of China* 1(4):419–38.

3. *Adult Morbidity: Limited Data and Methodological Uncertainty*

Christopher J. L. Murray, Richard G. A. Feachem,
Margaret A. Phillips, and Carla Willis

IF EVERY DISEASE CAUSED MORBIDITY in known proportion to the mortality it causes, then mortality rates would be an adequate proxy both for the overall burden of adult ill-health and for the contribution to that burden of each specific disease or cause. Some diseases, however, like onchocerciasis, epilepsy, and leprosy, cause substantial adult morbidity but little mortality. Consequently, adult mortality rates capture only a portion of the burden of illness, and cause-specific mortality undervalues the burden of certain causes of illness. Direct measurements of morbidity are needed to fill this gap in knowledge. Because of substantial conceptual and technical problems involved in measuring morbidity, adult morbidity in developing countries cannot be quantified to the same degree as adult mortality. This chapter discusses the different types of morbidity data, which illustrate the lack of consensus on how to quantify morbidity. Examples of adult morbidity surveys illustrate the importance of adult morbidity and show why there is no coherent empirical picture of the levels and causes of adult morbidity in developing countries.[1] The problems and issues raised in this chapter are not unique to developing countries. Morbidity in industrialized countries also defies valid and reproducible measurement.[2]

Measures of Morbidity

Morbidity measures can be classified as either observed or self-perceived.[3] Observed morbidity consists of reports from clinicians or other investigators about illnesses they have observed in the people they examine or test. Self-perceived morbidity consists of reports from people about their own illnesses. The deviation from a normal state of health is defined by the investigator in observed morbidity and by the individual in self-perceived morbidity. Self-perceived morbidity is closer to the concept of illness, while observed morbidity corresponds more closely to disease. Measures of observed morbidity have characteristic rates of false positives and false negatives associated with them; measures of self-perceived morbidity do not (if I think I am ill, then, by definition, I *am* ill).

Observed and self-perceived morbidity are fundamentally different because they change in response to overlapping but different sets of determinants. Rates of observed morbidity, when measurement error is minimized, respond only to changes in the underlying burden of disease or pathology.[4] A 50 percent increase in observed rates of arthritis is probably due to some shift in the epidemiology of the disease. Well-collected observed measures are repeatable and comparable across space and time. Conversely, rates of self-perceived morbidity are determined both by the underlying burden of disease or pathology (during an epidemic of malaria more people report having fevers) *and* by individual and community perceptions of illness and local patterns of illness behavior. The effects of illness perception and reporting behavior probably explain why the United States has higher rates of self-perceived morbidity than India. Because self-perceived morbidity responds to these two factors, gradual changes recorded over several years may be due to changes in the underlying pattern of disease or changes in how people perceive and report their illnesses. For the same reason, cross-sectional patterns of self-perceived morbidity analyzed according to socioeconomic variables can be difficult to interpret. The following sections of this chapter give several counter-intuitive examples in which self-perceived morbidity increases as income increases. How fast self-perceived morbidity rates change offers some help in interpreting these changes. Sudden changes in self-perceived morbidity are more likely to reflect changes in disease burden than changes in reporting behavior, because the latter tend to occur slowly.

Observed Measures of Morbidity

Observed measures of morbidity can be classified into four categories: physical and vital signs, physiologic and pathophysiologic indicators, functional tests and clinical diagnoses (table 3-1).

PHYSICAL AND VITAL SIGNS. In medicine, signs are evidence of disease that can be detected on physical examination. By tradition, they include vital signs such as blood pressure and temperature. Surveys based on physicians' examinations of large population samples are

Table 3-1. Measures of Morbidity

Observed measures	*Self-perceived measures*
Signs	Symptoms or impairments
Physiologic and pathophysiologic indicators	Functional disabilities
Functional tests	Handicaps
Clinical diagnoses	Utilization of health services[a]

a. See text for discussion of the relevance of utilization measures as indicators of self-perceived morbidity.

rare because of cost and logistical problems. While physicians are presumably better at making accurate physical diagnoses than surveyors with less training in medicine, observer error and variance in skill can be substantial problems in morbidity surveys based on physicians' examinations (Cochrane, Chapman, and Oldham 1951).

PHYSIOLOGIC AND PATHOPHYSIOLOGIC INDICATORS. A wide range of laboratory examinations (of blood, urine, feces, and other body fluids) and diagnostic imaging techniques (e.g., radiography) are included in this category. Tuberculin skin sensitivity surveys, mass miniature radiography surveys, and anthropometric surveys are examples of morbidity surveys that use this type of indicator commonly in developing countries. These survey results are repeatable and comparable to the extent they are well executed. One limitation of some data of this class is that values for any particular parameter may be defined as abnormal with respect to some arbitrary standard. For example, for anthropometry, the cutoff is often two standard deviations below the mean of a reference population. The health implications of deviations from normal, such as a low hemoglobin, can be difficult to assess.

Most epidemiologic studies of infectious diseases in developing countries measure infection, not disease. For example, the presence of *Ascaris* eggs in stool samples does not indicate necessarily the existence of clinical disease due to *Ascaris* infection. Similarly, a positive tuberculin skin test indicates infection with *Mycobacterium tuberculosis*, but only 6 to 8 percent of these infections progress to clinical disease (Murray, Rouillon, and Styblo 1990). It is important to distinguish observations of asymptomatic infections from observations of disease marked by specific pathologic changes.

FUNCTIONAL TESTS. Functional tests assess a person's ability to perform some function such as running, blowing up a balloon, lifting weights, or performing intellectual tasks. These tests rarely form the basis of morbidity surveys. Some groups studying disability advocate using functional tests as gold standards for assessing disability. To date, functional test data for adults in developing countries are scant.

CLINICAL DIAGNOSES. Clinical diagnoses are assessments that physicians or allied health professionals make on the basis of symptoms, signs and often laboratory results. Symptoms that are self-perceived are the key input to clinical diagnoses for a variety of disorders, most notably chronic pain and neuroses. In most surveys, clinical diagnosis is made without the benefit of laboratory results. For example, someone who has an enlarged spleen and fever in a country where malaria is endemic probably will be diagnosed without laboratory confirmation as having malaria. This limits the validity, repeatability, and comparability of clinical diagnoses because of variations in how physicians diagnose similar constellations of signs and symptoms (Elinson and Trussel 1957).

Self-Perceived Measures of Morbidity

Self-perceived measures of morbidity can be grouped into three categories: symptoms, functional disability and handicaps, and the utilization of health services (table 3-1).

SYMPTOMS OR IMPAIRMENTS. Most morbidity surveys collect information about symptoms or impairments. Respondents are asked about the occurrence of symptoms of illness in a defined time period. Such surveys are extraordinarily sensitive to the precise wording of questions and also may be affected by subtle cultural differences in the interpretation of these questions. Surveys vary in several ways. They differ in the way of identifying self-perceived symptoms. Some surveys ask questions about specific diagnoses or diseases as opposed to symptoms, such as ''Do you have tuberculosis or hemorrhoids?'' and presume respondents have enough medical knowledge to answer appropriately. Many surveys ask open-ended questions, such as ''Have you been ill in the last month? If so, from what?'' Others use lists of symptoms (tracer lists), which increase self-perceived morbidity rates by prompting respondents (Kroeger 1983; Linder 1965). Some surveys, like the United States National Health Interview Survey, use a salience principle or impact criteria to limit the information they collect; they ask only for morbidity that leads to visiting a doctor or to reducing normal activities for at least half a day (NCHS 1986). Surveys differ in how long ago they ask people to recall illness; some ask people about illnesses they have had in the last two weeks, others about illnesses in the last three months. The length of the recall period affects rates of self-perceived morbidity (Kroeger

1983; Linder 1965; Ross and Vaughan 1986). Longer periods increase reports of chronic disease and decrease reports of acute illness. Research on diarrhea has shown that using a two-week recall period may be too long when asking mothers about their children's diarrhea: mothers forget some of the episodes, especially if they are mild. Some surveys allow the head of the household to respond for all members, and this reduces the rates of reported morbidity for these other adults (Linder 1965; Mechanic 1965). Finally, surveys differ in their timing and duration, which matters because of the seasonality in disease incidence. Even when all these factors are the same, differences in morbidity rates may arise due to differences in illness perception and reporting behavior rather than differences in the underlying pattern of disease.

FUNCTIONAL DISABILITY AND HANDICAPS. Surveys of functional disability ask people about their ability to carry out specific functions or about restrictions of their activity. The most simplistic type asks about days out of work or school, days restricted to bed, or days of reduced function. Such surveys provide information only about illnesses and injuries serious enough to affect individual function. Functional disability surveys may ask also about the distance one can walk, the number of stairs one can climb, and the ability to dress oneself or prepare one's own meals. Many of the same limitations that apply to symptom surveys also apply to functional disability surveys. Illness perception and reporting behavior also affect rates of self-perceived functional disability. *Handicap* refers to functional disability in a particular social context. If a violinist and a banker lose their middle fingers, their functional disabilities are the same, but their degree of handicap is different. Few surveys measure handicaps. For a more detailed discussion, see Manton, Dowd, and Woodbury (1986) and Murray and Chen (1991).

UTILIZATION OF HEALTH SERVICES. The utilization of health services is a function of self-perceived illness and its severity and the availability, perceived efficacy, and price of health services. Therefore, changes in the use of health services cannot be ascribed simply to changes in the underlying burden of disease.

Interpretation of Differences in Self-Perceived Morbidity

Because all measures of self-perceived morbidity have two distinct sets of determinants—that is, underlying disease and perception of illness—they sometimes produce information that is counter-intuitive. The findings of a 1973–74 survey in India exemplify this.

The survey (Indian National Sample Survey 1974) reported overall self-perceived morbidity incidence rates for acute conditions that occurred in the two weeks before the survey. The state that had the lowest mortality rates, Kerala (chapter 2, table 2-6), had the highest reported morbidity. There are three possible interpretations of this finding: (a) the pattern of disease in Kerala is strikingly different, characterized by higher rates of nonfatal conditions than in other states in India; (b) the pattern of disease in Kerala is the same as in other states, but the burden of disease is greater, and the low mortality rates are due to extremely effective therapeutic health services; or (c) as health has improved in Kerala, illness perception and reporting behavior have changed so that the Keralese report more illness despite a lower disease burden. In the United States, the two-week incidence of self-perceived acute conditions is even higher than in Kerala. In the Living Standards Measurements Surveys (LSMS)[5] sponsored by the World Bank (various countries), the percentage of householders reporting illness in the previous month increases with increasing income in Côte d'Ivoire, Ghana, and Peru (see discussion under *Cross-Sectional Surveys of Self-Perceived Symptoms* in this chapter). Because the observed burden of disease is unlikely to be greater among the rich in these countries, the difference is likely to be due to variations in illness perception. However, when the incidence of self-perceived morbidity is greater in households without water, deciding whether this is due to disease or to perception is difficult. Causes of socioeconomic patterns in self-perceived data are difficult to determine. Meaningful comparisons of disease burdens over time or across communities cannot be made.[6] Self-perceived morbidity data, however, serve other purposes. In particular, they help characterize the demand for health services, community priorities and the effect of disability on the individual.

There is no single correct way to characterize morbidity among adults in developing countries. Each type of observed and self-perceived measure of morbidity provides a different way of looking at illness and disease, and no two are equivalent or even comparable. To provide some picture of adult morbidity, albeit an inadequate one, the next sections present the results of a few morbidity surveys, some using observed data, others using self-perceived data.

Selected Surveys of Observed Morbidity

National surveys of observed morbidity have been conducted in only a few developing countries (Kroeger 1983). Reports and results are available for even fewer; research for this chapter yielded surveys conducted in Colombia, Egypt, and Uruguay (Colombia, Ministerio de Salud Publica 1969; Egypt, Ministry of Health 1989; Rodriguez and Ospina 1987; Uruguay, Ministerio de Salud Publica 1985) and one survey underway in Pakistan. In addition, some small scale studies have been published, for example from Ghana (Belcher and others 1976).[7] This section reviews two physical examination surveys in Colombia (in 1968 and 1977–80) and the Egyptian health examination survey in Cairo (in 1981–82).

COLOMBIA. The Colombian National Morbidity Survey conducted physical examinations of 5,258 people in 1965–66 (Colombia, Ministerio de Salud Publica, 1969). The physical examinations were conducted by physicians and most participants had laboratory tests of blood, urine, and stool specimens. Some participants also had more intensive physiologic parameter tests. Physical examination results were reported by probable diagnostic category, but not age. High rates of helminthiases, tuberculosis, dysentery, acute and chronic respiratory infections, anemia, and injuries, as well as some less severe problems such as varicose veins and decreased visual acuity were observed. These observed data reveal some distinct differences when compared with self-perceived data: they include relatively high rates of thyroid disorder, diabetes mellitus, hernia, biliary tract disease and neoplasms, and low rates of musculoskeletal disorder. For a comparison, see discussion under *Selected Surveys of Self-Perceived Morbidity* in this chapter.

Specific data on parasitic infections are available by age and socioeconomic variables. Intestinal parasitic infections (detected by stool examinations) were found in 83 percent of those between fifteen and twenty-four years and 74 percent of those between both twenty-five and forty-four and forty-five and sixty-four years. These rates were more than double the disease rates discovered on physical examination by physicians. Lower parasitic burdens were associated with secondary or higher education and higher income (table 3-2), but rich and poor adults differed little in the prevalence of intestinal parasitic infection (70 versus 86 percent, respectively).

More than a third of older men and women in Colombia had hypertension (table 3-3) according to the standard definition of hypertension in the United States (systolic blood pressure greater than 140 millimeters of mercury or diastolic blood pressure greater than 90 millimeters of mercury). Hypertension prevalence was highest among men living in cities and lowest among women living in rural areas.

A second health examination survey was conducted in Colombia between 1977 and 1980 (Rodriguez and Ospina 1987). Clinical diagnoses were reported by age groups for men and women. Rates for

Table 3-2. Intestinal Parasitic Infections by Age, Education, and Income in Colombia, 1965–1966

Socioeconomic characteristic	*Prevalence rate (percent)*
Age	
15–24 years	82.6
25–44 years	73.8
45–64 years	74.0
Education (all ages)	
None	88.2
Primary	81.0
Secondary or higher	63.4
Household income[a]	
<3,600	85.6
3,601–6,000	80.7
6,001–12,000	78.5
12,000 +	69.6

a. 1965 pesos
Source: Colombia, Minísterio de Salud Pública (1969).

some causes of morbidity, like tuberculosis, were much lower than in 1968. Major health problems, however, were similar to those of 1968. High rates were observed for intestinal infections, helminths, respiratory infections, complications of pregnancy, urinary tract infections, and pelvic inflammatory disease. Major noncommunicable causes of morbidity included psychoses, varicose veins, chronic respiratory diseases, and digestive diseases (for example, ulcers, hernias, and biliary tract disease). Arthritis was a major problem in 1968 and continued to be a decade later. Because age-specific rates were not available for 1968, it is unclear whether the rates changed during the ten years between the surveys.

Table 3-3. Hypertension of Adults by Age and Gender in Colombia, 1965–1966

	Percent of men with hypertension		*Percent of women with hypertension*	
Age (years)	*Diastolic*	*Systolic*	*Diastolic*	*Systolic*
15–24	4.3	6.6	3.8	2.1
25–44	17.9	19.2	12.4	11.5
45–64	33.0	42.3	38.8	49.7

Note: Diastolic hypertension defined as >90 mm Hg, systolic as >140 mm Hg.
Source: Colombia, Minísterio de Salud Pública (1969).

EGYPT. The National Health Survey of Egypt was conducted in 1981 and 1982. Results were available only for the district of Cairo. More than 84 percent of men and 91 percent of women aged twenty to fifty-nine years had at least one health problem, although some of these were minor conditions like decreased visual acuity. Although high rates of endocrine and metabolic disorders were reported, no breakdown was provided to explain them. Anemia accounted for much of the high rate of blood and blood organ disorders. Musculoskeletal disorders affected less than three percent of men and four percent of women. Major parasitic and infectious diseases were amoebiasis, trachoma, ascariasis, schistosomiasis and pinworm (*Enterobius*) infestation.

Comparative Studies of Self-Perceived and Observed Morbidity

In the United States during the 1950s, several investigators studied the relationship between self-perceived morbidity and findings on clinical examinations (Elinson and Trussel 1957; Krueger 1957; NCHS 1967). For example, Krueger (1957) compared self-perceived and observed morbidity measures from the 1953–55 Baltimore Health Survey. His analysis indicated tremendous variance in the correspondence between the two types of measures depending on the cause. While only 2 percent of syphilis cases diagnosed by physicians were self-perceived, 100 percent of rheumatoid arthritis cases were.

At least one study in a developing country, the Dhanfa health project in Ghana, has made a direct comparison of self-perceived illnesses with clinical diagnoses (Belcher and others 1976). This study demonstrates how, even in a well-served population, there are substantial differences between self-perceived and observed morbidity (table 3-4). The ratio of self-perceived morbidity to clinically diagnosed morbidity in the general population was greater than 1.0 for blindness, back pain, and yaws. Eleven conditions—some minor, some severe—were discovered at least ten times more frequently on examination than reported by individuals (skin ulcers, malnutrition, pediculosis, intestinal parasites, splenomegaly, anemia, missing extremities, varicose veins, hypertension, upper respiratory infections, and injuries). Other studies have shown that the specific ratio of self-perceived to observed morbidity for each condition varies from community to community. In some communities in Egypt, more schistosomiasis is reported by individuals than is detected by physicians, while in other places the converse is true.

Table 3-4. Comparison of Self-perceived Conditions with Diagnoses Made from Physical Examinations of 3,653 Persons in Ghana, All Ages

Condition or diagnosis	Prevalence rate (percent) Interview	Examination	Ratio[a]
Tracer conditions			
Poliomyelitis	0.2	0.3	0.80
Pyoderma	10.3	15.6	0.66
Conjunctivitis	1.8	3.9	0.45
Diarrhea	0.9	3.2	0.27
Skin ulcer	0.1	3.7	0.04
Malnutrition	0.8	32.1	0.03
Pediculosis	0.0	3.1	<0.01
Intestinal parasites	0.2	55.0	<0.01
Splenomegaly	0.0	28.4	<0.01
Anemia	0.0	11.7	<0.01
Chronic conditions or impairments			
Blindness	0.5	0.4	1.29
Leprosy	0.2	0.2	1.00
Poliomyelitis	0.2	0.3	0.80
Inguinal hernia	0.6	1.9	0.29
Malignancy	0.0	0.2	0.19
Missing extremity	0.0	0.5	0.06
Varicose veins	0.0	0.7	<0.01
Hypertension	0.0	0.6	<0.01
Other conditions			
Low back pain	4.5	0.3	16.6
Yaws	1.2	0.3	3.9
Fever	5.2	13.9	0.37
Upper respiratory infection	3.5	35.1	0.1
Injuries	0.1	4.1	0.02

a. Ratio of interview to examination
Source: Belcher and others (1976).

Selected Surveys of Self-Perceived Morbidity

Many studies provide data on self-perceived symptoms of illness in developing countries. Since the 1960s, a variety of surveys and censuses have included morbidity questions.

Cross-Sectional Surveys of Self-Perceived Symptoms

The recent round of household surveys sponsored in part by the United Nations Statistical Office as part of the National Household Survey Capability Program has included morbidity questions. This section presents information from national surveys of Pakistan and

Thailand (and the United States, for comparison) and from the Living Standards Measurement Surveys (LSMS) of Côte D'Ivoire, Ghana, and Peru.

PAKISTAN. The Pakistan National Health Survey sampled 11,000 households in 1982–83 (Pakistan, Federal Bureau of Statistics 1986). Respondents were asked about illness in the previous month. A type of salience principle was employed so that illnesses were included only if the respondent had one or more of the following experiences:

- Was unable to perform his or her daily routine for at least twenty-four hours,
- Was unable to eat normal food for at least twenty-four hours, or
- Required bed rest for at least twenty-four hours.

These criteria are relatively strict and probably yielded much lower overall morbidity rates than would have a general question about illness in the previous month. Fourteen percent of men and 17 percent of women reported having been ill in the month before the survey. This corresponds to 1.7 episodes per man-year of reporting and 2.1 episodes per woman-year of reporting. Rates of self-perceived illness increased throughout the adult years (figure 3-1). Women reported having more episodes of illness than men, although adults reported that boys had more episodes of illness than girls. The latter may reflect more concern about male children in Pakistani culture. Self-perceived morbidity was lower among men who had more education, but lowest among women who had less than primary school education. Householders also were asked about the type of symptom. More than 50 percent of illness was due to acute respiratory infections and fevers or malaria. Other major causes included chronic respiratory and digestive disorders. Musculoskeletal complaints and trauma were not major causes of self-perceived morbidity.

THAILAND. The Thai Health and Welfare Survey of 21,680 households in 1981 asked each household member about illness in the previous month, using the same salience criteria as the Pakistan National Health Survey. The overall reported rate of self-perceived morbidity was 5.5 percent for men and 6.9 percent for women, the equivalent of 0.7 episodes per man-year of reporting and 0.8 episodes per woman-year of reporting. Because of probable differences in Thai and Pakistani reporting behaviors, to conclude that the burden of morbidity in Thailand is significantly less than in Pakistan would be unfounded despite the similarities in the designs of these surveys.

Figure 3-1. Age-Specific Morbidity Rates by Sex, Pakistan

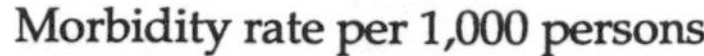

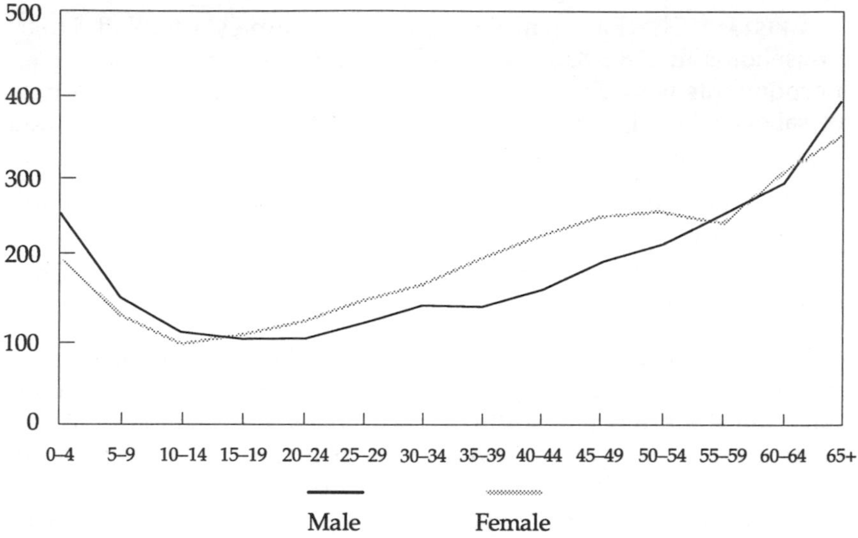

Source: Pakistan, Federal Bureau of Statistics (1986).

The age-specific pattern of self-perceived morbidity was similar in Thailand and Pakistan; although the reported rates for Thai children were much higher than in other age groups. As in Pakistan, adults in Thailand reported that boys had more episodes of illness than girls, and Thai women reported more illness than Thai men. The Thai survey collected data on employment status and reported illness. Unemployed Thai adults reported high rates of illness (table 3-5). Unfortunately, individual employment categories had different age distributions; consequently, it cannot be determined whether differences in morbidity rates among these categories are age-related.

UNITED STATES. For comparison, the 1985 United States National Health Interview Survey of 34,844 households found the number of acute conditions per person per year was 1.8 for eighteen to twenty-four year olds, 1.6 for twenty-five to forty-four year olds and 1.1 for forty-five to sixty-four year olds (NCHS 1986). The salience criteria were different from those used in the Pakistani and Thai surveys. Respondents were asked about illness or injury that lasted less than

Table 3-5. Self-perceived Morbidity Rates (One Month Recall) by Employment, Place of Residence, and Gender in Thailand, 1981
(percentage)

	Municipal areas		*Non-municipal areas*		
Employment status	*Men*	*Women*	*Men*	*Women*	*Total*
Employed					
Professional/administrative	3.4	3.3	4.1	3.2	3.7
Clerical/sales	2.9	4.6	5.5	6.1	4.0
Farmers/miners	3.8	4.7	5.7	7.7	5.6
Transportation	4.5		4.0		4.3
Craftsmen/laborers	5.0	5.8	4.6	6.9	4.8
Service	3.7	3.3	3.7	4.1	3.7
Unemployed					
Around house	3.4	5.8	7.7	8.0	6.6
Students	3.2	3.0	5.6	5.0	5.0
Other unemployed	15.3	14.8	18.8	19.3	17.9

Source: Thailand, National Statistics Office (1983).

three months, was first noticed less than three months before the survey, and was serious enough to a) cause the person to cut down for at least half a day on the things he usually does or b) cause the person to contact a physician regarding the illness or injury. In all adult age groups, women reported 25 to 37 percent more illness than men. Respiratory conditions accounted for roughly half of acute morbidity in adults, and injuries were the second most important cause. Reports of chronic conditions among forty-five to sixty-four year olds included arthritis (27 percent), glaucoma (16 percent), orthopedic impairment (16 percent), heart disease (13 percent), high blood pressure (26 percent), allergic rhinitis (18 percent) and ulcers (4 percent). In total, the annual number of days adults (aged eighteen to sixty-four years) spent in bed because of illness was 4.5 for men and 6.7 for women. Total days of reduced activity per year were twelve for men and sixteen for women.

CÔTE D'IVOIRE, GHANA, AND PERU. Designed principally to obtain detailed information on household income and expenditure, the LSMS also collect some basic health information. Household members are asked whether they had any illness or injury in the preceding four weeks, how many days they had been ill, and how many days they were unable to carry out their normal activities. No salience criteria are employed. This section reports results from surveys of Côte

Table 3-6. Characteristics of the Populations Surveyed by the LSMS in Côte d'Ivoire, Peru, and Ghana

Feature	*Côte d'Ivoire*	*Peru*	*Ghana*
Year of survey	1985	1985–1986	1987–1988
Size of population surveyed	13,270	25,630	15,550
Percentage of age group			
0–14	50	39	47
15–59	45	54	47
60+	5	7	6
Percentage male	48	50	49
Percentage rural	59	45	66
Number of households	1,380	5,090	3,140
Percentage of households without toilet	40	0	18
Main water source			
well water (percentage)	53		
inside tap (percentage)		45	
river/lake (percentage)			48
Main fuel source			
wood (percentage)	74		69
Median household size	7	4–5	4
Ratio of mean per capita household expenditure in the highest over the lowest decile households	20	23	14

Source: Living Standards Measurement Surveys in Côte d'Ivoire, Peru, and Ghana (World Bank various countries).

d'Ivoire (in 1985), Ghana (in 1987–88) and Peru (in 1985–86),[8] that each covered between fifteen hundred and five thousand households in communities selected from cities, villages, and rural areas in a two-stage sampling procedure. The nature of the populations surveyed is described in table 3-6.

Age. In Côte d'Ivoire, self-perceived illness and treatment-seeking behavior increased with age (table 3-7). The combination of higher rates and longer periods of self-perceived illness yielded markedly higher proportions of days ill, inactive and hospitalized among older adults and the elderly: forty to fifty-nine year olds had roughly double the levels of fifteen to thirty-nine year olds and half the levels of the elderly. This pattern of higher illness rates and longer duration of illness with age was also evident in Ghana and Peru (table 3-8). In Côte d'Ivoire, adults were responsible for 50 percent of all reported illness, 53 percent of all days ill, and 59 percent of all hospitalization days. More than 60 percent of private medical expenditure was for adults (table 3-9).

Distribution of illness in households. In Côte d'Ivoire, 87 percent of all households reported at least one household member ill in the pre-

Table 3-7. Illness and Care-Seeking Behavior by Age in Côte d'Ivoire, 1985

						For those ill					
Age (years)	*Sample population (number)*	*Percentage of persons ill during past month*	*Percentage of days ill*	*Percentage of days decreased activity*	*Percentage of days hospitalized*	*Percentage seeking consultation*	*Percentage hospitalized*	*Per capita medical expenditure (CFA[a])*	*Mean days ill*	*Mean days decreased activity*	*Mean days hospitalized*
0–4	2,148	32.2	11	7	0.06	59	2	2,773	9.7	5.8	0.05
5–14	4,070	22.1	7	4	0.07	50	2	1,705	8.5	4.6	0.09
15–39	4,582	27.8	10	6	0.19	56	3	3,830	10.2	6.0	0.19
40–59	1,723	46.4	22	13	0.35	47	3	4,035	13.5	7.9	0.21
60+	659	57.1	38	27	0.88	39	8	3,835	18.4	13.2	0.43

a. 1985 Franc de la Communauté Financière Africaine.
Source: Living Standards Measurement Survey in Côte d'Ivoire (World Bank).

Table 3-8. Illness by Age in Ghana, 1987–88, and Peru, 1985–86

Age (years)	*Percentage of persons ill during past month*		*Percentage of days ill*		*Percentage of days with decreased activity*		*Percentage of days hospitalized*	
	Ghana	*Peru*	*Ghana*	*Peru*	*Ghana*	*Peru*	*Ghana*	*Peru*
0–4	41	52	11	15	6	5	0.28	0.15
5–14	29	35	7	9	3	2	0.23	0.05
15–39	36	39	9	12	5	3	0.30	0.18
40–59	42	53	18	21	10	15	0.39	0.32
60+	49	61	21	32	12	8	0.46	0.33

Source: Living Standards Measurement Surveys in Ghana and Peru (World Bank various countries).

Table 3-9. The Impact of Ill-Health at Different Ages in Côte d'Ivoire, 1985

	Illness		*Hospitalization*		*Private medical expenditure*	
Age (years)	*Number of days ill*	*Percentage of all ill days*	*Number of days*	*Percentage of all hospital days*	*1,000 CFA*[a]	*Percentage of all private expenditure*
0–4	6,709	15	34	5	1,918	15
5–14	7,645	17	81	12	1,534	12
15–39	12,993	29	242	35	4,879	37
40–59	10,739	24	168	24	3,226	25
60+	6,924	15	162	24	1,443	11
Total	45,064	100	687	100	13,000	100

a. 1985 Franc de la Communauté Financière Africaine.
Source: Living Standards Measurement Survey in Côte d'Ivoire (World Bank various countries).

Table 3-10. Proportion of Adults Ill or Inactive for Long Periods in Côte d'Ivoire, 1985

Illness and illness-induced inactivity during the preceding twenty-eight days	*Percentage of ill adults*	*Percentage of all adults*
Ill for all twenty-eight days	20	7
Ill for one week or more	62	20
Inactive for all twenty-eight days	9	3
Inactive for one week or more	37	12
Ill but active	31	10

Source: Living Standards Measurement Survey in Côte d'Ivoire (World Bank various countries).

vious twenty-eight days, and 41 percent reported three or more members ill. Individuals in smaller households (one to three members) were two to three times more likely to report being ill than those in larger households. This is explained only partly by the fact that adults report more illness on average than the rest of the population and that smaller households tend to have a higher proportion of adults; disaggregation into adults and nonadults showed that the pattern of high reported illness in small households held for both. It is unclear to what extent this picture may be explained by smaller households existing in areas where disease is more common, or to what extent individuals who are prone to disease end up in smaller households, or to what extent being in a smaller household itself imposes risks (perhaps coping mechanisms of various sorts are absent). Perhaps individuals in small households have different perceptions and illness behavior, or households with sick members send some of their family members to live in other households. The pattern of higher illness rates in smaller households is not unique to Côte d'Ivoire. Reported illness rates were about 50 percent higher in small Peruvian households, and the pattern in Ghana was similar, although less striking.

Severity and length of illness. One fifth of Côte d'Ivoirian adults who reported illness said they had been ill for the entire month (table 3-10). About half of these adults appeared to be relatively seriously affected by this illness; they reported that for the entire month they were unable to carry out their normal activities. At any point in time, about three percent of all adults claim not to be functioning at their full capacity because of illness and might describe themselves as being chronically disabled.

Sex and pregnancy. As in most cross-sectional surveys of self-perceived illness in adults, women reported more illness than men (table 3-11). In Côte d'Ivoire, 29 percent of all self-perceived morbidity was among women and 22 percent was among men. In Ghana

Table 3-11. Adult Illness and Care-Seeking Behavior in Côte d'Ivoire, 1985

						For those ill					
Age, sex and pregnancy status	*Sample population (number)*	*Percentage of persons ill during past month*	*Percentage of days ill*	*Percentage of days with decreased activity*	*Percentage of days hospitalized*	*Percentage seeking consultation*	*Percentage hospitalized*	*Per capita medical expenditure (CFA[a])*	*Mean days ill*	*Mean days decreased activity*	*Mean days hospitalized*
Adults aged 15–39											
Men	2,050	25.4	9	5	0.15	53	2	2,374	9.4	5.2	0.16
Women[b]	2,532	29.8	11	7	0.20	49	3	4,834	10.8	6.5	0.19
Pregnant	124	36.3	12	7	0.00	58	0	2,604	9.0	5.2	0.00
Nonpregnant	675	34.2	13	7	0.40	55	4	5,779	10.3	6.1	0.33
Adults aged 40–59											
Men	803	46.7	21	12	0.30	48	2	4,310	12.4	7.3	0.18
Women	920	46.1	24	14	0.48	58	4	3,792	14.6	8.3	0.29

a. 1985 Franc de la Communauté Financière Africaine.

b. A subsample of women was asked the question concerning pregnancy

Source: Living Standards Measurement Survey in Côte d'Ivoire (World Bank various countries).

Table 3-12. Adult Illness and Care-Seeking Behavior by Per Capita Household Expenditure in Côte d'Ivoire, 1985

						For those ill					
Household expenditure quartile	*Sample population (number)*	*Percentage of persons ill during past month*	*Percentage of days ill*	*Percentage of days with decreased activity*	*Percentage of days hospitalized*	*Percentage seeking consultation*	*Percentage hospitalized*	*Per capita medical expenditure (CFA[a])*	*Mean days ill*	*Mean days decreased activity*	*Mean days hospitalized*
1 (lowest)	1,845	29.7	13	8	0.30	44	4	2,671	12.7	7.9	0.28
2	1,704	32.3	13	8	0.14	49	2	2,742	11.3	6.9	0.12
3	1,490	33.9	13	8	0.24	60	2	3,831	11.1	6.5	0.20
4 (highest)	1,266	37.1	14	7	0.28	58	3	6,805	10.8	5.2	0.21

a. 1985 Franc de la Communauté Financière Africaine.

Source: Living Standards Measurement Survey in Côte d'Ivoire (World Bank various countries).

and Peru, women reported somewhat higher rates of general morbidity than men and substantially higher rates of hospitalization. Pregnancy in women aged fifteen to thirty-nine years appeared to make relatively little difference in self-perceived illness or care-seeking behavior in Côte d'Ivoire. Pregnant women reported illness slightly more often than nonpregnant women, although for shorter periods and with less hospitalization (table 3-11). In Ghana and Peru, pregnant women reported illness more often and for longer periods than nonpregnant women; in Ghana, pregnant women reported illness 20 percent more often and, when ill, for 25 percent more days than nonpregnant women.

Poverty and location of household. Adults from richer households in Côte d'Ivoire (those that had higher per capita expenditure) reported higher levels of morbidity (table 3-12). The average period of inactivity and hospitalization tended to be smaller for the ill from richer households in Côte d'Ivoire but not in Ghana. Wealthier adults did spend more on the treatment of illness, which might explain the shorter duration of their illnesses. In Ghana and Peru, richer households also reported more illness, higher rates of consultation and higher levels of medical expenditure on any given episode of illness (table 3-13). In all three countries, higher rates of morbidity were reported in urban areas, although these illnesses were perceived to be less disabling than rural illnesses. Nevertheless, the urban ill were more likely to seek medical consultation and spend considerably more on their health problems (table 3-14). Regression analysis of Côte d'Ivoire data indicated that these relationships were significant even when a variety of potentially confounding variables were controlled.

Employment. A high proportion of adults (about 31 percent of men and 40 percent of women) in Côte d'Ivoire had not been working in the seven days before the study and were not looking for work. Being a housewife or being a student were reasons most adults aged less than forty years gave for not seeking employment (table 3-15). Illness, however, was an important reason that adults aged forty to fifty-nine years gave for not seeking employment. Adults who gave illness as a reason for not seeking work also reported higher rates of illness: 92 percent reported having been ill in the previous four weeks for an average of twenty days and having been inactive for an average of seventeen days; 7 percent of those reporting illness were hospitalized.

Illness as an explanation for being unemployed and not seeking work was four times more common in older adults. However, because a substantially higher proportion of younger adults were unemployed and not seeking work, the population subgroups had

Table 3-13. Adult Illness by Per Capita Household Expenditure in Ghana, 1987–88, and Peru, 1985–86

Household expenditure quartile	Percentage of persons ill during past month		For those ill: Mean days decreased activity		For those ill: Percentage seeking consultation		For those ill: Per capita medical expenditure[a]	
	Ghana	Peru	Ghana	Peru	Ghana	Peru	Ghana	Peru
Adults aged 15–39 years								
1 (lowest)	27	34	3.4	2.2	35	27	444	17
2	32	38	3.8	1.9	46	36	578	36
3	35	40	3.6	1.5	48	42	662	51
4 (highest)	45	41	3.5	1.6	56	51	805	91
Adults aged 40–59 years								
1 (lowest)	38	50	4.0	2.6	33	27	550	18
2	41	54	4.6	2.8	46	38	980	38
3	41	55	4.3	2.4	47	49	671	64
4 (highest)	49	52	4.5	1.9	53	52	888	88

a. In 1987 cedis (Ghana) and 1985 intis (Peru)

Source: Living Standards Measurement Surveys in Ghana and Peru (World Bank various countries).

Table 3-14. Adult Illness and Care-Seeking Behavior in Rural and Urban Areas of Côte d'Ivoire, 1985, Ghana, 1987–88, and Peru, 1985–86

				For those ill								
	Percentage of persons ill during past month			Mean days decreased activity			Percentage seeking consultation			Per capita medical expenditure[a]		
Age and location	Côte d'Ivoire	Ghana	Peru	Côte d'Ivoire	Ghana	Peru	Côte d'Ivoire	Ghana	Peru	Côte d'Ivoire	Ghana	Peru
15–39 years												
Urban	30[b]	38	41	4.9[b]	3.0	1.5	62[b]	54	46	6,880[b]	760	62
	29[c]			4.8[c]			58[c]			3,250[c]		
Rural	26	34	35	7.2	4.0	2.3	51	46	30	2,500	600	35
40–59 years												
Urban	37[b]	43	53	6.4[b]	3.0	2.0	60[b]	54	51	10,480[b]	910	70
	46[c]			6.1[c]			58[c]			5,430[c]		
Rural	48	42	53	8.6	5.1	2.9	42	41	32	2,560	780	36

a. In CFA (Côte d'Ivoire), cedis (Ghana) and intis (Peru)
b. Abidjan
c. Other
Source: Living Standards Measurement Surveys in Côte d'Ivoire, Ghana and Peru (World Bank various countries).

Table 3-15. Adult Illness as an Explanation for Unemployment in Côte d'Ivoire, 1985

Age and sex	Sample population (number)	Population not looking for work		Of those unemployed and not looking for work, reasons given (percentage)				Percentage of population unemployed and not looking for work due to illness
		Number	Percentage	Sick	Student	Housewife	Other	
15–39 years								
Men	2,050	748	38	6	54	0.4	40	2
Women	2,532	1,157	46	7	22	37	34	3
40–59 years								
Men	803	140	17	32	1	0	67	5
Women	920	250	28	24	1	30	46	7

Source: Living Standards Measurement Survey in Côte d'Ivoire (World Bank various countries).

similar rates of illness-related failure to seek work: at least 3.5 percent of the population (and 7 percent of older women) claimed to be unemployed due to illness (table 3-15). These figures may underestimate the effect of illness on employment, because they explain only why individuals were not seeking work when surveyed and do not address the question of why the individuals were unemployed originally.

Cross-Sectional Surveys of Impairment

The self-perceived morbidity surveys reviewed so far have measured mostly the acute symptoms of relatively common causes of ill-health. Larger surveys or censuses are required to measure chronic and rare impairments because of their lower prevalence rates. The most comprehensive source of data on impairments is the United Nations International Disability Statistics Data Base (DISTAT), developed by the Statistics Office, Department of International Economic and Social Affairs (United Nations 1988), which has consolidated data on impairments and functional disabilities from censuses and surveys in more than 50 countries.[9] Because these national data sets are highly heterogeneous in the quality and type of information they collected, they cannot be used for comparisons across countries. Nevertheless, they do provide information on the age, sex, residence, education, and work status of people who have self-perceived impairments, as well as providing information on the types of disabilities.

EGYPT, BAHRAIN, AND SRI LANKA. This section examines surveys of impairments in three countries—Egypt (in 1976), Bahrain (in 1981) and Sri Lanka (in 1981).[10] These national data sets all derive from national censuses, use both observed and self-perceived reports,[11] and use similar classifications of impairments. Although Egypt, Bahrain, and Sri Lanka may not be representative of developing countries, their data show general patterns of impairments that may apply to many developing countries. Some developing countries may have significantly higher impairment rates, but unfortunately the countries where impairments are likely to be most prevalent tend to have the least detailed and reliable data.

Figures 3-2 through 3-4 present overviews of impairment in Egypt, Bahrain, and Sri Lanka. Data from these countries are not directly comparable,[12] but do show similar patterns. Impairment rates increased with age and were higher for men than for women. The majority of those impaired were adults, in all three countries. Blindness was a prominent cause of adult impairment and was more important both absolutely and relatively with age, causing about one

(Text continues on p. 144.)

Figure 3-2. Adult Disability in Egypt

Disability Among Adults

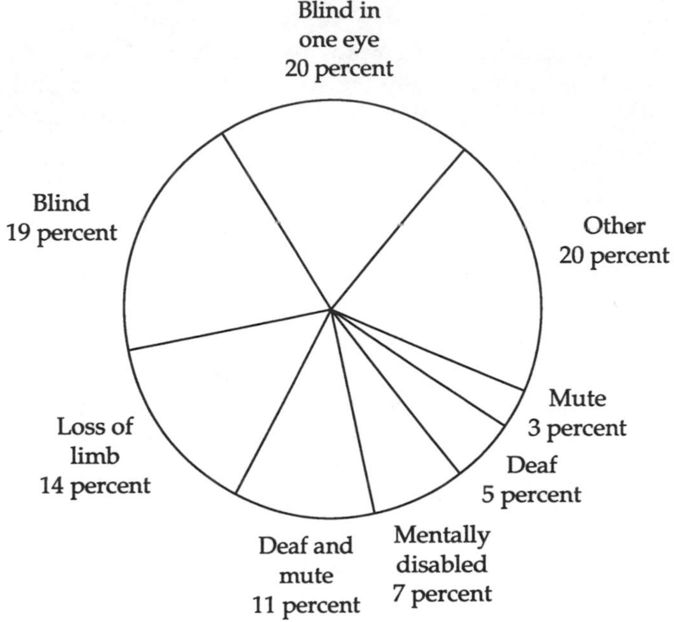

Disability Rates by Age and Gender

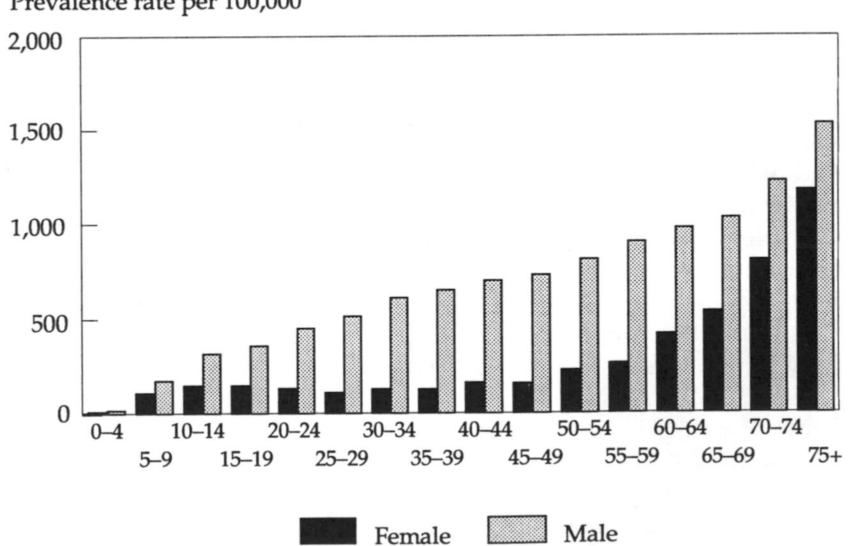

Source: UN International Disability Statistics Database.

Changing Composition of Disability with Age

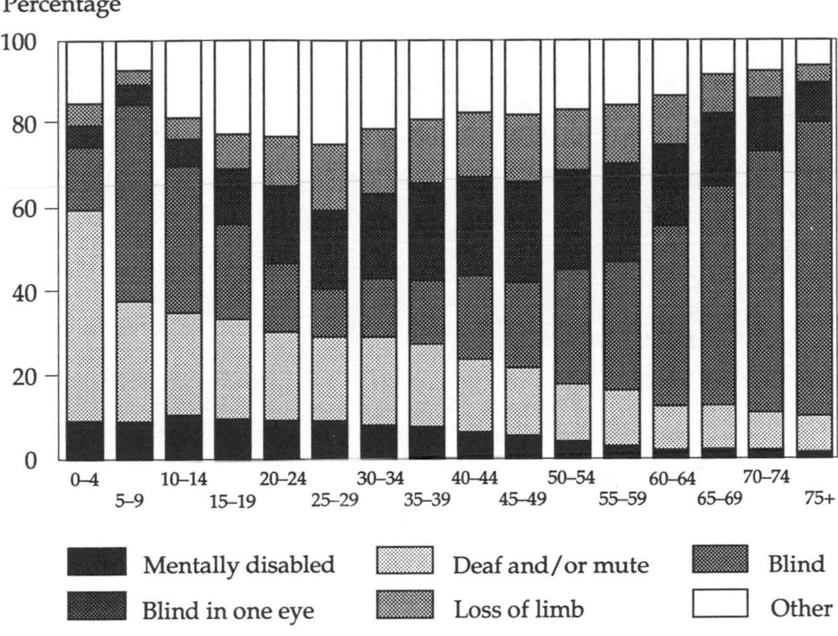

Disabled Population by Age Group and Gender

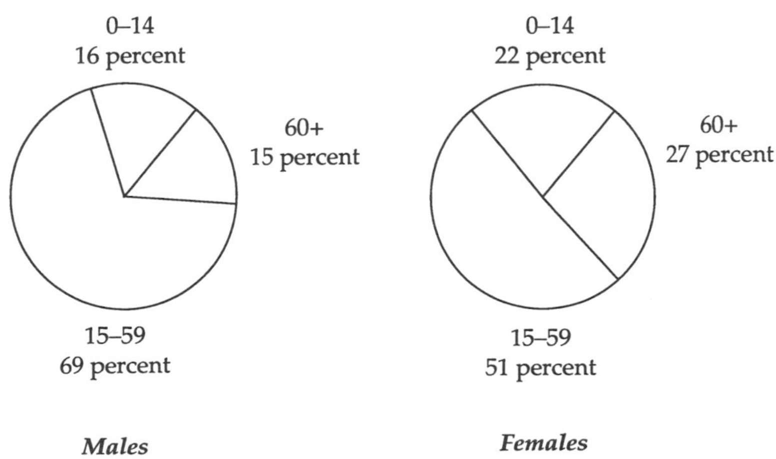

Figure 3-3. Adult Disability in Bahrain

Disability Among Adults

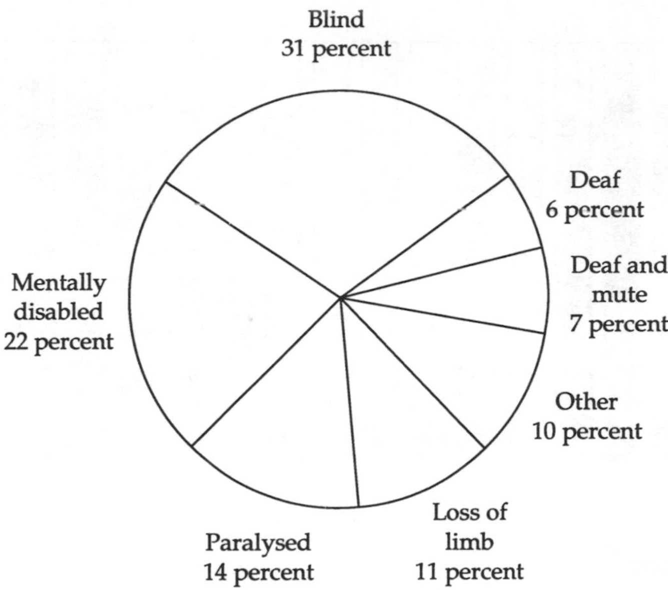

Disability Rates by Age and Gender

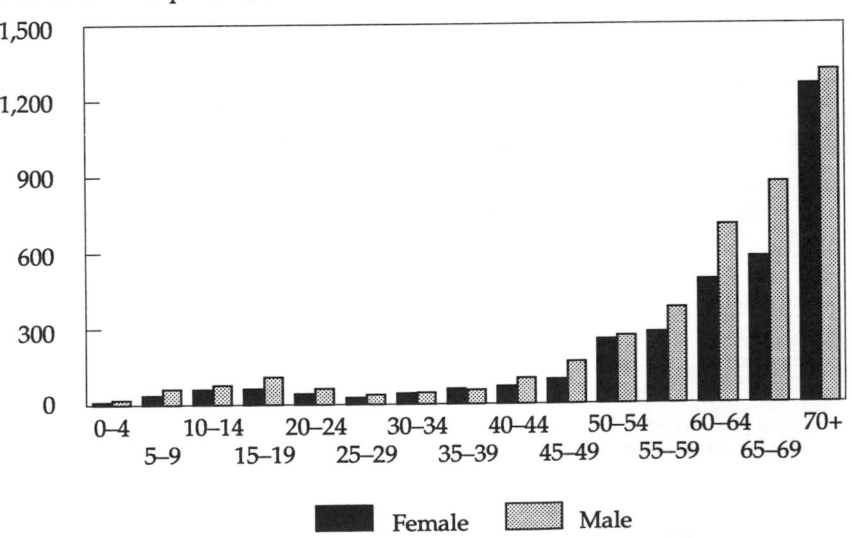

Source: UN International Disability Statistics Database.

Changing Composition of Disability with Age

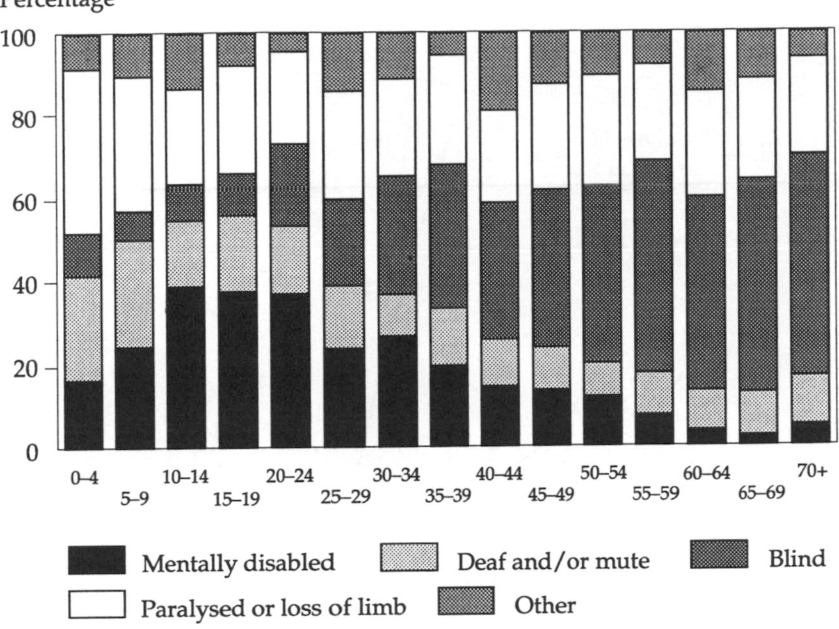

Disabled Population by Age Group and Gender

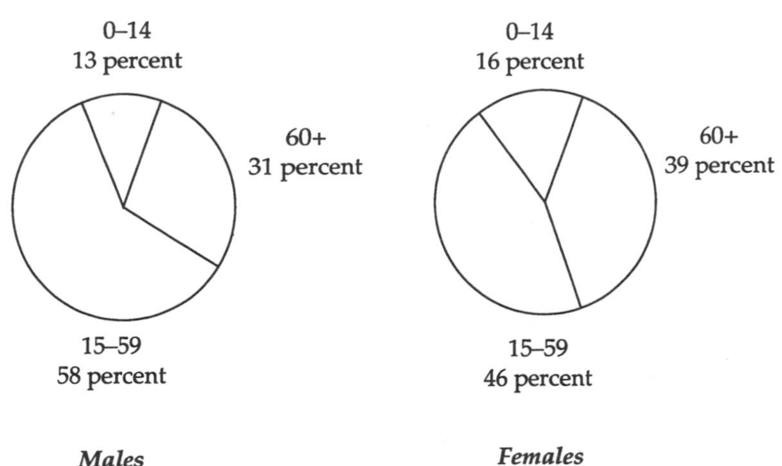

Figure 3-4. Adult Disability in Sri Lanka

Disability Among Adults

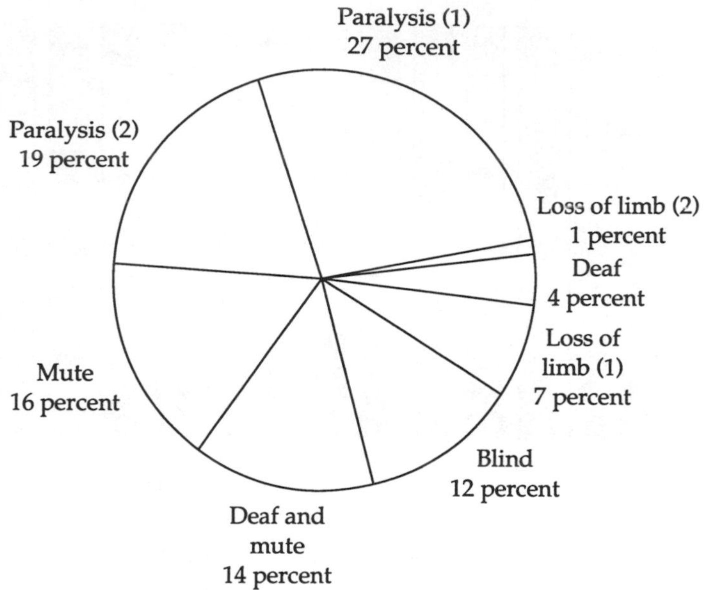

Disability Rates by Age and Gender

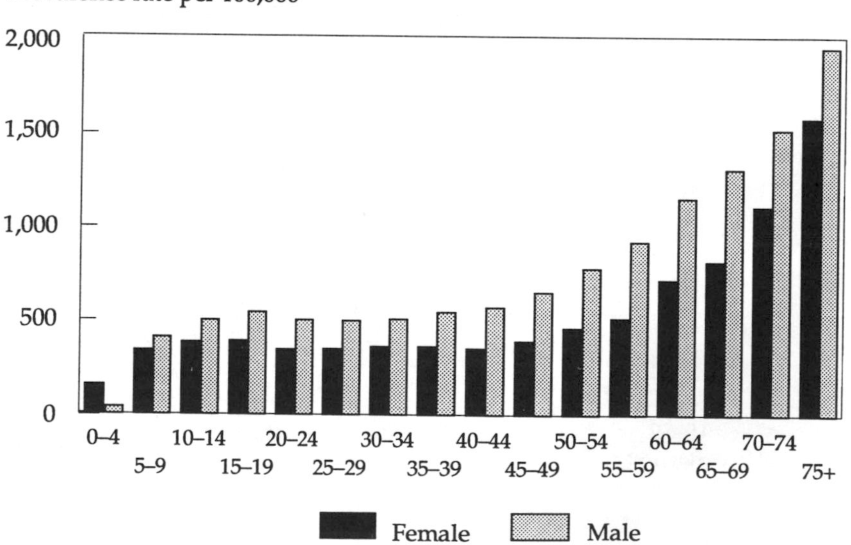

Source: UN International Disability Statistics Database.

Changing Composition of Disability with Age

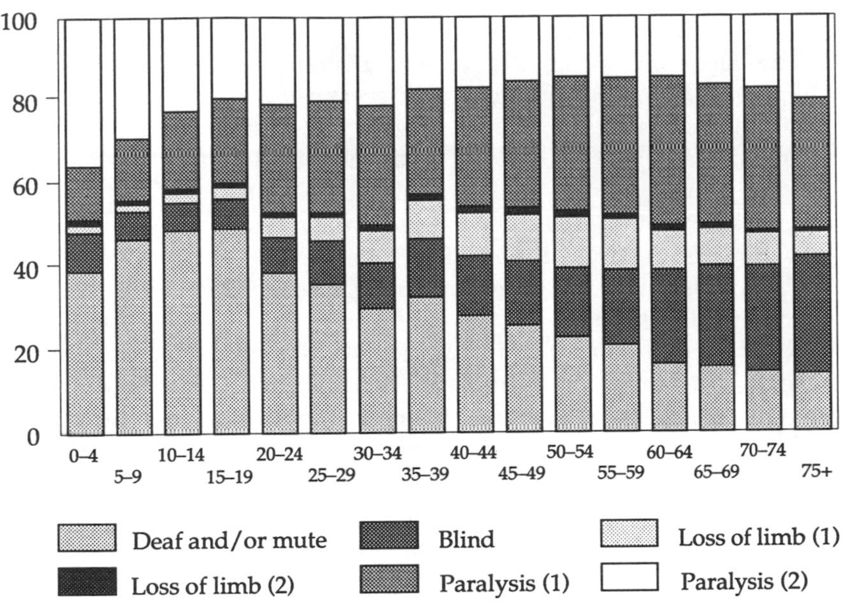

Disabled Population by Age Group and Gender

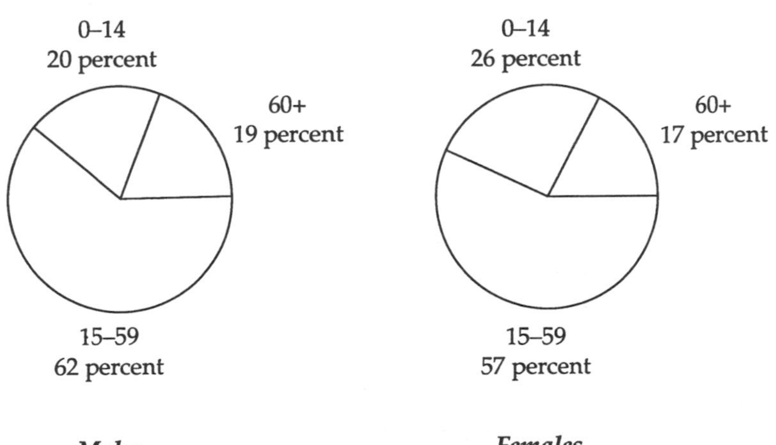

fifth of all reported adult impairment in Egypt and nearly one third of all adult impairment in Bahrain. Blindness may be more prevalent among older adults and the elderly both because of age-related ocular changes and because of decreasing rates of communicable diseases that cause blindness (a cohort effect).

The data from these surveys may overstate differences between child and adult rates and gender differences because impairments of children and females of all ages may be underreported. Impairments frequently are not recognized or acknowledged until a child has reached school age (United Nations 1986), and fewer girls attend school. Women of marriageable age may be reluctant to report impairments. Some of the difference between men's and women's rates of impairment, however, may reflect men's greater exposures to occupational hazards.

Ninety-seven percent of impairments in Bahrain were due to disease, injury, and birth defects. Most of the impairments were preventable, although "preventable impairment" was not rigorously defined. A substantial portion of adult impairment was acquired during childhood, indicating that efforts to improve adult health should include preventive programs that target children.

The Bahrain data provide evidence that self-reported impairment correlates with low socioeconomic status. People who had impairments were three and a half times more likely to be illiterate and twelve times less likely to have received a college degree. Similarly, people who had impairments were nearly three and a half times less likely to be employed. More than half of the impaired were reported to be unable to work. This is in contrast to the higher rates of symptoms reported for upper income groups in the LSMS data. The Sri Lanka census concentrated on highly visible impairments and, consequently, identified relatively many cases of paralysis and loss of limb. Prevalence of adult impairments ranged from 1 per 100,000 for loss of both arms to 65 per 100,000 for paralysis of one leg. It is unlikely that the true mix of impairments (e.g., blindness versus paralysis or loss of limb) differs among Egypt, Bahrain, and Sri Lanka as much as these data suggest. Sixteen percent of people who had impairments in Sri Lanka had more than one impairment, the most common multiple impairment being paralysis of one leg and one arm. Self-reported impairment was more prevalent in rural than urban areas, and men in rural areas had the highest rates. One fifth of all impairments in Sri Lanka were reported as starting during adulthood. Violence was reported rarely as a cause of impairment.

In Sri Lanka, less than 10 percent of all those who had impairments supported themselves through employment. Family members supported 77 percent, underscoring the economic and social consequences that impairment presents to families and communities. Men who had impairments were more likely than women to beg for a living, although begging was by far the least frequently reported means of support. Impairments that seemed to interfere least with employment were deafness and loss of one limb, whereas paralysis of two limbs and blindness interfered most. Nearly 20 percent of the deaf supported themselves through employment, compared with less than 3 percent of those who had paralysis in two limbs.

The methods and definitions of Sri Lanka's 1963 census were roughly comparable to the 1981 census. Between 1963 and 1981, both the blindness rate and the deaf-muteness rate declined by about one-third. The proportion of impairment caused by disease (as opposed to injury or birth defect) declined from 49 to 33 percent for blindness, 9 to 3 percent for deaf-muteness, and 45 to 26 percent for disability in both legs. Because mortality rates from injury have been increasing among men in Sri Lanka since the early 1960s (chapter 2, figure 2-12a), impairments from injuries are likely to have been increasing also, although this could not be analyzed using the data from these two censuses.

Prospective Studies of Self-Perceived Symptoms

The previous section presents prevalence rates derived from cross-sectional surveys. To characterize adult morbidity fully, it is necessary to know the incidence rates—the numbers of episodes per unit of population during a specified time—for particular diseases or impairments or for disease and impairment in general. To examine the incidence rates of adult morbidity, this section summarizes prospective data collected in Kenya, Egypt, and Mexico over a period of a year or more. Data comparisons among these countries are generally not possible because, even though the investigations were linked by a common protocol, differences in detailed methods and definitions make it difficult to distinguish genuine contrasts and similarities from artifacts.

The three studies took place between January 1984 and May 1986 and were the components of an investigation of the functional consequences of chronic mild-to-moderate malnutrition.[13] Table 3-16 summarizes the main features of these three studies and their locations. The special feature of these studies is their longitudinal design. Most other comprehensive and detailed adult morbidity data come from cross-sectional surveys of relatively large samples of households of the kind summarized in the previous section. In Kenya, Egypt, and Mexico, a small sample of households were visited weekly for a year or more and all forms of adult morbidity were recorded. This makes it

Table 3-16. Features of the Prospective Studies in Kenya, Egypt, and Mexico

Feature	*Kenya*	*Egypt*	*Mexico*
Site	Embu	Kalama	Solis
Distance from capital	120 km from Nairobi	47 km from Cairo	240 km from Mexico City
Altitude	1,000–1,500 m	Sea level	2,500 m
Setting	Rural	Periurban	Rural
Economy	Subsistence and cash agriculture	Agriculture and urban wage labor	Agriculture and urban wage labor
Staple crops	Maize and beans	Wheat and rice	Maize and beans
Electrification	None	All households	Not known
No. of households studied	285	290	284
Sample size			
Lead males	249	81	286
Lead females (nonpregnant)	126	36	287
Lead females (pregnant)	124	42	156

Mean age			
Lead males	37	35	37
Lead females	31	29	32
Percentage illiterate			
Lead males	25	50	50
Lead females	49	90	50
Data collection	Weekly household visit by high school graduate	Weekly household visit by physician	Weekly household visit by physician or health auxiliary
Illness recall	Past 7 days	Past 7 days	Past 24 hours

Note: Participant households were chosen on the basis of the presence of a woman in the first trimester of pregnancy or likely to become pregnant, a young infant, a toddler, or a school-aged child. The parents of the infant, toddler, or child, or the pregnant woman and her husband, became the so-called lead males and females, about whom detailed longitudinal data on the incidence, severity, and duration of morbidity were collected. Less detailed data, both longitudinal and cross-sectional, were collected for all other adults living in the participant households. Morbidity data were collected by weekly home visits over one year or more. Monthly, quarterly, and semi-annual special surveys were conducted also. The investigators believe that the participant households are representative of households in which a married couple, with the wife in her reproductive age span, reside. The participant households cannot, however, be expected to be representative of all households. For example, households with single parents, especially those in which the husband has left or died, may be expected to be poorer and less healthy than the households studied.

Source: See note 13 at the end of this chapter.

possible to measure the incidence of acute morbidity and to analyze the determinants and consequences of adult morbidity in more detail than is possible in cross-sectional surveys.

KENYA. The most comprehensive data are available from Kenya. Ninety-nine percent of women surveyed were aged fifteen to forty-four years, and 95 percent of men were aged twenty-five to fifty-five years. This highly clustered age distribution reflects the sampling method used in all three studies (see the footnote to table 3-16). Incidence rates of illness were between seven and seventeen episodes per person per year in various groups (table 3-17), were higher in pregnant than in nonpregnant women, and were almost twice as high in women as in men.[14] The majority of these episodes were mild and were experienced by most adults—only 2 percent of women and 7 percent of men reported no mild episodes during eighteen months of observation. Severe episodes were reported by 35 percent of nonpregnant women, 52 percent of pregnant women and 37 percent of men. The causes of adult illness were mainly communicable diseases (especially respiratory disease, fever [including malaria], and diarrhea) and musculoskeletal problems (table 3-18). The distribution of broad causes was almost identical for pregnant women, nonpregnant women, and men. No strong seasonal pattern of morbidity emerged over the two years (1984 and 1985) of study, although there was a

Table 3-17. Incidence Rates of Morbidity for Adults in Kenya, 1984–86
(episodes per person per year)

	Women		
Age and severity	*Nonpregnant*	*Pregnant*	*Men*
Age groups (years)			
<34	14	14	7
35+	13	17	8
All	14	15	8
Severity of illness			
Mild	13	15	7
Severe	0.6	1	0.6

Note: The definition of mild and severe was complex, and investigators followed a long checklist of mild and severe conditions. Examples of mild episodes were localized skin diseases, conjunctivitis, otitis media, oral thrush, common cold, mild diarrhea, headache, joint pain, sprains, bruises, cuts, and abrasions. Examples of severe episodes were extensive skin disease, burns, trachoma, mastoiditis, pneumonia, bronchitis, severe diarrhea or diarrhea with dehydration, genital discharge or lesions, pelvic inflammatory disease, malaria, meningitis, severe trauma, and fever greater than 39°C. In general, a severe episode was one that was expected to limit usual activities.

Source: See note 13 at the end of this chapter.

Table 3-18. Proportional Morbidity Rates of Adults in Kenya, 1984–86
(percentage of all episodes due to a particular cause)

	Women		
Cause	*Nonpregnant*	*Pregnant*	*Men*
I. Communicable and reproductive	64	64	65
Respiratory	28	29	29
Fever	13	12	17
Diarrhea and other gastrointestinal	11	11	9
Eye and ear	5	6	4
Skin	3	3	5
Genitourinary	2	2	1
Oral cavity	1	1	1
Maternal or reproductive	1	1	0
II. Noncommunicable	34	34	31
Musculoskeletal (including arthritis)	20	20	21
Psychologic, emotional	7	6	4
Headache, fainting, dizziness, seizures	6	5	4
Dental	2	1	2
III. Injuries	2	2	4

Note: Some of the respiratory disease may be chronic and noncommunicable rather than acute and infectious. Some of the musculoskeletal illness may come from previous injury.

Source: See note 13 at the end of this chapter.

near-doubling of morbidity rates at the time of a severe drought-induced food scarcity.

The proportions of time spent ill, in decreased activity and bedridden are shown in table 3-19. Men were ill roughly one fifth of all days, had decreased activity 4 percent of all days (fifteen days per year) and were bedridden 0.3 percent of all days (one day per year). Women were sick one third to one half of all days, had decreased activity 9 to 13 percent of all days (thirty-three and forty-seven days per year for nonpregnant and pregnant women, respectively), but were bedridden to a similar extent as men. Severe episodes accounted for few days of illness, but more days of decreased activity and more days bedridden. Of all episodes of illness, 21 percent caused decreased activity, and 1 percent caused the individual to stay in bed. These incapacities varied by cause of illness and were highest for episodes of fever (43 percent decreased activity and 4 percent bedridden) and episodes of diarrhea (33 percent decreased activity and 3 percent bedridden). Twenty-one percent of all episodes also caused decreased food intake.

Table 3-19. Proportion of Days Adults in Kenya Spent Ill, with Decreased Activity and Bedridden, 1984–86
(percentage of days)

	Women						Men		
	Nonpregnant			Pregnant					
Age and severity of illness	*Percentage of days ill*	*Percentage of days with decreased activity*	*Percentage of days bedridden*	*Percentage of days ill*	*Percentage of days with decreased activity*	*Percentage of days bedridden*	*Percentage of days ill*	*Percentage of days with decreased activity*	*Percentage of days bedridden*
Age (years)									
<34	41	10	0.3	43	10	0.6	19	4	0.1
35+	35	9	0.4	53	20	0.3	22	5	0.4
All	38	9	0.3	46	13	0.5	21	4	0.3
Severity of illness									
Mild	38	8	0.3	40	11	0.4	19	4	0.2
Severe	2.2	1	0	4.4	1	0.2	1.6	1	0.2

Source: See note 13 at the end of this chapter.

Lower socioeconomic status, older age, and illness of their children and wives were the factors most strongly associated with increased morbidity in men. For women, illness in other family members (especially toddlers), poor household sanitation, and chronic undernutrition (as measured by head circumference) were the factors most strongly associated with increased morbidity.

Sick men and women required, in some cases, help in daily tasks, or task reassignment (table 3-20). In about one quarter of their illnesses, pregnant women required help with daily tasks, and a further one quarter required task reassignment. Nonpregnant women were notably more able to cope with daily tasks. When women were ill, help was provided by, or tasks were reassigned to, their husbands, other household adults, friends or household school children, in roughly decreasing order of frequency. Illnesses requiring most help or task reassignment were fever and diarrhea.

Other findings of interest in this Kenyan rural community were as follows:

- A high prevalence of anemia in women (49 percent had < 12 g/dl hemoglobin)
- Roughly half of all adults carried hookworms
- Women reported much more anxiety and depression than men
- Hypertension was very rarely recorded
- On average, men consumed seven liters of traditional beer and three liters of commercial beer per week.

EGYPT. Sample sizes in the Egypt survey were small (table 3-16) and the age range was broader than in Kenya (a few individuals were aged sixty years and older). As in Kenya, the greater part of acute self-perceived morbidity was reproductive or communicable. Respiratory disease, fever, and diarrhea were prominent. Respiratory disease was most common in the winter (October to March), and diarrhea was most common in the summer (April to September). Morbidity of women was associated significantly with the morbidity of their husbands and their young infants. Out of a wide range of socioeconomic, environmental, and physiological variables studied, the variables associated significantly with higher adult morbidity were: taking water from a public tap (rather than a private well or tap), smaller house size, more people per room, absence of grandparents, older age, and lower hemoglobin levels.

The morbidity patterns of pregnant and lactating women in the Egypt sample have been the subject of more detailed analyses.[15] Eighty-four women, aged seventeen to forty-five years, were studied

Table 3-20. Percentage of Adult Illness Episodes Requiring Help or Task Reassignment in Kenya, 1984–86

	Women[a]				Men[b]	
	Nonpregnant		Pregnant			
Daily activity	Help required	Task reassigned	Help required	Task reassigned	Help required	Task reassigned
Salaried jobs	n.a.	n.a.	n.a.	n.a.	1	2
Animal and agricultural work on own farm	5	1	18	9	19	6
Housekeeping and compound care	7	8	21	20	0.2	9
Child care	2	11	11	26	n.a.	1
Food procurement, preparation and cooking	8	6	17	24	n.a.	1
Fetching fuel and water	8	4	27	8	n.a.	1

n.a. = not applicable
a. No women engaged in salaried employment
b. Men engaged in almost no child care, food preparation and cooking, or fetching of water and fuel, unless they were assisting a wife who was ill
Source: See note 13 at the end of this chapter.

Table 3-21. Morbidity among Pregnant and Lactating Women in Egypt, 1984–86

Morbidity measure	*Pregnant (last two trimesters)*	*Lactating (first six months)*
Percentage of women having no morbidity	54	54
Incidence rate (episodes per woman per year)[a]	2.6	2.0
Percentage of days ill	4.7	3.2
Percentage of all time ill due to respiratory disease, diarrhea, and skin disease	42	59

a. The incidence rate during the six month period multiplied by 2

Source: Data provided by Avanelle Kirksey and Atassa Rahmanifar of Purdue University.

during the last six months of pregnancy and the first six months of lactation. Half the women were between twenty and thirty years of age, the mean birth interval was thirty months and the mean parity was four. Eighty-one percent had no formal education and 82 percent were illiterate. The average household had seven people, of whom three were children under six years of age. Just more than half of the pregnant and lactating women reported no illness (table 3-21). Annual incidence rates were similar for pregnant and lactating women (2.6 and 2.0 episodes per woman per year, respectively), but duration of illness was somewhat longer for pregnant women, raising their prevalence rates of illness (4.7 versus 3.2 percent of days ill). Roughly half of all time spent ill was due to three conditions: respiratory disease, diarrhea, and skin disease. Neither socioeconomic status, sanitation, education, nor household composition was associated significantly with percentage of time ill.

MEXICO. In the Mexico survey, 97 percent of women were aged fifteen to forty-five years, and 97 percent of men were aged fifteen to fifty-five years. Women were sick for more than twice as long as men (table 3-22). Sixty-two percent of men, but only 36 percent of women, reported no illness during the thirteen to fourteen months of participation in the study. Respiratory illness was by far the largest cause of reported morbidity, and fever and diarrhea were second and third. The distribution of symptoms varied little by sex or pregnancy status. No seasonal pattern of morbidity was detected. Men and women reported being mildly incapacitated by illness 0.7 to 1.8 percent of all days (three and seven days per year) and severely incapacitated 0.1 to 0.3 percent of all days (<1 and 1 day per year). Of the factors significantly associated with increased morbidity, several were counter-

Table 3-22. Morbidity of Adults in Mexico, 1984–86
(percentage of days)

Condition	Women: Nonpregnant	Women: Pregnant	Men
Ill	4.1	3.7	1.8
Mildly incapacitated[a]	1.2	1.8	0.7
Severely incapacitated[b]	0.3	0.2	0.1

Note: In Mexico, a twenty-four-hour, rather than a seven-day, morbidity recall was used. It is not possible, therefore, to construct incidence rates. The rates presented here are prevalence rates (percentage of days ill) based on the assumption that days on which households were visited were representative of all days.

a. Stayed at home

b. Stayed in bed

Source: See note 13 at the end of this chapter.

intuitive. Higher calorie intake, cleaner houses and yards, better personal hygiene, and higher literacy were associated with increased morbidity of some type in women or men.

Other findings of interest in this Mexican rural community were as follows:

- Sixteen percent of women and 21 percent of men had had surgery
- Blood pressure was substantially higher in men than in women, but the prevalence of hypertension in men was <10 percent
- Forty-one percent of women and 64 percent of men said they drank pulque (a fermented drink made from the sap of the agave plant) daily
- Thirty-eight percent of men, but no women, said they smoked cigarettes.

DISCUSSION. The incidence and prevalence rates of self-perceived morbidity varied greatly between Kenya, Egypt, and Mexico. Annual incidence rates varied from as many as seventeen episodes (older pregnant women in Kenya) to two episodes (lactating women in Egypt). Illness prevalence rates varied from 53 percent of all days (older pregnant women in Kenya) to 3 to 5 percent of all days (women in Egypt and Mexico) and 2 percent of all days (men in Mexico). These data are shown on tables 3-19, 3-21, and 3-22. Although rates in Kenya may be higher because of greater poverty, these huge differences almost certainly reflect differences in survey methods and perception of illness and illustrate the extreme difficulty of gathering comparable data on morbidity. The physicians who collected data in

Egypt and Mexico may have screened out a large amount of mild morbidity, whereas the high school graduates who collected data in Kenya probably included all such morbidity. Thus, the figures from Egypt and Mexico of women being ill 3 to 5 percent of all days (eleven to eighteen days per year) and men being ill 2 percent of all days (seven days per year) may be more reliable estimates of adult morbidity prevalence in rural and peri-urban communities in developing countries (tables 3-21 and 3-22). Interestingly, these figures correspond closely to the prevalence rates of severe illness in Kenya (women ill for 2 to 4 percent of all days, men for 2 percent), suggesting that what was measured as overall illness in Egypt and Mexico corresponds to what was measured as severe illness in Kenya.

Percentage of time of decreased activity and percentage of time bedridden were reported from Kenya and Mexico. Kenyan rates for decreased activity (9 to 13 percent of female days) were much higher than Mexican rates (1 to 2 percent of female days), but decreased activity in Kenya due to severe illness (1 percent of days) corresponded closely with that of Mexico. Data on the proportion of time spent bedridden agreed well between Kenya and Mexico, perhaps because this is a more objective measure. In both countries, adults reported spending 0.4 to two days per year in bed because of illness, substantially less than the number of days (4.5 for men and 6.7 for women) in the United States (NCHS, 1986).

Overall, adults in these three countries have fairly frequent mild infectious morbidity, resulting sometimes in a need to reallocate tasks, but causing very little time severely incapacitated or bedridden. It is quite probable that these adults cannot afford the luxury of being bedridden and that the same level of morbidity in more affluent communites would cause a higher percentage of time to be spent in bed.

Conclusions

Mortality, without attribution of cause, is a bedrock measure. It is objective and, assuming good registration systems are in place, it can be compared between age groups, places, and times, and confident conclusions about differences can be drawn. When cause is added, a major element of uncertainty and subjectivity is introduced. Nonetheless, reasonably valid data exist and international comparisons and time trends can be discussed, as in chapter 2. Morbidity is quite different. Reasonable comparability across age, time, and place can be obtained by using standardized measures of specific diseases or infections—for example, antibodies to *Schistosoma mansoni* or ocular signs of vitamin A deficiency. However, most multiple disease surveys cannot conduct enough tests with sufficient care to allow such comparisons, and so comparison of data even from observed morbidity surveys using laboratory tests and physical examinations becomes problematic. Interpreting data from self-perceived morbidity surveys is even more difficult. There is no method for measuring in a comprehensive and comparable way the burden of morbidity experienced by adults in developing countries or, indeed, by any age group anywhere.

Only rarely have observed data been collected for all causes of morbidity. Data from studies on specific diseases are much more common. This chapter has not reviewed all these sources because it is difficult to provide a balanced picture of the burden of morbidity using cause-specific studies of infection or disease. At the local level, however, such information can be useful for initially characterizing the important causes of morbidity (e.g., Ghana Health Assessment Project Team 1981).

The surveys of self-perceived morbidity reviewed in this chapter show a high incidence of relatively minor respiratory and musculoskeletal complaints in developing countries, as is also true in most developed countries. In addition, the three studies of impairments in Bahrain, Sri Lanka and Egypt indicated a more serious burden of visual, auditory, and locomotive impairments. These self-perceived morbidity data, however, have several counter-intuitive patterns. The United States, for example, has higher acute and chronic morbidity rates and bed disability rates than any of the developing countries discussed. Likewise, higher income groups in Ghana, Côte d'Ivoire, and Peru reported more morbidity than lower income groups. Because of the difficulty in separating the variation in self-perceived morbidity rates due to illness perception from the variation due to differences in the burden of pathology, it would be premature to draw conclusions about morbidity patterns in developing countries from these sources.

Chapter 2 used empirical data to identify key causes of adult death in developing countries. The same type of robust observations cannot be made about the causes of adult morbidity. Nevertheless, this review of adult morbidity in developing countries and the experience of the authors suggest some general observations about the causes of adult morbidity. While these observations all do not flow directly from the data reviewed in this chapter, they are included here to offset the tendency to ignore subjects that are difficult to measure.

Many causes of morbidity are common in both developed and developing countries. Examples include arthritis, thyroid disorders, cerebrovascular accidents, angina pectoris, epilepsy, and psychoses. The incidence and prevalence of these morbidity causes vary among communities, but they are morbidity problems that concern all communities. Some causes of adult morbidity are much more common in developing countries. Those that cause irreversible damage (such as paralysis due to polio or blindness from trachoma) deserve special attention. Causes of adult morbidity that lead to reversible damage (such as upper respiratory infections or infected skin ulcers) are by their very nature less important, and mortality data capture symptom-free causes (such as aneurysms or hypertension) which substantially raise mortality risks.

What message should policymakers and researchers take away from this discussion of morbidity? First, many, although not all, major causes of morbidity also cause mortality and therefore are captured in good quality mortality data. Second, morbidity is extremely difficult to measure adequately, and no developed country has a system in place yet for measuring morbidity from several major causes. Third, surveys of particular diseases or infections, especially if based on observation or laboratory tests, are extremely useful in planning and evaluating public health programs that target those particular diseases. Fourth, good quality data on utilization of health services, although saying very little about morbidity burdens in the community, measure the burden and pattern of morbidity that presents for attention and cure, and this can be useful for projecting future demand.

In view of the above, many developing countries may wish to select a policy that emphasizes first and foremost the collection, analysis, and use of high quality cause-specific mortality data. They may wish also to collect reliable data on health services utilization for planning purposes. Finally, they may wish to conduct surveillance of particular causes of morbidity in order to better design and evaluate specific programs of intervention.

Notes

1. This chapter has benefited from supporting research by Carlos Dora and the comments and suggestions of Lincoln Chen, Monica Das Gupta, Ed Dowd, Arthur Kleinman, and Robert Levine.

2. The major exception concerns the incidence rates of site-specific cancers, which are measured accurately in many developed, and some developing, countries.

3. This discussion draws on Murray and Chen (1991). Their terminology for different types of morbidity does not correspond exactly with other classifications such as the International Classification of Impairments, Disabilities, and Handicaps (WHO 1980).

4. Some psychiatric illnesses may be exceptions for which the boundaries between observed and self-perceived are too blurred for discrimination.

5. The LSMS is a research project which the World Bank (various countries) started in 1980 to improve the quantitative basis for the design and monitoring of development policy.

6. These problems are not unique to developing countries. Self-perceived morbidity (both total and that which limits activity) has increased steadily and substantially in the United Kingdom between 1976 and 1988 among nonmanual and manual occupational groups (Acheson, 1990).

7. Several longitudinal surveys, some of observed morbidity and some of self-perceived morbidity, have been conducted in Sub-Saharan Africa since 1950. The longer of these, in The Gambia, Ghana, Kenya, Nigeria, and Tanzania, are reviewed in Feachem and Jamison (1991).

8. Computer analysis of the data was performed by Butch Arroyo from the Department of Economics, Rice University, Houston, Texas (for Côte d'Ivoire) and Frederic Louat, Welfare and Human Resources Division of the World Bank's Population and Human Resources Department (for Ghana and Peru).

9. The DISTAT data base was compiled under the direction of Mary Chamie, Demographic and Social Statistics Branch of the Statistics Office of the United Nations. A technical description of the data base is available in United Nations (1988).

10. The United Nations compiled these data from the following original sources: Government of Egypt, Central Agency for Public Mobilization and Statistics: Population and Housing Census, 1976, vol. 1, Cairo; State of Bahrain, Cabinet Affairs, Directorate of Statistics: Bahrain Census of Population and Housing, 1981; Government of Sri Lanka, Department of Census and Statistics: Statistics on Physically Disabled Persons, 1981.

11. Because counts were based on self-reporting or on observations by census workers rather than medical examinations or laboratory tests, the studies tend to favor readily apparent conditions.

12. For example, mental impairment was reported as the second most common impairment in Bahrain, whereas it was not included at all as an impairment category in Sri Lanka. Prevalence of mental impairment is particularly difficult to gauge and compare because reported rates are very sensitive to lay reporting, scope and phrasing of survey questions, availability and quality of diagnostic services, cultural definitions of mental impairment, and the degree of stigma associated with mental impairment. Another difference between the censuses was that Bahrain and Sri Lanka included paralysis as a category whereas Egypt did not. Finally, the unit of analysis in Sri Lanka was *impairments* rather than people who had impairments; therefore, people who had multiple impairments were counted more than once. Consequently, figure 3-4 presents only a rough gauge of impairment rates by age and sex.

13. The studies in Egypt, Kenya, and Mexico were part of the Collaborative Research Support Program on Food Intake and Human Function (CRSP) supported by the United States Agency for International Development. Similar but not identical studies were conducted in each country by a team of specialists at local institutions and staff from universities in the United States. In Kenya, the investigators were Nimrod Bwibo (University of Nairobi) and Charlotte Neumann and colleagues from the University of California, Los Angeles. In Egypt, the investigators were Osman Galal (Nutrition Institute, Cairo) and Gail Harrison, Avanelle Kirksey and Norge Jerome from the Universities of Arizona, Kansas and Purdue. In Mexico, the investigators were

Adolfo Chavez and Homero Martinez (Insituto Nacional de la Nutrición, Mexico City) and Lindsay Allan and Gretel Pelto of the University of Connecticut. The three studies were coordinated and overseen by Doris Calloway and colleagues at the University of California, Berkeley. The data presented here were obtained with the particular assistance of Charlotte Neumann and Leslie Wanek (Kenya), Gail Harrison (Egypt) and Gretel Pelto (Mexico).

14. This large gender differential, although consistent with the results of other surveys of self-perceived morbidity, may be partly an artifact. Women were more often available for interview during house visits than men, and a higher proportion of information on men is derived from reports of their wives than vice versa—an example of the proxy respondent effect discussed in the first part of this chapter.

15. These analyses were conducted by Avanelle Kirksey and Atossa Rahmanifar of Purdue University.

References

Acheson, E. D. 1990. "Edwin Chadwick and the World We Live in." *Lancet* 336:1482–85.

Belcher, D. W., A. K. Neumann, F. K. Wurapa, and I. M. Lourie. 1976. "Comparison of Morbidity Interviews with a Health Examination Survey in Rural Africa." *American Journal of Tropical Medicine and Hygiene* 25(5):751–58.

Cochrane, A. L., P. J. Chapman, and P. D. Oldham. 1951. "Observer's Error in Taking Medical Histories." *Lancet* i:1007–10.

Colombia, Minísterio de Salud Pública. 1969. *Estudío de Recursos Humanos para la Salud y Educación Médica en Colombia: Investigación Nacional de Morbilidad: Evidencia Clínica.* Bogotá: Minísterio de Salud Pública.

Egypt, Ministry of Health. 1989. *Final Report: The Health Examination Survey; Morbidity, Nutritional, and Dental Status in Cairo, 1989.* Ministry of Health Publication No. 38/4. Cairo.

Elinson, J., and R. E. Trussel. 1957. "Some Factors Relating to Degree of Correspondence for Diagnostic Information as Obtained by Household Interviews and Clinical Examinations." *American Journal of Public Health* 47:311–21.

Feachem, R. G. A., and D. T. Jamison, eds. 1991. *Disease and Mortality in Sub-Saharan Africa.* New York: Oxford University Press for the World Bank.

Ghana Health Assessment Project Team. 1981. "A Quantitative Method of Assessing the Health Impact of Different Diseases in Less Developed Countries." *International Journal of Epidemiology* 10(1):73–80.

Indian National Sample Survey. 1974. *On Morbidity: National Sample Survey, Twenty-Eighth Round.* Schedule 12. October 1973–June 1974.

Kroeger, A. 1983. "Health Interview Surveys in Developing Countries: A Review of Methods and Results." *International Journal of Epidemiology* 12(4):465–81.

Krueger, D. E. 1957. "Measurement of Prevalence of Chronic Disease by Household Interviews and Clinical Evaluations." *American Journal of Public Health* 47:953–60.

Linder, F. E. 1965. "National Health Interview Surveys." *Public Health Papers* Vol. 27. Geneva: World Health Organization.

Manton, K. G., J. E. Dowd, and M. A. Woodbury. 1986. "Conceptual and Measurement Issues in Assessing Disability Cross-Nationally: Analysis of a WHO-Sponsored Survey of the Disablement Process in Indonesia." *Journal of Cross-Cultural Gerontology* 1:339–62.

Mechanic, D. 1965. "Some Problems in the Analysis of Morbidity Data." *Journal of Chronic Diseases* 18:569–80.

Murray, C. J. L., and C. C. Chen. 1991. "Health Transitions: Patterns and Dynamics." In A. Kleinman, L. L. Chen, and J. Caldwell, eds., *Social Change and Health. (In press)*

Murray, C. J. L., A. Rouillon, and K. Styblo. 1990. "Tuberculosis in Developing Countries: Burden, Intervention and Cost." *Bulletin of the International Union Against Tuberculosis and Lung Disease* 65(1):2–20.

NCHS (National Center for Health Statistics). 1967. "Interview Data on Chronic Conditions Compared with Information Derived from Medical Records." *Vital and Health Statistics* Series 2, No. 23. Washington, D.C.: United States Department of Health and Human Services.

———. 1986. "Current Estimates from the National Health Interview Survey, United States." *Vital and Health Statistics* Series 10, No. 160. Washington, D.C.: United States Department of Health and Human Services.

Pakistan, Federal Bureau of Statistics. 1986. *National Health Survey 1982–83.* Karachi: Government of Pakistan.

Rodriguez, A. P., and E. R. Ospina. 1987. "Estudio Nacional de Salud: Morbilidad General." In: *Vol. II: Diagnosticós Médicos y Consumo de Medicamentos.* Bogotá: Instituto Nacional de Salud.

Ross, D. A., and J. P. Vaughan. 1986. "Health Interview Surveys in Developing Countries: A Methodological Review." *Studies in Family Planning* 17:78–94.

Thailand, National Statistics Office. 1983. *Health and Welfare Survey 1981.* Bangkok.

United Nations. 1986. "Development of Statistics of Disabled Persons: Case Studies." *Statistics on Special Population Groups* Series Y, No. 2. New York.

United Nations. 1988. United Nations International Disability Statistics Data Base, 1975–86: Technical Manual. *Statistics on Special Population Groups* Series Y, No. 3. New York: UN Department of International Economic and Social Affairs.

Uruguay, Minísterio de Salud Pública. 1985. *Estudio Sobre Enfermedades Crónicas y Ancianos Basados en la Encuesta Familiar de Salud del Uruguay: Percepción y Evaluación Clínica de la Prevalencía de Enfermedades Crónicas.* Uruguay.

World Bank. (various countries)."Living Standards Measurement Surveys." Washington, D.C.

World Health Organization. 1980. *International Classification of Impairments, Disabilities and Handicaps: A Manual of Classification Relating to the Consequences of Disease.* Geneva.

4. *The Consequences of Adult Ill-Health*

Mead Over, Randall P. Ellis, Joyce H. Huber, and Orville Solon

THIS CHAPTER PRESENTS EVIDENCE that the consequences of adult ill-health are substantial, larger than had been supposed previously, and larger than the consequences of illness in non-adults. The chapter explores the consequences of adult ill-health on the health of other household members, on medical treatment costs, and on nonmedical consumption, investment, production, earnings, and income distribution. The chapter also addresses the costs of the coping mechanisms that households and communities use to mitigate or to insure against the consequences of adult ill-health.

The most obvious effects of ill-health are the immediate subjective suffering of the person who becomes ill or injured or dies and the sympathetic grief of his or her family and friends. The reduction of these psychic costs is an important goal of all health policy. Any intervention that reduces this suffering improves human welfare and deserves consideration when resources are allocated. The full consequences of adult ill-health, however, go beyond this direct suffering and include effects that harm society indirectly or over longer periods. These indirect and long-term consequences substantially increase the cost of adult ill-health in developing countries and make improving adult health important to the economic well-being of these countries.

The realization that the nonmedical effects of adult illness in developing countries are substantial is new. Gwatkin (1983) reviewed the strengths and weaknesses of studies and concluded that the research findings were too mixed and uncertain to endorse an inevitable link between improved health and greater productivity and wealth. Andreano and Helmeniak (1988) came to a similar conclusion based on evidence through 1985. The discrepancy between these negative findings and the obvious suffering and economic disruption which exists has an explanation: households and firms cope (Gwatkin 1983; Popkin 1982; Rosenfield, Golladay, and Davidson 1984; Stevens 1977). When an adult household member becomes ill or injured, that individual and his or her family members and friends try to minimize the effects of the illness on the welfare of all concerned. At the level of the work group, other workers may work harder to cover the reduction in effort by an ill or injured colleague—perhaps with the expectation of similar help when they might need it. Employers who hire from a sickly workforce build slack into their production schedules and require less specialization of employee job descriptions. This chapter refers to these efforts as *coping processes*. To the extent that these coping processes reduce the effects of illness, they hide them from traditional empirical studies.

Coping processes are costly. At the individual level, coping may consist of doing less work at home to maintain one's productivity on the job. At the household or community level, those who fill in for an ill or injured adult may be drawn away from other productive activities. Investment may be sacrificed by keeping a child home from school to compensate or care for the ill adult. The employer who sacrifices specialization deprives his enterprise of many of the benefits of mass production, as described originally by Adam Smith (1776).

Unless the cost of these coping processes is included in an appreciation of the economic impact of ill-health, that impact will be underestimated. Table 4-1 presents a typology of the effects of adult ill-health and death which includes the coping responses as well as the direct psychic and economic losses.[1] The table distinguishes effects of ill-health and death on production and earnings, on investment and consumption and on the health and composition of the household and community. The table lists the effects that occur during an illness, of which the cost of medical care is only one, and distinguishes effects that occur at the time of death from those that may be felt months or years later. It also captures effects of ill-health on households whose members are currently healthy, including the costs of avoiding ill-health and helping the households of ill or injured relatives or community members. Because these costs would be reduced if ill-health were less prevalent, a comprehensive typology of the effects of adult ill-health must include them.

Table 4-1 also identifies which economic effects are direct and which are the manifestations of the coping process. Only recently has research begun to estimate the cost of these coping mechanisms, identifying for the first time their importance in the total economic effect of adult death. A major theme of this chapter is to point out these processes and begin to estimate their contribution to the total cost of adult ill-health in developing countries.[2]

A second theme of this chapter is how the burden of ill-health is distributed in the population. Because a full accounting of the costs of

Table 4-1. Economic Effects of Fatal Illness on the Household: Type and Timing of Impact

	Timing of impact			
Type of impact	*Before illness*	*During illness*	*Immediate effect of death*	*Long term effect of death*
Effect on production and earnings	a Organization of economic activity b Residential location	**a Reduced productivity of ill adult** b Reallocation of labor	**a Lost output of deceased**	**a Lost output of deceased** b Reallocation of land and labor
Effect on investment and consumption	a Insurance b Medical costs of prevention c Precautionary savings d Transfer to other households	**a Medical cost of treatment** b Dissaving c Changes in consumption and investment	**a Funeral costs** b Transfers **c Legal fees**	a Changes in type and quantity of investment and consumption
Effect on household health and composition	a Extended family b Fertility	a Reduced allocation of labor to health maintaining activities	**a Loss of deceased**	**a Poor health of surviving household members** b Dissolution or reconstitution of household
Psychic costs		**a Disutility of ill individual**	**a Disutility to individual** b Grief of loved ones	

Note: Direct economic effects appear in **bold type.** Manifestations of the coping process appear in normal type.
Source: Assembled by authors of chapter.

an illness or injury includes the burdens on others, it alters the estimated distribution of the burden of ill-health by age, gender and region. The fact that adult ill-health harms children more than the reverse implies that the share of the total ill-health burden borne by children is even larger than would be estimated from examining only the age distribution of ill-health.

Effects on the Health and Composition of the Household

Adult ill-health can harm the health of, and even kill, other household members.

Health of the Household

In the midnineteenth century, when Sweden was a developing country, the death of a Swedish mother during her infant's first year reduced the infant's probability of surviving that year from 0.97 to 0.50 and the probability of surviving the next four years from 0.94 to 0.02 (Hogberg and Brostrom 1985). These patterns persist in developing countries today.

A long-term study in the rural community of Matlab, Bangladesh showed that infant and child mortality were highly correlated with maternal mortality. A 1974 study in Matlab found that only 12 percent of infants whose mothers died during delivery survived two months and only 5 percent survived one year (Chen and others 1974). More recent data permit comparison of the survival of 125 infants whose mothers died in childbirth to the survival of 1,469 infants whose mothers survived childbirth (Koenig and others 1988). An enormous gap exists between the one-year survival rates of infants whose mothers died (25 percent) and infants whose mothers lived (91 percent). See figure 4-1.

Analysis of 1983–85 Matlab data on the survival of children aged less than ten years confirms the strong correlation between maternal and child mortality. Figure 4-2 presents mortality rates per thousand sons, daughters and other (for example, foster) children in households with an adult death compared to households without an adult death, by whether the adult who died was the father or mother. A father's death was associated with an increase of about 6 per thousand in the child mortality rate, regardless of the child's gender. A mother's death was associated with an increase of almost 50 per thousand for sons and 144 per thousand for daughters. Without an adult death, the two-year mortality rates per thousand were 27 for boys and 42 for girls. Therefore, the death of a mother was associated with almost a 200 percent increase in the mortality of her sons and more than a 300 percent increase in the mortality of her daughters.[3]

Figure 4-1. Effect of Maternal Death on Infant Survival in Matlab, Bangladesh

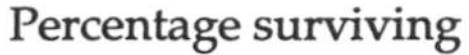

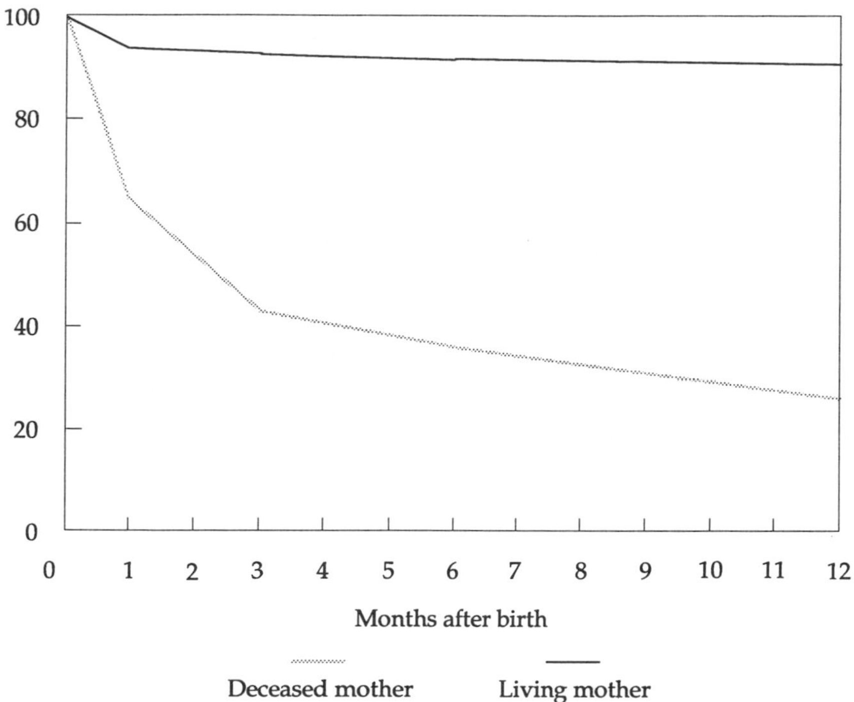

Source: Koenig and others (1988).

The ill-health of an adult may be associated with higher infant and child mortality in developing countries for several possible reasons. Before dying from a communicable disease, an adult may transmit it to other family members with fatal consequences, especially for infants. Although tuberculosis is less infectious than many other communicable diseases, each year of residence in the same household with someone who has tuberculosis incurs a 30 percent risk of infection and a 1 to 2 percent risk that the new infection will progress to disease (Benenson 1985). Similarly, household exposure to leprosy over a prolonged period may be important in the transmission of leprosy (Benenson 1985).

Some diseases are passed in utero from an infected mother to her fetus. Transmission from mother to fetus during pregnancy appears to account for clinical signs of malaria in 22 percent of all newborns in

Figure 4-2. Effect of Adult Death on Childhood Death (< 10 years) in Matlab, Bangladesh: 1983–85

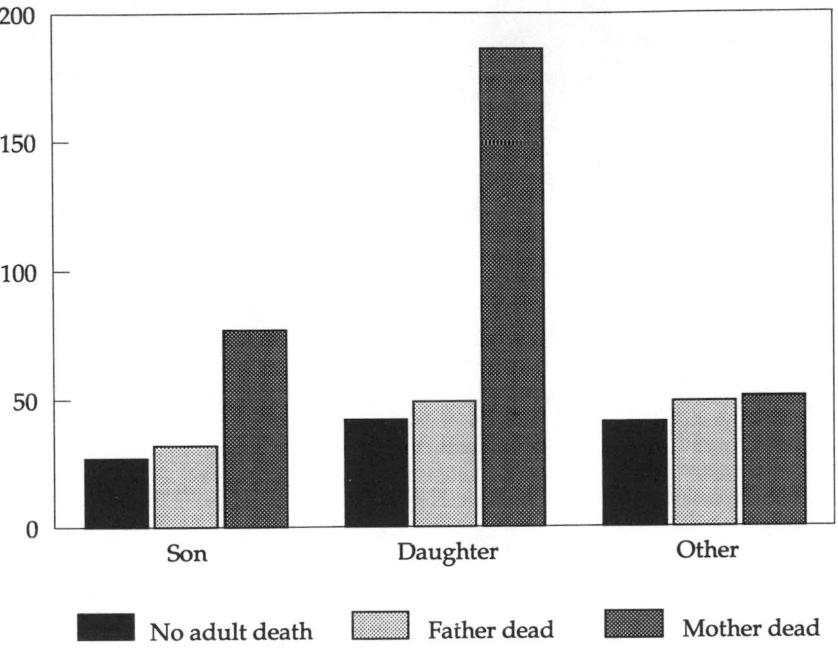

Source: Michael Strong, International Centre for Diarrhoeal Disease Research, Bangladesh.

Liberia (Jackson 1985). Congenital transmission of several other infectious diseases—including herpes simplex, rubella, toxoplasmosis and syphilis—causes still births, infant deaths and severe congenital malformations and disabilities (Walsh 1988). Women who are malnourished or have chronic anemia, malaria, intestinal diseases, diabetes or high blood pressure are more likely to suffer complications in childbirth, endangering their infant as well as themselves (Starr 1987). Likewise 25 to 50 percent of babies born to HIV infected mothers contract AIDS. Ninety-five percent of these die within two years, and the remaining 5 percent are expected to live no more than ten years (Over and Piot forthcoming).

The household's attempt to cope with the death or ill-health of an adult may shift household labor away from health maintaining activities such as cleaning, collecting water, hygienic food preparation, and breast-feeding. Evidence of increased infant mortality associated with less time spent by women on household chores is available for Gambia (Chambers 1982). In a study of the nutritional status of the young children of Filipino working mothers (Popkin 1980), 55 percent of children younger than thirty-six months who were cared for by siblings (aged six to eight years) were malnourished, compared with only 8.5 percent who were cared for by their mothers. Grandparents or other elderly people were more effective care givers than siblings, but still induced malnutrition in 21 percent of the young children. Ill women in rural Mexico have been known to stop breast-feeding their infants, claiming that illness soured their breast milk (Fink 1985). In a recent study on Chinese babies (Tu 1989), replacement of breast milk with the low cost alternatives available in China was estimated to increase infant mortality rates by seventy to eighty per thousand. In poor countries, when a mother dies and her child is bottle fed, the child is at greater risk of dying from diarrheal disease and dehydration.

To thrive, infants need a great deal of affection and contact; when a mother dies and the attention she gave her infant is not replaced by that of another care giver, the probability of infant death may rise. Adult mortality also can be associated with infant and child mortality when certain determinants (such as household poverty and its correlates of poor nutrition, sanitation, shelter, and clothing) independently affect the mortality rates of all ages. Unsanitary disposal of human waste or contamination of food and drinking water can spread a variety of diseases, including polio, hookworm, diarrhea, and ascariasis, among household members.

The relative contributions of these various influences to the excess mortality of the Matlab orphans is impossible to determine without further study. However, the preference for sons in rural Bangladesh and the much higher mortality of daughters strongly suggest that lack of attentive care is responsible for some of the excess mortality in Matlab of both sons and daughters whose mothers die. In Matlab and elsewhere in the developing world, policies that protect adults will also protect children to the extent that adult mortality directly causes a higher risk of illness among infants and children. To the degree that some external environmental hazard simultaneously causes excess mortality of both parents and children, selectively protecting only adults from these hazards will not help children.

Composition of the Household

Adult ill-health can affect household composition through its effects on fertility, foster child care, and marriage behavior. Some of these are the immediate effects of ill-health; others are the result of various coping responses.

Although most adult illnesses do not affect fertility (Menken, Trussel, and Watkins 1981), sexually transmitted diseases frequently cause infertility in women, especially in central and eastern Africa where primary infertility rates average 10 percent and can be as high as 33 percent of all women (Benenson 1985; Farley and Belsey 1988; Frank 1983). Conversely, the perceived risk of future infertility may contribute to less birth control among young women, and thereby increase total fertility (Wasserheit 1989). When young women have unprotected sex with multiple partners, they spread sexually transmitted diseases, which in turn increase the infertility rate and exacerbate the infertility worries of the next cohort of young women (Over and Piot forthcoming). Thus, once women understand that sexually transmitted diseases cause infertility, treatment and prevention of these diseases should increase the demand for birth control among younger women. The net effect of decreasing prevalence rates of sexually transmitted diseases could be a decrease, rather than an increase, in total fertility rates.

Recent research on child fostering is beginning to reveal the role adult illness plays in the decision to foster. While a family may foster out a child for many reasons, Bledsoe, Ewbank, and Isiugo-Abanihe (1988) suggested that children are more likely to receive foster care when the mother is severely ill or dies. In the latter event, the family is likely to disintegrate, which can lead to child fostering (Starr 1987). Support for these hypotheses comes from data on children aged seven to fourteen years in a national household sample in Côte d'Ivoire. Among those with two living parents, 18 percent were fostered (that is, living away from both parents) at the time of the survey. Among children with only one surviving parent, the percent fostered (that is, living in a different household from the surviving parent) was 38 or 49 percent, depending on whether the surviving parent was the father or the mother.[4]

Death of a man who is the household head usually creates a household headed by a woman, at least until remarriage. The child fostering patterns of these households reveal some strategies used to cope with the loss of the man. In Côte d'Ivoire, households headed by women are less likely to foster out children of either sex and are more likely to provide foster care for girls than are households headed by men (Ainsworth 1988). Because a woman who heads a household is likely to seek additional income outside the home, older foster children, especially girls, may provide important substitute child care and other home production activities.

Although foster children may help a widowed adult, they do so at a cost to their own future contribution to society. Bledsoe, Ewbank, and Isiugo-Abanahie (1988) found in Sierra Leone that, in comparison with a family's own children, foster children tended to be disadvantaged nutritionally, to have less access to modern health care, to work longer hours and to receive less schooling. Similar differences between a family's own children and foster children in the same household occur in Côte d'Ivoire (figure 4-3) and are statistically significant ($p = 0.05$), as shown by data from a national probability sample of households (Ainsworth 1988).

Thus the health of adult household members affects the size and composition of the household and the welfare of other household members. Adult ill-health is likely to increase the desired family size because the ability to share work increases the family's ability to cope when illness occurs. Adult ill-health or death has a negative effect on the health of other family members, especially children. This is partly due to direct transmission of disease but mostly due to the increased

Figure 4-3. Increased Work and Reduced Schooling of Foster Children in Côte d'Ivoire, 1985

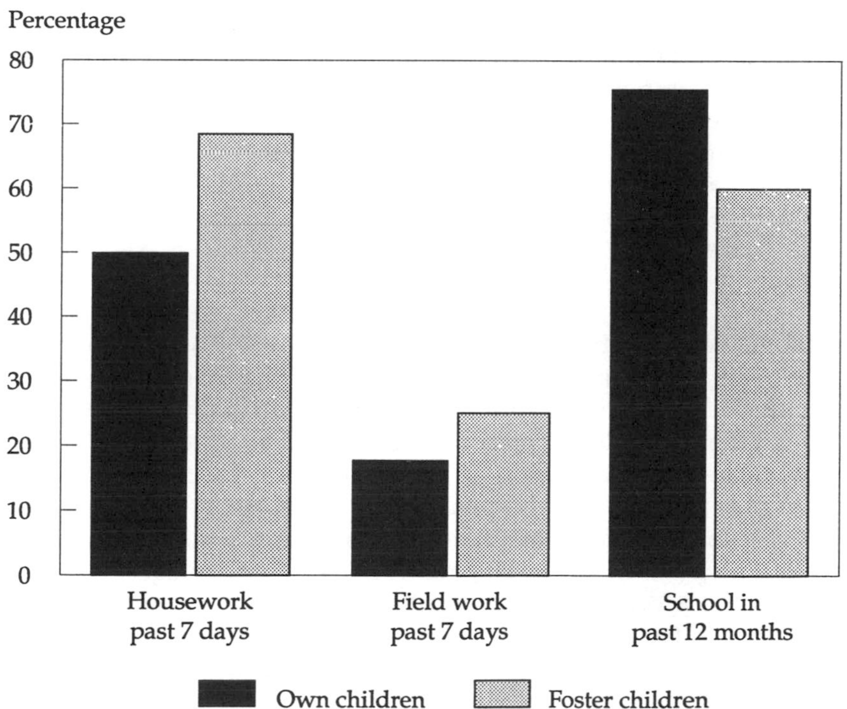

Source: Ainsworth (1988).

burden that adult ill-health or death places on other family members, reducing their ability to perform adequate health and child care activities.

Medical Costs of Treating Adult Illness

Adults are important consumers of both primary and secondary curative health care services. If adults suffered no ill-health, their households and the society at large would be spared the costs of this curative care. To estimate the magnitude of this potential savings in developing countries requires estimates of the total cost of health care and of the proportion of this cost attributable to adults. Neither of these is well known in any developing country. This section assembles the available information on both total cost and adult share for hospital and primary care.

The average low to middle income country spends about 4 percent of its central government budget on health services. Such countries individually spend from 1 percent (Nigeria) to 19 percent in Costa Rica (World Bank 1989b).[5] Central government health care expenditure in such countries typically constitutes between 1 and 2 percent of gross national product (GNP). Private households and employers spend an additional 1 to 5 percent of GNP on health care, with larger percentages in richer countries and countries where the government health care system is less comprehensive (de Ferranti 1985). Some of this expenditure is for preventive care, but the greater part is for curative care, much of which is delivered in a hospital, rather than a primary care setting.

Costs of Adult Hospital Care

Despite the efforts by many countries over the last ten years to reallocate financial resources towards primary care, few countries manage to spend less than half their budgets on hospitals and many spend up to two thirds. Table 4-2 presents estimates of the proportion of the national health budget spent on hospital care for selected countries.

Within nonpediatric hospitals worldwide, most resources are devoted to adult care. One index of this pattern that is available for several hospitals in the developing world is the percentage of hospital admissions accounted for by adults and elderly. Of the hospitals described in table 4-3, all use at least 70 percent of their resources on adult and elderly patients.[6] A more detailed breakdown of both admissions and costs by five broad age categories of insured Korean patients is presented in figure 4-4. Note that two-thirds of both cases and costs of inpatient care are attributable to adults in these hospitals.

Table 4-2. The Share of Hospitals in Total Public Recurrent Health Expenditure
(percentage)

Country	*Hospital share*	*Year*
Bangladesh	52	1984–1985
Botswana	49	1984
Brazil	68	1984
Burundi	66	1986
China	66	1987
Colombia	67	1984
Côte d'Ivoire	46	1984
El Salvador	62	1985
Ethiopia	49	1983–1984
Gambia	45	1985–1986
Indonesia	37	1985–1986
Jamaica	72	1986–1987
Jordan	75	1987
Kenya	73	1985–1986
Korea	34	1986
Lesotho	74	1986–1987
Malawi	81	1985–1986
Malaysia	65	1985
Mexico	58	1986
Mozambique	36	1987
Nepal	25	1987–1988
Philippines	71	1985
Senegal	50	1982
Somalia	70	1989
Sri Lanka	70	1977–1986
Swaziland	52	1983–1984
Thailand	53	1985
Turkey	63	1987
Uganda	43	1982–1983
Zimbabwe	54	1987

Source: Barnum and Kutzin (forthcoming). See the same authority for details on how estimates were constructed. See also Mills (1990b).

These figures are consistent with the cruder estimates from other countries (table 4-3). Most relatively inexpensive cases in adults from age fifteen to thirty-nine are maternity admissions. The fact that adults from age forty to fifty-nine have a greater share of costs (33 percent) than of admissions (23 percent) reflects the greater expense per hospitalization of older adults—due both to the onset of noncommunicable diseases and to the greater willingness of these adults to pay.

Hospitals also deliver outpatient care, some of which is appropriate secondary care (because the patient has been referred by primary care

Table 4-3. Percentage of Hospital Admissions of Adults and Elderly and of Children Compared, in Selected Countries, Various Years

Country	*Hospital*	*Admissions of adults and elderly*	*Admissions of children*
Belize	Belize City Hospital	77	23 (< 12 years)
China	County hospitals	88	12 (< 15 years)
Jamaica	Acute care public hospitals	84	16 (< 10 years)
Malawi	Salima District Hospital	73	27 (< 12 years)
Niger	Niamey Hospital	71	29 (< 12 years)
Papua New Guinea	Southern Highlands Provincial Hospital	82	18 (< 15 years)
Uganda	Keluva Hospital	70	30 (< 15 years)

Note: Adults and *elderly* were defined as all those aged ten, twelve, or fifteen years or older, depending on the definition of *children* used in each country.

Source: Belize: Raymond (1987); China: Cai (1989); Jamaica: Jamaica, Ministry of Health (1986); Malawi: Mills (1990a); Niger: Wong (1989); Papua New Guinea: Pust and Burrell (1986); Uganda: Williams, Hayes, and Smith (1986).

Figure 4-4. Inpatient Cases and Costs by Age for Insured Patients in Korean Hospitals, 1986

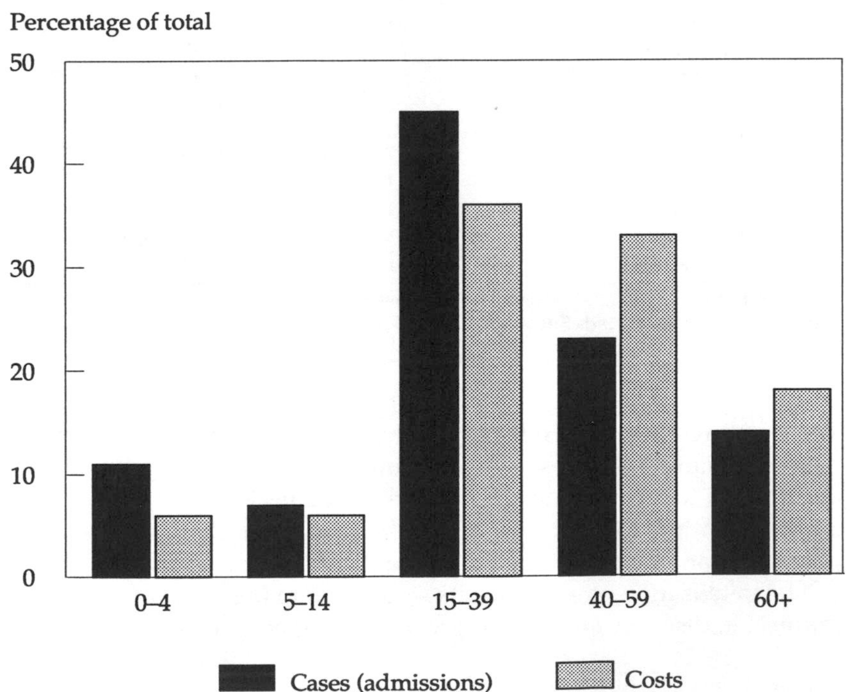

Source: Korea Medical Insurance Corporation (1987).

providers) and some of which is primary care that could be delivered usually at lower cost in a more conventional primary care setting. In Korean hospitals approximately two-thirds of the total operating costs are due to outpatient rather than inpatient care. In these Korean institutions, nonadults represent a higher proportion of outpatient than of inpatient cases and costs. However, figure 4-5 demonstrates that adults still dominate, representing more than 50 percent of all visits and commanding more than 50 percent of hospital outpatient resources.

Although breakdowns of hospital utilization data by age are rare, additional data supporting the greater burden of adults on hospitals can be derived from population based studies. Figure 4-6 presents the results of illness prevalence studies of random samples of the populations of four countries (China, Côte d'Ivoire, Ghana and Peru). To control for different survey methods, all the prevalence statistics have

Figure 4-5. Outpatient Cases and Costs by Age of Insured Patients in Korean Hospitals, 1986

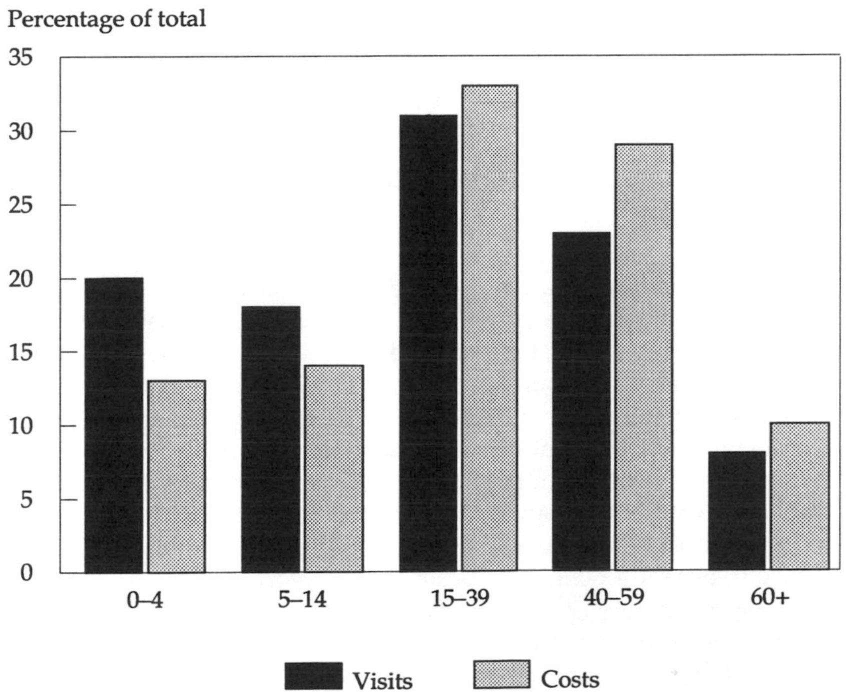

Source: Korea Medical Insurance Corporation (1987).

Figure 4-6. Proportion Ill Relative to Illness Among Five to Fourteen Year Olds

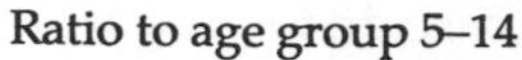

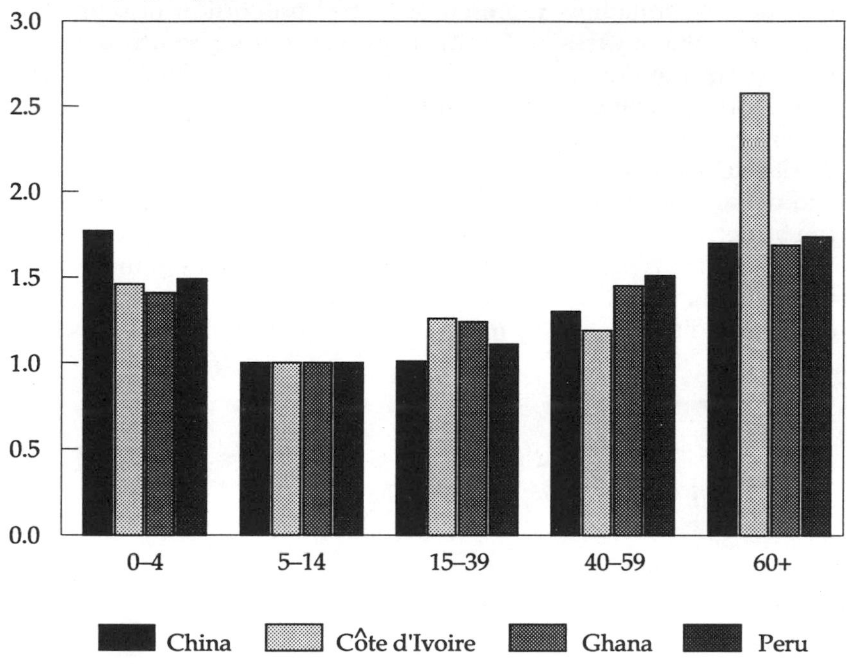

Source: Cai (1989); LSMS (World Bank various countries).

been scaled relative to the rate of the five to fourteen year age group, the group that had the least illness in all the survey samples.[7] The pattern of illness shows the expected decline from infancy and then a steady increase of about 20 percent between each successive age group. The patterns are remarkably consistent across countries except for the prevalence of illness in the elderly in Côte d'Ivoire, which was 260 percent greater than in the five to fourteen year age group and fully 80 percent greater than in the other countries. These data make it clear that illness episodes are not restricted to the very young and very old, but rather begin increasing on entry to adulthood.

Not every illness episode leads to the seeking of health care. Data from China and Côte d'Ivoire make it possible to examine the probability of hospital admission given an illness episode. Again, care must be taken in comparing the data across countries. If, for example, the definition of illness used in one survey is more all-embracing, then the probability of hospitalization given an illness will, other things being equal, be smaller. Figure 4-7 presents data on the propensity to hospitalize in China and Côte d'Ivoire, scaled to be proportional to the rate of hospitalization among five to fourteen year olds in each country. Five to fourteen year olds were not only least likely to be ill, but also least likely to be hospitalized when ill. In contrast, adults were more likely to be ill and more likely to incur the substantial expense of hospitalization. This pattern is driven partly by the greater severity of illness among older people and partly by the greater willingness of households to spend time and money on health care for older members. The greater willingness may reflect the power of adults to spend more on their own illnesses or the perception that

Figure 4-7. Probability of Hospitalization when Ill Relative to Hospitalization of Ill Five to Fourteen Year Olds

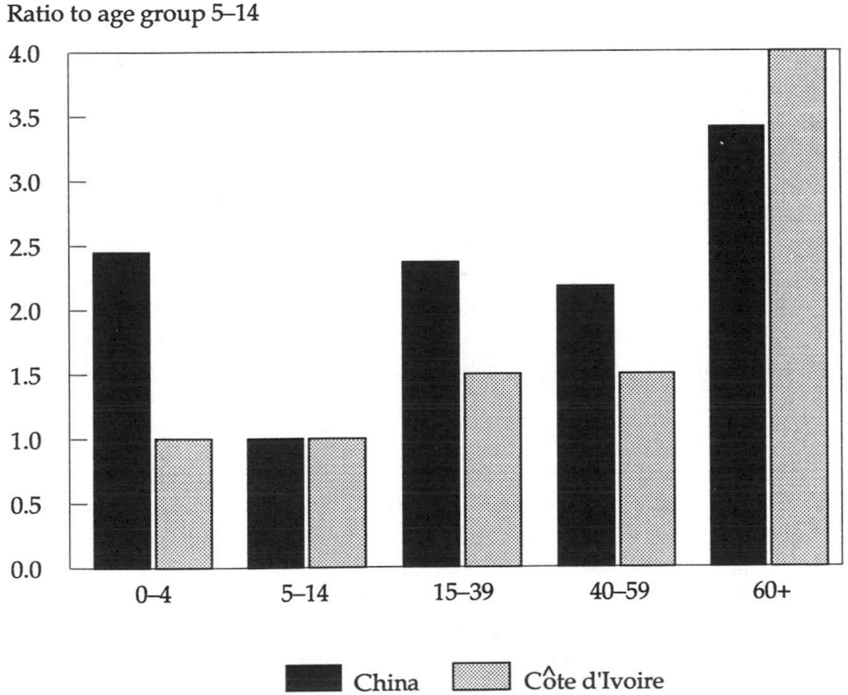

Source: Cai (1989); LSMS (World Bank various countries).

adult ill-health harms the entire household and therefore deserves priority attention.

Another perspective on the costs of adult hospital care is provided by disaggregating hospital use data by disease or condition. Table 4-4 presents such data aggregated across all ages. As demonstrated in chapters 1, 2, and 3, adults suffer more from noncommunicable diseases and from injury than do younger age groups, and the demographic component of the health transition increases the incidence of these health problems over time. Injuries represent from 3 to 13 percent of all admissions (and 28 percent of all male admissions in Jamaica). Noncommunicable diseases are a large burden on hospitals in developing countries, accounting for 20 to 44 percent of admissions.

Further insight can be obtained by breaking down the distributions of Korean hospital cases by the three diagnostic categories used in chapters 2 and 3. Figure 4-8 reproduces from figures 4-5 and 4-6 the age distributions of admissions and outpatient visits, but adds a breakdown by disease category.[8] Adults dominate Korean hospital activity (68 percent of admissions and 54 percent of outpatient visits). They seek care usually because of noncommunicable disease (56 percent of admissions and 62 percent of outpatient visits). In the forty to fifty-nine year age group, noncommunicable diseases represent 82 percent of admissions and 76 percent of outpatient visits. Among younger adults, the communicable and reproductive category assumes a much greater role in admissions due to maternity cases. However, noncommunicable diseases still account for 36 percent of admissions and 68 percent of outpatient visits in this younger group. Noncommunicable diseases are important also among children aged five to fourteen years (61 percent of admissions and 51 percent of outpatient visits), as well as among younger children and the elderly. By this indicator Korea is well advanced in the health transition described in chapter 1 and displays patterns that other developing countries will encounter in the future.

As described in chapter 1, the demographic component of the health transition will inexorably increase the proportion of adults in developing country populations. The current 60 to 80 percent of hospital care devoted to adults will increase even further. The implication of the large role that noncommunicable disease plays in the adult demand for hospital care is that the demand for the treatment of these noncommunicable diseases will also increase. The risk factor component of the health transition will cause a relatively more rapid decline in communicable than noncommunicable disease, thus further exacerbating this trend. Because noncommunicable diseases are the most costly to treat per episode, the projected future increase in their share of admissions will drive hospital costs upward.

Table 4-4. Inpatient Hospital Use by Disease or Condition as a Percentage of Total Discharges, Various Years

Region/ country	*Hospitals/patients*	*Year*	*Communicable and maternal and child health*	*Noncom-municable*	*Injuries*	*Other—not classified*
Africa						
Kenya	Reporting government	1968	59	26	10	5
Malawi	All	1986	67	26	5	3
Nigeria	All government	1984	64	22	5	8
Tanzania[a]	All government	1977	58	10	1	31
Uganda	All government	1968–1969	58	29	11	2
	All mission	1968–1969	63	31	3	3
Asia						
Korea	Insured patients	1986	46	44	7	3
Malaysia[a]	All government	1973	12	11	13	61
		1984	17	15	13	55
Middle East						
Oman	All government	1984	62	24	8	5
Caribbean						
Belize	All government	1984–1985	59	22	10	9
Jamaica	All acute public	1985	54	30	11	5
	All female		68	23	4	4
	All male		19	45	28	8

a. Data available for only ten leading causes of admission. Difference between total admissions and ten leading causes grouped into "Other."

Source: Belize, Jamaica, Korea, Malawi, Nigeria, Oman: derived from Barnum and Kutzin (in preparation) by aggregating their categories of "pregnancy and perinatal" and "communicable"; Kenya: Vogel and others (1974); Malaysia: Ghazali, Salam, and Baba (1987); Tanzania: Henn (1980); Uganda: Dunlop (1973).

Figure 4-8. Inpatient and Outpatient Cases by Age and Disease Group in Korean Hospitals, 1986

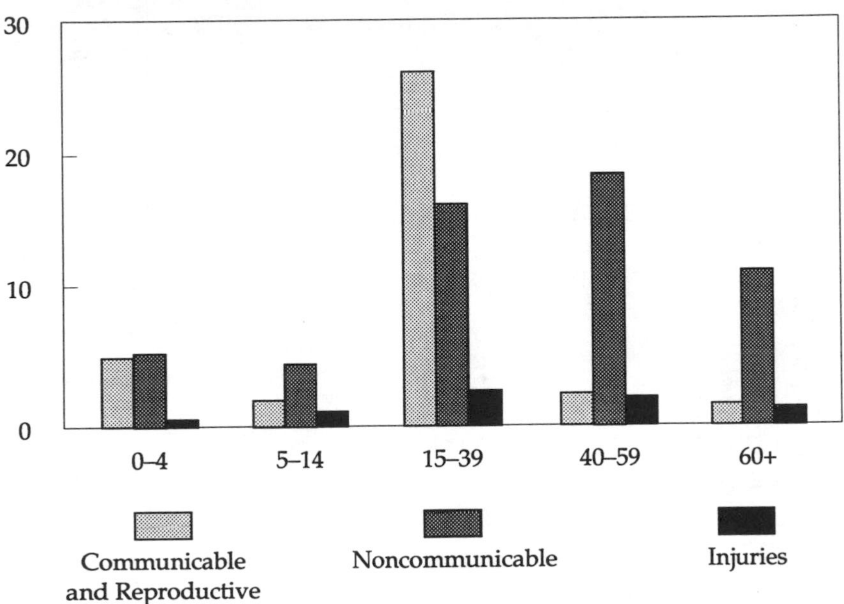

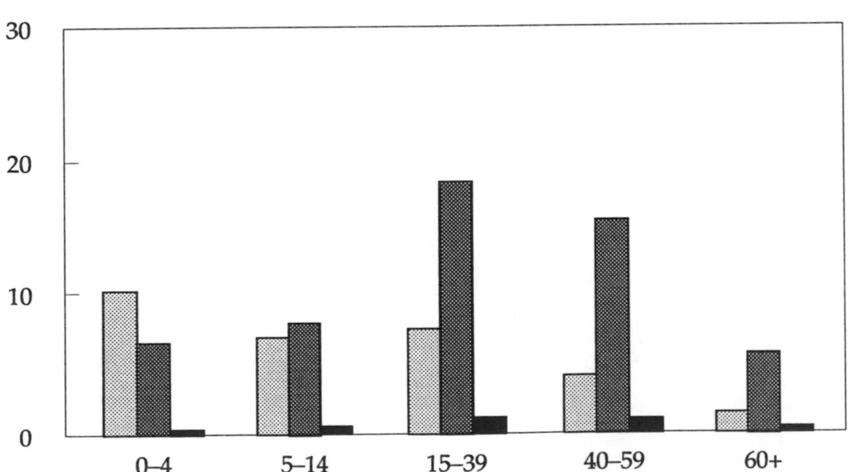

Note: The admissions distribution from figure 4-4 appears in the top chart; the outpatient distribution from figure 4-5 appears in the bottom chart.
Source: Korea Medical Insurance Corporation (1987).

The speed with which these health care costs increase depends upon the speed of the health transition, which in turn depends partly on economic growth. In Malawi, a relatively poor country not yet far advanced in the health transition, noncommunicable diseases do not yet appear to be an important component of hospital workloads.[9] The pattern for middle income countries, however, is different. In Jamaica, for example, noncommunicable diseases and injuries are four of the five leading causes of hospital admissions, the other being maternity (Jamaica, Ministry of Health 1987). Similar patterns have been observed for other (and poorer) countries. Osuntokun (1985) reported that Nigeria and some of the East African countries have the highest number of motor vehicle accidents per vehicle-mile in the world.

The increasing incidence of injuries in developing countries has prompted researchers to evaluate the benefits of introducing advanced trauma life-support programs. Ali and Naraynsingh (1987), using data from Trinidad and Tobago, argue that advanced trauma life-support programs would greatly reduce trauma deaths. Currently, hospitals do not have the capability of dealing with trauma cases; 73 percent of patients who die arrive at the hospital alive and of these deaths, 65 percent die within six hours of being admitted alive to the hospital. Of all deaths, 69 percent were of adult males, the majority of whom were twenty to thirty years old. In contrast to developed countries, in developing countries, pedestrians represented the highest percentage of people killed in motor vehicle accidents (47 percent).

Cardiovascular diseases are also becoming a leading cause of hospitalization in the developing world, particularly in middle-income countries. In Jamaica, cardiovascular diseases are the leading cause of hospitalization of adults aged between forty-five and sixty-four years. In India, data from various medical college hospitals show that nearly 2 percent of all hospital cases, 4.5 percent of medical cases, and 20 percent of admissions are of stroke patients (Dalal and Dalal 1986). Data from the Hindustan Aeronautics Limited Hospital show that 16 percent of heart patients admitted to the hospital were younger than forty years.[10] In Sudan, cardiovascular disease patients constituted 6 percent of total admissions to the Bahri Hospital during 1981–83 (El Samani 1986). Most of these patients were aged between forty and fifty-nine years.

Cost of Primary Care for Adults

Many developing countries spend 50 percent or more of their government budget on hospitals (table 4-2), where adults consume up to two-thirds of the resources. Primary care is often thought of as inexpensive preventive care for mothers and children. Even in the relatively well functioning primary care system of Tanzania, in which the lowest level dispensaries and health centers focus more on mothers and children than do the other centers, 64 percent of the patients at the lowest level are older than six years (figure 4-9). This percentage increases at higher levels of the health care referral system, where 77 percent of health center patients are older than six years.

A 1987 population based study in Jamaica provides evidence of the higher out-of-pocket expenditure per medical service for adults compared with other age categories (McFarlane and McFarlane 1987). Figure 4-10 shows that the 14 percent of the Jamaican population aged between forty and fifty-nine years spent more on their last medical service than any other age group, while the 42 percent aged be-

Figure 4-9. Age of Patients at Each Level of the Health Care Pyramid in Tanzania

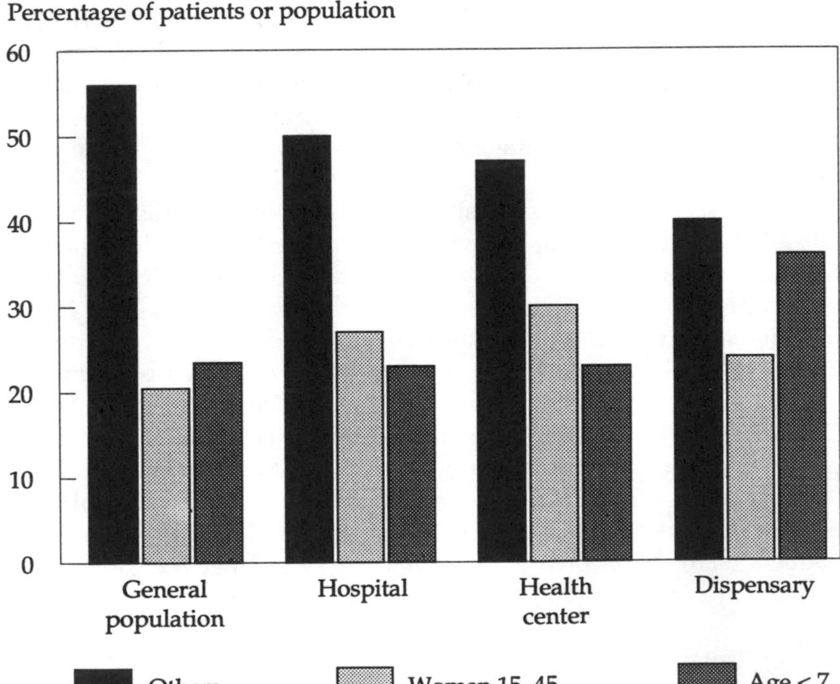

Source: Authors' calculations.

tween fifteen and thirty-nine years had the second highest average expenditure.

A population-based survey in Côte d'Ivoire estimated total medical expenditure within the last four weeks (Grootaert 1986).[11] The profile of out-of-pocket expenditure by age follows a similar pattern to that in the Jamaican survey; the age group between forty and fifty-nine years spent the most. In Côte d'Ivoire, however, the drop in expenditure at surrounding ages was smaller; the age groups between fifteen to thirty-nine years and from sixty years both spent only about 5 percent less in the most recent four weeks than the age group forty to fifty-nine years. More detailed medical expenditure data for Côte d'Ivoire, Ghana, and Peru are given in chapter 3, tables 3-7, 3-9, and 3-11 through 3-14.

Figure 4-10. Percentage of Population and Average Expenditure for Most Recent Medical Service, by Age Group, Jamaica, 1987

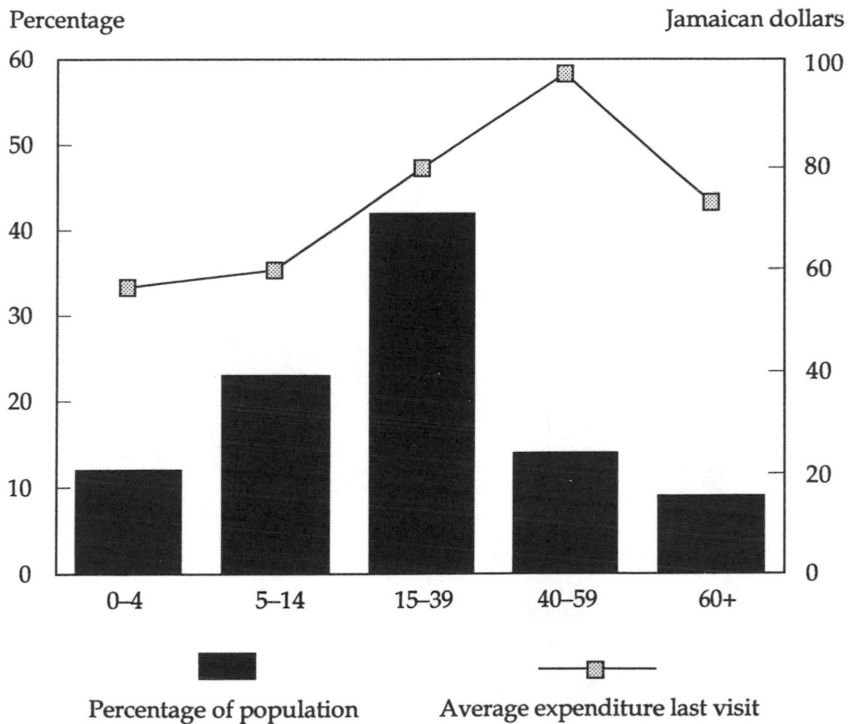

Source: McFarlane and McFarlane (1987).

Effects on Production, Consumption, Investment and Income

The effect of disease on income is mediated, and therefore obscured, by the effect of disease on health status, of health status on functional capacity, of functional capacity on productivity, and of productivity on income (figure 4-11).[12] Furthermore, the strength of the link between productivity and income depends critically on the incentives provided by the economic and institutional context. Another impediment to disentangling these relationships is that income, in turn, affects the probability of disease and influences the strength of the links between infection and disease, disease and health status, and health status and functional capacity. If any of the clockwise links from disease to income in figure 4-11 is weak in a specific empirical context, a researcher will fail to find evidence of a strong relationship between health and income. Only if every link is strengthened might a health intervention have a substantial observable effect on income. Even then a researcher must be careful to disentangle the effect of health on income from the simultaneous reverse effect of income on health.

Figure 4-11. Links between Health and Income

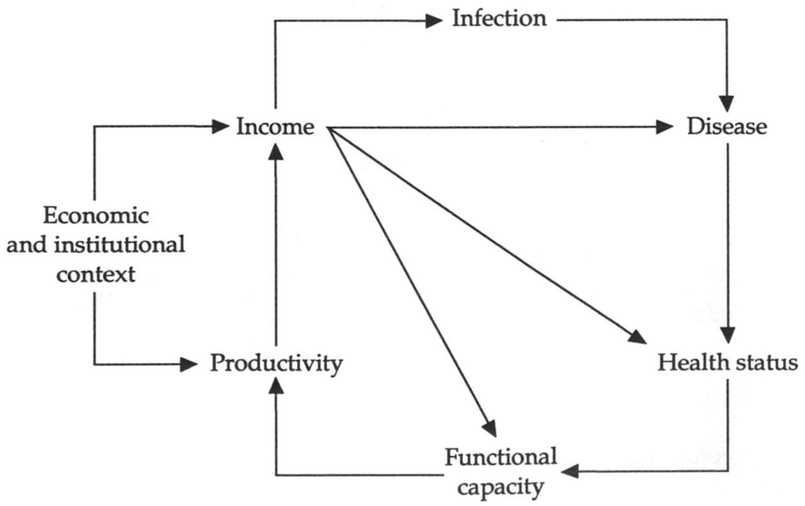

Source: Authors' design.

Effects of Adult Ill-Health on Individual Productivity and Income-Generating Potential

The evidence that disease reduces output is weak and conflicting. For example, a study in Colombia recorded reductions in the school and work time of malaria-infected students, laborers and household workers, whose average episodes of illness lasted from seven to ten days and whose morbidity rates were 3 to 14 percent per year (Castro and Mokate 1988). The study, however, did not report tests of statistical significance and omitted discussion of the net effect of morbidity on output. Other studies reviewed in Gwatkin (1983) found statistically insignificant effects; one Sudanese study even found a positive association between schistosomiasis infection and the output of sugar-cane workers (Collins and others 1976).[13]

The authors of the above studies have argued that various artificial features of the plantation environment make it unlikely that a negative effect of ill-health will be observed there. First, workers who appear too ill will be dismissed. Second, sick workers may strive to maintain their productivity on the plantation only to collapse at home, allowing other household members to take up the slack in home production. One study avoids these problems by focusing on household rather than plantation production among a sample of peasant farmers in Northern Cameroon (Audibert 1986). In this sample the proportion of individuals in each household infected with malaria and schistosomiasis was 0.10 and 0.14 respectively, but the standard deviations of these proportions in the sample were larger than the means (0.17 and 0.21 respectively) and all members of some households were infected. After controlling for other farm inputs, Audibert found that the prevalence of schistosomiasis had a statistically significant ($p = 0.001$) negative effect on the household's marketed farm output per acre.[14] The estimated elasticity with respect to household prevalence of -0.5 is so large that the the marketed yield per acre of a household whose infection prevalence is one standard deviation larger than average would be reduced by 75 percent.[15]

The link between better nutrition and better economic performance is mediated by both health status and functional capacity (figure 4-11). The literature on these links introduces another complication: the distinction between short- and long-term effects.

The link between short-term nutrition, in terms of caloric intake, and productivity is weak. Experimental studies that supplemented the diets of one group of workers with a sucrose drink and then compared their productivity either to their own previous productivity or to the productivity of unsupplemented workers found no effect (Immink and Viteri 1981; IBRD 1977). However, the participants in the study were likely to have been nutritionally disadvantaged in many ways, and calories alone may not have been the constraining factor. Iron supplements did appear to increase productivity, even in the short term.

Attempts to estimate the short-term effects of caloric intake on productivity using nonexperimental data require multivariate analyses to control for interactions between income and calories. Analyses that control for this problem are available for India, Sri Lanka, and Sierra Leone. In India, caloric intake did not significantly affect wages or farm output in regressions that included weight/height as a separate regressor (Deolalikar 1988). In Sri Lanka, the elasticity of the rural male wage rate with respect to caloric intake, as proxied by food prices, was a statistically significant 0.21 (Sahn and Alderman 1988). However, if food prices are autocorrelated over time in each locality, this Sri Lankan result may actually reflect longer-term relationships. In Sierra Leone, the output elasticity with respect to household caloric intake was estimated to be 0.33, but failure to control for functional capacity makes these results suspect as estimates of the short-term impact (Strauss 1986).

Conversely, studies in Indonesia, Sri Lanka, and the United States that have focused on the longer term have established a link between sustained nutrition intake and functional capacity as measured by performance on various tests of physical fitness (Gardner and others 1977; Karyadi and Basta 1973; Keys 1950). Other authors have found strong evidence in India and Kenya of a link between measures of long-term nutrition and health status (for example, weight-for-height, arm circumference and skinfold thickness) and productivity (Behrman, Deolalikar, and Wolfe 1988; Chesher 1979; Deolalikar 1988; IBRD 1975; IBRD 1977). For example, Deolalikar (1988) estimates that the elasticity of agricultural output with respect to average weight/height is 1.3 to 1.9 and the elasticity of wage with respect to average weight/height is 0.28 to 0.66.[16]

The significantly smaller estimated responsiveness of wage to weight-for-height than of productivity may reflect either the cost of monitoring agricultural wage labor or, alternatively, a social convention that redistributes wage income from the more to the less productive workers. Such a convention would help the society to cope with the poor health and the consequent low productivity of some of its members. Either explanation is an example of how economic institutions and social norms can mediate the relationship between productivity and income.

Because of the complexity of the linkages between adult ill-health, productivity and income, the earlier studies of these linkages tended to find few effects. Only recently, as study designs have improved (for example, Audibert 1986), and new econometric techniques have been applied (for example, Behrman, Deolalikar, and Wolfe 1988; Deolalikar 1988), have researchers begun to uncover the negative effects that seem obvious intuitively. As researchers learn from these experiences to design their studies to control for more of the complexities in figure 4-11, the true magnitude of the effect of ill-health on productivity will be revealed.

Reallocation of Labor Force

When an adult is ill or injured, the value of other household members' time increases in both home production (because of the needs of the ill or injured adult) and in market work (because of the increased marginal value of income). Household reallocations of labor in response to these changed relative values are an important part of the household's attempt to cope with adult ill-health, the costs of which vary depending on the activities from which the compensating labor is withdrawn. Table 4-5 lists studies on the magnitude of the reallocation response to illness in several countries.[17]

Table 4-5. Studies of Lost Labor Due to Ill-Health, Various Countries, Various Years

Country	*Year of study*	*Condition studied*	*Source*
Guinea	1987	Onchocerciasis	Evans 1989
Indonesia	1978	Self-reported illness in previous week	Pitt and Rosenzweig 1986
St. Lucia	1966–67	Schistosomiasis	Baldwin and Weisbrod 1974
Sudan	Undated	Malaria	Nur and Mahran 1988
U.S.A.	1966	Self-reported health status	Parsons 1977
U.S.A.	1966 1970	Self-reported work-limiting problem	Berger and Fleisher 1984
U.S.A.	1975	Myocardial infarction, stroke, cancer, motor vehicle injuries	Hartunian, Smart and Thompson 1981
U.S.A.	1977	Self-reported conditions or death	Berger 1983
U.S.A.	1981–82	Self-reported new health problems or death	Haurin 1989

Source: As shown on table.

In the United States, where families are less poor and the lost income of the ill or injured adult is partly replaced by formal insurance benefits, two studies found only small increases in a wife's work associated with her husband's illness (Haurin 1989; Parsons 1977) and a third found such effects only after controlling for disability benefit payments and other transfers (Berger and Fleisher 1984).[18] Conversely, husbands' deaths do significantly increase the labor market participation of American women (Haurin 1989).

In developing countries, where formal insurance is rare and poverty has precluded household asset levels that could substantially cushion income levels, the labor of other household members plays a larger role in replacing the work of the ill or injured adult. In a study of Indonesian farm households, work reallocation and other coping mechanisms were so successful that the agricultural profits of households with ill or injured adults were unaffected, despite the reduced labor input of these adults (Pitt and Rosenzweig 1986). In Sudan, where 250 households lost an average of forty hours per household per year due to the direct or indirect effects of malaria, the labor of other family members, mainly women (58 percent) and children (37 percent), substituted for 68 percent of the lost agricultural labor (Nur and Mahran 1988). Two other studies of malaria also found that decreased days worked by the affected individual were at least partly compensated for by other members of agricultural households (Castro and Mokate 1988; Conly 1975).

Available evidence suggests that these substitute workers usually do not fully compensate for the lost income of the ill or injured adult, and their increased labor allocation comes at the expense of other important activities. One study in the United States found that, in spite of statistically significant increased work by the household members of disabled husbands, only twenty-three cents of extra income was earned for every hour's reduction in the husband's labor supply—clearly much too little to compensate for that reduction. In agricultural households in Paraguay, a study showed that the increased farm labor of healthy household members was related to a reduction of their household production activities (Conly 1975). In Colombia, however, the increased workload of healthy household members did not affect the time allocated to their own work, but only reduced their leisure (Castro and Mokate 1988). In the Philippines, Popkin (1980) found that increased labor allocation to market activities increased household food consumption only marginally, decreased a woman's leisure dramatically and decreased her time allocated to child care somewhat, with the slack in child care and production of food taken up by older children.

In summary, the ill-health of an adult family member increases the labor demands on other household members, either in the form of increases in labor allocated to market or home production, depending on the economic needs of the family. That many studies have not shown significantly reduced agricultural output attributable to ill-health may be explained partly by the household structure of production and the success of other family members in compensating for the lost labor of the ill or injured individual. This extra effort, however, is likely to take its toll on the health and welfare of the household, as discussed previously in this chapter, and on the long-term productivity of the household, as discussed in the following section.

Change in Investment/Consumption Patterns

Investment and consumption patterns can be affected in anticipation of the probability of ill-health and after the fact as the household alters behavior to cope with the effects of ill-health of a household member. This subsection addresses only the consequences for investment and consumption of adult ill-health, after the fact. A discussion of the anticipatory effects appears later in the chapter (see *Costs of Avoiding or Ameliorating the Effects of Adult Ill-Health*).

Medical expenditure differs from other household expenditure by its high variance across households and across time for a given household. Most households spend only a small proportion of their income on medical care, but a small number of households spend a great deal. An expenditure survey of a random sample of households in a developing country will find only a few households with acutely ill or injured adults at the time of the survey. The resulting subsample of households harboring catastrophic ill-health is so small that sampling error prevents using observed average expenditure as a reliable estimator of average expenditure in the population. Furthermore, survey designers cannot justify asking all participants the full range of questions regarding medical expenditure that would be useful to ask this small subsample. Until special surveys are conducted that oversample households with seriously ill and injured adults, anecdotal evidence from small focus group studies provides the only basis for understanding the consequences of such ill-health for investment and consumption patterns.

At the onset of illness, household disinvestment, dissaving and borrowing help to finance medical care and maintain consumption. For example, in urban Bangladeshi households, expenditure on treatment was strongly correlated with the availability of assets, and once all assets were sold, expenditure on treatment stopped (Pryer 1989). In West African households afflicted by onchocerciasis, assets like bridewealth are often used to finance medical care (Evans 1989). In

Côte d'Ivoire, average medical expenditure of households where expenditure occurred was higher per unit of time than full-time employment earnings at the local minimum wage (Corbett 1988). Sale or slaughter of livestock has been cited often as a coping response to consumption shortages (Campbell and Trechter 1982; Corbett 1988; de Waal and el Amin 1986). One study in Thailand found that 60 percent of involuntary land sales were due to ill-health (Corbett 1989). In coastal Kenya, ill-health was the reason for selling land in 24 percent of land transactions (Chambers 1982).

Borrowing and the solicitation of transfer income are other frequent responses to income shocks, with transfers preferred to borrowing (Campbell and Trechter 1982; Pryer 1989; Rosenzweig 1988). When transfers are difficult to obtain or insufficient, a catastrophic adult illness can lead to serious debt and thence to impoverishment. For example, six of the seven Bangladeshi households with an ill breadwinner in one study had debts averaging over four times their monthly income and five times the average level of household indebtedness in that urban slum (Pryer 1989).

However, the ability of households to sell land or borrow depends on markets for credit and assets, particularly land, that are specific to a region and may in turn depend on the overall economy of that area. If an area is experiencing economic hardship, such as drought, widespread illness, or a large number of adult deaths, this would reduce the availability of credit to individual households, and depress the market for land and other assets. For example, in a ten-year longitudinal sample of ninety-three Indian households, a 10 percent decrease in village income decreased net loans to each household by 4 percent (Rosenzweig 1988). An example of depressed asset prices during periods of hardship was provided by the 1981–85 drought in northern Ethiopia, where the mean price of sheep fell 50 percent and the mean price of goats fell 33 percent (Cutler 1986).

The authors of this chapter are unaware of any studies that focus on the effect of adult ill-health on household investment in children's education. However, if adult ill-health causes children to be fostered out and, as mentioned before, foster children receive less education than the family's own children, then adult ill-health reduces children's education. Also, because education often requires out-of-pocket expenditure and always subtracts students from the household labor supply, the financial hardships imposed by adult ill-health reduce children's opportunities for education, both at home and in school.

The growing literature on the price elasticity of the demand for medical care in developing countries has not yet examined the effects of health care prices on, for example, food consumption. It would be useful to attempt such estimates from existing data sets. However, because most adult ill-health is less serious, these existing data sets will reveal only the responses of the average household, adding relatively little to an understanding of the plight of the household in which an adult is seriously or fatally ill or injured. To capture accurately the full negative effects of catastrophic adult ill-health on household consumption and investment, a survey must be designed specifically for this purpose, oversampling afflicted households and measuring the full array of consumption and investment responses. The desirable attributes and potential policy relevance of such a survey are described in the conclusions of this chapter.

Income Distribution

Wealthier households in developing countries are protected from some of the consequences of adult ill-health in two ways: a) their higher living standard permits them to protect themselves from malnutrition and from diseases related to poor environmental conditions, and b) their assets help them absorb the negative impacts of health shocks through self insurance.

Mortality data by income class are extremely scarce, especially for developing countries. Two Brazilian studies that used proxies for income class inferred higher mortality rates for lower socioeconomic categories. A 1980 study of Pôrto Alegre classified residential areas as "rich" or "poor" and found a 75 percent higher adult mortality rate in the poor areas (Barcellos and others 1986, as summarized in Briscoe 1990). A 1980–82 study on São Paulo classified occupations as "professional" and "nonprofessional" and found adult mortality rates of nonprofessionals to be 100 to 200 percent higher than those of professionals (Rumel 1987, as summarized in Briscoe 1990). Although these studies are consistent with the hypothesis that higher living standards protect health, neither contains sufficient statistical controls to identify the role played by income as distinct from the roles played by better sanitation available in rich areas and better education possessed by professionals. More research is needed to disentangle these causes.

It is possible to relate morbidity to income class using household surveys that measure both. As discussed in chapter 3, these surveys tend to display the counter-intuitive result that members of wealthier households report more illness than members of poor households. The most likely explanations for this finding are concerned with the self-perception of illness and illness behavior, as discussed in chapter

Table 4-6. Effect of Income on Illness, Medical Expenditure and Activity of Adults in Côte d'Ivoire, Ghana, and Peru

		Ghana		Peru	
Effect measure and income	*Côte d'Ivoire*	*Ages 15–39*	*Ages 40–59*	*Ages 15–39*	*Ages 40–59*
Percent ill in last four weeks					
Highest income quartile	37	45	49	41	52
Lowest income quartile	30	27	38	34	50
Ratio	1.23	1.67	1.29	1.21	1.04
Medical expenditure in last four weeks[a]					
Highest income quartile	6,805	805	888	91	88
Lowest income quartile	2,671	444	550	17	18
Ratio	2.55	1.81	1.61	5.35	4.89
Days decreased activity in last four weeks					
Highest income quartile	5.2	3.5	4.5	1.6	1.9
Lowest income quartile	7.9	3.4	4.0	2.2	2.6
Ratio	0.66	1.03	1.13	0.73	0.73

a. In 1987 CFA (Côte d'Ivoire), 1988 cedis (Ghana) and 1985 intis (Peru). See also tables 3-12 and 3-13.

Source: Living Standards Measurement Surveys in respective countries (World Bank, various countries).

3. Close examination reveals that higher income households do protect their members from serious adult ill-health and especially from death.

For Côte d'Ivoire, Ghana, and Peru, table 4-6 compares adults in the highest quartile of the income distribution with adults in the lowest quartile on the following three relevant measures: the percent who declare they have been ill in the last four weeks, the amount spent on their illness, and the days of decreased activity resulting from the illness. The percentage declaring themselves to have been ill is typically about 25 percent larger in the high income group. And the high income group spends much more on its illness—from 61 percent more among Ghanaian adults aged from forty to fifty-nine years to as much as 400 percent more in Peru where the income distribution is more widely dispersed. Days of decreased activity for those ill were fewer for the high income group in Côte d'Ivoire and Peru. These fewer days may be caused either by less severe illness among the higher income group or by more effective curative care bought by higher expenditure per episode. Data from the same surveys are presented in greater detail in tables 3-11 and 3-13 in chapter 3.

If a household is to recover from an adult death or serious illness, it must be able to weather a period of hardship with its fundamental human and productive capital intact. If it is forced to sell its productive assets or sacrifice the health of its other members by undernourishing and overworking them, it may pass below a threshold of poverty from which it cannot escape. The contribution of excess adult mortality and ill-health to the existing levels of poverty in developing countries is currently unknown and deserves study.

The effect of adult ill-health on the income distribution and on related poverty indices may be similar to the effect of such random shocks to household income as bad weather for an agricultural household. If this is so, a paper by Ravallion (1988) is relevant. This paper shows that for a poverty line below the modal value of household income, an increase in the variance of income will increase the expected degree of poverty. For a sample of Indian households, the contribution of income variability to the expected poverty gap was large, ranging from 26 to 54 percent. By implication, poverty would be reduced if health care expenditure risks were reduced through a government insurance mechanism. Furthermore, the effect of public health intervention would be to reduce the mean as well as the variance of medical expenditures and thus reduce expected poverty by an even greater amount.

Costs of Avoiding or Ameliorating the Effects of Adult Ill-Health: Informal and Formal Insurance Mechanisms

Although much of the research literature to date has focused on the consequences of adult ill-health once a person has become ill or injured or has died, these consequences may themselves be influenced heavily by actions taken prior to the onset of ill-health or death. These insurance mechanisms are the anticipatory coping strategies and are designed to mitigate the adverse consequences of adult ill-health. Because these mechanisms are costly, an assessment of the consequences of adult ill-health that ignores them underestimates the total burden of adult ill-health substantially.

The range of actions that can be attributed to insurance motives is quite large. Because many of these actions provide insurance against several risks simultaneously, it is difficult or impossible to allocate the insuring function of these actions entirely to adult ill-health. Formal mechanisms, which include health, disability, and life insurance, are explicit financial arrangements designed to compensate individuals for losses. In developing countries, although the government sector often does provide some formal insurance, financial constraints and the inherent difficulties of managing a health insurance program often limit the coverage actually provided.

In contrast with formal insurance mechanisms, informal mechanisms, such as seat belt use, job safety, and inheritance patterns, are widespread in both developed and developing countries. Other informal mechanisms that are especially important in developing countries include extended families, social networks, and community organizations (Rosenzweig 1988). Some authors have referred to these informal social conventions for coping with risk as the "implicit markets" of a "moral economy" (Ravallion and Dearden 1988; Scott 1976).

Both informal and formal insurance mechanisms are imperfect and involve both administrative costs and efficiency losses. In the United States, administrative costs account for 4.5 percent of all health insurance premiums and even more of life and disability insurance premiums (Hartunian, Smart, and Thompson 1981). Administrative costs for most informal insurance mechanisms have not been quantified. However, the West African credit clubs called *tontines* are known to pay zero or even negative interest to depositers, with the resulting profit going to the individual who administers the club.

All voluntary insurance contracts, whether informal or formal, are subject to two types of efficiency losses, which must be included in computing their costs. The first of these, called "adverse selection," occurs when high risk individuals seek out the insurance and low risk ones avoid it. A formal insurance program can avoid adverse selection in part by requiring enrollment, but an individual can always escape contributing to an informal system by migrating. The second source of efficiency loss is "moral hazard." It results when the insured individual is willing to incur greater health risks, or to consume more health care, than the uninsured. It seems likely that informal systems are less subject to moral hazard, because members of the risk-pooling group can monitor each other's behavior more effectively.

Insurance mechanisms may help explain why the direct effects of adult ill-health are often found to be small. Later productivity, income, and welfare losses of an adult who has been ill, or of survivors following an adult's death, may be smaller than expected if households have anticipated their occurrence and taken actions to reduce their consequences. The organization of economic activity itself may be designed to insure against the effects of illness in the work force. Two potential mechanisms for reducing reliance on workers who may become ill or injured are maintenance of a labor surplus and minimization of labor specialization. Such economic organization lowers the average productivity of all workers and conceals the productivity effects of illness. Although there is no evidence concerning this issue, the effect on output is potentially large.

Informal Insurance Mechanisms

In the absence of formal insurance markets, households can cushion the effects of adult ill-health on their income either by establishing prior claims on other households, to be called in when needed, or by borrowing later in the local credit market. The principal strategies for establishing claims on other households in poor countries are a) fertility, b) alliances through marriage of offspring, and c) transfers to other households in their time of need. All three of these strategies have substantial costs in the short run, which the household must be willing to incur to reap benefits in times of its own need. As with all insurance contracts, some of the household's expenditure will never be recouped. This excess of outlays over receipts is the cost of these mechanisms, a cost that would be unnecessary in the absence of risks like adult ill-health.

FERTILITY BEHAVIOR. High fertility in the developing world has been examined often in the context of demand for children's labor and insurance against risk. Children provide household labor when young (Ainsworth 1988) and investing in children through their marriages or education can insure against periodic crises by allowing parents to draw on the resources of their children in emergencies (Caldwell and Reddy 1986). Children have been a traditional form of insurance for the inevitable ill-health and loss of productivity that comes with age (King 1987).

Nevertheless, the desire for insurance can also be consistent with reduced fertility if the household takes account of the extra returns available from investing in well-educated children. For example, the periodic risk of drought and its accompanying risk to life and health in rural South India from 1980–1983 contributed to a decline rather than an increase in fertility, probably because parents responded to the increased risk by investing more in the education of fewer children (Caldwell and Reddy 1986).

MARRIAGE AND SOCIAL NETWORKS. For extended family structures, social networks, and community organizations to function effectively as methods of insurance and risk pooling, they must be able to spread risk, discourage moral hazard, enforce reciprocity, and control adverse selection. Consider first the risk-spreading requirement. In a poor agricultural economy both the weather and the prevalence of communicable diseases result in a higher correlation among the incomes of nearby households than of distantly separated ones. Because of this spatial covariation, a household will be less well insured by claims it makes on nearby households than by claims it makes on distant ones.

The implications that Caldwell and Reddy (1986), Lucas and Stark (1985) and Rosenzweig (1988) deduced from these observations are that poor agricultural households have an incentive to marry their children into households that are sufficiently distant to reduce the covariation of incomes but still close enough to call upon in times of need. Caldwell and Reddy (1986) and Lucas and Stark (1985) present evidence from cross-sectional surveys in India and Botswana that households in drought-stricken areas receive more transfers from outside than from inside the home village. Although this evidence supports the hypothesis that exogamy is motivated by a desire to insure against hard times, more convincing evidence in support of this hypothesis is provided by Rosenzweig (1988) from his longitudinal data that follow a sample of 201 households in six Indian villages over nine consecutive years. Loans account for more than six times as much income supplementation as transfers in the average household (1,289 rupees compared with 213). A larger proportion of the transfers come from outside the village (59 versus 27 percent) and the transfers come from farther away (25 versus 13 kilometers). In the average year, an average household pays out 231 rupees and receives 213 in return, for a net outlay of 18 rupees. If 231 rupees is considered as the insurance premium, the household is paying only about 8 percent of its total premium for ''administrative overhead,'' a figure which compares favorably with the overhead expenditures by the United States formal insurance system.[19]

Rosenzweig (1988) also shows the substantial difference in the roles of transfers and loans by income class. If income is short by 100 rupees one year, perhaps because of adult ill-health, a poor household will replace 37 rupees of the shortfall with a loan and 2.1 additional rupees with a transfer. The average household receives almost the same transfer (1.7 rupees), but a much smaller loan (23.9 rupees). A relatively wealthy household whose inheritance is 200,000 rupees receives a 0.9 rupee transfer, but would not borrow at all. In all income classes, every 100 rupees of transfer received reduces borrowing by 539 rupees, and the age of the head of household reduces borrowing by 280 rupees per year of age and transfers by 20 rupees per year of age.

These empirical results are consistent with the hypothesis that households that have access to their own reserves of wealth or to transfers from other households prefer to draw on those resources before resorting to loans. The fact that transfers tend to come from farther distances than loans is consistent with the view that credit arrangements require more monitoring than the less formal transfers within kinship groups and that the cost of monitoring increases sharply with distance.[20]

In a village that is having a bad year, households with low inheritance and young household heads have no effective safety net in the informal economy of loans and transfers. The substitution of transfers for loans occurs at richer rather than poorer levels of wealth. Young household heads receive more transfers, but also borrow much more in an average year. Households in hard-hit villages receive no more transfers, but substantially less credit than other households. In these Indian villages the transfer mechanism provides the best insurance for those who least need it.

Because the marriage contract and the resulting dispersion of children can play such an important role in spreading household risk, it is not surprising that households everywhere would seek to guard these contracts against risk. In particular, the traditional legal practices of some groups permit or require the dissolution of the contract and the return to the husband's family of the brideprice if one or the other partner is found to be in poor health.

Table 4-7 gives examples of health conditions traditionally considered to be legitimate reasons for dissolving the marriage contract in two Tanzanian ethnic groups. In these groups, divorce involves returning the brideprice, so that the cost of ill-health is borne partly by the parents of the ill spouse.

Social organizations, labor exchange pools and cohort groups that have insurance mechanisms are also common in developing countries. Knudsen (1977) reported the traditional work associations of the Sukuma ethnic group in Tanzania. Pryer (1989) reported a case study of a very successful informal insurance mechanism among a work group in Bangladesh. The five members of the group would pool their wages and divide them six ways, with the remaining one-sixth share used to provide income for members who could not work. The system was able to sustain one worker through a prolonged illness.

Table 4-7. Poor Health as a Justification for Divorce among the Haya and Sukuma of Tanzania

Ethnic group/ health problem	*Wife may divorce husband*	*Husband may divorce wife*
Haya		
Leprosy	Yes	Yes
Epilepsy	Yes	Yes
Syphilis	No	Yes
Impotence	Yes	n.a.
Sukuma		
Sterility	Unknown	Yes
Premature death	Unknown	Yes

Source: Cory and Hartnoll (1945); Cory (1953).

Investment and Savings

Many investments made before ill-health or death are motivated by the desire to insure against ill-health and other household risks. To the extent that precautionary motives induce the investor to sacrifice return for liquidity, the forgone earnings are a private and social cost of this form of insurance. Jewelry and small livestock (goats and sheep) are purchased often for insurance purposes (Corbett 1988; Campbell and Trechter 1982). Small livestock are more liquid than cattle but have fewer productive uses. Because of their demand for precautionary saving, pastoralists invest in their herds beyond the point of optimal return (de Waal and el Amin 1986).

An important investment choice in which return must sometimes be traded off against risk of ill-health is the choice of residential location. Diseases such as onchocerciasis and malaria are location specific and have been shown to discourage settlement on and development of fertile land. Onchocerciasis has been shown to contribute to the depopulation of river valleys in Nigeria (Bradley 1976) and in the Volta River Valley (Prescott, Prost, and LeBerre 1984). Conversely, many of the benefits attributed to the near eradication of malaria in Sri Lanka in the 1960s were due to migration into and development of areas which had been infested previously by malaria (Barlow 1967).

Motives for saving in developing countries are different from those in developed countries (Deaton 1989). Family sizes tend to be larger, with several generations living together, reducing incentives for life-cycle saving because most assets are shared across generations. Income derived from agriculture is inherently uncertain and shortfalls often pose serious threats to household well-being. Borrowing constraints are more serious in developing countries. Furthermore, the absence of formal insurance markets tends to increase the riskiness of income and consumption in developing countries, and health expenditure is important as an uncertain component of consumption. All of these factors imply that savings in developing countries are influenced heavily by the desire to smooth consumption over time rather than by life-cycle motives or intergenerational transfers. The need to maintain assets in a relatively liquid form to assure their availability as a buffer against bad times tends to reduce the scope and hence productivity of investments.

Formal Health Insurance

The term *insurance* typically refers not to the informal mechanisms discussed above, but to an institutionalized formal contract between an insurer, public or private, and an individual. Insurance in this latter sense has a long history in China and in many Latin American countries, but is a more recent innovation in Korea and is only beginning to be discussed in African countries. Figure 4-12 displays the degree of coverage by insurance programs in sixteen Latin American countries and twelve Asian countries. The fitted regression lines demonstrate the positive correlations between per capita GNP and insurance coverage in both regions.

Table 4-8 provides a detailed breakdown of health sector financing in Brazil, China, and the Republic of Korea, three countries with well-established health insurance programs. The proportion of total

Figure 4-12. Insurance Coverage and GNP per capita in Selected Asian and Latin American Countries, circa 1985 and 1977, Respectively

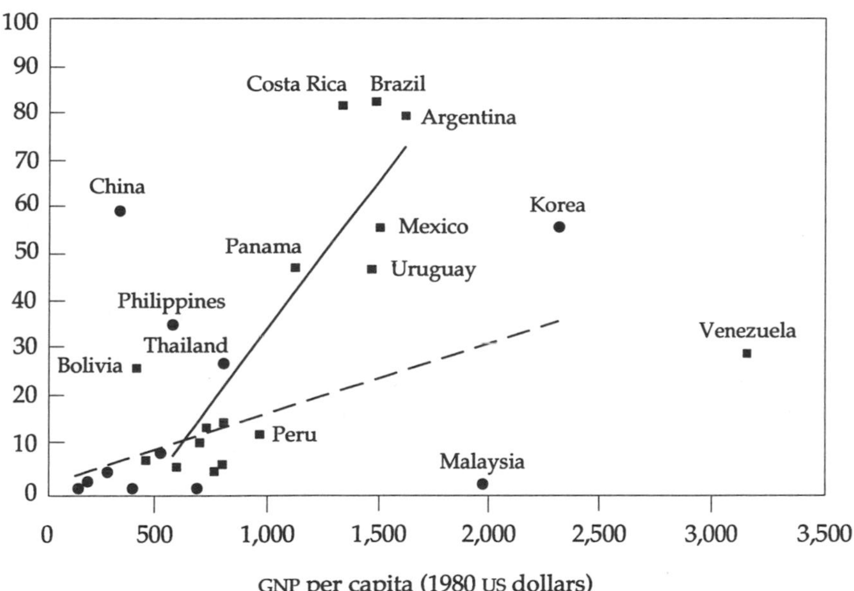

a. Latin America/Caribbean.
Source: Zschock (1986) and Griffin (1990).

Table 4-8. Sources of Recurrent Health Sector Financing in Brazil, China, and Korea, Selected Years
(percentage)

Year	*Public noninsurance*	*Private*	*National insurance program(s)*	*Total*
Brazil[a]				
1986	24.6	50.0	25.4	100.0
China[b]				
1980	31.4	17.7	50.8	100.0
1987	14.4	32.6	53.0	100.0
Korea				
1978	19.0	76.0	5.0	100.0
1985	12.0	67.0	21.0	100.0

a. Brazil: Survey estimated private expenditure as half of total expenditure on health. *Private* includes claims from private health insurance.

b. China: The *national insurance program* category includes the government insurance system, financed out of the ministry of finance budget, which accounted for 14 percent of insurance total in 1980 and 11 percent in 1987.

Source: World Bank (1989a, 1989c); Briscoe (1990).

health care costs covered by national insurance programs is highest in China (about 50 percent) and lowest in Korea (21 percent). This mode of financing, however, has grown rapidly in Korea, where expansion of the national health insurance program has been an explicit goal of government policy for more than a decade.

Ten years ago the public financing and supply of health care was more important in China than in the other two countries. But as a result of Chinese reforms in their communal system of production—and the repercussions of those reforms in their health system—public provision of health care has decreased in relative importance and been replaced by out-of-pocket private coverage.

Insurance provides the benefit of sharing risk only at the cost of the three sources of inefficiency mentioned above: adverse selection, administrative cost, and moral hazard. Adverse selection can be minimized by mandatory universal coverage, but such coverage has yet to be achieved in any developing country; even those with the highest incomes and the longest tradition of social insurance do not have mandatory universal coverage (table 4-8 and figure 4-12). Thus cost escalation and efficiency losses from adverse selection are a problem to various degrees in all of these national systems. Although administrative cost estimates are unavailable for developing countries, it is reasonable to assume that 4 percent (the loss in the United States) is the minimum loss each of these countries incurs from administrative expenses.

Finally, all insurance alters the incentives of the insured, increasing the probability of, or the size of, the event insured against. People with fire insurance are more likely to have fires, people with life insurance are more likely to die prematurely, and people with health insurance are more likely to go to the doctor. The degree of moral hazard varies, but is systematically higher for health insurance than for life insurance. To the degree that insured individuals consume more health care than they would if they were uninsured and non-poor, the moral hazard produces a loss of welfare for society at large, including both its insured and uninsured members. This welfare loss is one of the costs of insurance—and therefore one of the costs of adult ill-health that motivates that insurance.[21]

Formal insurance, like its informal cousins, is a social coping mechanism, the costs of which must be attributed to the ill-health of adults and non-adults. Although the proportion of total insurance expenditure and the attendant inefficiencies and costs due to adult ill-health are unknown, a reduction in adult ill-health will reduce total costs as it reduces this proportion. The full dimensions of these costs and their determinants deserve greater study, especially now that health insurance programs are expanding rapidly in Korea and being considered seriously in other Asian countries and Africa.

Conclusions

The consequences of adult ill-health extend far beyond increased consumption of medical care and range from dramatic effects on the health of other household members to subtle but probably costly effects on the efficiency with which a society organizes its currently healthy workers. Because of the success of social mechanisms for coping with illness, the measurement of the cost of ill-health must include the costs of coping—a challenging research task that has not yet been addressed fully by the research community. Available information suggests that the costs of coping often are extremely high, especially for future generations who must sacrifice their education to maintain household production and consumption when their adult family members become ill or injured or die.

Although it is not yet possible to measure the total cost of adult ill-health by adding together a measure of the welfare loss from all the cells in table 4-1, each of the separately enumerated effects of adult ill-health is negative. By robbing the individual and therefore the household, the community and the employer of time and resources, adult ill-health limits the development potential of the societies which it burdens. As research advances the precision of measuring each direct and indirect consequence of ill-health, stronger arguments will be made for preventing or curing adult ill-health.

Notes

1. For other typologies, see Andreano and Helmeniak (1988), Popkin (1982), Rice (1965, 1966, 1967, 1969), Rice and Cooper (1967), and Rosenfield, Golladay, and Davidson (1984).

2. When research is sufficiently advanced to attempt a calculation of the total cost of adult ill-health, care will be necessary to avoid double counting.

3. The increased mortality rate associated with death of the father is not statistically significant ($p > 0.10$), but that associated with the mother is ($p = 0.07$, one-tailed), as is the interaction effect between mothers' and daughters' deaths ($p < 0.001$). All data and analysis for figure 4-2 were provided by Michael Strong, International Center for Diarrhoeal Diseases Research, Bangladesh.

4. Data provided by Martha Ainsworth from background files for Ainsworth (1988).

5. In a large developing country with many states, central government expenditure may represent only a small part of total government health expenditures. In Nigeria, for example, the breakdown of government expenditure on health by level of government is approximately 30 percent federal, 50 percent state and 20 percent local (World Bank 1990).

6. Information on the proportion of hospital costs attributable to adults is difficult to acquire because of the scarcity of specific information linking age of patients and/or diagnosis of illness with hospital cost data in developing countries.

7. The base prevalence rates per thousand for the five to fourteen year age group were: 9.7 in China, 221 in Côte d'Ivoire, 29 in Ghana and 35 in Peru. The China rates for all age groups were averages for the counties of Shanghai, Fen-xian and Wu (Cai 1989). Other data were from Living Standards Measurement Surveys (World Bank various countries) carried out by the respective governments.

8. There are a total of 263,856 admissions and 12,274,521 oupatient visits in the data.

9. Personal communication from Anne Mills.

10. At Hindustan Aeronautics Limited, 53 percent of heart patients were among the lowest paid employees (earning less than US$46.88 per month) and 48 percent were manual laborers (Keshavamurthy and Gemson 1980).

11. Although the survey requested all hospital and drug expenditure in the preceding four weeks, it asked only about the first health provider seen and thus underestimates total expenditure by the expenditure on subsequent health care providers visited within those four weeks.

12. In infectious disease, infection intervenes between income and disease.

13. The authors hypothesized that the confounding variable of worker experience was causing both greater productivity and, because of prolonged exposure, higher infection rates.

14. Due to the difficulty of observing total farm output, the study was forced to use marketed output as the dependent variable.

15. Conversely, the prevalence rate of malaria infection in this group did not significantly affect marketed output. The author speculated that the episodic nature of both malaria and the demand for labor on household farms

prevents the former from significantly interfering with the latter when the average prevalence rate is only 10 percent.

16. The former, smaller estimates are from a random effects specification and the latter from a fixed effects one.

17. The studies are not directly comparable because of differences in analytical methods, in the definition of illness, in the normal number of hours worked per year, in the initial household assets and in the magnitude of transfer payments.

18. At the time the husband became ill, the average household in the Haurin sample held assets of US$55,000 (1981), a substantial cushion unavailable to most households in developing countries.

19. The positive net borrowing could be explained by a high default rate on the 10 percent of all loans that are from a cooperative bank or simply by a secular increase in borrowing over the period.

20. Hypotheses relevant to adult ill-health that Rosenzweig (1988) did not or could not test included: a) households define risk with reference to discretionary income, calculated by subtracting expenditures on needs like food and health care from total household income; b) the transfers and loans contracted for by an individual household are determined by both the household's demand and the outside world's supply, the latter being determined partly by the household's previous investments in exogamous marriage contracts; c) supply of transfers depends upon the nature of the household's income or expenditure shock, and ill-health attracts more transfers than high food prices; d) a household's demand for transfers is a nonlinear function of its wealth and of the age of the head—larger transfers are made at lower household incomes and younger ages; e) the insurance strategies of villages vary depending on the nature and degree of the risks inherent to them—some villages are healthier than others and therefore require less insurance; f) on average, loans have a lower fixed cost per transaction and a higher variable cost per dollar provided than do transfers.

21. To the extent that the consumption of a health service like a vaccination confers benefits on neighbors of the consumer (by preventing their exposure to infection), the additional consumption of such services caused by moral hazard might increase rather than reduce social welfare. However, there are few examples of such positive externalities among health care services for adults.

References

Ainsworth, M. 1988. ''Child Fostering and the Demand for Child Labor in Côte d'Ivoire.'' New Haven: Yale University, unpublished paper.

Ali. J., and V. Naraynsingh. 1987.''Potential Impact of the Advanced Trauma Life Support (ATLS) Program in a Third World Country.'' *International Surgery* 72:179–84.

Andreano. R., and T. Helmeniak. 1988. ''Economics, Health, and Tropical Diseases: A Review.'' In A. N. Herrin and P. L. Rosenfield, eds., *Economics, Health and Tropical Diseases*. Manila: School of Economics, University of the Philippines.

Audibert, M. 1986. "Agricultural Nonwage Production and Health Status: A Case Study in a Tropical Environment." *Journal of Development Economics* 24:275–91.

Baldwin, R. E., and B. A. Weisbrod. 1974. "Disease and Labor Productivity." *Economic Development and Cultural Change* 22:414–35.

Barcellos, T. M. and others. 1986. *Segregação Urbana e Mortalidade em Porto Alegre*. Porto Alegre: Fundação de Economia e Estatística.

Barlow, R. 1967. "The Economic Effects of Malaria Eradication." *American Economic Review* 68:130–44.

Barnum, H. N., and J. Kutzin. Forthcoming. *Public Hospitals in Developing Countries: Resource Use, Cost, Financing*. Washington, D.C.: World Bank.

Behrman, J. R., A. B. Deolalikar, and B. L. Wolfe. 1988. "Nutrients Impacts And Determinants." *World Bank Economic Review* 2:299–320.

Benenson, A. S., ed. 1985. *Control Of Communicable Diseases in Man*. 14th edition. Washington, D.C.: American Public Health Association.

Berger, M. 1983. "Labor Supply and Spouse's Health: The Effects of Illness, Disability, and Mortality." *Social Science Quarterly* 64:494–509.

Berger, M., and B. M. Fleisher. 1984. "Husband's Health and Wife's Labor Supply." *Journal of Health Economics* 3:63–75.

Bledsoe, C. H., D. C. Ewbank, and U. C. Isiugo-Abanihe. 1988. "The Effect of Child Fostering on Feeding Practices and Access to Health Services in Rural Sierra Leone." *Social Science and Medicine* 27(6):627–36.

Bradley, A. K. 1976. "Effects of Onchocerciasis on Settlement in the Middle Hawal Valley, Nigeria." *Transactions of the Royal Society of Tropical Medicine and Hygiene* 70(3):225–29.

Briscoe, John. 1990. *Brazil: The New Challenge of Adult Health*. World Bank Country Study. Washington, D.C.

Cai, J. 1989. "The Economic and Social Determinants of the Demand for Medical Care in a Rural Area in China." Research paper for the Takemi Program in International Health. Boston: Harvard School of Public Health.

Caldwell, J. C., and P. H. Reddy. 1986. "Periodic High Risk as a Cause of Fertility Decline in a Changing Rural Environment: Survival Strategies in the 1980–83 South Indian Drought." *Economic Development and Cultural Change* 34:677–701.

Campbell, D. J., and D. D. Trechter. 1982. "Strategies for Coping with Food Consumption Shortage in the Mandara Mountains Region of North Cameroon." *Social Science and Medicine* 16:2117–27.

Castro, E. B., and K. M. Mokate. 1988. "Malaria and its Socioeconomic Meanings: The Study of Cunday in Colombia." In A. N. Herrin and P. L. Rosenfield, eds., *Economics, Health, and Tropical Diseases*. Manila: School of Economics, University of the Philippines.

Chambers, R. 1982. "Health, Agriculture, and Rural Poverty: Why Seasons Matter." *Journal of Development Studies* 18(2):217–38.

Chen, L. C., M. C. Gesche, S. Ahmed, A. I. Chowdhury, and W. H. Mosley. 1974. "Maternal Mortality in Rural Bangladesh." *Studies in Family Planning* 5(11):334–41.

Chesher, A. 1979. "Worker Productivity and its Relation to Health." *World Bank Kenya Health and Nutrition Study (March)*. Washington, D.C.: World Bank.

Collins, K. J., R. J. Brotherhood, C. T. Davies, C. Dore, A. J. Hackett, F. J. Imms, J. Musgrove, J. S. Weiner, M. A. Amin, M. El Karim, H. M. Ismail, A. H. Omer, and M. Y. Sukkar. 1976. "Physiological Performance and Work Capacity of Sudanese Cane Cutters with *Schistosoma mansoni* Infection." *The American Journal of Tropical Medicine and Hygiene* 25(3):410–21.

Conly, G. N. 1975. *The Impact of Malaria on Economic Development: A Case Study.* Scientific Publication No. 297. Washington, D.C.: Pan American Health Organization.

Corbett, J. 1988. "Famine and Household Coping Strategies." *World Development* 16(9):1099–122.

———. 1989. "Poverty and Sickness: The High Costs of Ill-Health." *IDS Bulletin* 20(2):58–62.

Cory, H. 1953. *Sukuma Law and Custom.* London: Oxford University Press.

Cory, H., and M. N. Hartnoll. 1945. *The Customary Law of the Haya Tribe.* London: Percy Lund, Humphries.

Cutler, P. 1986. "The Response to Drought of Beja Famine Refugees in Sudan." *Disasters* 10(3):181–88.

Dalal, P. M., and K. P. Dalal. 1986. "Cost and Value of Technical Medicine for Diagnosis and Treatment of Cerebrovascular Disease Problems in the Developing Countries." *Japan Heart Journal* 27(6):901–10.

Deaton, A. 1989. "Saving in Developing Countries: Theory and Review." Princeton: Woodrow Wilson School, Princeton University, unpublished paper. (March).

De Ferranti, D. 1985. "Paying for Health Services in Developing Countries: An Overview." *World Bank Staff Working Papers* No. 721. Washington, D.C.: World Bank.

Deolalikar, A. B. 1988. "Nutrition and Labor Productivity in Agriculture: Estimates for Rural South India." *Review of Economics and Statistics* 70(3):406–13.

De Waal, A., and M. el Amin. 1986. *Survival in Northern Darfur 1985–86.* Report. Nyala, Sudan: Save the Children Fund.

Dunlop, D. W. 1973. "The Economics of Uganda's Health Service System: Implications for Health and Economic Planning." East Lansing: Michigan State University. PhD. Diss.

El Samani, El Fatih Z. 1986. *Cardiovascular Diseases Hospital Load in a Sudanese Urban Center.* Research paper for the Takemi Program in International Health. Boston: Harvard School of Public Health.

Evans, T. 1989. "The Impact of Permanent Disability on Small Households: Evidence from Endemic Areas of River Blindness in Guinea." *IDS Bulletin* 20(2):41–48.

Farley, T. M. M, and E. M. Belsey. 1988. "The Prevalence and Aetiology of Infertility." *Proceedings of the African Population Conference, Dakar, Senegal, November 7–12 1988.* Liege, Belgium: International Union for the Scientific Study of Population.

Fink, A. E. 1985. "Nutrition, Lactation and Fertility in Two Mexican Rural Communities." *Social Science and Medicine* 20(12):1295–1305.

Frank, O. 1983. *Infertility in Sub-Saharan Africa.* Working Paper No. 97. New York: The Population Council, Center for Policy Studies.

Gardner, G. R., V. R. Edgerton, B. Senewiratne, R. J. Barnard, and Y. Ohira.

1977. "Physical Work Capacity and Metabolic Stress in Subjects with Iron Deficiency Anemia." *The American Journal of Clinical Nutrition* 30(6):910–17.

Ghazali, A. A., H. Salam, and A. B. Baba. 1987. *Health Care Financing: Malaysia.* Paper prepared for the Seminar on Health Care Financing. Manila, Philippines: Asian Development Bank.

Griffin, C. C. 1990. *Health Sector Financing in Asia.* Report No. IDP-68. Washington, D.C.: World Bank.

Grootaert, C. 1986. "Measuring and Analyzing Levels of Living in Developing Countries." *LSMS Working Paper* No. 24. Washington, D.C.: World Bank.

Gwatkin, D. R. 1983. "Does Better Health Produce Greater Wealth? A Review of the Evidence Concerning Health, Nutrition, and Output." Overseas Development Council. (August). Unpublished paper.

Hartunian, N. S., C. N. Smart, and M. S. Thompson. 1981. *The Incidence and Economic Costs of Major Health Impairments: A Comparative Analysis of Cancer, Motor Vehicle Injuries, Coronary Heart Disease, and Strokes.* Lexington, Massachusetts: Lexington Book.

Haurin, D. R. 1989. "Women's Labor Market Reactions to Family Disruptions." *The Review of Economics and Statistics* 71(1):54–61.

Henn, A. E. 1980. *Tanzania Health Sector Strategy.* Washington, D.C.: USAID.

Hogberg, U., and G. Brostrom. 1985. "The Demography of Maternal Mortality: Seven Swedish Parishes in the Nineteenth Century." *International Journal of Gynecology and Obstetrics* 23(6):489–97.

Immink, M., and V. Viteri. 1981. "Energy Intake and Productivity of Guatemalan Sugarcane Cutters: An Empirical Test of the Efficiency Wage Hypothesis, Parts I and II." *Journal of Development Economics* 9:251–287.

IBRD (International Bank for Reconstruction and Development). 1975. *Effect of Health and Nutrition Status of Road Construction Workers in Northern India on Productivity.* Technical Memorandum No. 4. Washington, D.C.: International Bank for Reconstruction and Development.

———. 1977. *The Relation of Nutrition and Health to Worker Productivity in Kenya.* Technical Memorandum No. 26. Washington, D.C.: International Bank for Reconstruction and Development.

Jackson, L. C. 1985. "Malaria in Liberian Children and Mothers: Biocultural Perceptions of Illness vs Clinical Evidence of Disease." *Social Science and Medicine* 20(12):1281–87.

Jamaica, Ministry of Health. 1986. *Hospital Statistics Report 1985.* Kingston: Health Information Unit, Ministry of Health.

———. 1987. *Hospital Restoration Project.* Loan application document prepared by the Pan-American Health Organization (PAHO), Jamaica, and submitted to the Inter-American Development Bank. Kingston.

Karyadi, D., and S. Basta. 1973. *Nutrition and Health of Indonesian Construction Workers: Endurance and Anemia.* Staff Working Paper No. 152. Washington, D.C.: International Bank for Reconstruction and Development.

Keshavamurthy, N. K., and K. Gemson. 1980. "Observations on the Epidemiology of Coronary Heart Disease from an Industrial Hospital." *Tropical Doctor* 10:103–05.

Keys, A. B. 1950. *The Biology of Human Starvation.* Minneapolis: University of Minnesota Press.

King, E. M. 1987. "The Effect of Family Size on Family Welfare: What Do We

Know?'' In D. G. Johnson and R. D. Lee, eds., *Population Growth and Economic Development: Issues and Evidence.* Madison: University of Wisconsin.

Knudsen, B. R. 1977. ''Dance Societies: The Voluntary Work Associations of the Sukuma.'' *Tanzania Notes and Records* 81–82:66–74.

Koenig, M. A., V. Fauveau, A. I. Chowdhury, J. Chakraborty, and M. A. Khan. 1988. ''Maternal Mortality in Matlab, Bangladesh: 1976–85.'' *Studies in Family Planning* 19(2):69–80.

Korea Medical Insurance Corporation. 1987. *1986 Medical Insurance Statistical Yearbook, Eighth Issue.* Seoul.

Lucas, R. E. B., and O. Stark. 1985. ''Motivations to Remit.'' *Journal of Political Economy* 93:901–18.

McFarlane, D. H. C., and C. McFarlane. 1987. *Appraisal of an Analytical Report on a Survey of New Initiatives in Health Finance and Administration.* Kingston, Jamaica: Statistical Institute of Jamaica and Ministry of Health.

Menken, J., J. Trussel, and S. Watkins. 1981. ''The Nutrition Fertility Link: An Evaluation of the Evidence.'' *Journal of Interdisciplinary History* 11(3):425–41.

Mills, A. J. 1990a. *The Costs of the District Hospital: A Case Study from Malawi.* London: London School of Hygiene and Tropical Medicine. Unpublished.

———. 1990b. ''The Economics of Hospitals in Developing Countries: I. Expenditure Patterns.'' *Health Policy and Planning* 5(2):107–17.

Nur, E. T. M., and H. A. Mahran. 1988. ''The Effect of Health on Agricultural Labor Supply: A Theoretical and Empirical Investigation.'' In A. N. Herrin and P. L. Rosenfield, eds., *Economics, Health, and Tropical Diseases.* Manila: School of Economics, University of the Philippines.

Osuntokun, B. O. 1985. ''The Changing Pattern of Disease in Developing Countries.'' *World Health Forum* 6(4):310–13.

Over, M., and P. Piot. Forthcoming. ''HIV Infection and Other Sexually Transmitted Diseases.'' In D. T. Jamison and W. H. Mosley, eds., *Disease Control Priorities in Developing Countries.* New York: Oxford University Press for the World Bank.

Parsons, D. O. 1977. ''Health, Family Structure, and Labor Supply.'' *American Economic Review* 67:703–12.

Pitt, M. M., and M. R. Rosenzweig. 1986. ''Agricultural Prices, Food Consumption, and the Health and Productivity of Indonesian Farmers.'' In I. Singh, L. Squire, and J. Strauss, eds., *Agricultural Household Models: Extensions, Applications, and Policy.* Baltimore: Johns Hopkins University Press for the World Bank.

Popkin, B. M. 1980. ''Time Allocation of the Mother and Child Nutrition.'' *Ecology of Food and Nutrition* 9(1):1–13.

———.1982. ''A Household Framework for Examining the Social and Economic Consequences of Tropical Diseases.'' *Social Science and Medicine* 16:533–43.

Prescott, N., A. Prost, and R. Le Berre. 1984. ''The Economics of Blindness Prevention in Upper Volta under the Onchocerciasis Control Program.'' *Social Science and Medicine* 19(10):1051–55.

Pryer, J. 1989. ''When Breadwinners Fall Ill: Preliminary Findings from a Case Study in Bangladesh.'' *IDS Bulletin* 20(2):49–57.

Pust, R. E., and J. M. Burrell. 1986. ''Paramedical's Clinical Accuracy in 102 Cases Referred to a Hospital.'' *Tropical Doctor* 16:38–43.

Ravallion, M. 1988. ''Expected Poverty under Risk-Induced Welfare Variability.'' *Economic Journal* 98:1171–82.

Ravallion, M., and L. Dearden. 1988. ''Social Security in a 'Moral Economy': An Empirical Analysis for Java.'' *The Review of Economics and Statistics* 70:36–44.

Raymond, S. U., B. Lewis, P. Meissner, and J. Norris. 1987. *Financing and Costs of Health Services in Belize.* USAID Contract No. LAC 0632-C-00-5137-00, HCF/LAC Report. Stony Brook, New York: State University of New York at Stony Brook.

Rice, D. P. 1965. ''Estimating Costs of Cardiovascular Diseases and Cancer 1962.'' In *Report to the President, a National Program to Conquer Heart Disease, Cancer and Stroke* Vol. 2. Washington, D.C.: United States Government Printing Office.

———. 1966. *Estimating the Cost of Illness.* Public Health Service Publication No. 947-6. Washington, D.C.: United States Department of Health, Education and Welfare.

———. 1967. ''Estimating the Cost of Illness.'' *American Journal of Public Health* 57(3):424–40.

———. 1969. ''Measurement and Application of Illness Costs.'' *Public Health Reports* 84(2):95–101.

Rice, D. P., and B. S. Cooper. 1967. ''The Economic Value of Human Life.'' *American Journal of Public Health* 57(11):1954–66.

Rosenfield, P. L., F. Golladay, and R. K. Davidson. 1984. ''The Economics of Parasitic Diseases: Research Priorities.'' *Social Science and Medicine* 19(10):1117–26.

Rosenzweig, M. R. 1988. ''Risk, Implicit Contracts and the Family in Rural Areas of Low-Income Countries.'' *Economic Journal* 98:1148–70.

Rumel. 1987. ''Indicadores de Mortalidade per Categoria Occupacional e Nivel Social–Estado de São Paulo–1980–82.'' Dissertação de Mestrado, Universidade de São Paulo.

Sahn, D. E., and H. Alderman. 1988. ''The Effect of Human Capital on Wages, and the Determinants of Labor Supply in a Developing Country.'' *Journal of Development Studies* 29(2):157–83.

Scott, J. 1976. *The Moral Economy of the Peasant. Rebellion and Subsistence in Southeast Asia.* New Haven: Yale University Press.

Smith, Adam. 1776. ''An Inquiry into the Nature and Causes of the Wealth of Nations.'' *Works and Correspondence of Adam Smith* Vol. II. Oxford: Clarendon Press.

Starr, A. 1987. *Preventing the Tragedy of Maternal Deaths: A Report on the International Safe Motherhood Conference.* Nairobi, Kenya: World Health Organization.

Stevens, C. M. 1977. ''Health and Economic Development: Longer-Run View.'' *Social Science and Medicine* 11:809–17.

Strauss, J. 1986. ''Does Better Nutrition Raise Farm Productivity?'' *Journal of Political Economy* 94(2):297–320.

Tu, P. 1989. ''The Effects of Breastfeeding and Birth Spacing on Child Survival in China.'' *Studies in Family Planning* 20(6):332–42.

Vogel, L. C., A. S. Muller, R. S. Odingo, Z. Onyango, and A. de Geus, eds. 1974. *Health and Disease in Kenya.* Nairobi: East African Literature Bureau.

Walsh, J. A. 1988. *Establishing Health Priorities in the Developing World.* United Nations Development Program Task Force for Child Survival. New York: United Nations.

Wasserheit, J. N. 1989. "The Significance and Scope of Reproductive Tract Infections among Third World Women." *International Journal of Gynecology and Obstetrics* Supplement 3:145–68.

Williams, E. H., R. J. Hayes, and P. G. Smith. 1986. "Admissions to a Rural Hospital in the West Nile District of Uganda over a 27 Year Period." *Journal of Tropical Medicine and Hygiene* 89(4):193–211.

Wong, H. 1989. *Cost Analysis of Niamey Hospital.* USAID Project No. 683-0254. Washington, D.C.: Abt Associates.

World Bank. 1989a. "China: Long-term Issues and Options in the Health Transition." Report No. 7965-CHA. Washington, D.C.

———. 1989b. "Costa Rica: Public Sector Expenditure Review." Report No. 7877. Washington, D.C.

———. 1989c. "Korea: Health Insurance and the Health Sector." Report No. 7412-KO. Washington, D.C.

———. 1990. "Federal Republic of Nigeria: Health Care Cost, Financing and Utilization." Report No. 8382-UNI. Washington, D.C.

Zschock, D. K. 1986. "Medical Care under Social Insurance in Latin America." *Latin American Research Review* 21(1):99–122.

5. Current and Future Determinants of Adult Ill-Health

Tord Kjellstrom, Jeffrey P. Koplan, and
Richard B. Rothenberg

As previous chapters demonstrate, adults in developing countries experience substantially higher mortality than do adults in developed countries. The consequences of adult ill-health extend well beyond the affected individuals and their immediate families. Increased consumption of medical care distorts the balance between preventive and curative services, and has a negative effect on development itself. Yet many adult health problems are associated with determinants that can be reduced or eliminated. This chapter provides an overview of these determinants—recognizing that data specific to developing countries may not be available in some instances—and shows how their amelioration can reduce the loss of human capital.

Introductory Issues

The data presented in chapter 2 show that there is a negative correlation between economic development and overall adult mortality. This is seen both in cross-sectional analyses comparing countries at different development levels and in longitudinal analyses of time trends within countries. Communicable disease mortality shows the most consistent decrease with economic development. Injury mortality appears to be stable or, in some instances, increasing. The trend for noncommunicable disease is less clear, but noncommunicable mortality has declined in aggregate and for most specific causes. Noncommunicable diseases and injuries play an increasingly important role during periods of transition—that is, they have an increasing share of the decreasing burden. This changing pattern is due mainly to the demographic component of the health transition, as discussed in chapter 1.

Identifying the Determinants: The Basis of Prevention

This chapter, however, concentrates on the risk factor component. Three major trends in determinants of adult ill-health in developing countries can be identified. First, there has been a steady decrease in the importance of the traditional health hazards, such as disease vectors, poor sanitation and housing, and dietary deficiences. Second, there is the potential for a major increase in the modern health hazards, such as tobacco smoking, motor vehicle collisions, and environmental pollution. Third, there is the effect of the therapeutic component of the health transition—namely, the changing pattern of use and effectiveness of curative services.

This chapter gives examples of how specific determinants cause specific adult health problems in developing countries. In doing so, the chapter refers to past situations in developed countries. The influence that modern health hazards have had on adult ill-health in developed countries is relevant for the future health trends of many developing countries. The epidemics of lung cancer from tobacco smoking, injuries from motor vehicle collisions, and mesothelioma from asbestos in the workplace are being controlled in developed countries, but not so in developing countries where they are just starting to emerge.

As the title of this chapter indicates, developing countries need to consider both current determinants (mainly traditional health hazards) and future determinants (modern health hazards) to deal effectively with adult ill-health. This creates extra difficulties in setting priorities, because the benefits from preventing the health effects of future determinants may only be fully realized many years later. Conversely, developing countries have an opportunity to deal with future determinants before they cause the serious health effects that they have caused in developed countries. For instance, the public health effect of tobacco smoking in developed countries only became known at a stage when smoking habits were already widespread, and the entrenched interests of the tobacco industry made it difficult to reduce this determinant of adult ill-health. In those developing countries in which tobacco smoking is still rare, an opportunity exists to prevent smoking habits from becoming widespread. This is likely to be a lesser task than turning back the tide at a later stage.

A broad definition of the term *determinant* is used in this chapter. A determinant is any factor that can directly or indirectly cause or influence the progression of ill-health. The focus is on major determinants that can be controlled so that health can be improved. The mere existence of a determinant (e.g., motor vehicles, a determinant of injuries) does not necessarily lead to a fixed incidence of adverse health outcomes (for example, injuries). The effect can be attenuated by various factors (for example, speed limits, seat belts, quality of roads, driving behavior). Thus, countries with very similar determinants (for example, per capita motor vehicle densities) may have great differences in the rates of mortality and morbidity caused by these determinants. This attenuation of the effect of a determinant has been called the intervention transition (Kjellstrom and Rosenstock 1990). Because specific interventions often have limited consequences when used separately, attenuation of the effects of a determinant often can be improved by the simultaneous use of several interventions.

For some diseases and health conditions, an individual's genotype appears to influence susceptibility and severity. Such genetic predisposition may act by modifying a risk factor for disease, such as the tendency to have high or low serum cholesterol or blood pressure. It may also influence a disease directly, as in sickle cell disease. The 1990s will see an explosion in the understanding of the genetic basis of susceptibility to disease.

For many of the determinants, preventing adult ill-health is linked strongly to preventing the ill-health of children and the elderly. Improvements in indoor air quality, housing, sanitation, traffic safety, and maternal health benefit all age groups, either directly or indirectly. Actions to improve adult health therefore should not be seen as competing with actions to improve child health. In addition, preventive actions can contribute to health equity by focusing on those determinants that are of greatest importance in the least developed countries or in underprivileged sections in developed countries.

The actual effectiveness of preventive action depends on the interaction of a number of factors—determinants, conditions, tools, skills, and resources. Not only must the determinants, and their interaction with target conditions, be understood. Tools for disease control must be developed in the locality, and their fundamental technology must be appropriate to local circumstances. Skills and resources must be mobilized to deliver the preventive program. Many of these factors are not directly quantifiable, and recommendations for developing nations must frequently rest on relevant information from developed countries and qualitative assessment of local circumstances. The recommendations in chapter 6 recognize this multifactorial process and present those interventions that have the greatest chance for immediate success.

The Underlying Socioeconomic Factors: Poverty and Adult Ill-Health

Several examples of poverty as a determinant for adult ill-health are given in the preceding chapters. The cross-sectional and longitudinal analyses in chapter 2 show that 45Q15 decreases as economic development progresses in different countries. Detailed data from one developing country, China, also show that people with lower incomes have higher mortality rates than people with higher incomes. This inverse correlation between mortality and income is present for all three groups of causes of death. The greatest relative reduction of mortality with higher income is seen with communicable and reproductive diseases (Group I). In the least developed countries and among the poorest people, much of adult mortality is due to communicable and reproductive diseases—mainly tuberculosis, maternal causes, diarrheal diseases and respiratory infections. These diseases of the poor are also major killers of children, and the associated specific determinants are the same for children and adults: lack of safe drinking water and food, poor sanitation, poor housing conditions, undernutrition, chronic parasitic infection, and lack of effective curative services. Economic development has helped meet these basic human needs in the past and must continue to do so in the future. Most adults in developing countries are still at risk from these traditional hazards.

Higher mortality rates among the poor are caused also by noncommunicable diseases. As pointed out in chapter 2, adult mortality rates from these diseases are lower in developed countries than in developing countries. The specific determinants of these differences are difficult to ascertain, but poor nutrition, stress, indoor air pollution (in certain countries), smoking, and workplace hazards are important factors. Access to effective medical care is likely also to have a considerable influence on mortality from noncommunicable diseases.

There is no reason to believe that the association between socioeconomic status and health is due to genetic factors or that low status itself leads to disease, except in so far as low socioeconomic status may reduce people's expectations of health. The lower health status of the poor is likely to be caused by greater exposures to specific determinants, often superimposed upon a nonspecific increase in susceptibility, reflecting such things as long-term dietary deprivation and recurrent infections.

Illness itself may lead to lower socioeconomic status (see chapters 3 and 4). The interaction between ill-health and poverty may make it extremely difficult for affected individuals to improve their situations, reflecting the vicious cycle of poverty, unhealthy environments, and ill-health. This interaction between poverty and environment has been highlighted in the report of the World Commission for Environment and Development—also called the Brundtland Commission (WCED 1987). Poor living conditions and rapid population increases have led to overuse of agricultural lands and destruction of forests. Some industrialization projects have compounded these problems by causing pollution that further reduces the availability of food and firewood. Improved adult health in developing countries requires action against poverty itself as well as action against specific determinants.

The Impact of Case Management

The availability of health services that treat the sick and rehabilitate the impaired is important to adult health. Many deaths occuring in developing countries could be avoided with appropriate treatment. For some diseases, treatment and appropriate case monitoring may be more cost-effective than prevention. For many infectious and some vector-borne diseases (such as tuberculosis and malaria), the treatment of the sick is in itself a part of the prevention of the spread of the disease. Of the different approaches for controlling tuberculosis, existing diagnostic techniques and therapeutic drugs can be used effectively in developing countries to cure tuberculosis, making good case management an effective intervention for this disease (Murray, Rouillon, and Styblo forthcoming). Improving housing and reducing crowding help reduce tuberculosis, but these measures alone are insufficient.

The situation is quite different for chronic obstructive lung disease (COPD) according to Bumgarner and Speizer (forthcoming), for which case finding and treatment have mainly a palliative and rehabilitative effect. Reducing COPD morbidity and mortality requires actions to reduce smoking, air pollution, and occupational dust exposures. Acute respiratory infections and pneumonia can be prevented also by reducing air pollution, but, as for tuberculosis, drugs are effective in treating these infections, and the availability of drugs has been an important factor in the reduction of the mortality caused by these diseases.

The dramatic improvements in maternal health that occur with development (chapter 2) may be due to a combination of reduced fertility rates and improved prenatal and obstetric care (Walsh and others forthcoming). Family planning programs for reducing fertility are required. So are effective screening programs for detecting high risk mothers and better facilities and better trained staff for dealing with emergencies during birth. Similarly, medical care that targets the needs of other specific groups (for example, rehabilitation therapy for people with injuries or musculoskeletal disorders, treatment for diabetics, pain relief for people with cancer) improves the health and functional status of people who might otherwise be totally incapacitated.

The absence of adequate medical care is not a determinant for all adult ill-health problems. For example, the mortality rates of stomach cancer and lung cancer appear to be affected very little by different types of treatment (Stanley, Stjernsward, and Koroltchouk 1988). However, early detection and treatment of breast cancer does play a role in reducing mortality. This is the purpose of screening. The cost-effectiveness of breast cancer screening or any screening program needs to be evaluated before screening is implemented. Many screening programs assume that sophisticated medical care facilities are available to treat the cases identified by the screening. If such facilities are not available, the screening may achieve nothing. On the other hand, if the medical services required to restore or protect the health of cases found by screening are economical and can be made available easily, then screening may be an effective tool in adult health protection.

Assessing the Importance of Different Determinants

In setting priorities for prevention in developing countries, governments and development agencies must consider the relative importance of different determinants and the effectiveness and cost of interventions. To assess which determinants are most important for a developing country, the following questions must be asked.

- *Does this determinant cause a high individual risk?* Tobacco smoking increases the risk of lung cancer tenfold and doubles the risk of heart disease. These are substantial increases in individual risk. Similarly, certain workplace hazards (e.g., the use of organic solvents in inadequately ventilated areas) create very high risks of acute poisoning and brain damage.
- *Is the exposure widespread in the population?* Widespread exposure plus high individual risk is the worst combination. Widespread exposure at low individual risk may lead to few cases with serious effects and few deaths but to a large number of cases with less serious effects. An example is exposure to lead. The general environmental contamination caused by the use of lead in gasoline and lead solder in food cans increases the lead exposure of the population. The exposure is not sufficient to cause acute poisoning, but many children may suffer minor brain dysfunction. This is in contrast to the high exposures, which may lead to acute poisoning and brain damage, of a relatively small number of lead industry workers.
- *Is the exposure likely to increase or decrease in the future?* For noncommunicable diseases, the current disease pattern is the product of past exposures. Changes in smoking habits, motor vehicle use, and occupational hazards change the disease pattern of the future and make analysis restricted to the current adult ill-health pattern mis-

leading. Prevention priorities must include those determinants that will cause increasingly more ill-health in the future.

• *Is it feasible and cost-effective to reduce the exposure?* Some exposures that have major health consequences may be more difficult to control than exposures with less effect. The latter may be the first priority for action because the control can be done at low cost and with a high degree of success. Reducing drunk driving in a country in which alcohol consumption is high may be difficult to accomplish. For such countries, introducing other traffic safety measures, such as seat belt legislation, may be more cost-effective. If seat belts may not be accepted readily, controlling traffic speed may be more cost-effective.

As a rule, an effective program to protect health must be multifaceted and take advantage of different opportunities to reduce ill-health. A number of specific determinants should be considered in prevention programs, and the questions listed above should be answered for each of these determinants. The prevention process is dynamic because exposures change with time. Thus, epidemiologic monitoring programs are essential and descriptive data on exposures and health status should be evaluated regularly to set the best priorities for local action.

Lifestyle factors, such as tobacco and alcohol use, are voluntary exposures in that people choose them. Such exposures may be seen as less important for government action than exposures that people do not choose and cannot easily escape, such as urban air pollution. However, the advertising and other marketing practices of tobacco and alcohol manufacturers encourage people, especially the young, to start and continue using these substances. When people choose to smoke or drink, they do so in an environment of conflicting promotional messages in which the message to smoke or drink is often put across more frequently and persuasively than the message not to smoke or drink. In addition, depending upon the system of health care financing in a particular country, the costs of treating the disease caused by voluntary exposures may be paid with public funds, thus providing the government with a strong incentive to intervene.

Major Determinants at Early Stages of Development

The least developed countries need an intensive effort to reduce the effect of traditional hazards. Disease vectors still threaten many adults by spreading tropical diseases, such as malaria, schistosomiasis, onchocerciasis, filariasis, leishmaniasis, African trypanosomiasis and Chagas disease. Climatic and geographic conditions determine whether people in a specific country are at risk for a particular disease. About one half of the world's population (2.2 billion people) live in areas in which malaria can occur, and more than 100 million people (mostly the rural poor) are affected each year (WHO 1987a). The reduced productivity of adults who have malaria may affect economic development in endemic areas (chapter 4). Other tropical diseases, such as Chagas disease, also affect millions of people.

In high risk areas, mosquitos, flies, snails and other animals that spread these diseases are endemic and cannot be eliminated with a single method. Chemical pesticides (particularly DDT) were used extensively in the 1960s to try to eradicate malaria, but after initial success, the incidence of the disease increased again as mosquitos became resistant to the pesticide, the parasite became resistant to the drugs, and health services could not cope with the resurgence of cases. This experience emphasized the importance of good case-finding and treatment as well as vector control. Impregnated bed-nets are increasingly used in control programs in Africa and Asia.

The Precarious Coexistence With Infectious Disease

Tuberculosis is one of the most important infectious diseases of adults and contributes to the high adult mortality risks in developing countries. Without treatment, the case-fatality rate is more than 50 percent (Murray, Rouillon, and Styblo forthcoming). Infection is life-long and reactivations cause severe clinical illness. Early drug treatment is very effective if sustained for a long time (months to years). The spread of tuberculosis is associated with crowding and poor housing conditions, and better socioeconomic and environmental conditions reduced the incidence and mortality of tuberculosis considerably before antibiotics were available (McKeown 1976). Infection as well as the development of clinical tuberculosis are facilitated by weakened immune systems. Poor nutrition, silicosis, other lung diseases, and infection with the human immunodeficiency virus (HIV) increase the incidence and severity of tuberculosis. In communities with a high prevalence of tuberculosis, the first indication of an increase in HIV transmission is likely to be an increased incidence of tuberculosis (WHO 1989b).

Other major contributors to high adult mortality and morbidity rates in developing countries are respiratory infections other than tuberculosis (chapters 2 and 3). Crowded and poor housing conditions increase the incidence of these diseases. Family members infect each other, and for these diseases, poor child health leads to poor adult health. Serious bacterial respiratory diseases (e.g., pneumonia) often develop in conjunction with a viral respiratory disease or at a late stage of debilitating chronic disease, such as heart disease or cancer. The recorded cause of death may be pneumonia or the primary disease, depending on local recording practices, and this contributes to the difficulties of comparing mortality data from different countries (see chapter 2). The case-fatality rate of pneumonia depends on the treatment given. Antibiotics are effective, and a large part of the difference in pneumonia mortality rates between developing and developed countries, particularly among younger adults, is likely to be the lack of treatment in developing countries.

Diarrheal diseases are also important causes of adult morbidity and mortality in the least developed countries (Martinez, Phillips, and Feachem forthcoming). The conditions that facilitate the transmission of these diseases are all related to poverty and unhealthy living conditions.

Unfinished Business: Providing the Basic Necessities for a Healthy Life

From 1990 to 2025, the urban population in developing countries will almost triple (from 1.4 billion to 3.8 billion), and the rural population will increase about 10 percent, from 2.7 billion to 3.0 billion (United Nations 1987b). Most of the new urban residents will live in slums, marginal housing or without shelter, conditions that will result in serious health problems (Tabibzadeh, Rossi-Espagnet, and Maxwell 1989). As rural people emigrate to cities, their social structures break down. Single parent households become common, and the missing support structures for child care and care of sick family members create severe stress, particularly for women. The adult health problems associated with urbanization cannot be solved solely by actions in urban areas. Poor conditions in rural areas are a major reason for migration to cities. Improved conditions in rural areas might slow migration and make it possible to provide better for people in the poor areas of cities.

Another problem caused by unsatisfactory shelter and housing is indoor air pollution from cooking and heating with wood, cow dung, low grade coal, or agricultural waste (Anon 1990a; WHO 1984). The design of kitchens and stoves in many of the poorest communities creates substantial smoke exposure, particularly for women (appendix 5-A). Three hundred million to 400 million people may be at risk from using such types of biomass fuel (WHO 1984), and an additional 400 million people in China may be exposed to coal smoke from stoves without chimneys. The main health effects of such exposure are COPD, carbon monoxide poisoning and lung cancer (WHO 1984).

Studies in India and Nepal have shown strong associations between smoke from kitchen stoves and COPD and that women are affected more than men, despite women's lower rates of tobacco smoking. In many cases, COPD leads to a secondary heart condition, cor pulmonale. This is one of the most common types of heart disease in northern India (WHO 1984), and it is particularly common among women. A number of studies linking indoor air pollution to health effects have been carried out in China (Chen and others 1990; appendix 5-A). Because high exposures to indoor air pollution are very common in China, mortality rates from COPD and pulmonary heart disease are high for both men and women, despite women's low tobacco use (chapter 2, table 2-16).

Water and food pollution in developing countries (associated with poor waste disposal, poor sanitation, and lack of water treatment and food hygiene) creates a major problem of diarrheal disease, particularly among children but also among adults. In some countries with high total 45Q15, such as India, diarrheal diseases are a major cause of death among adults (chapter 2, table 2-14). These diseases also can be a major cause of morbidity, even when mortality has decreased. Epidemics of typhoid fever, cholera, and other severe diarrheal diseases continue to be major threats in many developing countries, and many people die because treatment is unavailable. A recent example is the large epidemic of cholera that occurred in Peru in 1991, which also seriously undermined the Peruvian economy. Less severe diarrheal diseases reduce adult productivity and increase adults' dependency on other members of the family (chapter 3). Diarrheal diseases spread via water and food contaminated with feces and via direct contact with infected people when personal hygiene is poor. The supply of safe drinking water and the protection of food during production, transport, storage, and preparation reduce these diseases (Huttly 1990). However, most studies of such interventions concern children's health, and the results are not consistent (Feachem 1984; Martinez, Phillips and Feachem forthcoming). The technology for filtering and protecting water supplies is well known, and a number of appropriate methods are available for developing countries (Drangert and Lundquist 1990). Appropriate methods for ensuring food safety are also available, but may be difficult to implement successfully because of the great potential for food contamination during preparation.

In spite of a major effort by international agencies during the 1980s, which was designated the International Drinking Water Supply and Sanitation Decade, about half of the population in developing country urban areas still lacks safe water and adequate sanitation (WHO 1987c). The proportion in rural areas is even greater. About 85 percent of people in rural areas have inadequate sanitation. Population proportions provided with these services increased between 1980 and 1985, but due to the population increase, the number of people who lack safe water and adequate sanitation is increasing. In 1985, about 1.1 billion people were without safe water, and 1.7 billion were without basic sanitation.

Hunger: A Persistent Threat

Malnutrition and deficiency diseases are important problems in developing countries because of deficient diets. To a great extent these are health hazards for children, but many adults are affected also, and childhood dietary deficiencies may lead to adult ill-health. The major hazards affecting both children and adults are protein-energy malnutrition (PEM) and vitamin A, iodine and iron deficiencies (WHO 1990c).

PEM affects a large proportion of the developing world population (Burger and others forthcoming). PEM is caused by a combination of insufficient food intake and infectious diseases and is related closely to inadequate knowledge, poor sanitation, poverty and insufficient access to health care. Several intervention programs have focused on PEM in children (Burger and others forthcoming). One program in India reduced the prevalence of PEM in young children from 19 to 12 percent as the prevalence in a control area increased from 16 to 30 percent (Berg 1987).

The prevalence of PEM among adults in the least developed countries is high, although the exact level is unknown. The worst situation occurs in Africa; in 1980, 23 percent of the African population was undernourished (Burger and others forthcoming). Even if most of the affected are children, several million adults are likely to have inadequate food for maintaining their health and remaining minimally active. The situation is worse for women in societies in which women eat less well than men and children.

It is hard to measure what effect supplementing adult diets with protein and energy might have on improving productivity. However, results from a few econometric analyses show a positive effect of reduced energy deficits (Burger and others forthcoming). Transfers resulting from food pricing and subsidy policies and from food stamp programs significantly reduce PEM in adults as well as children. Well-designed and well-funded education programs have improved nutritional status also.

Vitamin A deficiency is widely prevalent in the developing world. This deficiency causes considerable childhood morbidity and mortality. Blindness caused by vitamin A deficiency in childhood later contributes significantly to adult impairment (chapter 3, figures 3-2 to 3-4). Moreover, vitamin A (or beta carotene) may play an important role in reducing cancer risk.

Iodine deficiency is widespread in developing countries. It causes goiter, a severe disease of the thyroid gland manifested as thyroid enlargement and hormonal disturbances including cretinism. Even mild iodine deficiency can decrease child survival, slow physical and intellectual development, and lead to diminished adult productivity. About one billion people (children and adults) in more than eighty countries are at risk of iodine deficiency (Hetzel 1983). Severe iodine deficiency causes endemic cretinism, a condition characterized by irreversible mental deficiency and other neurological impairment.

Iron deficiency is widespread also, with possibly 460 million adults affected worldwide (WHO 1990c). Iron deficiency leads to anemia, which limits both children's and adults' capacities for physical activity. Iron deficiency also impairs intellectual development, reduces immune competence, and increases susceptibility to infection. The amount of iron available in the diet in developing countries is decreasing rather than increasing (United Nations 1987a; WHO 1990c).

Giving Birth: A Frequent and High Risk Activity

Diseases and death related to pregnancy complications cause a substantial share of avoidable mortality (chapter 2). In rural India, as much as 10 percent of adult female mortality is related to childbirth (chapter 2, table 2-14). The maternal mortality ratio (the number of maternal deaths per 100 thousand live births) is in the range of 100 to 2,000 in developing countries, compared with less than 30 in most developed countries. The lifetime risk of dying of maternal causes (which combines maternal mortality ratios with fertility rates) is 1 in 20 in much of Africa and 1 in ten thousand in northern Europe. As seen in a study in Nigeria (Harrison 1985), the most common causes of maternal morbidity and mortality are uncontrolled bleeding, incomplete delivery, and infection. The effect of these complications of pregnancy and childbirth is reduced if the pregnant woman is well nourished and in good health. But a substantial reduction of maternal mortality requires access to health care services for the early detection and treatment of complications. Properly trained staff in primary health care settings can greatly reduce maternal mortality caused by pregnancy complications, as seen for instance in Jamaica (Walker and others 1986).

Induced abortions create a major health hazard for women in developing countries. It is exceptionally difficult to obtain data on induced abortions, especially in countries in which abortion is legally or socially prohibited. Most statistics come from the complications of abortion. Crude estimates indicate a ratio of abortions to thousand live births varying from 9 in east Africa to 325 in Latin America (Rochat and others 1980) to more than 1,000 in parts of the Czech and Slovak Federal Republic (Feachem and Preker 1991). Induced abortion is estimated to be directly responsible for 7 to 50 percent (median, 15 percent) of all maternal deaths in developing countries (WHO 1986). The prospects for improving the situation involve the legalization of abortion and the provision of safe, accessible and affordable services, and/or the increased availability and use of contraception to avoid unwanted pregnancies (Feachem, Graham, and Timaeus 1989).

To deal with these problems, a number of international agencies established the Safe Motherhood Initiative (Starrs 1987), which aims to reduce the health risks of pregnancy and childbirth worldwide. The actions proposed by this initiative include better community-based health care, referral facilities, and emergency referral and transport systems (Herz and Measham 1987). The initiative stresses the importance of good nutrition and prenatal health care as the most important methods of reducing the need for emergency interventions at childbirth.

Being an Unhealthy Child

In general, poor and disadvantaged children become poor and disadvantaged adults. There is growing interest in the hypothesis that sick children become sick adults and the implications that intervening in child health might have for improving adult health. Evidence is growing that small children (of low body mass index and height) become small adults and that smaller adults have higher age-specific mortality rates (Beaton 1989). This relationship has been investigated in, for example, Norway (Waaler 1984) and Brazil (de Azevedo 1989). In urban Bangladesh, an association was found between increased morbidity and low body mass index (Pryer 1990). Links between specific childhood illness and cause-specific adult mortality have been suggested—for example, between childhood nutrition and adult ischemic heart disease in England and Wales (Barker and Osmond 1986). However, such links are generally geographically (or ecologically) determined and are difficult to interpret. Is adult mortality higher because these adults were deprived as children or because the conditions of deprivation still exist and affect them as adults? One study in the United Kingdom indicated that the latter explanation might be more likely (Ben-Shlomo and Davey Smith 1991). These issues have been recently reviewed (Elford, Whincup, and Shaper

1991). Not in question is the fact that chronic pathology acquired in childhood—for example, from infection or trauma—affects the health of adults (see chapter 3, figures 3-2 through 3-4).

Other Traditional Health Hazards of Adults

Determinants such as transportation hazards, environmental pollution, workplace hazards and violence have been common during the early stages of development in some developing countries. These hazards are described in the following section on emerging determinants. The types of injuries and diseases caused by such determinants in developing countries differ from those in developed countries, and their overall health consequences are probably greater. A lack of awareness about such hazards places developing country adults at greater risk of injury and disease, and the lack of emergency medical care in developing countries increases the severity of the outcomes.

Natural toxins in grains, nuts, toadstools, and seafood have caused mass outbreaks of poisoning in several countries. These hazards may increase when the foods at risk are transported and sold in distant markets. The industrialization of food production and distribution may lead to large-scale chemical contamination of foods. Bacterial contamination can also affect large amounts of food and result in bacterial food poisonings, including botulism, which is difficult to diagnose and highly fatal. Poisoning may result also from the drinking of home distilled alcohol that contains methanol or from the intentional sniffing of gasoline vapors that contain tetraethyl lead.

Burns are a major cause of injuries for women in developing countries (chapter 2, table 2-14). Many of these injuries involve open flame stoves (e.g., pressurized kerosene stoves) and flammable loose clothing. In India, about half of the fatal burns among young Hindu housewives involve these two risk factors; the other half are the result of murder or forced suicides related to marital disharmony (Stansfield, Smith, and McGreevey forthcoming).

Drownings and falls are important causes of adult deaths. Distinguishing whether these deaths are unintentional or suicides can be difficult. Some are associated with epilepsy and some with alcohol consumption. In urban areas of developing countries, the design of windows and verandas may increase the risk of falls. Hong Kong has a relatively high incidence of falls (Stansfield, Smith, and McGreevey forthcoming), which may reflect the large proportion of its population that lives in highrise apartments. In island countries and countries with large fishing industries, mortality rates from drowning are high.

Other hazards include animal bites, snake bites, guns, sharp agricultural tools and, increasingly, various types of sports. These are more likely to be important causes of temporary impairment rather than death, although skin wounds may lead to fatal infection from tetanus bacilli commonly found in soil. Tetanus can be prevented by preexposure vaccination or treated by prompt vaccination after an injury has occurred. Tetanus vaccination is a highly cost-effective means of reducing maternal and other adult mortality (Steinglass and others, forthcoming).

Major Determinants Emerging With Economic Development

Economic development brings the so-called modern determinants of adult ill-health. These arise mainly from changes in behavior and from the hazards of new and imperfectly understood technology.

Developing Unhealthy Habits

Changes in behavior can give rise to the development of unhealthy habits.

TOBACCO USE. The causal relationship between tobacco smoking and several major noncommunicable diseases is well established (USDHHS 1989; WHO 1988b). Cigarette smoking causes lung and laryngeal cancer, coronary heart disease, COPD, peripheral vascular disease, oral cancer, esophageal cancer, intrauterine fetal growth retardation, and low birthweight babies. Cigarette smoking is a probable cause of unsuccessful pregnancies, increased infant mortality, and peptic ulcer disease. It is a contributing factor for cancer of the bladder, pancreas, and kidney, and is associated with cancer of the stomach and the cervix. Smokeless tobacco, in the form of snuff and chewing tobacco, causes oral cancer. Involuntary smoking has been established as a cause of disease, including lung cancer, in nonsmokers and leads to an increased incidence of respiratory illness among children living with smokers. Cigarette smoking and other forms of tobacco use are addictive and constitute the most common form of drug dependency in the world.

Tobacco consumption in different countries during 1970 to 1985 was reviewed by Masironi and Rothwell (1988). In North America, much of western Europe, Australia, and New Zealand, annual cigarette consumption decreased 5 to 10 percent from about three thousand cigarettes per capita in 1970. The reverse was true in developing countries. Per capita consumption increased by about 40 percent in

Africa (from about five hundred cigarettes per year in 1970) and by about 20 percent in Asia and Latin America (from about one thousand cigarettes per year in 1970). Reasons for the decreasing per capita consumption in developed countries include the antismoking measures and campaigns carried out in these countries (Warner 1989). It should be remembered that the protobacco advertising and sponsorship activities in these developed countries have continued despite legal restrictions. In developing countries, few restrictions on advertising and promotion of tobacco smoking are in place (Nath 1986), and consumption is likely to continue to increase.

The tar content of manufactured cigarettes in developed countries has decreased steadily during the last decades, which may have contributed to decreasing lung cancer rates in these countries (WHO 1988b). In developing countries, cigarette tar content is still high (IARC 1986), making smoking more hazardous than in developed countries.

The overall effect tobacco smoking has on health is substantial (chapter 2, appendix 2-D). In Europe, 500 thousand people die each year because of tobacco smoking (WHO 1988b), and worldwide the figure is about three million (Peto and Lopez 1990). By 2025, about ten million people—many of whom will be adults in developing countries—will die each year because of tobacco smoking. China and India will have most of these deaths (Gupta and Ball 1990; World Bank 1989b). The possibilities for reducing tobacco use in the developing world are just beginning to be explored, and there are a few examples of early success (appendix 5-B).

ALCOHOL USE. Ethyl alcohol, the active ingredient in all alcoholic drinks, is a toxic organic compound with addictive properties. The consumption of alcohol may lead to a number of acute and chronic health problems as well as social problems. Alcohol use can cause acute alcohol poisoning (similar to poisoning from other organic solvents), suicidal behavior, and acute gastritis and contributes to injuries. Chronic alcohol exposure can cause liver cirrhosis, various psychiatric symptoms, dementia, stomach ulcers, pancreatitis, diabetes, fetal alcohol syndrome, and cancers of the gastrointestinal tract (Grant and Ritson 1983). Alcohol dependency can lead to debt, employment problems, family breakdown, homelessness, and social isolation.

In the United States, excessive alcohol consumption causes at least eleven thousand deaths from liver cirrhosis and twenty-five thousand deaths from traffic collisions annually (USDHHS 1983). The risk of illness and injury increases with the amount of daily consumption (WHO 1980). People who take more than two drinks of spirits (or the equivalent in beer and wine) per day have more serious health effects. Cancers of the esophagus and other parts of the gastrointestinal tract are strongly associated with alcohol consumption (IARC 1988).

Individual alcohol consumption is distributed unevenly in all countries. A few people consume most of the alcohol (Walsh and Grant 1985). In New Zealand, for example, 11 percent of the population drinks more than half of the alcohol. The consumption of home brewed or distilled alcohol, not included in official statistics, may mean heavy drinkers consume even more alcohol (Walsh and Grant 1985), and some of this may be contaminated by toxic substances (Nikander and others 1991).

Average alcohol consumption per capita is increasing in most countries. The increase is particularly large in developing countries and other countries that had low consumption rates thirty years ago (table 5-1). The adult health consequences of this trend are serious. In all countries and cultures, increases in potentially harmful drinking tend to accompany increases in average consumption (WHO 1980). Alcohol consumption habits of young adults set the scene for ill-health problems later in life. In addition, development itself is affected, because young urban people, particularly young males, are the first to adopt heavy drinking patterns, thereby reducing the human resources available for development.

Table 5-1. Alcohol Consumption Per Capita in Selected Countries, 1960 and 1981
(liters/year)

Country	*1960*	*1981*
Beer consumption		
Denmark	71	131
Gabon	12	135
Mexico	23	40
Philippines	3	15
United States	58	93
Venezuela	36	80
West Germany	96	147
Spirits consumption[a]		
Hungary	1.4	4.8
Mexico	0.5	0.9
South Korea	0.7	5.4
Sweden	2.3	2.8
United States	2.1	3.0
West Germany	1.9	2.9

a. As 100 percent alcohol.
Source: Walsh and Grant (1985).

INTENTIONAL VIOLENCE: SUICIDES, HOMICIDES AND WARFARE. Suicides are major causes of death in both developed and developing countries. Worldwide, about one million adult suicides occur each year. Deaths from suicides represent only a small portion of suicidal behavior. In developed countries about 10 times as many people are admitted to hospitals for suicide attempts as the number who die from suicides. In many countries the incidence of suicidal behavior is increasing.

Several psychosocial factors contribute to suicidal behavior. Social isolation, crises (bereavement, unemployment, or other personal loss), depression, alcoholism, and other mental or social changes often precede suicidal behavior. People who give warnings of suicide or who attempt suicide are at high risk of dying from suicide, even though many of those who attempt suicide are relieved when their attempts do not succeed (WHO 1981a). Suicidal behavior is complex and few effective preventions are available, although some data suggest ''life-line'' telephone counseling services are useful (WHO 1981a). Good socioeconomic conditions and supportive community attitudes seem to play a great role in prevention. Further, it has been proposed that better health and social services and a reduction in the availability of lethal poisons will help to reduce the case-fatality rates, (WHO 1981a). As mentioned previously, easy access to highly toxic pesticides facilitates suicides in developing countries.

Adult homicide rates are associated with a variety of psychosocial factors, just as suicides are, but homicides vary more across countries, possibly reflecting differences in laws and cultures. Homicide rates are higher in most developing countries than in most developed countries. Homicide rates vary greatly within countries by gender (males have higher rates), income (the poor have higher rates), place of residence (urban areas have higher rates) and ethnicity.[1] Homicide is an extreme form of interpersonal violence. A much larger number of assaults, rapes and other violent attacks occur. Many of these are not reported because the victim fears retribution or social stigma. For these reasons, family violence in particular is likely to be underreported.

Warfare kills and disables adults in many developing countries, especially in the Middle East, southern Africa, Central America, and Southeast Asia. Accurate data are seldom available because of the difficulties of maintaining vital registration systems in war conditions and because of deliberate attempts to distort mortality statistics. Many of the current conflicts are internal, with open or hidden support from factions in other countries. Important phenomena in some countries are the conflicts between criminal gangs and police agencies or among the gangs themselves. The lucrative trade in illegal drugs has led to warfare of this type in both developed and developing countries, and the toll on adult health is substantial.

DIETARY IMBALANCE. As noted earlier, the major dietary problem in the developing world is lack of food. However, as nations develop, food supplies increase and diets change. Often, the new diet is characterized by more meat, animal fat and processed foods. The traditional diet, when adequate, usually consists of a source of carbohydrate such as rice, tapioca, or platano, a source of vegetable protein such as soy or lentil, and possibly some fish or meat. In comparison, the new diet is high in saturated fat, cholesterol, simple carbohydrates, and sodium and low in fiber (WHO 1990c).

Though debate continues concerning the exact role of nutrients and calories in disease causation, there is now considerable evidence to link this new diet with a number of important chronic diseases. Coronary heart disease (appendix 5-C), still the chief cause of mortality in many developed nations despite declines in recent years, is strongly linked to saturated fat and cholesterol in the diet. Hypertension is influenced substantially by obesity and high salt intake. Though an area of some controversy, ecologic evidence suggests an important association between fat in the diet and breast cancer. Other cancers—cancer of the colon, pancreas, and perhaps the lung—may be causally linked to fat as well; some protection against these cancers may be afforded by consumption of fruits and vegetables.

The role of calcium in osteoporosis, mediated through an interaction with estrogen and exercise, is well established. Similarly, the importance of fluoride in preventing dental disease has been clearly demonstrated. Excess calories may be as important as specific constituents of the diet. Obesity, particularly in its most severe form, is an important risk factor for premature mortality. The control of diabetes in adults is directly linked to dietary composition, but of greater interest is the potential for primary prevention of diabetes by prevention of excessive caloric intake. The specific role of obesity as a causative agent in other chronic disease is under active investigation. It seems clear, at the very least, that obesity may potentiate the effect of other risks, such as physical inactivity.

Early policy formation by developing nations may play a substantial role in mitigating the effects of dietary distortion. The behavioral changes required are straightforward. In a recent review (USDHHS 1988), a number of simple recommendations were made to promote better nutrition: eat a variety of foods; maintain desirable weight; avoid too much fat, saturated fat, and cholesterol; eat foods with adequate starch and fiber; avoid too much sugar and salt; drink alcohol only in moderation. But a variety of social and economic forces are brought to bear in a developing nation and can hamper individual efforts at dietary change. Nutritional policy, agricultural policy, and control of food distribution systems may play an even larger role in effecting behavioral change (WHO 1990c). By shaping the diet of the population, such policies may be particularly appropriate during a period of economic transition.

CHANGES IN PHYSICAL ACTIVITY. Regular physical activity promotes improved health. There is a growing body of evidence that regular physical activity, whether occupational, recreational, or part of daily chores, is associated with decreased risks of coronary heart disease (Powell and others 1987). Other studies suggest that risks for colon cancer, stroke, and hypertension are reduced and that exercise can assist in the management of persons with non-insulin-dependent diabetes mellitus, depression, and obesity. Physical fitness is associated with lower rates of all causes of mortality as well as cardiovascular disease and cancer mortality (Siscovich, La Porte, and Newman 1985).

In developing countries, most people have adequate physical activity (Koplan, Cooperson, and Powell 1989) in the routine aspects of their work, home life, and mode of transportation to confer a health benefit.[2] However, in more developed countries, levels of activity have been declining with the increased use of motor vehicles and labor-saving devices. Recent surveys in the United States indicate that fewer than 10 percent of Americans older than eighteen years have enough physical activity. Developing nations may need to monitor the levels of activity in their own populations and be prepared to develop programs aimed at encouraging activity and exercise if needed.

OTHER BEHAVIORAL RISKS. Many health and disease states are influenced by individual behavior, a health determinant sometimes referred to as "lifestyle." In a developed country context, *lifestyle* usually refers to individual choice in diet, physical activity, and use of tobacco, alcohol, and drugs and actions taken to prevent injuries. Thus, someone who chooses a diet low in fats, maintains a low body mass index, is physically active, does not use tobacco or drugs, drinks in moderation and not when driving a motor vehicle, and who always wears a seat belt when in an automobile would be considered as having a healthy lifestyle.

Behavior influences diseases as diverse as enteric infection and cervical cancer. Knowledge and practice of basic hygiene (for example, food handling and preparation, fecal disposal) markedly reduce diarrheal disease rates. Planned versus unplanned pregnancy and the use of contraception illustrate the importance of behavioral determinants. Monogamy or the use of condoms probably reduces the likelihood of papilloma virus infection of the cervix and the subsequent development of cervical cancer. Regular participation in cervical cancer screening increases the probability that if a cancer occurs, it will be detected early, in a premalignant or readily treatable stage.

AIDS: An Infectious Disease of New Dimensions

Among modern adult health hazards, AIDS poses particularly difficult problems. It is spread mainly via sexual intercourse,[3] has a very long incubation period, and has no effective cure or preventive immunization (Mann 1989). Health education about the use of condoms and other methods for safer sex is the main approach for controlling the spread of this disease. The AIDS epidemic is not directly linked to economic development. Some of the most affected countries are those that are least developed, but in some of them, it is the more wealthy and educated who are experiencing the highest rates of HIV infection.

The first case of AIDS was diagnosed in 1981. By 1991, more than one million cases of AIDS had occurred worldwide, and about nine million people had been infected with HIV (table 5-2). Approximately 50 percent of HIV-infected persons will develop AIDS within ten years (Moss and Bacchetti 1989), and it seems likely that the remainder will develop AIDS within fifteen to twenty years.

A major concern is the growth of HIV infection via heterosexual intercourse, which has so far been relatively uncommon in developed countries, but common in the developing countries of Sub-Saharan Africa. Among monogamous heterosexual couples in which one partner has HIV infection, the prevalence of HIV transmission is 10 to 50

Table 5-2. Global Distribution of the Number of People Estimated to Have HIV Infections and Reported or Estimated to Have AIDS as of April 1, 1991

Area	*HIV*	*AIDS (Reported)*	*AIDS (Estimated)*
Africa	>5,500,000	86,000	800,000
Americas	2,000,000	208,000	320,000
Asia	500,000	1,000	3,000
Europe	500,000	48,000	65,000
Oceania	30,000	<3,000	4,000
Total	<9,000,000	<350,000	<1,200,000

Source: WHO data.

Table 5-3. Age- and Sex-Specific Motor Vehicle Accident Mortality Rates (per 100,000) in Five Countries

	Age group				
Country	*15–24*	*25–34*	*35–44*	*45–54*	*55–64*
Chile					
Men	8.6	13.3	14.0	22.9	21.3
Women	2.2	2.0	2.3	2.8	2.2
Egypt					
Men	8.0	18.9	18.8	14.6	9.6
Women	2.2	2.3	2.3	2.3	4.2
Sri Lanka					
Men	8.8	13.7	18.1	18.2	19.2
Women	1.1	1.5	1.8	2.9	4.8
Switzerland					
Men	46.3	21.7	13.2	17.7	18.7
Women	11.5	4.4	2.8	4.2	8.4
United States					
Men	57.3	37.0	27.3	21.4	20.5
Women	19.4	10.7	8.5	8.5	9.7

Source: WHO (1989a).

percent without the use of condoms and spermicide (Piot and others 1987). Even after a single act of intercourse with an HIV-infected individual, the risk of infection may be as high as 3 to 14 percent, if either person has ulcerous lesions of venereal disease (Piot and others 1987). The foremost risk factors for AIDS are having more than one sexual partner and not using condoms.

The public health effect of the AIDS epidemic is substantial and growing (chapter 2, appendix 2-C). In some developing countries, particularly in Sub-Saharan Africa, AIDS is becoming one of the most common causes of death among young men and women (de Cock and others 1990). In some African countries, AIDS rates are higher among highly educated people holding key positions in local industry and government (Over and Piot forthcoming). Thus, the AIDS epidemic is a great threat to development as well as to the health of adults in developing countries (Okware 1988).

The Motorized Epidemic

Motor vehicle collisions are one of the major causes of adult mortality in the developing world (chapter 2), causing about 0.5 million deaths a year. Injuries from motor vehicle collisions affect ten to twenty-five times more people, with as many as half of these requiring hospitalization (United Nations 1989). About as many people have permanent impairments as die from motor vehicle collisions (Thorson 1975). As the number of motor vehicles increases in developing countries, the number of motor vehicle collisions causing injury and death is likely to increase. Analysis of crude traffic fatality rates and motor vehicle density (vehicles per thousand inhabitants) in twenty-one developing countries showed that in most countries one person is killed each year for every four hundred vehicles (WHO 1989a).

Types of motor vehicles, and consequently types of injuries from motor vehicle collisions, vary among developing countries. Countries with a high proportion of motorcycles and other unprotected vehicles (such as the countries in Southeast Asia) have higher risks of driver and passenger injury (WHO 1989a). Conversely, these countries are likely to have relatively lower injury rates for pedestrians, as cars and trucks generally cause more severe injuries in collisions involving pedestrians. For example, in a national survey of 765 motor vehicle collisions in Malaysia (Malaysia 1985), a country with a very high proportion of motorcycles, more than six hundred people were injured, of whom only 91 were pedestrians.

Differences in the age distribution of injuries (table 5-3) also reflect differences in motor vehicle use. Developed countries tend to have the highest mortality rates among those fifteen to twenty-four years

Figure 5-1. Incidence of Fatalities from Motor Vehicle Collisions in Relation to Number of Vehicles per Thousand Inhabitants

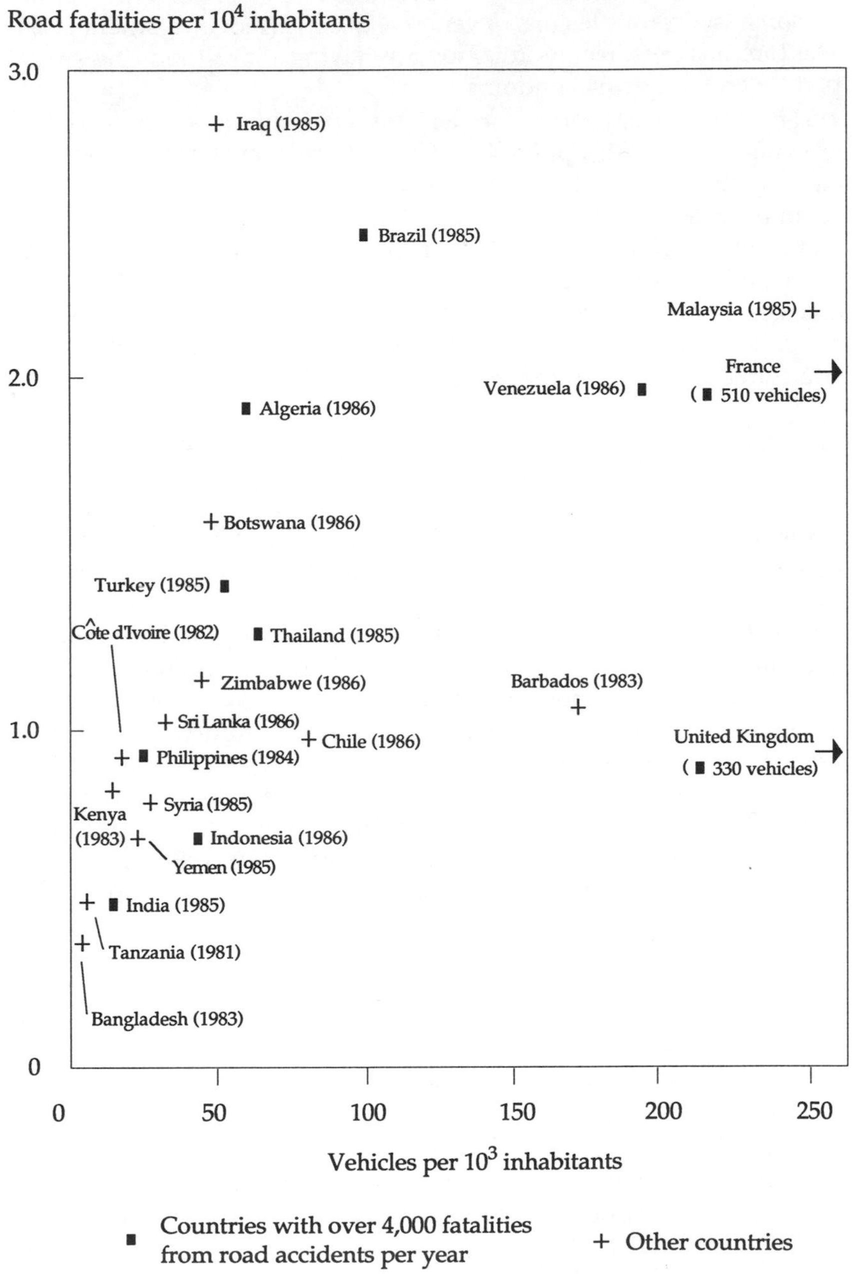

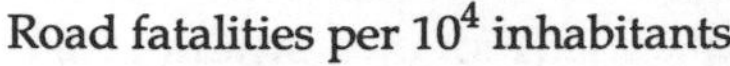

Source: WHO (1989a).

old, reflecting car ownership and travel patterns of young adults in these countries. In developing countries, the highest mortality rates occur after age twenty-five. In Chile and Sri Lanka, the rate increases throughout the adult years. When car ownership becomes more accessible for younger people in these countries, increases in injury rates will be particularly great for fifteen to twenty-four year olds.

Mortality rates in some developing countries (Barbados, Malaysia, and Venezuela) have increased more slowly as vehicle density has increased (figure 5-1), possibly because of enforced seat belt and crash helmet legislation and generally more advanced prevention programs (WHO 1989a). The same is likely to apply to developed countries, such as Sweden, France, and the United Kingdom, which in spite of high vehicle densities have relatively low traffic fatality rates. In the 1950s and 1960s, when mass car ownership was increasing in developed countries and the awareness of traffic safety was poor, the mortality rates and vehicle densities in these countries were similar to those of most developing countries today (WHO 1989a). Since the 1960s, several effective safety measures have been instituted in most developed countries. These include speed limits, car safety inspections, seat belts, improved roads and car design, and the use of running lights in daylight.

Future trends in motor vehicle collisions in developing countries will depend on vehicle densities and the preventive measures that are taken. If vehicle densities increase without effective safety measures, mortality rates will increase to levels much higher than those currently occurring in developed countries (appendix 5-D). Assuming some preventive actions will be taken, the contribution of motor vehicle collisions to adult mortality risk (45Q15) can be estimated. If a developing country progresses with vehicle density and preventive measures like those of France, the male 45Q15 from motor vehicle collisions would be at least 1.4 percent. With further preventive measures, the male 45Q15 could be 0.7 percent or less, as in Sweden and England (see statistical appendix table A-3b).

Destroying the Environment

As discussed in a preceding section (see *Unfinished Business*), contaminated drinking water, food and indoor air are major determinants of adult ill-health at early stages of development. Industrialization and economic development create new sources of water, food, and air pollution that can become important determinants of adult ill-health unless preventive measures are taken. Experience from developed countries shows that the adult health risk due to pollution is likely to increase at the beginning of the development process. If appropriate preventive technology is applied, however, the risk can decrease in spite of continued industrial development. Air pollution is a growing problem in some developing countries. The main sources of pollution vary from country to country, but in general they are of three types: power plants, industry, and residential heating and cooking in urban areas; road traffic in urban areas; and industry or power plants in rural areas. These sources of pollution give rise to a varying mixture of chemicals and dusts that can damage the lungs and other organs, depending on the actual chemical composition of the pollution. There are three main types of such pollution mixtures: a) ash and carbon dust (suspended particulate matter, SPM) and sulfur dioxide (SO_2) from the burning of coal and heavy oil in power plants and industrial or home furnaces; b) ozone, nitrogen oxides (NO_x), carbon monoxide and hydrocarbons from motor vehicle engine exhaust; and c) specific heavy metal (for example, lead) or other chemical pollution from industries using or producing these substances. The predominant health problems due to air pollution are acute lung and heart disease, COPD and various types of chemical poisoning such as from lead or cadmium.

A review of global air pollution (WHO 1988a) found many urban areas have air pollution levels in excess of World Health Organization guidelines for different chemicals (WHO 1987b). Large cities in developing countries generally have the worst pollution from SPM and SO_2. In some cities the average levels—several hundred to a thousand micrograms per cubic meter ($\mu g/m^3$) are close to the levels occurring in severely polluted areas of certain developed countries thirty to fifty years ago. In general, air pollution is increasing in cities in developing countries and decreasing in cities in developed countries. The highest levels of NO_x pollution generally occur in cities of developed countries, with a few exceptions such as Mexico City and São Paulo. Respiratory effects have been documented among children living in these two cities, and a recent public health impact analysis (Romieu, Weitzenfeld, and Finkelman 1990) found that the health of adults and the elderly living in Latin American cities with air pollution may be affected considerably.

The number of people living in urban areas with poor air quality may be substantial (WHO 1988a). Of a global urban population of 1.85 billion people, about 625 million live in areas in which annual average SO_2 levels are unacceptable, and about 975 million live in areas in which peak levels are unacceptable. Similarly, 1.25 billion live with unacceptable annual average or peak levels of SPM.

In urban areas of China and India, SPM and SO_2 pollution is increasing (WHO 1988a). Some cities in China have peak levels (one thousand to five thousand $\mu g/m^3$) during winter—as high as the infamous London smog in 1952, when about four thousand people died in one week from acute lung and heart effects (UKMOH 1954). China has high adult mortality rates from COPD (chapter 2, table 2-16), a disease associated with high levels of air pollution (WHO 1979). Indoor air pollution contributes to this health problem (appendix 5-A). If extreme air pollution conditions occur during two one-week periods each year and the increased acute mortality lasts for four weeks, overall adult mortality would increase by 1.5 times 4/52, or 0.12 times the total 45Q15 of 20 percent. This is based on the figures for increased mortality that occurred during the London fog (Preston, Keyfitz, and Shoen 1972). This is equivalent to a 45Q15 from air pollution of 2.4 percent.

The dose response relationship between mortality rates and air pollution levels appears to exist over a wide range of air pollution levels. Substantial mortality rate increases have been found where SPM and SO_2 levels were 500 $\mu g/m^3$, and higher rates of respiratory diseases have been found where SPM and SO_2 levels were 250 $\mu g/m^3$ (WHO 1987b). A multiple regression analysis of London data for 1958 to 1972 showed a statistically significant increase of daily mortality even when SPM levels were less than 150 $\mu g/m^3$ (Ostro 1984). SPM and SO_2 levels often exceed 250 $\mu g/m^3$ in Beijing, Shenyang, Xian, Calcutta, and New Delhi (WHO 1988a). The long-term effect of air pollution in these cities may be a considerable increase in adult mortality and morbidity.

The effects of motor vehicle exhaust pollution (particularly ozone and NO_x) are less dramatic than the effects of severe SPM/SO_2 pollution. Ozone and NO_x increase the incidence of asthma attacks and upper respiratory infections and reduce lung function. Ozone exposure may induce headache, coughing, and eye irritation. Studies of the day-to-day correlation between exposure levels and symptoms (WHO 1978) showed that peak levels of ozone (more than 500 $\mu g/m^3$) increased the prevalence of headache by 30 percent, cough by 50 percent, and eye irritation by 400 percent. If high levels of carbon monoxide pollution accompany high levels of ozone and NO_x, the incidence of heart attacks increases among people with preexisting heart disease. Lung cancer has also been reported to be associated with motor vehicle exhaust (Buell, Duam, and Breslow 1967). Many of these effects are likely to interact with the effects of tobacco smoking.

Industrial air pollution from a variety of chemicals has caused several large-scale tragedies (UNEP 1989) that have attracted considerable attention, but unrecorded outbreaks caused by pollution from small factories may contribute more to overall ill-health. Cadmium and lead poisoning around smelters and mines has been studied in a few developing countries (such as China). These studies show prevalences of adverse health effects as high as 46 percent among people living nearby (Cai and others 1990). Children have the highest risk for lead poisoning, but adults can also be at risk, particularly when working in cottage industries. For toxic metals, air pollution often indirectly leads to water, soil, and food contamination, and the consumption of local foods may be the main route of exposure.

The health hazards of industrial and agricultural chemicals and the toxic wastes created by their production and use pose increasing problems in many developing countries. Catastrophic outbreaks of poisoning have had disastrous effects. In Bhopal, India, at least two thousand people died and 200 thousand were poisoned when isocyanate was released from a pesticides factory (ICMR 1987). In Iraq, almost five hundred people died and more than six thousand were poisoned by eating bread made from grains treated with methylmercury fungicide (Bakir and others 1973; WHO 1976).

Adverse health effects increase with increasing pesticide use (WHO 1990b). These chemicals are widely used in rural areas of developing countries. Poisoning occurs among people who mix and spray pesticides, people exposed to spray drifts, people who eat contaminated foods, and people who use pesticides for suicide. The latter may in fact be the most common type of pesticide poisoning. The worldwide annual incidence of suicide attempts using pesticides is about two million, most of which occur in developing countries and more than 200 thousand of which result in death. Easy access to pesticides and the high toxicity of some of these chemicals make them particularly hazardous and increase the likelihood of death from suicide attempts. About four million pesticide poisonings occur each year, most of which involve adults. The number of agricultural workers experiencing some symptoms of pesticide poisoning each year may be as many as twenty-five million (Jeyaratnam 1990).[4]

Chemical contamination of food and water are increasing in importance. Many industries in developing countries use water in their processes, and this often leads to water pollution. When polluted waterways are used for drinking water, irrigation, or as a source of shellfish or fish, chemical contaminants can cause severe health problems. Drinking water contaminated with arsenic from mining activities in Chile and China has led to an increase of heart disease and skin cancer (WHO 1981b). Natural arsenic contamination of well water in India has caused liver poisoning (Guha Mazumder and others 1988). The use of polluted water for irrigation causes considerable problems in rice growing countries. Cadmium pollution from mines has caused large areas of rice cultivation in China and Japan to be contaminated with cadmium (Cai and others 1990; Friberg and others 1985). Farmers who ate the rice suffered cadmium poisoning of the kidneys, which in severe cases led to a disabling bone disease. At extreme levels, agriculture itself is affected, because crops cannot survive when cadmium levels get too high.

When chemical contamination kills fish and other forms of seafood, people avoid eating these foods. A more dangerous situation is when seafood looks normal but has toxic levels of chemical contaminants. The most well known example is methylmercury contamination caused by chemical industries, pulp and paper production, geothermal power plants and gold refining. Methylmercury accumulates in fish and first caused poisoning in the 1950s in the town of Minamata, Japan, for which this type of poisoning is named (WHO 1976). Pregnant women are especially sensitive to this poison, and children may be poisoned in utero. The economic conditions in Minamata in the 1950s were similar to current conditions in some developing countries. Industries generating mercury pollution are present in Brazil, Chile, China, and India. Without proper safeguards, the effects of this pollution may be as bad as in Minamata.

Food contamination in developing countries is mainly a problem of biological contamination, but chemical contamination during bulk food processing needs to be monitored carefully. Poisoning outbreaks from chemical contamination of these processes can affect large populations, as when fourteen thousand people in Taiwan were poisoned by cooking oil contaminated during production with polychlorinated biphenyls (Shu and others 1984). Several incidents of pesticide contamination of flour have occurred during transport. For instance, in Sierra Leone, poor cleaning of a truck used for transporting first parathion and then wheat flour caused acute poisoning in forty-nine people (Etzel and others 1987).

The global environmental threats of depletion of the ozone layer and creation of the greenhouse effect have aroused major international debate. Calls for action have come mainly from developed countries, but the health consequences are likely to affect most countries in the long term. Ozone layer depletion may lead to a higher influx of ultraviolet light, causing more skin cancers and cataracts. The most serious skin cancer is malignant melanoma, which is highly fatal and occurs mainly among adults. A 1 percent reduction of the ozone layer may increase the risk of malignant melanoma by 0.1 percent (Lee 1989). In the northern hemisphere, the ozone layer in summer already has been reduced by 2 percent within the last twenty years. Because skin cancer is mainly a problem for light-skinned people, the incidence of skin cancer will increase more in developed countries than in developing countries (Urbach 1987).

The greenhouse effect is caused by carbon dioxide and other gases that trap heat radiation from the earth's surface. Global warming from this effect may raise ocean levels and flood the areas where as

Table 5-4. Mortality from Workplace Injuries, Estimates for 1984–1987

		Rate ratios between the mortality rates of specific occupations and the crude rate					
Country	*Crude rate (per 1,000 workers)*	*Agriculture*	*Mining*	*Industry*	*Construction*	*Transportation*	*Services*
Developing countries							
Cuba	0.097	0.7	—	1.2	2	3	0.3
Egypt	0.16	0.4	1	1	1.6	1.5	0.3
Guatemala	0.54	1	3	1.3	2	2	0.5
Hong Kong	0.075	—	23	0.4	12	7	0.4
Peru	0.057	0.1	7	3	2	1	0.1
South Korea	0.33	—	13	0.5	1	2	0.7
Zimbabwe	0.28	1	4	0.5	1.5	3	0.7
Industrialized market economies							
Japan	0.020	8	19	1	4	3	—
Sweden	0.036	5	6	1.7	2	3	0.5
United Kingdom	0.017	5	10	1	6	2	0.2
United States	0.060	3	5	0.7	3	3	0.3

— Not available.

Source: Estimates were based on data from the International Labour Office (ILO, 1988).

many as 100 million people live in developing countries. In addition, heat stress in tropical countries will increase, and endemic areas of tropical vector-borne disease may expand. Food production will be decreased in many countries, and massive emigration will exacerbate the problems of urbanization. The potential public health consequences of the greenhouse effect have been reviewed by the World Health Organization in collaboration with the World Meteorological Organization and the United Nations Environment Program (WHO 1990a).

Safety Shortcuts and Dangerous Jobs

Deaths from workplace injuries are about ten times more common in developing countries than in developed countries (table 5-4). Injuries are common in agriculture, construction, transport, and the primary industries, such as mining—important sources of employment in developing countries. Agricultural injury mortality rates are three to eight times higher than the average for all occupations in developed countries; mining mortality rates are five to nine times higher (table 5-4). Underreporting of agricultural injuries may be common, as these injuries may only be recorded if the injured are covered by insurance or by government inspection services. The vast majority of agricultural workers in developing countries have no such coverage, and so the risks of injury listed in table 5-4 may be gross underestimates. Even with underreporting, the risk of dying from injury while working in agriculture is substantial (45Q15 of 0.3 to 2.4 percent). Mortality data from China (chapter 2) highlight high injury mortality rates in rural areas where agricultural work predominates. Specific hazards in agricultural work include falls, exposures to pesticides, injuries from cutting instruments and tractors, and drowning. The introduction of new agricultural equipment and chemicals to developing countries without the simultaneous introduction of sufficient safeguards for their use contributes to the high rates of injury (table 5-4). Common chemical exposure in the early stages of developing country industrialization is to lead (in car battery factories), to organic solvents (in paint and painting industries), to acids and other corrosive agents (in metal-plating industries, paper plants, tanneries), and to silica or asbestos dust (in quarries and the building materials industry). All of these chemicals can cause serious chronic disease and death. High lead exposure and poisoning have occurred among people who work in cottage industry lead smelters in several countries (appendix 5-E). Children of these workers are at particular risk. Even when the adverse health effects are temporary, their social consequences may be considerable, because in many developing countries employees lose their jobs for any absence from work.

The cumulative effect of workplace hazards is substantial. Worldwide, at least thirty-three million occupational injuries and poisonings occur each year, 145 thousand of which are fatal (WHO 1988c). These are likely to be underestimates, because the statistics from most countries are poor. Most of these injuries and deaths occur in developing countries. About 10 percent of nonfatal injuries lead to some permanent impairment. Thus, the annual number of work-related impairments (about 3.3 million per year) is about the same as the number of new cases of tuberculosis (Murray, Rouillon, and Styblo forthcoming).

Workplace safety measures are lacking in many developing country industries, even in recently constructed facilities. Many improvements can be achieved without costly investments, and, as shown in Brazil (Nogueira 1987), active worker involvement increases the success of health and safety programs. A cost-benefit analysis of these preventive actions is not available, but given the direct link between loss of productivity and illness or injury in the workplace, reducing specific major occupational hazards is likely to be cost-effective.

Reducing the Impact of Determinants

Methods of reducing the effects of determinants of ill-health are available and have been successfully applied in some settings.

Modes of Intervention

The potential for reducing the effects of determinants is clear from the reductions in 45Q15 seen in many developing and developed countries during the twentieth century (chapter 2). If a traditional or modern health hazard can be controlled in one country, it should be possible to achieve the same result in another country at a similar development stage. The general improvements of housing and community infrastructure that usually accompany economic development lead to a reduction of the determinants for tuberculosis, malnutrition, diarrheal diseases, and other poverty-related diseases. To achieve the most cost-efficient improvement in public health as economic development progresses, however, it is necessary to target preventive actions on specific determinants. This section describes some of the approaches that can be used for prevention and gives examples of interventions that have been effective. Chapter 6 draws conclusions concerning priority interventions in developing countries.

Prevention can be classified according to different determinants or according to different types of intervention, some of which reduce health risks from several determinants. Preventive measures that address the health needs of children and the elderly as well as adults, and that reduce exposure to risk factors for several diseases, will be among the more cost-effective. Interventions may be classified in six groups.

- Technology development and application (e.g., installation of seat belts in cars and environmental sanitation).
- Medical interventions (e.g., immunization).
- Health promotion and health education.
- Community involvement (e.g., organization of common efforts for controlling pollution; social support for preventing suicides).
- Legislation.
- Economic measures (including tax incentives and disincentives that influence the actions of individuals, the private sector, and health care providers).

All these modes of intervention can be very effective in modifying the determinants of health discussed in this chapter. We illustrate, in appendix 5-B on tobacco, how a mixture of interventions can be symbiotic in reducing health risks and improving outcome. In any given national or cultural setting, a given intervention may be more or less effective.

Different sectors must contribute to interventions against the determinants of adult illness. The health sector has a major role to play in providing information on health effects and coordinating intervention activities. The roles of other sectors include the following:

- Agricultural sector: Dietary improvement
- Education sector: Health education and promotion
- Energy sector: Pollution control
- Housing sector: Shelter, town planning, sanitation
- Industry sector: Pollution control, occupational hazards control
- Transport sector: Traffic safety
- Women's affairs sector: Community involvement, health promotion.

Legislative and economic measures are a responsibility of governments, whereas nongovernmental community organizations can develop community involvement and health promotion activities. Industry must invest in technology development and application partly in cooperation with the health professions, whose main focus is on medical intervention and health promotion.

Examples of Successful Interventions

The changing mortality and morbidity patterns associated with economic and health sector development suggest the relative success of different interventions. The success of interventions against biological factors causing infectious disease has been impressive, whereas interventions against some of the other causes of adult ill-health do not seem to work so well. As pointed out earlier in this chapter, the improvements in housing, sanitation, and nutrition that can be achieved when poverty is reduced are effective interventions against the determinants of a broad range of diseases. To achieve these improvements in the rapidly growing cities of developing countries requires major investment in the infrastructure and housing stock of these cities. The technology is well known and has been applied successfully in a short time frame in cities such as Hong Kong and Singapore.

In rural areas, interventions to supply safe drinking water, basic sanitation, and shelter can be very effective if their implementation is based on the participation of the community and on technology and materials appropriate for local conditions (Huttly 1990). Epidemiologic studies of interventions have documented the reduction in diarrheal diseases (for example, Daniels and others 1990) and vector-borne diseases (for example, Graves and others 1987) that can be achieved by the community itself if given the necessary knowledge and support. Initial sucess, however, often has been offset by poor maintenance of water supply or sanitation systems due to lack of an integration of the interventions into the social and administrative practices of the community.

Interventions against environmental and occupational hazards are effective if the right combination of technical, legislative, and economic measures is applied. For instance, the very serious air pollution in the United Kingdom in the 1950s was improved substantially during the 1960s and 1970s as a result of air pollution legislation requiring smoke-free zones, changes in the fuel used in power stations, industry and residences (from coal to oil, gas, or nuclear-power generated electricity), and application of new filter technologies (Weatherley, Gooriah, and Charnock 1976). The current situation in many large cities in China is similar to that of London in the 1950s. An analysis of the association of daily air pollution levels and daily mortality in London (Ostro 1984) found the dramatic epidemics of pollution-related deaths in the 1950s had been eliminated. If these interventions were applied in urban areas of developing countries, where severe air pollution occurs (WHO 1988a), many deaths and illnesses could be prevented.

Other effective interventions for controlling pollution and occupational hazards exist. For example, biogas plants and solar heaters reduce exposures to indoor smoke in rural areas; sedimentation ponds and chemical treatments greatly reduce water pollution from mines and metal refineries; using substitutes for asbestos reduces industrial exposure to asbestos; integrated pest management (WHO 1990b), which emphasizes the use of natural mechanisms to control pests and limited use of degradable chemicals, reduces exposure to toxic pesticides; and closed systems and improved ventilation reduce exposure to organic solvents in workplaces. Occupational injuries can be reduced by technical interventions, training, legislation, and worker involvement, as has been shown in Brazil (Nogueira 1987). Legislative interventions that force the polluter to pay for pollution, or that provide tax incentives for investment in pollution abatement, thus making pollution control more economically attractive, have been applied in some countries such as Brazil (Miglino and Harrington 1984). Another approach, used effectively in Sweden (SEPA 1991), is to force polluters by legal means to reduce emissions to as low a level as is technologically feasible at the time and further to reduce emissions whenever the technology to do so becomes available.

The ultimate effect of a combination of interventions against environmental and occupational hazards in developed countries has been a reduction of chronic lung disease, specific occupational diseases, and possibly also certain cancers. However, some of these effects may have been attenuated by concurrent negative trends, such as an increase in tobacco use or a deterioration in diet. Taken together, these and other changes in the determinants of adult mortality have produced the trends shown in the early sections of chapter 2.

Interventions against some safety hazards and injuries have been effective in developed countries. Seat belt legislation can reduce the injury and mortality rate from motor vehicle collisions by 50 percent (UKGSS 1984).

Community-based education and technical intervention programs have reduced substantially the incidence of residential and sports injuries in Sweden (Shelt 1987).

A broad range of activities has been undertaken in the United States, Australia, and other developed nations to counteract the effects of tobacco. These include information and education campaigns; advertising campaigns using techniques not usually employed in the public health setting; legislative efforts to restrict smoking in public areas and on airlines; development of school curricula that deal with smoking and other substance abuse; and regulation of tobacco advertising. Although it is difficult to connect any single effort to the prevalence of smoking, the net effect of these activities has been an inexorable downward trend of about 0.8 percent per year in the United States (USDHHS 1989). Price increases through increased taxation are a particularly effective measure for governments that have the political nerve to use them.

In developed countries, a number of large-scale clinical trials have been conducted to reduce the level of cardiovascular disease risk factors that affect both morbidity and mortality, some of which have been very successful. In the Oslo intervention study (Hjerman and others 1981), significant decreases of 17 percent in cholesterol level and 25 percent in smoking occurred in the intervention group. Similarly, in the United States, the Hypertension Detection and Followup Program demonstrated a 13 percent decline in hypertension in the intervention group (Hypertension Detection and Followup Program 1982). Controversy concerning the effectiveness of these interventions persists, because not all of the programs could demonstrate differences between intervention and control groups, nor a clear effect on outcome. Nonetheless, the ability to alter risk factor status has important implications for the risks that may become manifest in the developing world.

Recent successes with the World Health Organization's expanded program on immunization highlight the potential effectiveness of immunization campaigns. Some countries experience major adult mortality from hepatocellular carcinoma and chronic hepatitis, both of which are preventable with the use of hepatitis B vaccine. Clinical trials, conducted in Taiwan and elsewhere, have demonstrated the efficacy of the vaccine in the prevention of these long-term sequelae (Eddleston 1990).

Conclusions

Although the paramount determinants of adult ill-health in developing nations are poverty and the associated lack of proper nutrition, shelter, and basic sanitation, this observation offers little insight or solace. A group of more specific determinants—some representative of old or traditional problems in developing nations, some representative of new—has been identified in this chapter. The common factor among these determinants is their potential for remediation. These determinants relate in complex ways to a number of health problems. Their remediation and their ultimate effect on adult health depend on the presence of tools for disease and injury control and on skills for employing those tools.

A number of these determinants are amenable to alteration with currently available technology, and these alterations are within the current reach of many developing nations. Many developing nations face a variety of determinants simultaneously. Given the effect of adult mortality, this may spark a reexamination and possible reallocation of resources within this segment of health activities. As gains in adult health are achieved by reducing the exposures to traditional determinants, the relative importance of other determinants increases. These other determinants include tobacco and alcohol use, sexual behavior that spreads AIDS, motor vehicle collisions, and pollution inside and outside the workplace. The health effects of some of these determinants occur years after the exposure starts. Investment in prevention therefore needs to be made long before the health problem has become apparent. Because the emerging issues in adult mortality are noncommunicable disease and injuries (chapter 2), and because cost-effective preventive interventions are available (chapter 6), policymakers will need to consider a substantial reordering of priorities.

The determinants of adult ill-health are a concern for all sectors of society. Many of these determinants can be dealt with effectively, but not until the health sector has identified the determinants of local importance and the methods to deal with them. While current knowledge about determinants makes it possible to prevent and control some diseases and injuries, there are many gaps in this information. More information is needed about certain determinants, such as the primary remediable risk factors for breast cancer; about effective interventions for modifying these determinants, such as the components of a cost-effective community cardiovascular prevention program; and about the distribution in society of exposure to specific determinants (for example, who smokes and why?). Thus an important task for adult health programs in the developing world will be to acquire more information about determinants and their modification. Chapter 6 develops these ideas further and relates the acquisition of more and better information to the setting of health priorities and the development of adult health policy.

Appendix 5-A. Indoor Air Pollution from Domestic Fuel Use

In millions of kitchens throughout India, China and many other developing countries, cooking is done on an unvented open fire of wood, cow dung, rice straw or coal. The smoke from the fire fills the cooking area, reaching especially high concentrations during cold weather when the cooking area is least ventilated. The smoke is much more than a respiratory irritant. Accumulating evidence from epidemiologic studies shows that this smoke is a substantial health hazard (Chen and others 1990). The concentration of smoke particles (total suspended particulates or TSP) can be more than ten times higher than accepted air quality guidelines, and the concentrations of specific chemicals, such as benzo-alpha-pyrene (in wood smoke) or sulphur dioxide (in coal smoke), can be even higher.

A study in Chandigarh, India showed a significant increase of chronic bronchitis symptoms among women who used traditional unvented stoves fueled with wood and cow dung. The lowest prevalence of chronic bronchitis symptoms were reported by women who used gas or kerosene for cooking but who otherwise lived in the same socioeconomic conditions as women who used wood for cooking. In Nepal, a high prevalence of chronic bronchitis was found also among women using traditional stoves. Cor pulmonale was common among heart disease patients in Nepal, and all cases of cor pulmonale were complications of chronic bronchitis. In Nepal, acute respiratory infections were more prevalent among children living in households that used traditional stoves. Similar findings of increased lung disease in women and acute respiratory infections in children have been associated with biomass smoke exposure in The Gambia, Guatemala, India, and South Africa.

In China, most studies have focused on indoor air pollution from coal, even though in many rural areas biomass is the major source of cooking fuel. One study of about four hundred women compared the prevalences of respiratory symptoms and diseases between women who used coal in the kitchen and those who used gas. Neither of the stove designs included a chimney, so all smoke and fumes were unvented. The women who cooked with coal had higher prevalences of chronic bronchitis (25 percent versus 12 percent), emphysema (10 percent versus 2 percent), and current cough (40 percent versus 18 percent) than the women who cooked with gas. Other studies in China have shown similar results (Chen and others 1990). Another repeated finding in China has been the increased mortality rates (odds ratios of about 4.0) from lung cancer of nonsmoking women who use coal stoves without chimneys (Mumford and others 1987).

Quantitative estimates are not available of the number of children and women (adult and elderly) whose health is affected by indoor air pollution from cooking and heating. The number, however, is likely to be substantial as perhaps as many as 400 million people are exposed to excessive levels of this type of indoor air pollution.

Appendix 5-B. Tobacco Use and its Complex Determinants

Tobacco use is the single largest preventable cause of death in developed nations and unfortunately shows every sign of being well on its way to achieving the same status in developing countries. Eight of the ten countries with the highest rates of cigarette smoking by males are developing nations. China consumes more cigarettes than any other country (28 percent of the world's total). Cigarette consumption in China has grown annually over the past forty years at high rates (4.2 to 9.6 percent each year) and is estimated to account for over two million deaths per year by the time today's young smokers reach middle and old age (World Bank 1989b). Similarly, cigarette consumption in Brazil has increased steadily from the 1940s through the early 1980s. The usual twenty-five to thirty year lag between changes in rates of smoking and incidence of lung cancer has been observed in Brazil: an epidemic of lung cancer deaths began about 1970 and is continuing on an upward trend (World Bank 1989a). Africa increased its cigarette consumption by 42 percent from 1970 to 1985 (Masironi and Rothwell 1988).

Tobacco is a risk factor for many diseases, including lung cancer, oral cancers, coronary heart disease and COPD (chapter 2, appendix 2-D). Tobacco is first and foremost a commercial product for farmers, brokers, manufacturers, and retailers who are eager to make a profit from their sales. Multinational tobacco companies have sought both to increase their market share and, more importantly, to increase consumption through sophisticated marketing and advertising techniques (Yu, Shin, and Kim 1989). Governments may also seek financial gain through tobacco production and sales, either as tobacco growers themselves (as in China), or as beneficiaries of excise tax, or both. Ten percent of China's total tax revenue and 11 percent of Korea's is from tobacco taxes (Yu and Shopland 1989).

Economic incentives and disincentives can be used to control tobacco use. It has been demonstrated repeatedly that price increases can suppress tobacco use, particularly among the poor and young. Thus increases in cigarette taxes can be expected to lead to fewer smokers (Bal and others 1990; Chapman and Richardson 1990; Warner 1990). At the same time, such increases can increase government tax revenues because of the particular features of the price elasticity of cigarette consumption. Social pressures can influence tobacco use also, making smoking less socially acceptable in some socioeconomic classes (such as people with higher education in the United States), but more likely in others (such as professional women in Spain).

Cigarette composition (that is tobacco type and the presence or absence of a filter or chemical additives) determines the degree of toxicity, and tar and nicotine contents correlate with carcinogenicity and addictive strength, respectively. Legislation that limits the places where smoking is allowed may help smokers to quit and also provides a safer respiratory environment for nonsmokers, whose exposure to cigarette smoke increases their risk of disease.

The health care system itself can serve as a determinant of tobacco use. Health care providers can influence smoking behavior by encouraging smokers to quit and providing assistance for them to do so. Conversely, smoking by health care providers is a negative message to the general population. Low rates of smoking by health professionals appear to be associated with a more active role by this group in cessation efforts and serve as a harbinger of declining rates in the community at large.

For effective tobacco control, governments may need to pass legislation restricting areas for smoking, raise taxes, provide school health education, conduct mass media campaigns, and encourage the health care system to discourage smoking. Such an understanding of the multi-faceted nature of tobacco use has been recognized in Hong Kong (chapter 6, appendix 6-B) and has led to a comprehensive governmental policy of legislation, education, taxation, and publicity, resulting in a considerable decrease in the prevalence of smoking (MacKay and Barnes 1986).

Appendix 5-C. Determinants of Coronary Heart Disease

Socioeconomic status and behavioral factors play important contributory roles in the incidence of coronary heart disease (CHD). Elevated serum cholesterol—particularly low density lipoprotein (LDL) cholesterol—diabetes, hypertension, cigarette smoking, and sedentary lifestyle all have been shown to increase the relative risk of developing CHD. Most of the studies that reached these conclusions were done in the developed world. The relevance of these risk factors for different populations remains unknown. From a biological perspective, it is reasonable to assume that these risk factors are applicable to all populations, be they in Cardiff or in Cairo. However, some studies from the developing world offer other interesting perspectives.

In a small West Indian island with a high prevalence of smoking, sedentary lifestyles, and diets high in fat, no clinical CHD had been observed for fifteen years, and a study of lipoprotein patterns revealed high levels of high density lipoprotein (HDL) cholesterol and low levels of serum total triglyceride. The authors concluded "the lipoprotein lipid pattern in these people is consistent with a low cardiovascular risk status and might account for the apparent absence of CHD on the island" (Miller and others 1979).

The genetic contribution to CHD was pursued further in a ten-year community survey in Trinidad that compared ethnic differences in CHD and associated risk factors. The relative risk of a cardiac event due to CHD was twice as high in the Indian population as compared with other ethnic groups. The authors concluded that for men, blood pressure, diabetes mellitus, and LDL cholesterol levels were positively and independently related to risk of CHD, while alcohol consumption and HDL levels were inversely associated with risk. The higher rates of CHD found in individuals of Indian descent versus those of African descent persisted after the other factors were taken into account (Miller and others 1989). The increased susceptibility of persons of south Asian ancestry to CHD and diabetes, and the relationship between this susceptibility and obesity, has been reported also from the United Kingdom (McKeigue, Shah, and Marmot 1991).

There is evidence that the lifestyle shifts that occur in different geographic and sociocultural milieus can increase the cardiovascular risks of members of the same ethnic group. Japanese men living in Japan, Hawaii and California have different CHD risk factors. The respective prevalencies of CHD (2.5 percent, 3.5 percent, and 4.5 percent) are correspondingly different (Marmot and others 1975). Investigators have concluded that "these changes must be due to differences in environment or lifestyle" (Marmot and Davey Smith 1989).

The prevalence of CHD risk factors can be seen to change with development. For example, an urban population in Costa Rica had significantly higher total cholesterol and triglyceride levels along with a higher intake of dietary animal fat and saturated fat than the rural population (Campos and others in press). Similar observations have been made in Brazil and Puerto Rico (Costas and others 1978; Laurenti 1982).

How closely such lifestyle and physiological changes correlate with CHD rates in diverse developing country settings remains unclear. Little information on CHD trends is available from the developing world. A rapid increase in CHD mortality has been observed in some newly developed countries, such as Singapore (Beaglehole 1990). A study of twenty-one Pacific Island countries suggests that the more developed nations have lower overall mortality and relatively higher proportional mortality from cardiovascular disease than the lesser developed nations of the same region (Taylor, Lewis, and Levy 1989).

However, as emphasized in chapter 2, such rises in proportional mortality are of limited interest. The salient fact is that adult cardiovascular mortality rates and risks, including that due to CHD, have been stagnating or falling despite the increasing prevalence of some known risk factors. This suggests the effect of determinants that at present are not identified, understood or measured.

Appendix 5-D. Current and Future Motor Vehicle Collisions in Developing Countries

Vehicle density is an important determinant of mortality rates in developing countries (WHO 1989a). At the early stages of development, when safety awareness is marginal, many of the fatalities from motor vehicle collisions involve pedestrians (e.g., about half the collisions in Kenya, the Philippines and Thailand). At later stages of development, driving skills improve (e.g., drivers become accustomed to the long distances needed for braking), road construction and lighting improve, and fewer pedestrians are involved in motor vehicle collisions.

High mortality rates from motor vehicle collisions in developing countries are also due to the prevalence of unprotected two-wheeled vehicles. Voluntary use of crash helmets is minimal in developing countries because of cost, discomfort, and limited supplies. The value of enacting and enforcing strict crash-helmet legislation has been shown in Malaysia, where motorcylists who are caught riding without helmets instantly lose possession of their motorcycles. With this legislation, helmet use in Malaysia has increased to almost 100 percent, and injury rates have been reduced (WHO 1989a).

Overloading and poor vehicle maintenance also contribute to high injury and mortality rates from motor vehicle collisions during the early stages of development. Drunken driving and nonuse of seat belts are risk factors that persist at later stages of development and, indeed, are common in developed countries.

Integrated safety programs have been implemented in recent years in Botswana, Brazil, Colombia, Côte d'Ivoire, Kenya, and the Philippines. A follow-up analysis of the type presented in figure 5-1 is needed to assess the effect of these programs.

Appendix 5-E. Lead Exposures in Cottage Industries

Cottage industries, often located in or near dwellings, play important roles in developing economies. Lead-related cottage industries can be especially hazardous to workers and nearby residents. Lead batteries, used in almost all motor vehicles, are heavy and cumbersome to transport. Therefore, local production and recycling of batteries is an industry that emerges during the early stages of industrialization. In many developing countries, cottage industries recycle batteries in residential areas. Rudimentary smelters can be found in people's backyards in, for instance, Jamaica (Matte and others 1989), China and Vietnam.

A review of hospital records of lead poisoned children in Kingston, Jamaica showed that more than 80 percent of these hospitalized children lived at or near a backyard battery repair shop (Matte and others 1989). A follow-up investigation found that the average blood lead levels of those living in twenty-four households with repair shops were much higher than those living in eighteen control households. Children had the highest blood lead levels, and about half of them were greater than seven hundred micrograms per hundred milliliters (μg/100 ml). Overt symptoms of lead poisoning can begin when the blood lead level exceeds 50 μg/100 ml, but subclinical neurobehavioral effects have been identified at blood lead levels as low as 10 μg/100 ml. The study showed a correlation between dust and soil lead levels and blood lead levels, both among children and adults. Contaminated soil and dust may cause continuing lead exposure long after a battery repair shop has closed.

Cottage industry production of ceramics often involves the use of glazes containing lead and is another high-risk industry (Koplan and others 1977). Lead leaching into foods or beverages from ceramic pottery fired at low temperatures has been identified as a substantial source of lead exposure in Mexico (Hernandez-Avila and others 1990). Cottage industries that have been associated with excessive lead exposure in India include papier-mache work (Kaul and Kaul 1986) and silver jewelry making (Behari, Singh, and Tandon 1983).

Other sources of lead exposure in developing countries may cause more widespread lead exposure, albeit at lower levels than those associated with cottage industries. Use of lead in gasoline and in soldered cans, while being phased out in many developed countries, remains an ongoing source of lead exposure in many developing countries and in eastern Europe. The reduction of lead pollution from all sources and the cleanup of past contamination remain difficult challenges.

Notes

1. In the United States, homicide is the leading cause of death among young black males of between fifteen to twenty-four years and accounts for 42 percent of all deaths in this group. Firearms account for 78 percent of these homicides. Homicide rates among young black males are four to five times higher than among young black females, five to eight times higher than among young white males, and six to twenty-two times higher than among young white females (Anon 1990b).

2. This amount is thought to be at least twenty minutes a day, at least three times a week of an activity that will stress the musculoskeletal and cardiovascular systems enough to provoke perspiration.

3. The spread of HIV infection occurs only in four ways (Mann 1988): a) sexual intercourse, both homosexual and heterosexual; b) sharing needles for intravenous drug use (such spread also can occur if contaminated needles are reused in medical practice without adequate sterilization); c) blood transfusions with blood from an infected person; and d) transplacental spread or spread at birth from an infected mother to her child.

4. This problem is not assisted by the practice some developed countries have of exporting their own banned or restricted pesticides to the developing world. The United States exports large quantities of such pesticides, the main recipients being Brazil, Colombia, Japan, South Korea, Sri Lanka and Syria (FASE 1991).

References

Anonymous. 1990a. "Indoor Air Pollution in Developing Countries." *Lancet* ii:1548.

———. 1990b. "Homicide among Young Black Males—United States 1978–1987." *Morbidity and Mortality Weekly Report* 39:869–73.

Bakir, F., S. F. Damluji, L. Amin Zaki, M. Murtadha, A. Khalidi, N. Y. Al Rawi, S. Tikriti, H. I. Dhahir, T. W. Clarkson, J. C. Smith, and R. A. Doherty. 1973. "Methylmercury Poisoning in Iraq." *Science* 181:230–41.

Bal, D. G., K. W. Kizer, P. G. Felton, H. N. Mozar, and D. Niemeyer. 1990. "Reducing Tobacco Consumption in California." *Journal of the American Medical Association* 264:1570–74.

Barker, D. J. P., and C. Osmond. 1986. "Infant Mortality, Childhood Nutrition, and Ischaemic Heart Disease in England and Wales." *Lancet* i:1077–81.

Beaglehole, R. 1990. "International Trends in Coronary Heart Disease Mortality, Morbidity and Risk Factors." *Epidemiologic Reviews* 12:1–15.

Beaton, G. H. 1989. "Small but Healthy? Are We Asking the Right Questions?" *Human Organization* 48:30–39.

Behari, J. R., S. Singh, and S. K. Tandon. 1983. "Lead Poisoning among Indian Silver Jewelry Makers." *Annals of Occupational Hygiene* 27:107–09.

Ben-Shlomo, Y., and G. Davey Smith. 1991. "Deprivation in Infancy or in Adult Life: Which is More Important for Mortality Risk?" *Lancet* 337:530–34.

Berg, A. 1987. *Malnutrition: What Can Be Done?* Baltimore: Johns Hopkins University Press.

Buell, P., J. E. J. Duam, and L. Breslow. 1967. ''Cancer of the lung and Los Angeles type air pollution.'' *Cancer* 20:2139–47.

Bumgarner, J. R., and F. E. Spiezer. Forthcoming. ''Chronic Obstructive Pulmonary Disease.'' In D. T. Jamison, and W. H. Mosley, eds., *Disease Control Priorities in Developing Countries.* New York: Oxford University Press for the World Bank.

Burger, S., J. P. Habicht, K. Peterson, and P. Pinstrup-Andersen. Forthcoming. ''Protein-Energy Malnutrition.'' In D. T. Jamison, and W. H. Mosley, eds., *Disease Control Priorities in Developing Countries.* New York: Oxford University Press for the World Bank.

Cai, S. W., L. Yue, Z. N. Hu, X. Z. Zhong, Z. L. Ye, H. D. Xu, Y. R. Liu, R. D. Ji, W. H. Zhang, and F. Y. Zhang. 1990. ''Cadmium Exposure and Health Effects among Residents in an Irrigation Area with Ore Dressing Wastewater.'' *Science of the Total Environment* 90:67–73.

Campos, H., W. C. Willett, R. M. Peterson, X. Siles, S. M. Bailey, P. W. F. Wilson, B. M. Posner, J. M. Ordors, and E. J. Shaefer. In press. ''Nutrient Intake Comparisons between Framingham and Rural and Urban Puriscal, Costa Rica: Associations with Lipids, Lipoproteins, Apolipoproteins and LDL Particle Size.'' *Arteriosclerosis.*

Chapman, S., and J. Richardson. 1990. ''Tobacco Excise and Declining Tobacco Consumption: The Case of Papua New Guinea.'' *American Journal of Public Health* 80:537–39.

Chen, B. H., C. J. Hong, M. R. Pandey, and K. R. Smith. 1990. ''Indoor Air Pollution in Developing Countries.'' *World Health Statistics Quarterly* 43(3):127–38.

Costas, R., M. R. Garcia-Palmieri, E. Nazano, and P. D. Sorlie. 1978. ''Relation of Lipids, Weight, and Physical Activity to Incidence of Coronary Heart Disease: The Puerto Rico Heart Study.'' *American Journal of Cardiology* 4:653–58.

Daniels, D. L., S. N. Cousens, L. N. Makoae, and R. G. Feachem. 1990. ''A Case-Control Study of the Impact of Improved Sanitation on Diarrhea Morbidity in Lesotho.'' *Bulletin of the World Health Organization* 68:455–63.

De Azevedo, I. C. B. 1989. *Children's Growth Status and Adults' Body Size among Urban Poor Households: A Cross Sectional Study in São Luis, Maranhão, Northeast Brazil.* London: London School of Hygiene & Tropical Medicine, Ph.D. thesis.

De Cock, K. M., B. Barrere, L. Diaby, M. F. Lafontaine, E. Gnaore, A. Porter, D. Pantobe, G. C. Lafontant, A. Dago-Akribi, M. Ette, K. Odehouri, and W. L. Heyward. 1990. ''AIDS—The Leading Cause of Adult Death in the West African City of Abidjan, Ivory Coast.'' *Science* 249:793–96.

Drangert, J. O., and J. Lundquist. 1990. ''Household Water and Health: Issues of Quality, Quantity, Handling, and Cost.'' In E. Nordberg and D. Finer, eds., *Society, Environment and Health in Low-income Countries.* Stockholm: Department of International Health Care Research (IHCAR), Karolinska Institute.

Eddleston, A. 1990. ''Modern Vaccines: Hepatitis.'' *Lancet* i:1142–45.

Elford, J., P. Whincup, and A. G. Shaper. 1991. ''Early Life Experience and

Adult Cardiovascular Disease: Longitudinal and Case-Control Studies.'' *International Journal of Epidemiology* 20:833–44.

Etzel, R. A., D. N. Forthal, R. H. Hill, and A. Demby. 1987. ''Fatal Parathion Poisoning in Sierra Leone.'' *Bulletin of the World Health Organization* 65:645–49.

FASE. 1991. ''Exporting Banned and Hazardous Pesticides.'' FASE Reports 9(1):51–58.

Feachem, R. G. 1984. ''Interventions for the Control of Diarrheal Diseases among Young Children—Promotion of Personal and Domestic Hygiene.'' *Bulletin of the World Health Organization* 62:467–76.

Feachem, R. G., W. J. Graham, and I. M. Timaeus. 1989. ''Identifying Health Problems and Health Research Priorities in Developing Countries.'' *Journal of Tropical Medicine and Hygiene* 92:133–91.

Feachem, R. G., and A. Preker. 1991. *The Czech and Slovak Federal Republic. The Health Sector: Issues and Priorities.* Washington, D.C.: Central and Eastern Europe Department, World Bank.

Friberg, L., C. G. Elinder, T. Kjellstrom, and G. F. Nordberg. 1985. *Cadmium and Health.* Vols. 1 and 2. Boca Raton, Florida: Chemical Rubber Company Press.

Grant, M., and B. Ritson. 1983. *Alcohol: The Prevention Debate.* London: Croom Helm.

Graves, P. M., B. J. Brabin, J. D. Charlwood, T. R. Burkot, J. A. Cattani, M. Ginny, J. Paino, F. D. Gibson, and M. P. Alpers. 1987. ''Reduction in Incidence and Prevalence of Plasmodium falciparum in under Five-Year Old Children by Permethrin Impregnation of Mosquito Nets.'' *Bulletin of the World Health Organization* 65:869–77.

Guha Mazumder, D. N., A. K. Chakraborty, A. Ghose, J. D. Gupta, D. P. Chakraborty, S. B. Dey, and N. Chattopadhyay. 1988. ''Chronic Arsenic Toxicity from Drinking Tubewell Water in Rural West Bengal.'' *Bulletin of the World Health Organization* 66:499–506.

Gupta, P. C., and K. Ball. 1990. ''India: Tobacco Tragedy.'' *Lancet* 335:594–95.

Harrison, K. A. 1985. ''Childbearing, Health and Social Priorities: A Survey of 22,774 Consecutive Hospital Births in Zaria, Northern Nigeria.'' *British Journal of Obstetrics and Gynecology* Supplement 5:1–119.

Hernandez-Avila, M., C. Rios, I. Romieu, E. Palazuelos, and A. Rivero. 1990. ''Determinants of Blood Lead Levels in a Random Sample of Women in Mexico City.'' Second Annual Meeting of the International Society for Environmental Epidemiology, August 13–15, Berkeley, California.

Herz, B., and A. R. Measham. 1987. *The Safe Motherhood Initiative: Proposals for Action.* World Bank Discussion Paper 9. Washington, D.C.: World Bank.

Hetzel, B. S. 1983. ''The Control of Diseases Related to Nutrition.'' In W. W. Holland, S. R. Detel, and G. Knox, eds., *The Oxford Textbook of Public Health.* Vol. 4. Oxford: Oxford University Press.

Hjerman, I., K. Velve Byre, I. Holme, and P. Leren. 1981. ''Effect of Diet and Smoking Intervention on the Incidence of Coronary Heart Disease: Report from the Oslo Study Group of a Randomised Trial in Healthy Men.'' *Lancet* ii:1303–10.

Huttly, S. R. A. 1990. ''The Impact of Inadequate Sanitary Conditions on Health in Developing Countries.'' *World Health Statistics Quarterly* 43(3):118–26.

Hypertension Detection and Followup Program Cooperative Group. 1982. "The Effect of Treatment on Mortality in 'mild' Hypertension." *New England Journal of Medicine* 307:976–80.

IARC (International Agency for Research on Cancer). 1986. *Tobacco Smoking*. Lyon.

———. 1988. *Alcohol drinking*. Lyon.

ICMR (Indian Council of Medical Research). 1987. "Studies of the Health Effects of the Bhopal Gas Leak Episode." *Indian Journal of Medical Research* Supplement 86:1–90.

ILO (International Labour Office). 1988. *Year Book of Labour Statistics* 48th issue. Geneva.

Jeyaratnam, J. 1990. "Acute Pesticide Poisoning: A Major Global Health Problem." *World Health Statistics Quarterly* 43(3):139–44.

Kaul, P. S., and B. Kaul. 1986. "Blood Lead and Erythrocyte Protoporphyrin Levels among Papier-Maché Workers in Kashmir." *Mount Sinai Journal of Medicine* 53:145–48.

Kjellstrom, T., and L. Rosenstock. 1990. "The Role of Environmental and Occupational Hazards in the Adult Health Transition." *World Health Statistics Quarterly* 43(3):188–96.

Koplan, J. P., A. V. Wells, H. J. Diggory, E. L. Baker, and J. Liddle. 1977. "Lead Absorption in a Community of Potters in Barbados." *International Journal of Epidemiology* 6:225–29.

Koplan, J. P., C. J. Caspersen, and K. E. Powell. 1989. "Physical Activity, Physical Fitness, and Health: Time to Act." *Journal of the American Medical Association* 262:2437.

Laurenti, R. 1982. "Epidemiologia das Doenças Cardiovasculares no Brasil." *Arquivos Brasileiros de Cardiologia* 38:243–48.

Lee, J. A. H. 1989. "The Relationship between Malignant Melanoma of Skin and Exposure to Sunlight." *Photochemical Photobiology* 50:493–96.

MacKay, J. M., and G. T. Barnes. 1986. "Effects of Strong Government Measures against Tobacco in Hong Kong." *British Medical Journal* 292:1435–37.

McKeigue, P. M., B. Shah, and M. G. Marmot. 1991. "Relation of Central Obesity and Insulin Resistance with High Diabetes Prevalence and Cardiovascular Risk in South Asians." *Lancet* 337:382–86.

McKeown, T. 1976. *The Modern Rise of Population*. New York: Academic Press.

Malaysia, Ministry of Health. 1985. *Epidemiology of Road Traffic Accidents in Malaysia. Report from the Epidemiology Unit*. Kuala Lumpur.

Mann, J. M. 1988. "A Global Strategy for a Global Challenge." *World Health* March:4–8.

———. 1989. *Global Aids into the 1990s*. Document GPA/DIR/89.2. Geneva: World Health Organization.

Marmot, M. G., S. L. Syme, A. Kagan, H. Kato, J. P. Cohen, and J. Belsky. 1975. "Epidemiologic Studies of Coronary Heart Disease and Stroke in Japanese Men Living in Japan, Hawaii, and California: Prevalence of Coronary and Hypertensive Heart Disease and Associated Risk Factors." *American Journal of Epidemiology* 102:514–25.

Marmot, M. G., and G. Davey Smith. 1989. "Why are the Japanese Living Longer?" *British Medical Journal* 299:1547–51.

Martinez, J., M. A. Phillips, and R. G. A. Feachem. Forthcoming. "Diarrhea." In D. T. Jamison and W. H. Mosley, eds., *Disease Control Priorities in Developing Countries*. New York: Oxford University Press for the World Bank.

Masironi, R., and K. Rothwell. 1988. "Smoking Trends and Effects Worldwide." *World Health Statistics Quarterly* 41:228–41.

Matte, T. D., J. P. Figueroa, S. Ostrowski, G. Burr, L. Jackson-Hunt, R. A. Keenlyside, and E. L. Baker. 1989. "Lead Poisoning among Household Members Exposed to Lead-Acid Battery Repair Shops in Kingston, Jamaica." *International Journal of Epidemiology* 18:874–81.

Miglino, L. C. P., and J. J. Harrington. 1984. "The Impact of Taxes on the Management of Industrial Discharges." *Revista DAE São Paulo* 44(138):1–20.

Miller, G. J., J. P. Koplan, P. Morgan, M. T. Ashcroft, M. Moinuddin, and G. L. A. Beckles. 1979. "High Density Lipoprotein Cholesterol Concentration and Other Serum Lipids in an Isolated Island Community Free of Coronary Heart Disease." *International Journal of Epidemiology* 8:219–25.

Miller, G. J., G. L. Beckles, G. H. Maude, D. C. Carson, S. D. Alexis, S. G. Price, and N. T. Byam. 1989. "Ethnicity and Other Characteristics Predictive of Coronary Heart Disease in a Developing Community: Principal Results of the St. James Survey, Trinidad." *International Journal of Epidemiology* 18:808–17.

Moss, A. R., and P. Bacchetti. 1989. "Natural History of HIV Infection." *AIDS* 3:55–61.

Mumford, J. L., X. Z. He, R. S. Chapman, S. R. Cao, D. B. Harris, X. M. Li, Y. L. Xian, W. Z. Jiang, C. W. Xu, J. C. Chuang, W. E. Wilson, and M. Cooke. 1987. "Lung cancer and indoor air pollution in Xuan Wei, China." *Science* 235:217–20.

Murray, C. J. L., A. Rouillon, and K. Styblo. Forthcoming. "Tuberculosis." In D. T. Jamison, and W. H. Mosley, eds., *Disease Control Priorities in Developing Countries*. New York: Oxford University Press for the World Bank.

Nath, U. R. 1986. *Smoking, Third World Alert*. Oxford: Oxford University Press.

Nikander, P., T. Seppala, G. P. Kilonzo, P. Huttunen, L. Saarinen, E. Kilima, and T. Pitkanen. 1991. "Ingredients and Contaminants of Traditional Alcoholic Beverages in Tanzania." *Transactions of the Royal Society of Tropical Medicine and Hygiene* 85:133–35.

Nogueira, D. P. 1987. "Prevention of Accidents and Injuries in Brazil." *Ergonomics* 30:387–93.

Okware, S. I. 1988. "AIDS Control in Uganda." *World Health* March:20–21.

Ostro, B. 1984. "A Search for a Threshold in the Relationship of Air Pollution to Mortality: A Reanalysis of Data on London Winters." *Environmental Health Perspectives* 58:397–99.

Over, M., and P. Piot. Forthcoming. "HIV Infection and Other Sexually Transmitted Diseases." In D. T. Jamison and W. H. Mosley, eds., *Disease Control Priorities in Developing Countries*. New York: Oxford University Press for the World Bank.

Peto, R., and A. D. Lopez. 1990. "The Future Worldwide Health Effects of Current Smoking Patterns: Three Million Deaths/Year in the 1990s, But over Ten Million/Year Eventually." 7th World Conference on Tobacco and Health, Perth, Australia.

Piot, P., J. K. Kreiss, J. O. Ndinya-Achola, E. N. Ngugi, J. N. Simonsen, D. W. Cameron, H. Taelman, and F. A. Plummer. 1987. "Heterosexual Transmission of HIV." *AIDS* 1(4):199–206.

Powell, K. E., P. D. Thompson, C. J. Caspersen, and J. S. Kendrick. 1987. "Physical Activity and the Incidence of Coronary Heart Disease." *Annual Review of Public Health* 8:253–87.

Preston, S. H., N. Keyfitz, and R. Schoen. 1972. *Causes of Death. Life Tables of National Populations.* New York: Seminar Press.

Pryer, J. A. 1990. *Socioeconomic and Environmental Aspects of Undernutrition and Ill-health in an Urban Slum in Bangladesh.* London: London School of Hygiene & Tropical Medicine, Ph.D. thesis.

Rochat, R. W., D. Kramer, P. Senanayake, and C. Howell. 1980. "Induced Abortion and Health Problems in Developing Countries." *Lancet* ii:484.

Romieu, I., H. Weitzenfeld, and J. Finkelman. 1990. "Urban Air Pollution in Latin America and the Caribbean: Health Perspectives." *World Health Statistics Quarterly* 43(3):153–67.

SEPA (Swedish Environmental Protection Agency). 1991. *The Development of an Environmental Policy. The Swedish Experience.* Solna.

Shelt, L. 1987. *Epidemiology as a Basis for Evaluation of a Community Intervention Program on Accidents.* Stockholm: Karolinska Institute.

Shu, T. H., I. M. Chao, S. K. H. Hsu, S. W. Shi, N. H. M. Hsu, and C. C. Yeh. 1984. "Discovery and Epidemiology of PCB Poisoning in Taiwan." *American Journal of Industrial Medicine* 5:71–79.

Siscovich, D. C., R. E. LaPorte, and J. M. Newman. 1985. "The Disease-Specific Benefits and Risks of Physical Activity and Exercise." *Public Health Reports* 100:180–88.

Stanley, K., J. Stjernsward, and V. Koroltchouk. 1988. "Cancers of the Stomach, Lung, and Breast: Mortality Trends and Control Strategies." *World Health Statistics Quarterly* 41:107–14.

Stansfield, S., G. S. Smith, and W. P. McGreevey. Forthcoming. "Injury and Poisoning." In D. T. Jamison and W. H. Mosley, eds., *Disease Control Priorities in Developing Countries.* New York: Oxford University Press for the World Bank.

Starrs, A. 1987. *Preventing the Tragedy of Maternal Deaths. A Report on the International Safe Motherhood Conference, Nairobi, Kenya, February 1987.* Washington, D.C.: World Bank.

Steinglass, R., L. Brenzel, and A. Percy. Forthcoming. "Tetanus." In D. T. Jamison and W. H. Mosley, eds., *Disease Control Priorities in Developing Countries.* New York: Oxford University Press for the World Bank.

Tabibzadeh, I., A. Rossi-Espagnet, and R. Maxwell. 1989. *Spotlight on the Cities. Improving Urban Health in Developing Countries.* Geneva: World Health Organization.

Taylor, R., N. D. Lewis, and S. Levy. 1989. "Societies in Transition: Mortality Patterns in Pacific Island Populations." *International Journal of Epidemiology* 18:634–46.

Thorson, J. 1975. *Long-term Effects of Traffic Accidents.* Lund, Sweden: Hakan Ohlssons Publishing Company.

UKGSS (United Kingdom, Government Statistical Service). 1984. *Press notice. December 1. on seat belt use in Great Britain.* London: Department of Transportation.

UKMOH (United Kingdom, Ministry of Health). 1954. *Mortality and Morbidity during the London Fog of December 1952.* London: Her Majesty's Stationery Office.

UNEP (United Nations Environment Program). 1989. *Environmental Data Report.* Oxford: Basil Blackwell Publishing Company.

United Nations. 1987a. *First Report on the World Nutrition Situation.* Rome: Administrative Committee on Coordination-Subcommittee on Nutrition, Food and Agriculture Organization.

———. 1987b. "The prospect of world urbanization." *Population Studies.* No. 101, ST/ESA/SER.A/101. New York.

———. 1989. *Statistics of Road Traffic Accidents in Europe.* Geneva: Economic Commission for Europe, United Nations.

USDHHS (United States Department of Health and Human Services). 1983. *Fifth Special report to the US Congress on Alcohol and Health.* Rockville, Maryland: National Institute on Alcohol Abuse and Alcoholism.

———. 1988. *The Surgeon General's Report on Nutrition and Health.* DHHS. PHS. Publication No. 88-50210. Washington, D.C.

———. 1989. *Reducing the Health Consequences of Smoking: 25 Years of Progress. A Report of the Surgeon General* DHHS Publication No. (CDC) 89-8911. Rockville, Maryland: Office on Smoking and Health, Centers for Disease Control.

Urbach, F. 1987. "Man and Ultraviolet Radiation." In W. F. Passchier, and B. F. M. Bosnijakovic, eds., *Human Exposure to Ultraviolet Radiation: Risks and Regulations.* Amsterdam: Elsevier Science Publishers.

Waaler, H. 1984. "Height, Weight and Mortality: The Norwegian Experience." *Acta Medica Scandinavica* Suppl 679:1–56.

Walker, G. J. A., D. E. C. Ashley, A. M. McCaw, and G. W. Bernard. 1986. "Maternal mortality in Jamaica." *Lancet* i:486–88.

Walsh, B., and M. Grant. 1985. *Public Health Implications of Alcohol Production and Trade.* Offset Publication No. 88. Geneva: World Health Organization.

Walsh, J. A., C. A. Feifer, A. R. Measham, and P. J. Gertler. Forthcoming. Maternal and Perinatal Health Problems. In D. T. Jamison and W. H. Mosley, eds., *Disease Control Priorities in Developing Countries.* New York: Oxford University Press for the World Bank.

Warner, K. E. 1989. "Effects of the Anti-Smoking Campaign: An Update." *American Journal of Public Health* 79:144–51.

———. 1990. Tobacco Taxation as Health Policy in the Third World. *American Journal of Public Health* 80:529–31.

WCED (World Commission on Environment and Development). 1987. *Our Common Future.* Oxford: Oxford University Press.

Weatherley, M. I., B. D. Gooriah, and J. Charnock. 1976. *Fuel Consumption, Smoke and Sulfur Dioxide Emissions and Concentrations, and Grit and Dust Deposition in the U.K. up to 1973–74.* WSL Report LR214AP. Stevenage, United Kingdom: Warren Spring Laboratory.

World Bank. 1989a. *Adult Health in Brazil: Adjusting to New Challenges.* Report No. 7807-BR. Washington, D.C.

———. 1989b. *China: Long-term Issues and Options in the Health Transition.* Report No. 7965–CHA. Washington, D.C.

WHO (World Health Organization). 1976. "Mercury." *Environmental Health Criteria.* No. 1. Geneva.

———. 1978. "Photochemical oxidants." *Environmental Health Criteria.* No. 7. Geneva.

———. 1979. "Sulfur oxides and suspended particulate matter." *Environmental Health Criteria.* No. 8. Geneva.

———. 1980. "Problems related to alcohol consumption." *Technical Report Series.* No. 505. Geneva.

———. 1981a. *Changing Patterns in Suicide Behavior.* Copenhagen.

———. 1981b. "Arsenic." *Environmental Health Criteria.* No. 18. Geneva.

———. 1984. *Biomass Fuel Combustion and Health.* Geneva.

———. 1986. *Prevention of Maternal Mortality.* Document WHO/FHE/86.1. Geneva.

———. 1987a. *Evaluation of the Strategy for Health for All by the Year 2000. Seventh Report on the World Health Situation.* Vol. 2. Geneva.

———. 1987b. *Air Quality Guidelines.* Copenhagen.

———. 1987c. *The International Drinking Water Supply and Sanitation Decade. Report of Mid-decade Progress.* Report CWS/87.5. Geneva.

———. 1988a. *Assessment of Urban Air Quality.* Geneva.

———. 1988b. *Tobacco or Health. Smokefree Europe:* 4. Copenhagen.

———. 1988c. *Workers Health. Global Medium-term Program.* Document OCH/MTP/88-1. Geneva.

———. 1989a. *New Approaches to Improve Road Safety.* Technical Report Series No. 781. Geneva.

———. 1989b. *Statement on AIDS and Tuberculosis.* Document WHO/GPA/INF/89.4. Geneva.

———. 1990a. *Potential Health Effects of Climatic Change.* Document WHO/PEP/90.10. Geneva.

———. 1990b. *Public Health Impact of Pesticides Used in Agriculture.* Geneva.

———. 1990c. *Diet, Nutrition, and Prevention of Chronic Diseases.* Technical Report Series No. 797. Geneva.

Yu, J. J., and D. R. Shopland. 1989. "Cigarette smoking, behavior, and consumption characteristics for the Asia-Pacific region." *World Smoking and Health* 14:7–9.

Yu, S. H., D. C. Shin, and C. B. Kim. 1989. "Korea: Health Implications of Cigarette Import Policy." *World Smoking and Health* 14:11–13.

6. *The Emerging Agenda for Adult Health*

Margaret A. Phillips, Richard G. A. Feachem, and Jeffrey P. Koplan

THIS BOOK PRESENTS AN OVERVIEW of the health of adults in developing countries: the patterns of mortality and morbidity (chapters 2 and 3); the consequences for the individual, family and community (chapter 4); and factors that influence health and ill-health (chapter 5). Such information is key to policy formulation in the health sector. But it has important gaps. This last chapter not only summarizes the key findings from earlier chapters, it also identifies areas of data collection and research needed to clarify further the health problems of adults in developing countries.

To move beyond this exposition of the problem to prescriptions for action requires information on the effectiveness of alternative interventions and their costs. This book does not attempt such an analysis. A companion volume to this book, entitled *Disease Control Priorities in Developing Countries* (Jamison and Mosley forthcoming), does. It reviews intervention options for the prevention and control of almost all major diseases in developing countries. That book and the analyses presented in chapters 2 through 5 of this book form the basis for the agenda for action proposed in this chapter. Prominent among these recommendations is the proposal that governments focus on reducing expenditure on inefficient and inequitable adult health care and thereby free resources for the implementation of cost-effective interventions, many of which are neglected preventive interventions. This reflects in part a concern that improvements in the health of adults should not be at the expense of children. Some of the important research issues raised by these recommendations are then addressed, and the chapter concludes with a plea to fill the policy vacuum in adult health.

The Findings

The review of adult health in this book supports some widely held views, but also challenges several generally accepted notions, especially regarding adult mortality. The key findings of this book are summarized below.

Surviving childhood is not the only health hurdle in developing countries (chapters 2 and 3).

• Mortality statistics (chapter 2) clearly support current international concern for the health of children in developing countries: 38 percent of all deaths in developing countries occur among children younger than five years old, and 97 percent of these deaths are avoidable. However, it is also true that 27 percent of all deaths in developing countries occur in the adult age group (fifteen to fifty-nine years), and 72 percent of these are avoidable. Deaths of adults account for about half of all potential years of life lost (using productivity weighting and discounting at 8 percent).

• In some developing countries (e.g., Sierra Leone), the probability of dying in the forty-five years between the ages of fifteen and sixty years (45Q15) is greater than 50 percent. The average in developing countries is 25 percent for men and 22 percent for women, very much higher than in the developed market economies, where the average is about 12 percent for men and 5 percent for women.

• The burden of adult ill-health is increasing. The adult population of developing countries is large (comprising 56 percent of the total) and growing at a faster rate than the whole population (chapter 1). If adult mortality rates do not decline steeply, adult deaths (particularly those from noncommunicable diseases and injuries) will increase, both in number and relative to all deaths.

• High adult mortality rates are accompanied by substantial levels of morbidity, although methodological problems frustrate efforts to quantify this in a consistent and comparable fashion (chapter 3).

The ill-health of adults has serious consequences for the individual, his or her family, and society (chapter 4).

• Adult ill-health consumes a major proportion of health care resources (more than three-quarters in some countries). Families bear an important part of this burden, spending on average at least as much as governments spend on health care.

• Adults comprise the majority of the labor force, and the ill-health or death of adults generally has deleterious effects on productivity. The losses are probably substantial, though difficult to measure because they are often obscured, deflected, or delayed through compensatory reallocation of labor away from income-generating activities, education, or child care. These coping mechanisms, which ameliorate the effect of adult ill-health, themselves impose costs.

• Adults are the ones on whom other family members depend. The death or ill-health of adults can harm the health of, or even kill, other members of the household—the mortality rates of infants whose mothers die can be as high as 90 percent.

• Poor adults suffer more frequently from severe ill-health, are more likely to depend on regular physical work, have fewer resources with which to cope, and consequently are more heavily penalized by ill-health. In the poorest households, ill-health can be catastrophic, leading to asset sales and irreversible impoverishment.

• Societies probably cope with the frequency and unpredictability of adult ill-health by maintaining a labor surplus and minimizing labor specialization. The efficiency losses from these coping processes may be of immense importance in understanding the slow pace of development in some countries.

The nature, distribution, and trends of adult mortality challenge preconceptions (chapter 2).

• Noncommunicable diseases (including cardiovascular diseases and cancers) and injuries are the leading causes of adult death in most developing countries with adequate mortality data.[1] Furthermore, these diseases, which are commonly thought of as diseases of the rich, in aggregate cause higher rates of death in poorer countries than in less poor countries and higher rates of death among poorer people within a country. Many developing countries face these major challenges from noncommunicable diseases and injuries while at the same time continuing to have high rates of certain communicable diseases of adults, such as tuberculosis.

• Age-specific adult death rates of most diseases, including many noncommunicable diseases, are falling. Fifty percent of the recent decline in 45Q15 in some countries is due to a fall in noncommunicable disease. Despite this, adult deaths from noncommunicable diseases are increasing both in absolute numbers (because of the growing number of adults) and in relative importance (because mortality rates from communicable and childhood diseases are decreasing even more rapidly).

• Men aged fifteen through fifty-nine years have higher mortality rates than women of the same ages in nearly all developing countries, and the difference in some countries is large. Even during the reproductive years (from fifteen to thirty-nine years), men in nearly all countries have higher mortality rates than women. Although death rates are lower among women than men, comparisons with developed countries reveal that women's avoidable mortality is higher.

• In countries with acceptable cause-specific data, injuries are responsible for about 25 percent of the male 45Q15 and 37 percent of age-standardized adult years of potential life lost. Rates are generally lower among women. There are no consistent patterns over time or in relation to overall mortality risk. Injury rates appear to be determined by distinct, location-specific sets of social, cultural and economic factors.

Although information on the determinants of adult health is incomplete, enough is known to improve adult health through preventive interventions (chapter 5).

• The determinants of adult health are many and diverse, providing multiple opportunities to promote health and prevent disease.

• Many determinants of adult ill-health in developing countries are behavioral, including smoking, alcohol consumption, and dietary habits. The prevalence of some important risk factors (notably smoking) is increasing. Past and present increases in these risk factors and the lag between exposure and disease development mean that death rates from some diseases (notably lung cancer) will rise inevitably over the next few decades.

• There is no clear relationship between overall adult mortality levels and the cause-of-death structure, which suggests that the health transition and its determinants are not the same everywhere (chapter 2). Child mortality is not closely associated with adult (especially male) mortality, and the socioeconomic correlates of adult mortality are distinctly different from those for child mortality (chapter 2). These observations suggest that developing countries cannot address adult health problems by expanding successful child health policies. They also suggest that countries are not locked into an inevitable experience of the health transition (Olshansky and Ault 1986) and that they can take action to avoid some of the undesirable manifestations of the transition—for example, by curbing tobacco use by women before it is too late.

The lack of data on adult ill-health in developing countries is a serious obstacle.

• The picture of adult health can be sketched only vaguely, and is least clear for mortality in poorer countries, for morbidity everywhere, and for the consequences of adult ill-health. This is not just a problem for statisticians and epidemiologists. Government policymakers need to know the rates and distribution of disease to plan new programs and evaluate them. Disease and risk factor surveillance systems are necessary for the development of rational and responsive public health and health care systems.

An Agenda for Improving the Information Available for Decision Making

The development of appropriate and effective health policies and programs needs to be based on relevant data. Such information can be obtained through two complementary approaches: the routine collection and analysis of health statistics, and a research program focusing on practical questions regarding the diseases, other health issues and the delivery system of a particular nation.

HEALTH STATISTICS. Basic health data collection is often considered in two categories: *surveillance* (including diseases and/or risk factors such as cases of tuberculosis or cervical cancer, numbers of cigarette smokers or alcohol drinkers) and *vital statistics* (birth and death records). Few developing countries give priority to either. Data quality may be questionable even when collection occurs. Data that are collected may not be analyzed or used to influence health policy.

RESEARCH. When countries are struggling to provide even basic health services, it is not difficult to view research as a luxury that they can ill afford.[2] The contrary view, cogently argued by the Commission on Health Research for Development, is that research is essential for these countries precisely because of the need to empower those who must accomplish more with fewer resources (Commission on Health Research for Development 1990). As chapters 2 through 5 of this book intimate, the research agenda to clarify the nature, causes, and consequences of adult ill-health is potentially a very large one. Ignorance in itself, however, is insufficient justification for research. Fortunately, the topics that merit investment in research (i.e., for which the benefits outweigh the costs of research) are a small subset of this vast sea of unknowing.[3] Without attempting to be rigorous, the following sections identify general areas in which ignorance is a serious obstacle to good decision making, and research has a high probability of providing the necessary information at reasonable cost. Some of these research topics are appropriate mandates of international and donor organizations. But the majority must be undertaken by developing countries themselves, with external assistance where necessary, for the purpose of establishing their own health policies. If the proposals by the Commission on Health Research for Development (1990) for fostering research on the health problems of developing countries are heeded, there is a good chance that the research topics outlined below will be more than a wish list. They will require the establishment of appropriate institutional and financing mechanisms to expand research capacities.

Levels and Causes of Adult Ill-Health

The analyses presented in this book provide a provocative counter to the argument that the study of the levels and causes of adult ill-health is unnecessary because enough is known already about the major problems. Without the evidence presented here, for example, how many policymakers would have predicted that the three leading causes of adult female death in El Salvador and Mauritius are the same as those in the United States—namely, cardiovascular diseases, cancer, and injuries? (See statistical appendix table A-3a.) These kinds of findings, based on the routine collection of mortality data, are an important start, but major information gaps remain.

Low health standards and poor data quality go together. The result is that the least is known about countries where adult health is the worst. For example, the mortality analysis in chapter 2, which includes only countries that have reasonably good cause-specific data, omits Sub-Saharan Africa, the poorest region in the world. The relative importance of causes of adult ill-health is likely to be different in the poorest countries. The data from India hint at this (chapter 2, table 2-14). Countries with good data may be an inappropriate basis from which to make global generalizations. More information is needed on adult mortality in the poorest countries, particularly those in Sub-Saharan Africa and South Asia.

There are good reasons why acceptable data have not been generated in many poorer countries: collecting data is expensive, and increasing coverage and accuracy adds substantially to costs. Modeling is a potential alternative. However, the dangers of using modeling to generate data on adult mortality are particularly severe for the least developed countries, for which the base-line data are poorest (chapter 2). Even for those countries that have reasonably reliable mortality data, questions remain about the real importance of certain causes of death. Current approaches to attributing cause of death can seriously underestimate the role of certain chronic conditions (e.g., diabetes and chronic obstructive lung disease). Inexpensive and easy-to-use methods for collecting and analyzing data on adult mortality, by improving vital statistics systems or adopting innovative approaches, need to be developed.[4]

Reliable, comparable data are even more scarce for adult morbidity than for mortality. It is tempting to conclude that any research on adult morbidity in developing countries would be worthwhile. This would be a mistake. Many previous studies, for example, have focused on single diseases—an approach which can lead to overestimates—and have employed inconsistent definitions and measurements of morbidity (chapter 3). Basic methodological work is needed to clarify the kinds of morbidity data that are useful and how they should be interpreted.[5] Once some consensus on methods is achieved, selected countries should collect data on the nature and level of community morbidity and disability. Determining the relationship between adult morbidity and mortality in these countries will clarify the ways in which mortality statistics are inadequate for identifying priority health problems and will help to generate simpler methods for estimating morbidity.

Evidence presented in chapter 3 suggests that much greater attention should be paid to the collection and use of good data on health services utilization. Such data tell policymakers precisely what kinds of morbidity prompt people to seek care and what demands are placed on private and public health care systems—information that is crucial for health care planning and resource allocation.

Consequences of Adult Ill-Health

Morbidity and mortality statistics are summary measures for distressing and sometimes catastrophic events, but inadequate for capturing the full effect of these events especially on poor families. Reliance on such indicators probably explains why the current understanding of the ramifications of adult ill-health and death is so rudimentary.

There are at least two important reasons for exploring further the consequences of ill-health and death. First, such exploration opens up new possibilities for ameliorating the effect of adult ill-health. These possibilities include attacking the root causes and reducing the occurrence of morbid events. There may also be opportunities to enhance existing coping strategies and to facilitate family recovery. Second, ill-health is not a homogeneous state and can have very different consequences from one individual to another depending not only on the nature of the ill-health but also on the social and economic environment. Rational justification of intervention priorities should take these differences into account.

What distinguishes the consequences of different kinds of ill-health, of ill-health experienced at different ages, or in different economic circumstances, or by men or women? The effect of catastrophic illness or injury and mortality in poorer households deserves particularly close attention. Studies to address these questions demand a more adequate understanding of the nature of the consequences of ill-health. They require the development of methods to measure and value these consequences with particular attention to identifying legitimate proxy measures based on highly correlated outcomes.

Coping processes that societies have evolved for mitigating the consequences of ill-health will need special attention both for an understanding of how they might appropriately be reinforced and to capture the full costs of adult ill-health and death. Formal and informal insurance are two coping mechanisms that should be studied in diverse cultural contexts. Too little is known about the efficiency losses incurred in developing countries that establish national insurance programs. An assessment of these costs arrayed against the benefits of such programs would provide information for making better decisions about the extension of insurance programs to other developing countries.

Determinants of Adult Ill-Health

The basic pathogenesis and pathophysiology of several important diseases of adults in developing countries (e.g., most cancers) are not understood adequately. This ignorance is an obstacle to the development of techniques for prevention or cure. Most of these health problems, however, are shared by developed countries that have both the incentive and the resources to undertake basic biomedical research, the results of which are likely to be broadly relevant elsewhere.

A similar rationale argues against major investments by developing countries in basic research on the nature of associations between adult diseases and their risk factors. Much of this basic research is being conducted already in developed countries and can be applied to less developed countries. It is highly likely, for example, that the relationship between the quantity, type and years of cigarette smoking and the risk of lung cancer is similar in Britain and Burkina Faso. Existing data and research on risk factors should be exploited.

Nevertheless, there is some justification for supporting certain original studies of certain risk factors in developing countries. In some settings, such research may play an important advocacy role. In addition, there may well be environmental or genetic factors that have received little attention because they occur infrequently in developed countries. Infectious causes of noncommunicable diseases are one example. Some puzzles, such as the apparently inverse trends in the rates of certain noncommunicable diseases and their putative risk factors (chapter 2), might be explained by previously unknown or underestimated etiologies. Furthermore, some risk factors have been evaluated inadequately in developed countries (for example, certain lifestyle and socioeconomic risk factors, various risk factor combinations, and exposure to risk factors in childhood). Examples of much needed research into risk factors in selected developing countries include the study of diet and indoor and outdoor air pollution in relation to a variety of diseases of the lungs and circulatory system.

In contrast to the transferability of data on the effects of risk factors, the level of exposure to these factors varies greatly by location. The high rates of smoking in Papua New Guinea tell nothing about smoking rates in Paraguay. Data on exposure to many key risk factors are poor and must be improved—alcohol and tobacco use, diet, exercise, sexual habits, environmental and workplace exposures, and injury are important examples. Without information on the nature, extent, time trends, and combinations of exposure to important risk factors, it is difficult to design appropriate preventive strategies. It is also important to know which people are at risk and how they are likely to respond to government action. This information helps to target and design interventions. Strategies may be different for men and women, for younger and older adults, for urban and rural populations, for industrial workers and bureaucrats. In the United States, for example, the young are more responsive to increases in the price of cigarettes than is the population as a whole (Lewit, Coate, and Grassman 1981).

For the same reason, it is crucial to understand the determinants of determinants—why, for example, do people smoke or not smoke? Information on the nature and relative importance of cultural, economic and educational factors in influencing risky behavior is needed for the design and delivery of interventions. Such information may be largely specific to a particular country or population group.

An Agenda for Action

The results from the research proposed above should arm developing countries with information on the major health problems of their adults, as well as the consequences and determinants of these problems. Good health policymaking depends on such information. But it requires more. It requires an understanding of the options available for tackling these problems and their full costs and benefits. That adult health problems exist, or even that they are demonstrably serious in their effects, is not enough to justify a role for government in prevention or treatment: the technology may not be available or may be hugely expensive and largely ineffective, or the private sector may provide services efficiently and equitably.

This book does not attempt to analyze policy options. Its objective—to document what is known of health problems facing adults in developing countries—is more modest. Nevertheless, the major findings of this book, outlined earlier in this chapter, are pregnant with implications for action. Not to clarify these, where possible, and warn against possible misreadings of the data would be both irresponsible and a wasted opportunity. Fortunately, a companion volume (Jamison and Mosley forthcoming) provides much of the data needed to make broad recommendations for action. That book and its cost-effectiveness analyses identify areas that merit more attention from developing countries and their collaborators.

Principles and Provisos

There are several observations and some caveats to stress in presenting this set of proposals. First, any analysis requires some organizing principle with which to categorize problems and responses. These categories inevitably impose limitations. Diseases and their determinants have largely structured the analyses in this book and in Jamison and Mosley (forthcoming) and have directed the nature of the recommendations that emerge. Reanalysis from a different perspective, perhaps using institutions, inputs, or income levels as the organizing principle, could reveal a complementary set of proposals.

Second, the database on the effectiveness and resource requirements of interventions is not very firm. Much of the information available about the costs and benefits of alternative strategies is limited to government costs and direct health outcomes and ignores equity despite the fact that most societies value it. Even within this limited framework, there is substantial ignorance about the achievements and costs of alternative approaches to improving adult health. Further research on this topic is strongly recommended.

Third, generalizations can be dangerous. Countries differ not only in the diseases with which they are grappling, but also the technical, economic, and political environments in which they must implement health policy. Not all the proposals have equal relevance everywhere. The focus on common, important, and generally poorly managed diseases has generated a list of interventions likely to be broadly relevant. These interventions need careful consideration by each developing country government in the light of its own particular circumstances.

One factor that may critically influence the desirability of investment in any given intervention in a particular country is the nature of the alternative investments that must be sacrificed. Appropriate decisions about government investment in adult health depend on how such investments would be used otherwise. If governments devote more resources to pain relief for cancer sufferers, would this be at the expense of fewer surgeries for advanced cancer patients, fewer actions for preventing motor vehicle collisions, fewer vaccinations for children, or fewer improvements in housing? Assessment of the desirability of investing in pain relief may well depend on the answer. Political, institutional, and financial structures all constrain choices for government spending in ways that have rarely been studied and are difficult to generalize. In the absence of information on the nature of these choices, the following are general observations on broadly defined options that developing countries may be considering.

• A shift of resources from direct investment in child health towards adults most probably would be inefficient and inequitable. This is particularly likely if resources were simply to follow current patterns of investment. Many interventions in child health are highly cost-effective[6] (Jamison and Mosley forthcoming), due both to the nature of the relatively inexpensive and effective interventions and the fact that they can be applied early in life with relatively immediate benefits. Moreover, income-related health differentials are greater among children than adults and the poor tend to be younger because of higher fertility rates. The implications are that investment in children is likely to address inequalities more effectively. If better evidence were available about the range and severity of the consequences of ill-health in adults and children, some rethinking of this position might be required.

• Communicable diseases of adults are generally more cost-effective to treat than noncommunicable diseases (Jamison and Mosley forthcoming). Many communicable diseases are readily cured with drugs (e.g., dysentery, bacterial pneumonia, and ascariasis). Noncommunicable diseases, conversely, are often difficult to manage. Some, like lung cancer, are essentially untreatable or involve high treatment costs with extremely modest benefits in terms of extra years of healthy life. Resources invested in noncommunicable diseases will benefit the poor and probably the poor more than the rich since many noncommunicable disease rates are higher among the poor (chapter 2), but investment in communicable disease control will probably be even more relatively beneficial to the poor. Major shifts in government health services from communicable to noncommunicable diseases, particularly while diseases like tuberculosis remain important problems, therefore do not seem appropriate. (Some important specific exceptions are discussed below).

• Cases of noncommunicable disease and injury in adults are increasing in number and in relative importance and are an appropriate target of concern for developing countries. Sizeable amounts of resources are already devoted to the treatment of these diseases with often questionable results. A redirection of some of these resources towards prevention is justified. Not only are some of these preventive strategies demonstrably more cost-effective than their therapeutic alternatives, but differences in the economic characteristics of treatment and prevention suggest that the private market in health is likely to underinvest (from a social perspective) in preventive strategies.

• It is hard to judge the relative merits of tradeoffs outside the health sector between economic development and health. A good case, however, probably could be made for some redistribution of the substantial resources employed by many governments in agriculture, industry, and price subsidies for the middle classes towards health and safety concerns.

• Finally, there is one transfer that is potentially efficient and dramatically equitable: shifting resources from developed countries to improve adult health in developing countries. A shift of resources for health research is similarly attractive (see note 2).

Ten areas of action are identified below. The first concerns the withdrawal of resources from some adult health programs. The other nine are specific interventions that merit more attention. All are highly cost-effective (less than $300 per discounted year of healthy life gained[7]) and address problems of importance in all developing countries (cancer, traffic injuries, maternal ill health, sexually transmitted diseases, tuberculosis, and diabetes).[8] Important tropical diseases are excluded. While some (e.g., malaria) are not being controlled adequately, others (e.g., onchocerciasis) are, and these diseases already receive considerable attention in international and national health programs.

Withdraw Resources from Inefficient and Inequitable Government Health Services for Adults

More than 60 percent of health care resources in some developing countries are spent on adult health care. Studies of how these resources are used and with what effect are rare. Anecdotal evidence, however, supports the suspicion that much of this investment is inefficient and inequitable. Cancer treatment is one example. An estimated two thirds of cancers in developing countries are incurable when diagnosed (WHO 1984). Technology offers little hope to those who contract stomach, esophageal, liver, or lung cancer. Even in the United States, the five-year survival rates of people who have these cancers are less than 15 percent, the survival rates of people with esophageal and liver cancers being only 2 to 3 percent (Greenwald and Sondik 1986). Overall, cancer treatment provides only small gains in life expectancy, and such gains often are associated with great discomfort and distress. Furthermore, cancer treatment is expensive, having cost-effectiveness estimates of more than $50,000 per discounted year of healthy life gained (Barnum and Greenberg forthcoming). Too often, the use of "aggressive therapeutic attempts to achieve minor prolongation of the act of uncomfortable dying predominate over the concern for the quality of death in a familiar environment" (Stjernsward 1988). Governments should withdraw resources from the nonpalliative treatment of most cancers. More appropriate approaches (cancer pain relief, cervical cancer screening and treatment, tobacco control and hepatitis B vaccination) are discussed below.

Jamison and Mosley (forthcoming) identify several other medical interventions that are highly costly in relation to adult health returns in terms of discounted healthy years of life gained. Medical management of hypertension (US$2,000), medical management of hypercholesterolemia (US$4,000), antiviral therapy for acquired immunodeficiency syndrome (AIDS) (US$5,000), and coronary artery bypass surgery (US$5000) are all immensely unattractive investments for public funds. Furthermore, these four conditions can be effectively and economically reduced by primary prevention involving behavioral and dietary practices.

This is a short list of some of the more obvious examples of technologies for which government spending should be discouraged. There are others. How commonly employed they are in developing countries has not been the subject of much attention. Health ministries should take a close look at the health services they provide to adults. An honest appraisal of the way existing health services meet the needs of adults is likely to reveal substantial room for improvement in a variety of administrative, training, financing, and technical areas. To constrain what would otherwise be a daunting task, the initial approach should focus on technical areas and, in particular, on those diseases of adults for which substantial resources are invested in treatment, such as injuries, cancer, cardiovascular diseases, diabetes, and tuberculosis. How do current services manage adult illnesses and injuries? What are the costs and effects and the factors important in determining them? What are the alternatives, their likely costs and effectiveness, and their effect on the poor? What are the implications of these findings for the broader health services issues of financing, administration, and training?

Minimizing government support for treatments of highly doubtful value may antagonize entrenched interests. For this reason, governments need to consider carefully their policies that influence health care staffing. Unless medical curricula, scholarships, specialty training, and salary structures all reflect identified health care priorities, powerful medical lobbies may seek to apply therapeutic advances in all areas without regard to cost-effectiveness. A decision to create a capability to do coronary angiography in a hospital needs to recognize the relationship of this diagnostic procedure with costly surgical treatment, the prevalence of the condition to be diagnosed and treated, the massive capital outlay required and opportunity costs of alternative health expenditure, the need for advanced training for a wide variety of personnel, and other hidden additional costs in infrastructure, training, and maintenance. Policies towards technology assessment and adoption need to be developed with great care and determination. This is an area in which developed-country governments are only just beginning to make progress, and some, such as the United States, have essentially no means of putting a brake on the use of excessively costly or ineffective technology.

Stop Smoking

Chapters 2 and 5 highlight the important role that tobacco use, particularly cigarette smoking, plays in undermining the health of adults in the developing world. The chapters discuss how tobacco use creates a burden of smoking-related morbidity and mortality, the full effect of which has yet to be felt. Recent estimates suggest a current worldwide annual toll of three million tobacco-related deaths—a quarter of which occur in India alone (Gupta 1988)—rising to more than ten million by the 2020s (Peto and Lopez 1990). Most of this increase will occur in developing countries. Fifty million Chinese alive today will die as a result of tobacco use (Novotny and Peto 1988).

Developed-country experience has clearly demonstrated that smoking habits can be changed. Changing public opinion through combined legislative and educational policies is promising. Effectively enforced legislation can hasten the decline of tobacco use, not only through direct restrictive action but also by conveying the idea that tobacco is harmful. Health warnings on tobacco product packages and bans on advertising and on smoking in public areas have been enacted in several developed countries and appear to be effective.

Education through individual counseling (e.g., by physicians) and high quality mass media campaigns have been shown to work in some countries, although more for encouraging nonsmokers never to start smoking than for helping smokers to stop. Education that targets children is especially promising and needs strengthening in most countries.

Taxing cigarettes is one of the most effective public health tools governments have for reducing cigarette smoking (appendix 6-A). Cigarette taxes deter nonsmokers from taking up the habit and reduce smoking among the poor and the young. Price increases of 10 percent are estimated to reduce consumption by 4 percent in the United States and Western Europe (WHO 1987). The first report from a developing country showed that an increase in tobacco tax (not price) of 10 percent in Papua New Guinea reduced demand for cigarettes by 7 percent (Chapman and Richardson 1990). Simultaneous increases in the cost of all tobacco products are necessary to discourage consumers from switching to cheaper (and perhaps even more hazardous) products (Warner 1990).

Barnum and Greenberg (forthcoming) analyzed the limited data available on the costs and effectiveness of strategies to reduce cigarette smoking and concluded that educational interventions are highly cost-effective. They found costs of about US$25 per discounted year of healthy life gained in countries with gross national products (GNP) of US$1,500 per capita, and they surmised that costs could be as low as US$15 if cigarette taxes are increased. There are other costs not captured by these figures. These costs include the discomfort suffered by individuals who give up smoking and the temporary unemployment and loss of national income suffered by those countries with large tobacco growing or cigarette manufacturing industries. But there are also additional benefits including reductions in smoking-related domestic fires and the saving of wood used for curing tobacco.

Demonstrating that the social benefits of reduced tobacco consumption exceed the costs does not imply that reforms can be implemented easily. Groups that have vested interests in maximizing cigarette consumption (cigarette manufacturers, distributors, and advertisers) have considerable influence. Consumers in developing countries have relatively weak lobbying power, are generally poorly informed, and do not currently face a major problem with tobacco-related diseases. They are less likely to play the role that their developed country counterparts have in stimulating antitobacco activities. The governments of developing countries, which almost universally benefit from taxation applied to cigarettes, may be reluctant to adopt measures they fear will harm this lucrative source of income. In fact, the demand-deterrent effect of moderate increases in tobacco taxes is less than the price increase, and the net effect is that a 10 percent increase in taxes is estimated to *increase* revenues by some 5 to 8 percent (Godfrey and Maynard 1988). Some governments have understood this and have taken firm action in the face of strong opposition from the tobacco industry (appendix 6-B).

The challenge is great. Each developing country should establish a national agency to plan and coordinate efforts against tobacco use. Procrastination cannot be justified. The control of tobacco use is one of the most, if not the most, important public health issue facing the world.[9]

Make Road Travel Safer

Injuries from motor vehicle collisions are a major cause of death for adults in developing countries and have become increasingly important in the last two decades: two- to three-fold increases in mortality rates were common during the 1970s (chapters 2 and 5). Crude death rates from motor vehicle collisions are higher in developing than developed countries, and when adjustments are made for the number of vehicles, the difference is even more dramatic: the number of fatalities per thousand motor vehicles is ten to twenty times greater in developing countries. These high death rates are accompanied by substantial levels of serious morbidity and disability and destruction of property. Motor vehicle collisions result in estimated economic losses of 1 to 2 percent of GNP in some developing countries (Fossberg 1986).

Two important features distinguish the developing country picture: the high percentage of people injured in motor vehicle collisions who are pedestrians, and the variety of vehicles on the road—bicycles, animal-drawn carts, and high-speed trucks all jostle for space in narrow roads. Fatalism is the first obstacle to overcome in reducing these deaths and injuries. Motor vehicle collisions are not accidents. They have determinants that are largely controllable. These include dangerous road design (characterized by poor lighting and lack of traffic segregation); dangerous driving (involving high speeds, young or inexperienced drivers, and drivers under the influence of alcohol); and dangerous vehicles (characterized by insufficient protection for drivers and passengers, poor maintenance, and oversized loads). Legislation, pricing policies, direct investment, and education are all potentially effective.

Alcohol plays an important but inadequately studied role in motor vehicle collisions in developing countries (chapter 5).[10] Several strategies, including price increases, have been successful in moderating general alcohol consumption (Curry 1987) and in reducing motor vehicle related mortality, especially among young drivers (Phelps 1988). Legislation, including penalties for drunk driving and limits placed on the hours and conditions of alcohol sales, is another approach, though generally less successful (IARC 1988).

Unfortunately, there is little evidence of the cost-effectiveness of any of these strategies in developing countries. Further investigations are urgently needed. The relative importance of different causes of traffic collisions varies in different countries, and the variation that this implies for specific preventive strategies suggests that governments should collect location-specific data as an essential complement to their efforts to make road travel safer. In the meantime, it would be highly prudent for governments to make traffic safety a high priority by focusing on improving road design and modifying driver behavior. The latter could be achieved through such measures as the enactment and enforcement of legislation governing speed limits, seat belt provision and use, and the use of helmets and headlights by motorcyclists. Special attention should be given to reducing alcohol use—which has health consequences beyond vehicle collisions (chapter 5)—improving pedestrian safety, and accommodating slow and mixed traffic.[11]

Vaccinate Against Hepatitis B

Worldwide, more than 300 million people are carriers of hepatitis B. Of these, 25 to 30 percent will die of hepatitis B virus-induced cirrhosis or hepatocellular carcinoma (Eddleston 1990). Hepatocellular carcinoma is one of the most common cancers in southeast Asia and the Pacific (for example, see the mortality rate from liver cancer for men in Hong Kong [statistical appendix table A-3b]) and is a common cancer in parts of Sub-Saharan Africa. It is essentially untreatable. Up to 80 percent of hepatocellular carcinomas are attributed to hepatitis B virus. The risk of developing liver cancer is two hundred times greater for hepatitis B carriers than non-carriers.

The cost of the hepatitis B vaccine recently fell as a result of technological developments and competitive pricing (from more than US$100 to less than US$3 for prophylaxis that is 75 to 95 percent effective in preventing the hepatitis B carrier state).[12] The vaccine, intended for administration to newborns and infants, can be delivered through the infrastructure already in place for other childhood vaccinations (Hall, Greenwood, and Whittle 1990), thereby increasing the feasibility and reducing the cost of delivery. Several developing countries, including Gambia and Taiwan, already have started national hepatitis B vaccination programs, and Italy is considering compulsory hepatitis B vaccination for all infants (Garattini 1991).

As with many preventive strategies, the financial attractiveness of vaccinating for hepatitis B is modified by the delay between investment in the intervention and the realization of benefits (that is, avoided cancers). Nevertheless, the cost per discounted year of healthy life gained is likely to be in the range of US$25 to US$50 (Barnum and Greenberg, forthcoming; Kane, Clements, and Hu forthcoming). This calculation takes into account all mortality related to hepatitis B—principally liver cancer, but also cirrhosis of the liver and hepatitis itself. Most developing countries will find hepatitis B vaccination a highly worthwhile investment.

Make Motherhood Safe

Maternal health problems are widespread and should be priorities for intervention. The maternal mortality ratio (the number of maternal deaths per 100 thousand live births) is in the range of 100 to 2000 in developing countries, compared to less than 30 in most developed countries. The lifetime risk of dying of maternal causes (which combines maternal mortality ratios with fertility rates) is one in twenty in much of Africa and one in ten thousand in northern Europe. Three quarters of all maternal deaths are caused by hemorrhage, sepsis, or eclampsia, and a considerable proportion of the hemorrhage and sepsis is attributable to abortion or obstructed labor.

The majority of these maternal deaths are preventable. Appropriate preventive activities vary from country to country, but developing country governments should consider a) screening to detect women at high risk (including very young women and women with sexually transmitted diseases and other reproductive tract infections), b) referring women with complicated pregnancies to higher level care and encouraging them to deliver in health facilities, and c) providing tetanus toxoid immunizations, iron/folate supplements and, where necessary, malaria prophylaxis. Other measures worth serious consideration are the monitoring of weight and blood pressure during pregnancy, the educating of pregnant women about signs of premature labor, and measures to ensure that all pregnant women receive pelvic examinations. High priorities for care at delivery include provision of hygienic supplies, the training of birth attendants (both traditional and health service staff), and the maintenance of referral systems for complications and emergencies. Programs that improve general education and literacy also benefit maternal health, and interventions that help women avoid unwanted pregnancies are highly cost-effective.

Cost and effectiveness data for these measures are scarce. However, the averting of maternal mortality through the combined effects of antenatal care, safe delivery, and emergency referral measures (that is, the package described above) is among the more cost-effective interventions for adults (Jamison and Mosley forthcoming).

Because the risk factors for maternal morbidity and mortality are almost identical to those for neonatal morbidity and mortality, these measures also benefit newborns by increasing birthweights and neonatal survival. If the effect on perinatal mortality is taken into account, the cost-effectiveness of this same package becomes even more favorable.[13]

Promote Safe Sex and Treat STDs

Sexually transmitted diseases (STDs), especially AIDS and syphilis, contribute considerably to morbidity and mortality in many parts of the developing world (chapters 2 and 5). AIDS, an incurable and fatal disease caused by infection with the human immunodeficiency virus (HIV), is a growing problem (chapter 2, appendix 2-C) and already the major cause of productive days of life lost in Africa.

A variety of strategies can be used to prevent the spread of HIV, which is transmitted through sexual contact, intravenous drug use, blood transfusions and intrauterine transmission. Legislative measures are controversial, but pricing policies (e.g., reducing the cost of condoms, needles, and syringes; stopping payment for blood donations), voluntary partner notification, and investment in improved blood screening may be effective and worthy of more attention. The success of educating individuals to have fewer sexual partners and use condoms to prevent the spread of HIV has been mixed and not always well evaluated. Education seems to be most cost-effective when mass media messages target high risk groups. Developing country governments should promote the use of condoms, especially among the promiscuous, and should screen blood donors for HIV antibodies. These interventions are cost-effective in reducing HIV transmission. Depending on the prevalence of HIV infection, the cost-effectiveness per discounted year of healthy life gained is US$8 to US$50 for condom promotion and US$1 to US$5 for blood screening. If the benefit of condom use in the prevention of other sexually transmitted diseases is taken into consideration, the cost-effectiveness of this intervention is even greater.

AIDS has provoked a global response, and substantial funding is being directed to AIDS research and prevention. All countries should exploit this opportunity to develop institutional capacities and effective ways of using health education to promote safe sex. The control and treatment of other sexually transmitted diseases is also highly cost-effective. Such control and treatment may also reduce HIV transmission, partly by the direct effect of interventions, such as safe sex promotion, and partly because some of these diseases are major risk factors for HIV transmission.[14]

Improve Case Management for Tuberculosis

Tuberculosis is widespread throughout the developing world and one of the major killers of adults (chapter 2). An estimated two million adults in developing countries die annually from tuberculosis, representing nearly 20 percent of all adult deaths and probably more than 25 percent of all avoidable adult deaths. Tuberculosis is one of the most common opportunistic infections of people in Africa who are HIV-positive, and the prevalence of tuberculosis is increasing in areas with epidemics of HIV infection and AIDS (Anon 1990b; Elliott and others 1990). Effective diagnostic tests and chemotherapeutic agents exist, but their use has been undervalued in recent years by much of the international health community. Vaccination with bacillus Calmette-Guerin (BCG) is an additional and cost-effective approach to control (Rodrigues and Smith 1990).[15]

Treatment of tuberculosis has been demonstrated to give excellent results in developing country field conditions, even in large-scale, national interventions (such as in Tanzania) in which the challenge of achieving compliance for the necessary six to eighteen months of treatment is great. Treatment is highly effective (cure rates approach 90 percent; reductions in transmission are parallel) and also inexpensive. Passive case detection (using sputum microscopy) combined with short course chemotherapy for sputum-positive cases appears to be the most cost-effective approach, having an estimated cost of less than US$10 per discounted year of healthy life gained.

Developing-country health ministries should devote special energies to reassessing their current approaches to tuberculosis control and to designing and implementing new programs using short course chemotherapy.[16]

Screen for Cervical Cancer

Cervical cancer is the most common cancer in developing countries and leads to substantial morbidity and mortality when it reaches an advanced symptomatic stage. If detected early, however, it is almost 100 percent curable.[17] The technology for early detection (cytological screening in the form of Papanicolaou tests) is technically straightforward, sensitive and relatively inexpensive. Well-organized cervical screening programs (for example, in Canada and Iceland) have reduced cervical cancer mortality by 50 to 60 percent, and cost-effectiveness calculations indicate that cervical cancer screening and early treatment are worthwhile investments. Screenings every five years of women aged thirty-five to sixty years are estimated to cost between US$75 and US$400 per discounted year of healthy life gained (depending, among other things, on the prevalence of cervical cancer and the ability to detect and treat cervical cancer in its earliest stages) in a country where the average GNP per capita is US$1,500.

Fewer than 5 percent of women in developing countries have been screened for cervical cancer in the last five years, and the little screening that has been done has tended to focus inappropriately on younger women who have lower risk (WHO 1986b). Developing countries should consider investing more in cervical cancer screening and treatment, especially for women aged 35 to 60 years. Developing countries (e.g., Brazil and China) that have extensive health care systems (including the ability to obtain pathology reviews, do surgical procedures and avoid postoperative infections) are more likely to be able to identify and treat cervical cancers cost-effectively than are countries with rudimentary health care systems.[18]

Relieve Cancer Pain

Cancer is one of the three leading causes of death in adults in developing countries and will continue to be important even if the cancer prevention and screening measures advocated in this chapter are adopted. An estimated 30 to 40 percent of people with early stages of cancer and 45 to 100 percent of people with advanced stages of cancer experience moderate to severe pain (Stjernsward 1988). The technology to alleviate this pain exists. The World Health Organization has developed a method to relieve 80 to 90 percent of pain by administering drugs on a schedule instead of on demand and moving from nonopiates to weak and then strong opiates until the patient is free from pain (WHO 1986a). The average cost (including the costs of drugs and outpatient services) is estimated at US$75 to US$250 per discounted year of healthy life gained.

Despite cheap and effective means for relieving cancer pain, most cancer patients in developing countries are not offered pain relief (Stjernsward 1988). For example, in India, which has about 20 percent of the cancers in the developing world, only about 5 percent of cancer patients are treated for pain at specialized treatment centers; the rest are largely neglected (Eddy 1985). In many countries, misguided national drug legislation limits the availability of pain relieving drugs, and poorly managed drug procurement and distribution systems further limit supplies. Among health specialists, ignorance about appropriate drug strategies and misplaced fears of creating addiction further constrain the use of these drugs. Developing countries should pay serious attention to the options for making cancer pain relief more widely available through appropriate legislative, logistic, and training arrangements. New legislation, training protocols, and retraining programs for physicians, although not without cost, are likely to involve relatively small one-time investments. Some controls on the use of addictive drugs are clearly appropriate. The challenge is to design systems that achieve this without penalizing the many people who, without access to these drugs, will suffer unnecessarily painful deaths.[19]

Treat Diabetes

Diabetes is a more serious problem for adults in developing countries than generally acknowledged. In some countries, diabetes accounts for more than 5 percent of the mortality risk of adult women; in Trinidad and Tobago (statistical appendix table A-3a) and Nauru (chapter 2), it is as high as 15 percent. Diabetic persons may develop a variety of serious complications—including blindness, renal disease, heart disease, and peripheral nerve damage—and have a shorter than average life expectancy. Treatment of complications imposes a substantial burden on health care facilities in some countries.

Treatment of non-insulin-dependent diabetes with oral hypoglycemic drugs may be a cost-effective proposition, at about US$330 per discounted year of healthy life gained, and many of the dietary and behavioral changes recommended for prevention of cardiovascular disease are very likely to assist in the prevention of diabetes. Treatment of insulin-dependent diabetes may be even more worthwhile. Characterized by lifetime dependence on daily insulin injections, without which the patient dies, insulin-dependent diabetes frequently goes untreated in developing countries. The basic costs for insulin and syringes are estimated at about US$150 per discounted year of healthy life gained. Although this is an underestimate of total costs, it suggests that insulin treatment is relatively cost-effective, even if costs are doubled to allow for patient monitoring and project administration.

Education programs for diabetic patients and their health care providers are highly cost-effective in some developed countries (e.g., the United States). Teaching diabetic patients proper foot care (i.e., how to bathe and dry feet, how to clip toenails, what types of footwear to use) reduces the rate of foot and leg infections and prevents amputations. Blindness can be prevented or delayed by opthalmologic screening (which relatively uneducated workers can be trained to do) followed by laser repair of pathologic changes in the retina. The relatively sophisticated technology is expensive, but so is the social and economic cost of blindness. A trial program of retinal screening for persons with diabetes should be done to determine the appropriateness of using this intervention in developing countries.

Policies towards diabetes in developing countries should be reviewed, and consideration should be given to additional subsidies for treatment of insulin-dependent and non-insulin-dependent diabetes and for patient and health care provider education.[20]

Other Important Agenda Items

The interventions highlighted above are those that are both relatively cost-effective and likely to have a substantial effect on morbidity and mortality levels in most developing countries. These interventions are not an exhaustive list of cost-effective options, and the reader should consult Jamison and Mosley (forthcoming) for a fuller account. Other interventions, mentioned in chapter 5, deserve close attention but do not lend themselves to global recommendations at this time.

DIETARY INTERVENTIONS. As discussed in chapter 5, diet plays a major role in a variety of adult illnesses—see also Leslie (1991) and National Research Council (1989). Specific dietary problems, however, differ markedly from one country to the next. Furthermore, good evidence on the cost and effectiveness of dietary interventions is not available. Dietary interventions may merit further research and experimental implementation in some developing countries.

POLLUTION CONTROL. Much is known about the hazards of severe pollution and specific toxic agents, the technology of pollution control, and government actions that are effective in controlling pollution (see chapter 5). Furthermore, pollution control is an area in which market failure demands some response from government. For some cities in the developing world, it would be foolish for governments not to take steps to control pollution through appropriate regulations and pricing policies. The specific strategies required will vary depending on the nature and extent of the pollution in these cities.

OCCUPATIONAL ILLNESS AND INJURY INTERVENTIONS. Occupational hazards are an important cause of adult morbidity and mortality (chapter 5), and many are preventable at reasonable cost. Although important and worthy of further research and intervention investment by developing countries, occupational hazards are too varied and too location-specific for global recommendations to be appropriate.

An Agenda for Intervention-Related Research

The interventions highlighted in the previous section simultaneously serve as proposals for action and provocations to research. They are some of the best bets, given present knowledge, but the evidence for them is by no means cut-and-dried.

Preventive programs as a whole are poorly developed in many countries. This is sometimes because determinants have not been identified or do not appear readily amenable to modification. Often, however, it is simply that prevention has been an unjustifiably low priority. Research is needed to evaluate how worthwhile selected preventive strategies are and to determine how best to implement such strategies. One way of accomplishing this is to conduct field trials of promising interventions. The results of these field trials (which should include an analysis of both costs and health consequences) should be used to select strategies for widespread adoption, and the experience gained in these field trials should be used to improve capacity for implementing these strategies. Several issues remain to be clarified

What are the spin-off effects for children and the elderly of investments to improve the health of adults?

• For children, the potential benefits (chapter 4) include those resulting from a) reduced exposure to risks (for example, passive smoking); b) averting the death or disability of parents; and c) improvements in treatment programs (for example, tuberculosis control). The effect of each of these has yet to be clearly and widely demonstrated.

• Saving the lives of adults simply to have them spend a disabled and unhappy old age is a questionable objective. Waiting until adults become ill and then treating them is a strategy that might increase the proportion of the elderly who are unwell. Preventing adult ill-health is probably an effective way to ensure a healthy old age. Some research supports this: morbidity can be postponed to later ages through mortality prevention strategies (even when these fail to reduce mortality) (Fries, Green, and Levine 1989; Heikkinen 1987; Rose and Shipley 1990). But more evidence is needed and uncertainty remains as to how the prevention of adult mortality affects the number of years spent subsequently in a state of frail health.

How best can equity objectives be served in meeting the health needs of adults?

• Equity considerations provide much of the rationale for the direct provision of health care services and other government interventions in the health sector. Yet the exact distributional consequences of different adult health interventions remain unclear.

• Noncommunicable diseases have been considered by some to be diseases of affluence—the result of lifestyle factors that the rich, in particular, can afford to adopt. This is a misconception. Although scarce, data on socioeconomic differentials and mortality rates in developing countries show that the poor have higher rates of noncommunicable diseases than the rich (chapter 2, appendix 2-B). This is unequivocally the case in developed countries.[21]

• The equity effect, however, of additional government investment in the prevention of noncommunicable diseases in adults is unclear. There are two dimensions of equity that need to be distinguished: equity of health outcomes and equity of health care costs. Whether equity of outcome is improved as a result of preventing noncommunicable diseases in adults depends on what other opportunities for health improvement are forfeited. Shifting resources from children to adults, or from communicable to noncommunicable disease control, may reduce equity. Investing in prevention at the expense of treatment is more likely to improve equity: therapeutic services are notoriously regressive, being demanded and consumed more by the wealthy than the poor. The outcome equity of prevention strategies is influenced also by the choice of medium, style, and geographic or commodity focus. Televising educational messages where few people own televisions and distributing brochures where few people read are strategies that are more likely to benefit the rich.

• Improvements in the equity of health outcomes are sometimes accompanied by a deterioration in the equitable distribution of costs. For example, taxes on cigarettes and alcohol will depress demand more among the poor, bringing them greater health benefits than the rich. However, this may well be achieved at a financial cost to the poor that is proportionally greater than that to the rich, for whom cigarette purchases constitute a relatively small share of total expenditure.

What are the appropriate sources of finance for the proposed adult health interventions?

• In addition to the finances generated by withdrawing government funds from inefficient and inequitable health care of adults, there are a number of potential sources of funding for the strategies proposed above. Nonhealth sectors can be called on (for example, to improve road construction) or fees can be charged for certain services. Several of the recommended interventions actually have the potential to generate resources for the health sector: taxation of cigarettes, alcohol, gasoline and private vehicles could increase government resources while at the same time reducing health risks, depending on the level of tax and the responsiveness of demand to price. If extra funds are generated, health ministries will be competing with other government bodies to secure these resources. Health ministries will, therefore, need carefully prepared proposals for taxation that stress the explicit objective of health improvement through the combined use of both price increases and additional health-related investments.

Beyond the provision of health services, what is the appropriate role for government in improving adult health?

• Much of the health care of adults takes place outside government health facilities. The government share in the health sector of developing countries is generally less than 50 percent (de Ferranti 1983). Government can still influence practices in the rest of the health services sector by, for example, governing medical training and certification and regulating the use of medical technology and drugs. Given the importance of the nongovernment health services sector, these avenues of influence deserve attention.

• Many of the attractive options for improving adult health are preventive and do not involve health services at all. Some take the form of direct investment, for example, in safer roads or working environments. Others imply a role for legislation and pricing policies. These tools have not been studied adequately, and their appropriate use needs to be better defined through careful analysis of costs and effects.

An Agenda for Policy

There is a policy vacuum in the field of adult health. Many, perhaps most, developing countries have an explicit policy for child health, supported by some form of systematic data collection on the incidence of disease and the use of services. This policy typically gives priority to common infectious diseases and perinatal ill-health and translates into action through national programs designed specifically to address these problems. Many governments supplement these targets with broader programs addressing family size, child spacing, and nutrition.

For adult health, the picture is strikingly different. Some governments maintain effective action against one or more of the major parasitic diseases such as malaria and schistosomiasis. Some governments are initiating measures to reduce maternal mortality. Some governments have tuberculosis control activities, although these have fallen into disrepair in many countries. Few countries, however, have a coherent policy about the health of adults or a plan for reducing and treating some of the major noncommunicable diseases and injuries that cause adult ill-health. In most countries, even the great killer tobacco is not the focus of any consistent government action.

The number of adults in developing countries is increasing rapidly—from 2.1 billion in 1988 to an estimated 3.8 billion in 2015 (chapter 1, table 1-1), and the increase is most rapid in the poorest countries. Adults are influential politically and likely to demand increasing expenditure on sophisticated curative health services. Developing countries cannot afford to delay the articulation of adult health policy and action. They need to identify important information gaps and fill them through the development of disease surveillance and improved vital statistics systems and through action-oriented research. They need to make strenuous efforts to reduce the prevalence of risk factors through prevention and to improve the cost-effectiveness of therapy. Governments must target specific modifiable determinants of adult ill-health—such as tobacco use, dangerous roads and hepatitis B infection—and take systematic action to reduce exposure to these risk factors. The cost-effectiveness of the substantial resources already expended on treating ill and injured adults should be examined carefully. Public funds should be spent on curative services that offer good value for the money and not on expensive means to achieve minor prolongation of life.

Policy formulation for adult health needs to start now. The longer it takes, the more vulnerable health resources will be to pressures from adults for high cost, marginally effective technology, and the greater the adult health problems of the future will be.

Appendix 6-A. Tobacco Pricing Policy

Governments play a substantial role in setting the price of cigarettes, primarily through taxes, and there is considerable variation in price among countries. For example, in northern and western European countries, the retail price of twenty cigarettes varied from US$4.17 in Norway and US$3.60 in Denmark to US$0.80 in France and US$1.21

in Italy in 1987 (United States dollars). The tax rate on cigarettes in European countries varies from 35 to 87 percent of the retail price, the average being about 53 percent. Tax rates are within this range for the majority of countries worldwide.

The largest reductions in tobacco consumption are produced by a combination of regular price increases of tobacco products in conjunction with an effective health education program. If either portion is missing, the effect is markedly reduced, and a decrease in tobacco tax rates can easily negate the effect of other components of a tobacco control program.

The effect of raising taxes on tobacco products is measured by the price elasticity of demand—the percentage of change in tobacco consumption associated with a 1 percent increase in price—adjusted for inflation. The price elasticity for cigarettes in North America and western Europe is approximately -0.4—that is, for every 10 percent increase in the price of cigarettes, consumption will fall 4 percent. The fall in consumption is greater among teenagers (an elasticity of -1.4 [Lewit, Coate, and Grossman 1981]), particularly among young teenage boys, and among lower socioeconomic groups. Furthermore, an increase in price will have a greater effect on people's decisions to start or stop smoking, rather than on the number of cigarettes smoked. Thus a price increase has an important role in reducing the number of people who start or continue a tobacco habit.

An increase in cigarette prices not only affects cigarette consumption, it also results in a switch to lower priced brands (often unfiltered), hand-rolled cigarettes and other tobacco products. Tobacco duties were increased by 39 percent in the Federal Republic of Germany in 1982. By the next year, the sale of name brands had dropped by 17 percent, but the sales of low-priced cigarettes and of tobacco for hand-rolled cigarettes had increased markedly, making up 60 percent of the decline of sales in name brand cigarettes. This problem can be largely solved by market-neutral simultaneous increases in the cost of all tobacco products, with greater proportional increases in the least expensive, such as tobacco for hand-rolled cigarettes.

The most frequent argument against the raising of tobacco prices is that it will lead to a decrease in governmental tobacco tax revenues. In reality, however, an increase in tobacco taxes will cause a rise rather than a fall in tax revenues (Warner 1984). The primary reason for this is that while a price increase (above the rate of inflation) will result in a decrease in consumption, the decrease in consumption is proportionally smaller than the increase in tax revenues (provided that the price elasticity of demand is greater than -1). It has been estimated that a 10 percent increase in the tobacco tax rate will result in a 5 to 8 percent rise in tobacco tax revenues (Godfrey and Maynard 1988; Jones and Posnett 1988). While this relationship will not continue to hold if prices are raised to astronomical levels, they can be raised considerably in all countries before a point of diminishing returns is reached. If price increases do not keep pace with inflation, consumption will increase and tax revenues will fall. This section draws on Stanley (forthcoming).

Appendix 6-B. Increase in Tobacco Taxation in Hong Kong

The following extract comes from a press release issued 8 March 1991

Hong Kong's Massive Tax Increase Stuns Tobacco Industry

The tobacco companies in Hong Kong this week were reported "stunned" by the massive and unexpected 200 percent increase in the rate of tobacco duty announced by Hong Kong's Financial Secretary. The cost of a packet of twenty cigarettes will increase from the present US$1.50 to between US$2.50 and US$3.00. For the first time in Hong Kong's history, the government stated that this increase was for health, not fiscal, reasons. In announcing the news, the Financial Secretary said, "It has been put to me persuasively that for health reasons a hefty increase is now justified. So, with a particular view to reducing the attractiveness of smoking to young people, I am proposing an increase of 200 percent in the rate of duty. Incidentally, although the proposed increases are for health and not fiscal reasons, it has not escaped my notice that the estimated additional revenue yield after allowing for consumer resistance will be about $1.9 billion [in Hong Kong dollars]."

Philip Morris' Director of Regional Corporate Affairs was quoted in the *South China Morning Post* (SCMP) as saying, "I think it is a cheap, underhanded, and punitive attack on the million or so people in Hong Kong who are adults and choose to smoke, and the 30,000 or so people who earn an income from the tobacco industry" (SCMP, 7 March 1991).

The General Manager of RJ Reynolds, who is also the newly elected Chairman of the Tobacco Institute of Hong Kong, said, "The enormous increase is disproportionate, regressive and runs contrary to Hong Kong's traditional policy of not adopting social engineering measures. This action will fuel inflation at a time when Hong Kong can ill afford it, and the lower income segment of the smoking population will be hit hardest" (SCMP, 7 March 1991).

Public and media interest has been intense. The health concerns have been emphasizing the beneficial effect of this increase, especially among the young and the poor, and have supported this commendable public health action by the government.

This press release was issued by Judith Mackay, Asian Consultancy on Tobacco Control, Hong Kong.

Notes

1. A major caveat on interpreting the mortality data presented in chapter 2 is that high mortality countries are seriously underrepresented in the analyses. High mortality countries, including all countries in Sub-Saharan Africa, lack cause-specific mortality data for adults and therefore were not included in the analyses in chapter 2. The extrapolation of the data to high mortality levels (see tables 2-13a and 2-13b) may underestimate the importance of communicable and reproductive causes of death in high mortality countries or, indeed, in most poor countries.

2. Global annual expenditure on health research was about US$30 billion in 1986 (Murray and others 1990). Of this, US$1.6 billion was spent on developing country health problems, including the US$685 million that was spent in the developing countries themselves.

3. Mosley, Jamison, and Henderson (1990) concluded that ''allocation of research resources to the health sector in developing countries virtually ignores the problems that will dominate the policy agenda in years to come.''

4. Problems with existing approaches for measuring overall and disease-specific adult mortality levels and possibilities for future research are described in detail in two World Bank publications (Hayes and others 1989; Timaeus and Graham 1989).

5. Important progress is being made already in selected areas—for example, in maternal morbidity (Graham and Campbell 1990).

6. This is only strongly true relative to adult health interventions when a year of healthy life gained in childhood is given equal value to a year in adulthood.

7. All cost-effectiveness data in this chapter are in 1989 United States dollars per discounted healthy life-year (DHLY) gained, at a discount rate of 3 percent and for a country with a gross national product (GNP) per capita of US$1,500.

8. Information on what governments and organizations are doing already to prevent and manage adult ill-health is not readily available. Nevertheless, anecdotal evidence suggests that the interventions recommended below are unlikely to be ''more of the same'' in most developing countries.

9. This section draws on Stanley (forthcoming).

10. This is also true in developed countries. In the United States, motor vehicle collisions are the leading cause of death of people at all ages from one to thirty-four years, and almost half of all motor vehicle related deaths are alcohol-related. Forty percent of all people in the United States are involved in an alcohol-related motor vehicle collision sometime during their lives (Anon 1990a).

11. This section draws on Stansfield, Smith and McGreevey (forthcoming), Barss and others (1991), Smith and Barss (1991), and additional work by Carlos Dora, London School of Hygiene & Tropical Medicine.

12. Hepatitis B is the only new vaccine recommended here for immediate adoption. Over the next two decades it is likely that several new vaccines will become available that have the potential to reduce the burden of adult disease considerably. These may include new vaccines against leishmaniasis, leprosy, malaria, schistosomiasis (Playfair, Blackwell, and Miller 1990), tuberculosis, and AIDS and other viral diseases.

13. This section draws on Walsh and others (forthcoming) and additional contributions from Kamal Ahmad, formerly of the World Bank and now of the Rockefeller Foundation. See also Herz and Measham (1987).

14. This section draws on Over and Piot (forthcoming).

15. In addition to its effect on pulmonary tuberculosis, which is highly variable, BCG also has an effect on tuberculosis, meningitis, and leprosy.

16. This section draws on Murray, Rouillon, and Styblo (forthcoming).

17. There are important parallels between cervical cancer and breast cancer. Both are cancers of women, both are among the most common cancers, and both can be treated if detected early by screening. The major difference is that cervical cancer mortality rates are declining with development while breast cancer mortality rates are rising (chapter 2, table 2-12). Barnum and Greenberg (forthcoming) take an optimistic view of the cost-effectiveness ($180 per discounted year of healthy life) of breast cancer screening by physical examination (rather than by mammography). However, in a recent and comprehensive review, Kalache (1990) doubts the feasibiity and effectiveness of this intervention in developing countries.

18. This section draws on Barnum and Greenberg (forthcoming).

19. This section draws on Barnum and Greenberg (forthcoming).

20. This section draws on Vaughan, Gilson, and Mills (1989).

21. For example, there is a strong social gradient in noncommunicable disease mortality rates in the United Kingdom, as shown by national and regional analyses and by the study of specific groups (Morris 1990; Strong 1990).

References

Anon. 1990a. ''Alcohol-Related Traffic Fatalities: United States 1982–89.'' *Morbidity and Mortality Weekly Report* 39:889–891.

———. 1990b. ''Africa's Tuberculosis Problem and Chemoprophylaxis.'' *Lancet* i:1249–50.

Barnum, H., and R. Greenberg. Forthcoming. ''Cancers.'' In D. T. Jamison and W. H. Mosley, eds., *Disease Control Priorities in Developing Countries.* New York: Oxford University Press for the World Bank.

Barss, P., G. S. Smith, D. Mohan, and S. P. Baker. 1991. *Injuries of Adults in Developing Countries: Epidemiology and Policy.* Washington, D.C.: Population, Health and Nutrition Division, World Bank.

Chapman, S., J. Richardson. 1990. ''Tobacco Excise and Declining Tobacco Consumption: The Case of Papua New Guinea.'' *American Journal of Public Health* 80:537–40.

Commission on Health Research for Development. 1990. *Health Research: Essential Link to Equity in Development.* New York: Oxford University Press.

Curry, R. L. 1987. "A Framework for National Alcohol Programmes in Developing Countries." *British Journal of Addiction* 82:721–26.

De Ferranti, D. 1983. "Background Information for Analysis of Financing and Resource Allocation Issues in Health Sector and Project Work." *PHN Technical Notes.* Gen 23. Washington, D.C.: World Bank.

Eddleston, A. 1990. "Modern Vaccines: Hepatitis." *Lancet* i:1142–45.

Eddy, D. 1985. *Priorities for Cancer Control in India.* Document WHO/SEA/CAN/64. Geneva: World Health Organization.

Elliott, A. M., N. Luo, G. Tembo, B. Halwiindi, G. Steenbergen, L. Machiels, J. Pobee, P. Nunn, R. J. Hayes, and K. P. W. McAdam. 1990. "Impact of HIV on Tuberculosis in Zambia: A Cross-Sectional Study." *British Medical Journal* 301:412–15.

Fossberg, P. 1986. "The World Bank's Approach to Road Safety." Paper presented to the 2nd World Congress on Road Safety; Luxembourg, September.

Fries, J., L. Green, and S. Levine. 1989. "Health Promotion and the Compression of Morbidity." *Lancet* i:481–83.

Garattini, S. 1991. "Italy: Compulsory Hepatitis B Vaccination." *Lancet* 337:228.

Godfrey, C., and A. Maynard. 1988. "Economic Aspects of Tobacco Use and Taxation Policy." *British Medical Journal* 289:339–43.

Graham, W. J., and O. M. R. Campbell. 1990. *Measuring Maternal Health: Defining the Issues.* London: London School of Hygiene & Tropical Medicine.

Greenwald, P., and E. Sondik, eds. 1986. "Cancer Control Objectives for the Nation 1985–2000." *National Cancer Institute Monograph* 2(1):1–105.

Gupta, P. C. 1988. "Health Consequences of Tobacco Use in India." *World Smoking and Health* 13:5–10.

Hall, A. J., B. M. Greenwood, and H. Whittle. 1990. "Modern Vaccines: Practice in Developing Countries." *Lancet* 335:774–77.

Hayes, R., T. Mertens, G. Lockett, and L. Rodrigues. 1989. "Causes of Adult Deaths in Developing Countries—A Review of Data and Methods." *Policy, Planning and Research Working Papers.* WPS 246. Washington, D.C.: World Bank.

Heikkinen, E. 1987. "Health Implications of Population Aging in Europe." *World Health Statistics Quarterly* 40:22–40.

Herz, B., and A. R. Measham. 1987. *The Safe Motherhood Initiative: Proposals for Action.* Discussion Paper 9. Washington, D.C.: World Bank.

IARC (International Agency for Research on Cancer). 1988. *Alcohol Drinking: IARC Monograph on the Evaluation of Carcinogenic Risks to Humans.* Lyon, France.

Jamison, D. T., and W. H. Mosley, eds. Forthcoming. *Disease Control Priorities in Developing Countries.* New York: Oxford University Press for the World Bank.

Jones, A., and J. Posnett. 1988. "The Revenue and Welfare Effects of Cigarette Taxes. *Applied Economics* 20:1223–32.

Kalache, A. 1990. "Risk Factors for Breast Cancer, with Special Reference to Developing Countries." *Health Policy and Planning* 5(1):122.

Kane, M. A., J. Clements, and D. Hu. Forthcoming. "Hepatitis B." In D. T. Jamison and W. H. Mosley, eds., *Disease Control Priorities in Developing Countries.* New York: Oxford University Press for the World Bank.

Leslie, J. 1991. "Women's Nutrition: The Key to Improving Family Health in Developing Countries?" *Health Policy and Planning* 6:1–19.

Lewit, E., D. Coate, and M. Grossman. 1981. "The Effect of Government Regulation on Teenage Smoking." *Journal of Law and Economics* 24:86–91.

Mackay, Judith. 1991. Press release. Asian Consultancy on Tobacco Control, Hong Kong. March 8.

Morris, J. N. 1990. "Inequalities in Health: Ten Years and Little Further On." *Lancet* 336:491–93.

Mosley, W. H., D. T. Jamison, and D. A. Henderson. 1990. "The Health Sector in Developing Countries: Problems for the 1990s and Beyond." *Annual Reviews of Public Health* 11:335–58.

Murray, C. J. L, D. E. Bell, E. DeJonghe, S. Zaidi, and C. Michaud. 1990. "A Study of Financial Resources Devoted to Research on Health Problems of Developing Countries." *Journal of Tropical Medicine and Hygiene* 93:229–55.

Murray, C., A. Rouillon, and K. Styblo. Forthcoming. "Tuberculosis." In D. T. Jamison and W. H. Mosley, eds., *Disease Control Priorities in Developing Countries.* New York: Oxford University Press for the World Bank.

National Research Council. 1989. *Diet and Health. Implications for Reducing Chronic Disease Risk.* Committee on Diet and Health, Food and Nutrition Board, Commission on Life Sciences, National Research Council. Washington, D.C.: National Academy Press.

Novotny, T. E., and R. Peto. 1988. "Estimates of Future Adverse Health Effects of Smoking in China." *Public Health Reports* 103:552–53.

Olshansky, S., and A. Ault. 1986. "The Fourth Stage of the Epidemiologic Transition: The Age of Delayed Degenerative Diseases." *Millbank Memorial Fund Quarterly* 64(3):355–91.

Over, M., and P. Piot. Forthcoming. "HIV Infection and Other Sexually Transmitted Diseases." In D. T. Jamison and W. H. Mosley, eds., *Disease Control Priorities in Developing Countries.* New York: Oxford University Press for the World Bank.

Peto, R., and A. D. Lopez. 1990. "The Future Worldwide Health Effects of Current Smoking Patterns: Three Million Deaths/Year in the 1990s, but over Ten Million/Year Eventually." 7th World Conference on Tobacco and Health, Perth, Australia.

Phelps, C. E. 1988. "Death and Taxes: An Opportunity for Substitution." *Journal of Health Economics* 7:1–24.

Playfair, J. H. L., J. M. Blackwell, and H. R. P. Miller. 1990. "Modern vaccines: parasitic diseases." *Lancet* 335:1263–66.

Rodrigues, L. C., and P. G. Smith. 1990. "Tuberculosis in Developing Countries and Methods for its Control." *Transactions of the Royal Society of Tropical Medicine and Hygiene* 84:739–44.

Rose, G., and M. Shipley. 1990. "Effects of Coronary Risk Reduction on the Pattern of Mortality." *Lancet* 335:275–77.

Smith, G. S., and P. Barss. 1991. "Unintentional Injuries in Developing Countries: The Epidemiology of a Neglected Problem." *Epidemiologic Reviews* 13:228–66.

Stanley, K. Forthcoming. ''Control of Tobacco Production and Use.'' In D. T. Jamison and W. H. Mosley, eds., *Disease Control Priorities in Developing Countries.* New York: Oxford University Press for the World Bank.

Stansfield, S., G. Smith, and W. McGreevey. Forthcoming. ''Injury.'' In D. T. Jamison and W. H. Mosley, eds., *Disease Control Priorities in Developing Countries.* New York: Oxford University Press for the World Bank.

Stjernsward, J. 1988. ''WHO Cancer Pain Relief Programme.'' *Cancer Surveys* 7:195–208.

Strong, P. M. 1990. ''Black on Class and Mortality: Theory, Method and History.'' *Journal of Public Health Medicine* 12:168–80.

Timaeus, I., and W. Graham. 1989. ''Measuring Adult Mortality in Developing Countries—A Review and Assessment of Methods.'' *Policy Planning and Research Working Papers* WPS 155. Washington, D.C.: World Bank.

Vaughan, P., L. Gilson, and A. Mills. 1989. ''Diabetes in Developing Countries: Its Importance for Public Health.'' *Health Policy and Planning* 4:97–109.

Walsh, J. A., C. M. Feifer, A. R. Measham, and P. J. Gertler. Forthcoming. ''Maternal and Perinatal Health Problems.'' In D. T. Jamison and W. H. Mosley, eds., *Disease Control Priorities in Developing Countries.* New York: Oxford University Press for the World Bank.

Warner, K. 1984. ''Cigarette Taxation: Doing Good by Doing Well.'' *Journal of Public Health Policy* 5:312–19.

———. 1990. ''Tobacco Taxation as Health Policy in the Third World.'' *American Journal of Public Health* 80:529–31.

WHO (World Health Organization). 1984. *Guiding Principles for the Formulation of National Cancer Programs in Developing Countries.* Document CAN/84.1. Geneva.

———. 1986a. *Cancer Pain Relief.* Geneva.

———. 1986b. ''Control of Cancer of the Cervix Uteri.'' *Bulletin of the World Health Organization* 64:607–18.

———. 1987. ''Tobacco Price and the Smoking Epidemic.'' *Smoke-free Europe Series* No. 9. Copenhagen.

Statistical Appendix

*Table A-1a. Country-Specific Estimates of Child and Adult Mortality Risk—**Asia***

			5Q0		45Q15	
Country	*Date*[a]	*Source*[b]	*Male*	*Female*	*Male*	*Female*
Bangladesh	1985–90	WB	18.3	16.5	33.7	37.9
Bhutan	1985–90	WB	22.7	20.5	29.5	37.0
Brunei	1985–90	WB	1.6	1.1	13.7	8.8
Burma	1985–90	WB	10.4	8.8	29.8	24.1
China	1986	CS	4.4	3.3	16.6	14.9
Fiji	1985–90	WB	2.8	2.1	19.6	13.1
French Polynesia	1985–90	WB	3.1	2.3	15.4	10.6
Guam	1985–90	WB	1.6	1.1	17.9	10.6
Hong Kong	1987	VS	0.8	0.7	12.2	5.7
India	1970–83	SR	19.9	22.0	32.8	29.4
Indonesia	1985–90	WB	10.6	9.0	28.8	23.2
Kampuchea	1985–90	WB	20.2	18.3	42.1	36.1
Kiribati	1985–90	WB	9.1	7.6	47.8	43.8
Korea, Democratic Republic	1985–90	WB	4.6	3.5	21.4	12.3
Korea, Republic	1985–90	WB	3.4	2.5	23.0	12.8
Laos	1985–90	WB	19.3	17.2	40.8	35.6
Macao	1985–90	WB	1.6	1.1	21.6	13.0
Malaysia	1985–90	WB	3.3	2.4	20.4	14.5
Maldives	1985–90	WB	11.9	10.2	27.5	22.8
Mongolia	1985–90	WB	6.4	5.1	28.7	22.2
Nepal	1985–90	WB	19.9	18.0	29.5	35.6
New Caledonia	1985–90	WB	5.0	3.8	21.3	14.9
Other Micronesia	1985–90	WB	4.4	3.3	21.2	14.9
Other Polynesia	1985–90	WB	4.0	3.2	20.3	11.1
Pacific Islands	1985–90	WB	2.7	1.9	16.1	8.0
Papua New Guinea	1985–90	WB	9.1	7.6	44.7	41.8
Philippines	1985–90	WB	6.4	5.1	28.6	22.7
Singapore	1987	VS	1.1	0.8	16.2	9.9
Solomon	1985–90	WB	6.1	4.8	19.3	19.3
Sri Lanka	1983	VS	4.3	3.9	22.5	12.7
Taiwan	1985–90	WB	2.3	1.6	13.0	8.3
Thailand	1985–90	WB	5.5	4.2	27.9	21.9
Tonga	1985–90	WB	3.6	2.6	28.0	22.0
Vanuatu	1985–90	WB	8.2	6.7	25.3	19.9
Vietnam	1985–90	WB	6.5	5.2	23.2	17.2
Western Samoa	1985–90	WB	7.2	5.8	23.7	16.1

a. Year(s) to which estimates apply.

b. WB—World Bank model-based estimates; CS—estimates based on a survey of one percent of the population; VS—estimates based on vital statistics; SR—estimates based on Sample Registration System data.

Source: See note b.

*Table A-1b. Country-Specific Estimates of Child and Adult Mortality Risk—**Latin America/Caribbean***

Country	Date[a]	Source[b]	5Q0 Male	5Q0 Female	45Q15 Male	45Q15 Female
Antigua/Barbuda	1983	VS	2.5	1.8	14.2	8.8
Argentina	1985	VS	3.1	2.5	19.7	10.7
Bahamas	1985	VS	3.4	3.3	23.2	12.3
Barbados	1984	VS	2.3	1.7	13.6	10.8
Belize	1985–90	WB	5.5	4.4	21.3	14.4
Bolivia	1985–90	WB	11.9	10.0	37.1	28.0
Brazil	1985–90	WB	6.9	5.6	23.5	14.5
Chile	1986	VS	2.6	2.1	18.9	10.2
Colombia	1985–90	WB	5.2	4.0	23.3	17.3
Costa Rica	1986	VS	2.5	2.1	14.5	7.7
Cuba	1986	VS	1.9	1.5	15.0	11.2
Dominica	1984	VS	2.1	1.5	14.3	15.0
Dominican Republic	1985–90	WB	7.2	5.8	19.3	13.2
Ecuador	1985–90	WB	6.9	5.6	21.0	14.5
El Salvador	1984	VS	4.0	3.4	24.6	12.4
Grenada	1985–90	WB	3.9	2.9	20.3	14.0
Guadeloupe	1985–90	WB	1.8	1.2	17.0	7.6
Guatemala	1984	VS	6.5	5.2	22.6	16.8
Guyana	1984	VS	3.1	2.5	24.0	14.7
Haiti	1985–90	WB	12.8	10.6	32.0	26.4
Honduras	1985–90	WB	7.6	6.2	22.7	16.1
Jamaica	1985–90	WB	2.0	1.6	14.4	7.0
Martinique	1985–90	WB	1.5	1.0	13.8	8.2
Mexico	1983	VS	3.9	3.2	25.1	14.4
Montserrat	1985–90	WB	3.6	2.8	18.3	12.3
Netherland Antilles	1985–90	WB	1.3	0.9	32.3	22.2
Nicaragua	1985–90	WB	6.9	5.5	22.6	20.0
Other	1985–90	WB	4.8	3.7	22.5	16.4
Panama	1985–90	WB	2.7	1.9	15.2	10.4
Paraguay	1985–90	WB	4.7	3.6	21.8	15.8
Peru	1985–90	WB	9.3	8.3	22.8	16.2
Puerto Rico	1985	VS	1.6	1.3	20.2	8.6
Saint Kitts/Nevis	1985–90	WB	4.5	3.5	19.3	13.3
Saint Lucia	1985–90	WB	2.4	1.7	18.9	13.4
Saint Vincent	1986	VS	2.9	3.0	21.4	11.5
Suriname	1985	VS	4.3	3.2	31.0	18.6
Trinidad and Tobago	1983	VS	2.5	2.0	21.9	14.8
Uruguay	1986	VS	3.3	2.7	18.3	10.1
Venezuela	1985–90	WB	4.0	3.2	19.4	9.4
Virgin Islands	1985–90	WB	2.2	1.6	16.3	8.1

a. Year(s) to which estimates apply.
b. WB—World Bank model-based estimates; VS—estimates based on vital statistics.
Source: See note b.

*Table A-1c. Country-Specific Estimates of Child and Adult Mortality Risk—**Middle East/North Africa***

Country	Date[a]	Source[b]	5Q0 Male	5Q0 Female	45Q15 Male	45Q15 Female
Afghan	1985–90	WB	30.3	27.5	39.3	40.5
Algeria	1985–90	WB	10.0	8.4	23.6	19.0
Bahrain	1985–90	WB	3.6	2.6	17.6	11.9
Egypt	1985–90	WB	11.7	9.9	24.8	21.0
Gaza	1985–90	WB	8.6	7.2	23.5	22.1
Iran	1985–90	WB	9.6	8.1	22.9	21.3
Iraq	1985–90	WB	9.2	7.7	20.3	18.7
Israel	1985–90	WB	1.6	1.1	11.1	7.3
Jordan	1985–90	WB	6.2	4.9	22.6	17.9
Kuwait	1987	VS	2.1	1.7	11.7	7.8
Lebanon	1985–90	WB	5.6	4.4	21.6	16.4
Libya	1985–90	WB	11.2	9.5	26.1	20.6
Morocco	1985–90	WB	11.2	9.5	26.1	20.6
Oman	1985–90	WB	15.3	13.5	31.4	27.4
Other North Africa	1985–90	WB	21.2	19.1	39.9	34.7
Pakistan	1985–90	WB	15.3	13.1	25.2	28.0
Qatar	1985–90	WB	4.3	3.2	20.0	13.0
Saudi Arabia	1985–90	WB	9.5	8.0	22.8	17.5
Syria	1985–90	WB	6.9	5.5	23.8	18.8
Tunisia	1985–90	WB	7.7	6.4	19.3	18.2
Turkey	1985–90	WB	10.3	8.7	19.6	15.2
United Arab Emirates	1985–90	WB	3.6	2.6	17.6	11.9
West Bank	1985–90	WB	6.2	4.9	22.6	17.9
Yemen Arab Republic	1985–90	WB	20.4	18.3	31.7	27.6
Yemen Democratic Republic	1985–90	WB	18.5	16.7	38.2	32.5

a. Year(s) to which estimates apply.
b. WB—World Bank model-based estimates; VS—estimates based on vital statistics.
Source: See note b.

*Table A-1d. Country-Specific Estimates of Child and Adult Mortality Risk—**Sub-Saharan Africa***

Country	Date[a]	Source[b]	5Q0 Male	5Q0 Female	45Q15 Male	45Q15 Female
Angola	1985–90	WB	24.3	21.9	42.8	36.9
Benin	1970	T	17.8	16.0	39.7	35.0
Botswana	1981	T	11.2	9.6	42.6	28.1
Burkina Faso	1985–90	WB	21.6	19.5	43.6	36.5
Burundi	1970–71	T	19.7	17.6	46.5	39.7
Cameroon	1975	T	14.3	12.5	30.1	21.9
Cape Verde	1985–90	WB	8.8	7.3	20.5	14.4

(*Table continues on the following page.*)

Table A-1d (continued)

Country	Date[a]	Source[b]	5Q0 Male	5Q0 Female	45Q15 Male	45Q15 Female
Central African Republic	1985–90	WB	20.5	18.6	37.5	30.8
Chad	1985–90	WB	23.4	21.1	40.1	36.9
Comoros	1985–90	WB	13.6	11.9	32.7	26.8
Congo	1967	T	10.9	9.3	24.6	15.5
Côte d'Ivoire	1978–79	T	16.6	14.7	35.5	33.5
Djibouti	1985–90	WB	21.6	19.4	40.8	34.9
Equatorial Guinea	1985–90	WB	22.5	20.3	42.0	38.5
Ethiopia	1985–90	WB	22.0	19.3	43.6	36.9
Gabon	1985–90	WB	15.7	13.9	40.2	33.2
Gambia	1978	T	25.4	22.9	28.4	23.7
Ghana	1968–69	T	15.4		41.2	36.8
Guinea	1985–90	WB	26.1	23.5	46.4	40.2
Guinea-Bissau	1985–90	WB	25.7	23.2	53.5	51.5
Kenya	1974	T	12.1	10.5	32.4	18.2
Lesotho	1976	T	15.3	13.5	48.3	25.9
Liberia	1971	T	14.9	13.1	43.9	38.1
Madagascar	1985–90	WB	16.9	14.6	34.3	28.7
Malawi	1971	T	23.5	21.2	34.8	41.4
Mali	1985–90	WB	24.2	21.3	38.7	32.7
Mauritania	1975	T	22.5	20.3	32.1	23.9
Mauritius	1987	VS	3.4	2.3	26.6	13.5
Mozambique	1985–90	WB	22.1	19.9	39.8	33.3
Namibia	1985–90	WB	16.4	15.1	27.0	22.5
Niger	1985–90	WB	24.0	21.6	43.4	37.3
Nigeria	1985–90	WB	18.3	16.3	36.1	30.3
Other West Africa	1985–90	WB	5.0	3.8	21.3	14.9
Reunion	1985–90	WB	1.9	1.3	24.9	10.3
Rwanda	1985–90	WB	21.6	19.4	36.5	31.0
Sao Tome and Principe	1985–90	WB	7.0	5.6	23.7	18.3
Senegal	1978	T	22.7	20.5	33.7	27.9
Seychelles	1987	VS	2.3	2.3	32.4	15.7
Sierra Leone	1970	T	26.8	24.2	57.9	54.1
Somalia	1985–90	WB	23.4	21.1	37.2	31.6
South Africa	1985–90	WB	10.8	9.1	30.8	19.8
Sudan	1985–90	WB	18.9	16.9	37.2	33.8
Swaziland	1972	T	16.6	14.4	49.4	32.8
Tanzania	1965	T	16.2	14.4	25.0	21.5
Togo	1985–90	WB	16.2	14.3	35.1	29.2
Uganda	1965	T	17.9	15.9	23.7	22.8
Zaire	1985–90	WB	14.9	13.2	40.8	34.2
Zambia	1985–90	WB	13.6	11.9	39.7	33.3
Zimbabwe	1975	T	12.1	10.5	26.2	15.7

a. Year(s) to which estimates apply.

b. WB—World Bank model-based estimates; T—estimates derived by the authors from life expectancies reported by Timaeus (for adults) and from 1985–90 World Bank model-based estimates (for children); VS—estimates based on vital statistics.

Source: See note b.

*Table A-1e. Country-Specific Estimates of Child and Adult Mortality Risk—**Industrialized Market***

Country	Date[a]	Source[b]	5Q0 Male	5Q0 Female	45Q15 Male	45Q15 Female
Australia	1986	VS	1.2	0.9	13.5	7.4
Austria	1987	VS	1.2	1.0	16.6	7.6
Belgium	1986	VS	2.0	1.6	15.3	8.2
Canada	1986	VS	1.1	0.9	14.2	7.6
Channel Islands	1985–90	WB	0.7	0.4	13.7	6.5
Cyprus	1985–90	WB	1.6	1.1	11.6	6.0
Denmark	1986	VS	1.1	0.9	15.6	10.0
Finland	1986	VS	0.8	0.5	18.7	7.1
France	1986	VS	1.1	0.9	17.4	7.2
Greece	1986	VS	1.4	1.1	12.0	6.0
Iceland	1987	VS	0.8	0.9	12.0	7.3
Ireland	1986	VS	1.1	0.9	14.8	8.8
Italy	1985	VS	1.3	1.0	14.4	6.7
Japan	1987	VS	0.6	0.6	11.3	5.7
Luxembourg	1987	VS	1.2	1.2	17.7	8.8
Malta	1987	VS	1.0	0.8	12.2	6.5
Netherlands	1986	VS	1.1	9.0	12.6	7.2
New Zealand	1986	VS	1.6	1.3	15.6	9.3
Norway	1987	VS	1.2	0.9	13.8	6.9
Other Europe	1985–90	WB	1.8	1.3	13.3	6.1
Other North America	1985–90	WB	4.1	3.0	18.2	13.2
Portugal	1987	VS	1.8	1.5	17.5	8.1
Spain	1985	VS	1.1	0.9	14.1	6.1
Sweden	1986	VS	0.8	0.7	12.3	6.6
Switzerland	1987	VS	0.9	0.6	12.8	5.3
United Kingdom	1987	VS	1.3	1.0	13.6	8.3
United States	1986	VS	1.4	1.1	17.5	9.3
West Germany	1987	VS	1.2	0.9	15.1	7.4

a. Year(s) to which estimates apply.

b. WB—World Bank model-based estimates; VS—estimates based on vital statistics.

*Table A-1f. Country-Specific Estimates of Child and Adult Mortality Risk—**Industrialized Nonmarket***

Country	Date[a]	Source[b]	5Q0 Male	5Q0 Female	45Q15 Male	45Q15 Female
Albania	1985–90	WB	5.0	4.0	14.2	7.8
Bulgaria	1987	VS	2.0	1.6	20.6	9.5
Czechoslovakia	1986	VS	1.7	1.3	22.8	10.0
East Germany	1985–90	WB	1.1	0.7	17.9	9.2
Hungary	1987	VS	2.2	1.7	27.7	12.7
Poland	1987	VS	2.1	1.6	24.8	10.3
Romania	1984	VS	3.3	2.7	22.4	11.5
Soviet Union	1985–90	WB	3.5	2.6	26.8	11.0
Yugoslavia	1987	VS	3.0	2.7	19.8	9.8

a. Year(s) to which estimates apply.

b. WB—World Bank model-based estimates; VS—estimates based on vital statistics.

Table A-2. Part I: Classification of Causes of Death in the Sixth and Seventh Revisions of the International Classification of Diseases (ICD)

Cause	*ICD6 & ICD7 A Codes*	*ICD6 & ICD7 B Codes*
I. Communicable and reproductive	001–043, 064, 087–092, 115–120, 130–135	001–017, 030–031, (84%)[a] 032, 040, 042–044
Diarrhea	012–014, 016	004–006
Tuberculosis	001–005	001–002
Malaria	037	016
Venereal diseases	006–011	003 (Syphilis)
Helminths	038–042	
Respiratory infections	087–092	030, 031, (84%) 032
Maternal	115–120	040
Perinatal	130–135	042–044
II. Noncommunicable	044–063, 065–086, 093–114, 121–129, 136–137	018–029, (16%)[a] 032, 033–039, 041, 045
Neoplasms	044–060	018–019
Esophagus	045	
Stomach	046	
Small intestine/colon/rectum	047, 048	
Liver		
Lung	050	
Breast	051	
Cervix	052	
Lymphatic/hematopoietic	058, 059	
Lip, oral cavity, pharynx	044	
Endocrine	061–063	
Diabetes mellitus	063	020
Cardiovascular	070, 079–086	022, 024–029
Hypertensive disease	083, 084	028
Ischemic heart disease	081	
Cerebrovascular	070	022
Vessels disease	085	
Respiratory	093–097	
COPD	093	(16%)[a] 032
Digestive	098–107	033–037
Chronic liver disease/ cirrhosis	105	037
Ulcers stomach/duodenum	099–100	033
Senile and ill-defined	136, 137	045
III. Injuries	138–150	047–050
Unintentional	138–147	047–048
Transport	138, 139	

Table A-2. Part I (continued)

Cause	*ICD6 & ICD7 A Codes*	*ICD6 & ICD7 B Codes*
Motor vehicle transport	138	047
Water transport		
Poisoning	140	
Falls	141	
Fires	143	
Drowning	146	
Intentional	148–150	049–050
Suicide	148	049
Homicide	149	050
War	150	050
Undetermined	n.a.	n.a.

a. Separating deaths from acute and chronic respiratory disease was not feasible for deaths coded according to early revisions of the International Classification of Diseases (ICD). Therefore, this separation was made by applying the proportions of deaths from acute (84 percent) and chronic (16 percent) respiratory disease coded according to the earliest year for which such separation could be made.

Source: WHO (1948, 1957, 1967, 1978), as cited in chapter 2.

Table A-2. Part II: Classification of Causes of Death in the Eighth and Ninth Revisions of the International Classification of Diseases (ICD)

Cause	*ICD8 A Codes*	*ICD9 B Codes*
I. Communicable and reproductive	001–044, 065, 089–092, 112–118, 131–135	01–07, 19, 310–312, 320–322, 38–41, 45
Diarrhea	001–005	01
Tuberculosis	006–010	02, 077
Malaria	031	052
Venereal diseases	034–038	06
Helminths	039–043	072–076
Respiratory infections	089–092	310–312, 320–322
Maternal	112–118	38–41
Perinatal	131–135	45
II. Noncommunicable	045–064, 066–088, 093–111, 119–130, 136, 137	08–18, 20–30, 313–319, 323–329, 33–37, 42–44, 46
Neoplasms	045–061	08–17
Esophagus	046	090
Stomach	047	091
Small intestine/colon/rectum	048–049 (Colon/rectum)	092, 093–094 (Small intestine/colon/rectum)
Liver		095
Lung	051	101
Breast	054	113
Cervix	055	120
Lymphatic/hematopoietic	059, 060	14
Lip, oral cavity, pharynx	045	08
Endocrine	062–064, 066	18
Diabetes mellitus	064	181
Cardiovascular	080–088	25–30
Hypertensive disease	082	26
Ischemic heart disease	083	27
Cerebrovascular	085	29
Vessels disease/atherosclerosis	086 (Vessels disease)	300 (Atherosclerosis)
Respiratory	093–096	313–319, 323–329
COPD	093	323–325
Digestive	097–104	33–34
Chronic liver disease/cirrhosis	102	347
Ulcers stomach/duodenum	098	341
Senile and ill-defined	136, 137	46
III. Injuries	138–150	47–56
Unintentional	138–146	E47–E53
Transport	138–139	E47

Table A-2. Part II (continued)

Cause	*ICD8 A Codes*	*ICD9 B Codes*
Motor vehicle transport	138	E471
Water transport		E473
Poisoning	140	E48
Falls	141	E50
Fires	142	E51
Drowning	143	E521
Intentional	147, 148, 150	E54–E55, E561
Suicide	147	E54
Homicide	148	E55
War	150	E561
Undetermined	149	E560

a. Separating deaths from acute and chronic respiratory disease was not feasible for deaths coded according to early revisions of the International Classification of Diseases (ICD). Therefore, this separation was made by applying the proportions of deaths from acute (84 percent) and chronic (16 percent) respiratory disease coded according to the earliest year for which such separation could be made.

Source: WHO (1948, 1957, 1967, 1978), as cited in chapter 2.

Note: On the following pages, countries listed in appendix tables A-3a and A-3b are organized alphabetically within developing world regions (Asia, Latin America/Caribbean, Middle East/North Africa) and industrialized economies (Industrialized Market and Industrialized Nonmarket). Data for the United Kingdom are presented by divisions (England and Wales, Scotland and Northern Ireland). See tables A-1a to A-1f for the specific year of each country's estimates.

*Table A-3a. Cause-Specific 45Q15 for Women in Countries with Complete Recent Vital Registration Data Classified According to Cause of Death—**Asia***

Cause	*Hong Kong*	*Singapore*	*Sri Lanka*
I. Communicable and reproductive	0.3	0.5	1.6
Diarrhea	0.0	0.0	0.5
Tuberculosis	0.0	0.1	0.3
Malaria	0.0	0.0	0.0
Venereal diseases	0.0	0.0	0.0
Helminths	0.0	0.0	0.0
Respiratory infections	0.1	0.3	0.3
Maternal	0.0	0.0	0.2
II. Noncommunicable	4.8	8.5	9.0
Neoplasms	2.7	3.9	1.8
Esophagus	0.0	0.0	0.1
Stomach	0.2	0.3	0.2
Colon/rectum	0.3	0.3	0.0
Liver	0.2	0.1	0.0
Lung	0.4	0.4	0.0
Breast	0.4	0.9	0.1
Cervix	0.2	0.4	0.1
Lymphatic/hematopoietic	0.1	0.3	0.1
Lip, oral cavity, pharynx	0.2	0.3	0.1
Endocrine	0.0	0.5	0.2
Diabetes mellitus	0.0	0.5	0.2
Cardiovascular	1.2	2.7	2.3
Hypertensive disease	0.1	0.3	0.3
Ischemic heart disease	0.3	1.1	0.3

Cerebrovascular	0.5	0.9	0.4
Atherosclerosis	0.0	0.0	0.0
Respiratory	0.2	0.3	0.6
COPD	0.2	0.3	0.5
Digestive	0.2	0.2	0.4
Chronic liver disease/cirrhosis	0.1	0.1	0.1
Ulcers stomach/duodenum	0.0	0.0	0.0
Senile and ill-defined	0.0	0.1	2.2
III. Injuries	0.7	0.9	2.2
Unintentional	0.2	0.3	0.6
Transport	0.1	0.2	0.1
Motor vehicle transport	0.1	0.2	0.1
Water transport	0.0	0.0	0.0
Poisoning	0.0	0.0	0.1
Falls	0.0	0.1	0.0
Fires	0.0	0.0	0.1
Drowning	0.0	0.0	0.1
Intentional	0.4	0.5	1.4
Suicide	0.4	0.5	1.3
Homicide	0.0	0.0	0.1
War	0.0	0.0	0.0
Undetermined	0.1	0.1	0.2
Total	5.7	9.9	12.8

(Next table section begins on the following page.)

Table A-3a (continued)—***Latin America/Caribbean***

Cause	*Argentina*	*Bahamas*	*Barbados*	*Chile*	*Costa Rica*	*Cuba*
I. Communicable and reproductive	0.8	1.5	0.5	0.9	0.4	0.5
Diarrhea	0.0	0.0	0.0	0.1	0.0	0.0
Tuberculosis	0.1	0.2	0.1	0.2	0.1	0.0
Malaria	0.0	0.0	0.0	0.0	0.0	0.0
Venereal diseases	0.0	0.0	0.0	0.0	0.0	0.0
Helminths	0.0	0.1	0.0	0.0	0.0	0.0
Respiratory infections	0.1	0.6	0.0	0.3	0.1	0.2
Maternal	0.2	0.0	0.1	0.1	0.2	0.1
II. Noncommunicable	9.2	9.6	9.6	8.3	7.5	8.7
Neoplasms	3.4	3.5	3.5	3.6	3.6	3.1
Esophagus	0.0	0.0	0.0	0.1	0.0	0.0
Stomach	0.1	0.2	0.2	0.3	0.5	0.1
Colon/rectum	0.2	0.1	0.2	0.1	0.2	0.2
Liver	0.1	0.0	0.0	0.1	0.1	0.0
Lung	0.2	0.3	0.0	0.2	0.1	0.4
Breast	0.9	0.4	0.7	0.5	0.5	0.6
Cervix	0.3	0.4	0.8	0.6	0.7	0.3
Lymphatic/hematopoietic	0.2	0.2	0.4	0.2	0.3	0.3
Lip, oral cavity, pharynx	0.0	0.1	0.0	0.0	0.0	0.0
Endocrine	0.3	0.4	0.8	0.3	0.4	0.5
Diabetes mellitus	0.2	0.1	0.8	0.2	0.4	0.4
Cardiovascular	3.4	3.0	3.3	1.9	1.8	3.4
Hypertensive disease	0.2	0.4	0.1	0.1	0.1	0.2
Ischemic heart disease	0.5	1.0	0.7	0.4	0.7	1.4

Cerebrovascular	1.1	0.8	0.8	0.9	0.6	1.1
Atherosclerosis	0.0	0.0	0.0	0.0	0.0	0.0
Respiratory	0.2	0.1	0.0	0.2	0.1	0.3
COPD	0.2	0.1	0.0	0.2	0.1	0.3
Digestive	0.7	1.4	0.5	1.1	0.5	0.5
Chronic liver disease/cirrhosis	0.2	0.8	0.1	0.8	0.2	0.2
Ulcers stomach/duodenum	0.0	0.0	0.0	0.0	0.1	0.0
Senile and ill-defined	0.3	0.3	0.3	0.5	0.1	0.0
III. Injuries	0.9	1.3	0.6	1.1	0.6	2.0
Unintentional	0.5	0.9	0.4	0.4	0.4	2.0
Transport	0.2	0.7	0.2	0.1	0.3	0.0
Motor vehicle transport	0.2	0.7	0.1	0.1	0.3	0.0
Water transport	0.0	0.0	0.0	0.0	0.0	0.0
Poisoning	0.0	0.0	0.0	0.0	0.0	0.0
Falls	0.0	0.0	0.0	0.0	0.0	0.0
Fires	0.0	0.0	0.1	0.0	0.0	0.0
Drowning	0.0	0.0	0.1	0.0	0.0	0.0
Intentional	0.3	0.0	0.2	0.1	0.1	0.0
Suicide	0.2	0.0	0.1	0.1	0.0	0.0
Homicide	0.1	0.0	0.1	0.0	0.1	0.0
War	0.0	0.0	0.0	0.0	0.0	0.0
Undetermined	0.1	0.4	0.1	0.6	0.0	0.0
Total	10.8	12.4	10.8	10.3	8.5	11.2

(Next table section begins on the following page.)

Table A-3a (continued)—***Latin America/Caribbean***

Cause	*Guyana*	*Martinique*	*Mexico*	*Panama*	*Puerto Rico*
I. Communicable and reproductive	1.1	0.3	2.1	1.1	0.5
Diarrhea	0.0	0.0	0.5	0.2	0.0
Tuberculosis	0.1	0.0	0.4	0.3	0.1
Malaria	0.0	0.0	0.0	0.0	0.0
Venereal diseases	0.0	0.0	0.0	0.0	0.0
Helminths	0.0	0.0	0.0	0.0	0.0
Respiratory infections	0.2	0.2	0.4	0.2	0.3
Maternal	0.2	0.0	0.4	0.2	0.0
II. Noncommunicable	12.7	10.0	11.0	6.5	7.1
Neoplasms	1.9	3.4	2.8	2.3	2.4
Esophagus	0.0	0.0	0.0	0.0	0.0
Stomach	0.1	0.1	0.2	0.1	0.1
Colon/rectum	0.0	0.1	0.1	0.1	0.2
Liver	0.0	0.2	0.0	0.0	0.0
Lung	0.0	0.2	0.1	0.1	0.2
Breast	0.3	0.9	0.3	0.3	0.7
Cervix	0.5	0.3	0.7	0.6	0.2
Lymphatic/hematopoietic	0.1	0.3	0.2	0.1	0.3
Lip, oral cavity, pharynx	0.0	0.0	0.0	0.0	0.0
Endocrine	1.6	0.3	1.4	0.4	0.5
Diabetes mellitus	1.3	0.1	1.2	0.3	0.5
Cardiovascular	5.8	3.6	2.8	1.8	2.4
Hypertensive disease	0.7	0.1	0.2	0.2	0.4
Ischemic heart disease	0.7	0.5	0.6	0.4	0.9

Cerebrovascular	2.4	1.8	0.7	0.8	0.3
Atherosclerosis	0.0	0.0	0.0	0.0	0.0
Respiratory	0.1	0.1	0.2	0.2	0.2
COPD	0.1	0.1	0.2	0.2	0.2
Digestive	1.1	0.6	1.6	0.4	0.6
Chronic liver disease/cirrhosis	0.3	0.2	0.8	0.2	0.3
Ulcers stomach/duodenum	0.2	0.0	0.1	0.0	0.0
Senile and ill-defined	0.9	0.6	0.6	0.7	0.0
III. Injuries	0.9	0.9	1.3	0.7	1.0
Unintentional	0.5	0.4	1.1	0.5	0.5
Transport	0.1	0.3	0.4	0.3	0.3
Motor vehicle transport	0.0	0.3	0.4	0.3	0.3
Water transport	0.0	0.0	0.0	0.0	0.0
Poisoning	0.0	0.1	0.0	0.0	0.0
Falls	0.1	0.0	0.1	0.0	0.0
Fires	0.0	0.0	0.0	0.0	0.0
Drowning	0.0	0.0	0.1	0.1	0.0
Intentional	0.3	0.3	0.2	0.1	0.3
Suicide	0.1	0.3	0.0	0.1	0.1
Homicide	0.0	0.0	0.2	0.0	0.2
War	0.2	0.0	0.0	0.0	0.0
Undetermined	0.1	0.2	0.0	0.0	0.1
Total	14.7	11.2	14.5	8.3	8.6

(Next table section begins on the following page.)

Table A-3a (continued)—***Latin America/Caribbean***

Cause	*St. Vincent*	*Suriname*	*Trinidad*	*Uruguay*	*Venezuela*
I. Communicable and reproductive	1.2	1.1	0.8	0.3	1.2
Diarrhea	0.0	0.3	0.0	0.0	0.1
Tuberculosis	0.2	0.0	0.0	0.1	0.2
Malaria	0.0	0.0	0.0	0.0	0.0
Venereal diseases	0.0	0.0	0.0	0.0	0.0
Helminths	0.0	0.1	0.0	0.0	0.0
Respiratory infections	0.7	0.4	0.3	0.1	0.2
Maternal	0.0	0.2	0.2	0.1	0.3
II. Noncommunicable	12.5	14.9	12.8	8.8	9.4
Neoplasms	3.6	3.8	2.7	4.0	3.2
Esophagus	0.0	0.0	0.0	0.1	0.0
Stomach	1.0	0.1	0.1	0.2	0.3
Colon/rectum	0.3	0.6	0.2	0.3	0.1
Liver	0.0	0.1	0.0	0.0	0.0
Lung	0.0	0.2	0.0	0.2	0.2
Breast	0.0	0.3	0.6	1.2	0.4
Cervix	1.1	1.1	0.4	0.3	0.5
Lymphatic/hematopoietic	0.0	0.3	0.2	0.3	0.2
Lip, oral cavity, pharynx	0.0	0.1	0.0	0.0	0.0
Endocrine	1.4	1.9	2.5	0.3	0.6
Diabetes mellitus	1.4	1.7	2.3	0.2	0.5
Cardiovascular	5.7	3.9	5.3	2.4	3.4
Hypertensive disease	2.1	0.2	0.4	0.1	0.3
Ischemic heart disease	1.7	1.6	2.4	0.5	1.3

Cerebrovascular	1.1	1.2	1.5	1.1	1.0
Atherosclerosis	0.0	0.0	0.0	0.0	0.0
Respiratory	0.3	0.6	0.3	0.2	0.2
COPD	0.3	0.6	0.3	0.2	0.2
Digestive	0.6	1.4	0.7	0.4	0.6
Chronic liver disease/cirrhosis	0.0	0.7	0.2	0.1	0.2
Ulcers stomach/duodenum	0.0	0.0	0.1	0.0	0.0
Senile and ill-defined	0.0	1.8	0.2	0.7	0.3
III. Injuries	0.9	2.4	1.2	1.0	1.1
Unintentional	0.6	1.2	0.8	0.7	0.8
Transport	0.3	0.7	0.4	0.2	0.5
Motor vehicle transport	0.3	0.6	0.4	0.2	0.5
Water transport	0.0	0.0	0.0	0.0	0.0
Poisoning	0.0	0.0	0.0	0.0	0.0
Falls	0.3	0.2	0.0	0.0	0.1
Fires	0.0	0.0	0.1	0.0	0.0
Drowning	0.0	0.0	0.1	0.1	0.0
Intentional	0.0	1.1	0.4	0.2	0.2
Suicide	0.0	0.9	0.2	0.2	0.1
Homicide	0.0	0.2	0.2	0.1	0.1
War	0.0	0.0	0.0	0.0	0.0
Undetermined	0.3	0.2	0.0	0.0	0.0
Total	14.6	18.5	14.8	10.2	11.7

(Next table section begins on the following page.)

Table A-3a (continued)—***Middle East/North Africa***

Cause	*Bahrain*	*Israel*	*Kuwait*	*Mauritius*	*Seychelles*
I. Communicable and reproductive	0.4	0.2	0.3	0.8	2.1
Diarrhea	0.0	0.0	0.0	0.1	0.0
Tuberculosis	0.0	0.0	0.1	0.0	0.0
Malaria	0.0	0.0	0.0	0.0	0.0
Venereal diseases	0.0	0.0	0.0	0.0	0.0
Helminths	0.0	0.0	0.0	0.0	0.0
Respiratory infections	0.2	0.1	0.1	0.2	0.1
Maternal	0.0	0.0	0.0	0.2	0.2
II. Noncommunicable	10.3	6.6	6.9	11.2	12.1
Neoplasms	2.1	3.3	2.0	2.3	5.3
Esophagus	0.2	0.0	0.0	0.0	0.0
Stomach	0.1	0.1	0.0	0.2	0.0
Colon/rectum	0.0	0.3	0.2	0.1	0.4
Liver	0.1	0.0	0.0	0.0	0.0
Lung	0.1	0.2	0.2	0.1	1.0
Breast	0.7	1.1	0.4	0.4	0.6
Cervix	0.1	0.1	0.1	0.2	1.3
Lymphatic/hematopoietic	0.2	0.3	0.2	0.2	0.4
Lip, oral cavity, pharynx	0.0	0.0	0.0	0.0	0.0
Endocrine	0.9	0.2	0.3	1.8	0.5
Diabetes mellitus	0.6	0.2	0.2	1.7	0.4
Cardiovascular	3.4	1.8	3.5	4.8	5.6
Hypertensive disease	0.9	0.1	1.4	0.3	0.8
Ischemic heart disease	1.3	0.8	0.9	1.6	1.6

Cerebrovascular	0.3	0.4	0.3	1.2	1.6
Atherosclerosis	0.0	0.0	0.3	0.0	0.4
Respiratory	0.1	0.2	0.3	0.5	0.0
COPD	0.0	0.1	0.2	0.3	0.0
Digestive	0.3	0.2	0.4	0.4	0.0
Chronic liver disease/cirrhosis	0.2	0.1	0.1	0.2	0.0
Ulcers stomach/duodenum	0.0	0.0	0.0	0.1	0.0
Senile and ill-defined	2.4	0.4	0.0	0.3	0.0
III. Injuries	0.8	0.9	0.6	1.5	1.9
Unintentional	0.4	0.5	0.5	0.9	1.5
Transport	0.4	0.2	0.4	0.1	0.4
Motor vehicle transport	0.4	0.2	0.4	0.1	0.4
Water transport	0.0	0.0	0.0	0.0	0.0
Poisoning	0.0	0.0	0.0	0.0	0.0
Falls	0.0	0.0	0.0	0.0	0.0
Fires	0.0	0.0	0.0	0.6	0.6
Drowning	0.0	0.0	0.0	0.0	0.3
Intentional	0.3	0.3	0.0	0.5	0.4
Suicide	0.1	0.2	0.0	0.5	0.0
Homicide	0.0	0.0	0.0	0.0	0.4
War	0.0	0.0	0.0	0.0	0.0
Undetermined	0.0	0.1	0.0	0.1	0.0
Total	11.5	7.7	7.8	13.5	16.1

(Next table section begins on the following page.)

*Table A-3a (continued)—**Industrialized Market***

Cause	*Australia*	*Austria*	*Belgium*	*Canada*	*Denmark*	*England*
I. Communicable and reproductive	0.1	0.1	0.1	0.1	0.1	0.2
Diarrhea	0.0	0.0	0.0	0.0	0.0	0.0
Tuberculosis	0.0	0.0	0.0	0.0	0.0	0.0
Malaria	0.0	0.0	0.0	0.0	0.0	0.0
Venereal diseases	0.0	0.0	0.0	0.0	0.0	0.0
Helminths	0.0	0.0	0.0	0.0	0.0	0.0
Respiratory infections	0.0	0.1	0.1	0.1	0.1	0.1
Maternal	0.0	0.0	0.0	0.0	0.0	0.0
II. Noncommunicable	6.3	6.3	6.6	6.4	8.4	7.3
Neoplasms	3.4	3.3	3.6	3.7	4.7	4.1
Esophagus	0.0	0.0	0.0	0.0	0.0	0.1
Stomach	0.1	0.2	0.1	0.1	0.1	0.1
Colon/rectum	0.4	0.3	0.3	0.3	0.4	0.3
Liver	0.0	0.0	0.0	0.0	0.0	0.0
Lung	0.4	0.3	0.2	0.7	0.7	0.5
Breast	0.9	0.9	1.2	1.1	1.2	1.3
Cervix	0.2	0.2	0.1	0.1	0.3	0.3
Lymphatic/hematopoietic	0.3	0.2	0.2	0.3	0.3	0.3
Lip, oral cavity, pharynx	0.0	0.0	0.0	0.0	0.0	0.0
Endocrine	0.1	0.1	0.2	0.2	0.3	0.1
Diabetes mellitus	0.1	0.1	0.1	0.1	0.2	0.1
Cardiovascular	1.7	1.7	1.5	1.5	1.6	1.9
Hypertensive disease	0.0	0.1	0.1	0.0	0.0	0.0
Ischemic heart disease	0.9	0.6	0.4	0.7	0.8	1.0

Cerebrovascular	0.4	0.5	0.4	0.4	0.5	0.5
Atherosclerosis	0.0	0.0	0.0	0.0	0.1	0.0
Respiratory	0.3	0.1	0.2	0.2	0.4	0.3
COPD	0.3	0.1	0.2	0.1	0.4	0.3
Digestive	0.3	0.6	0.4	0.3	0.5	0.3
Chronic liver disease/cirrhosis	0.1	0.5	0.3	0.2	0.3	0.2
Ulcers stomach/duodenum	0.0	0.0	0.0	0.0	0.0	0.0
Senile and ill-defined	0.0	0.0	0.4	0.1	0.4	0.0
III. Injuries	1.1	1.2	1.5	1.1	1.7	0.7
Unintentional	0.7	0.6	0.7	0.7	0.5	0.3
Transport	0.5	0.4	0.4	0.4	0.3	0.2
Motor vehicle transport	0.5	0.4	0.4	0.4	0.3	0.2
Water transport	0.0	0.0	0.0	0.0	0.0	0.0
Poisoning	0.0	0.0	0.1	0.1	0.1	0.0
Falls	0.0	0.1	0.1	0.0	0.0	0.0
Fires	0.0	0.0	0.0	0.1	0.0	0.0
Drowning	0.0	0.0	0.0	0.0	0.0	0.0
Intentional	0.4	0.6	0.8	0.4	1.0	0.2
Suicide	0.3	0.6	0.7	0.4	1.0	0.2
Homicide	0.1	0.0	0.1	0.1	0.0	0.0
War	0.0	0.0	0.0	0.0	0.0	0.0
Undetermined	0.0	0.0	0.1	0.0	0.2	0.1
Total	7.5	7.6	8.3	7.7	10.2	8.2

(Next table section begins on the following page.)

*Table A-3a (continued)—**Industrialized Market***

Cause	*Finland*	*France*	*Greece*	*Iceland*	*Ireland*
I. Communicable and reproductive	0.2	0.2	0.1	0.0	0.3
Diarrhea	0.0	0.0	0.0	0.0	0.0
Tuberculosis	0.0	0.0	0.0	0.0	0.0
Malaria	0.0	0.0	0.0	0.0	0.0
Venereal diseases	0.0	0.0	0.0	0.0	0.0
Helminths	0.0	0.0	0.0	0.0	0.0
Respiratory infections	0.1	0.1	0.1	0.0	0.2
Maternal	0.0	0.0	0.0	0.0	0.0
II. Noncommunicable	5.5	5.7	5.0	6.1	7.8
Neoplasms	2.7	2.9	2.7	4.8	4.3
Esophagus	0.0	0.0	0.0	0.0	0.1
Stomach	0.2	0.1	0.1	0.0	0.2
Colon/rectum	0.2	0.2	0.1	0.5	0.5
Liver	0.0	0.0	0.0	0.1	0.0
Lung	0.1	0.1	0.2	0.4	0.4
Breast	0.7	0.9	0.8	1.6	1.4
Cervix	0.1	0.1	0.1	0.2	0.1
Lymphatic/hematopoietic	0.3	0.2	0.2	0.3	0.3
Lip, oral cavity, pharynx	0.0	0.1	0.0	0.1	0.0
Endocrine	0.1	0.1	0.1	0.0	0.1
Diabetes mellitus	0.1	0.1	0.1	0.0	0.1
Cardiovascular	1.7	1.0	1.4	0.7	2.4
Hypertensive disease	0.0	0.0	0.0	0.0	0.0
Ischemic heart disease	0.7	0.2	0.4	0.3	1.2

Cerebrovascular	0.7	0.3	0.4	0.2	0.7
Atherosclerosis	0.1	0.0	0.0	0.0	0.0
Respiratory	0.1	0.2	0.1	0.1	0.4
COPD	0.1	0.1	0.0	0.1	0.3
Digestive	0.3	0.6	0.2	0.2	0.3
Chronic liver disease/cirrhosis	0.2	0.5	0.1	0.0	0.1
Ulcers stomach/duodenum	0.0	0.0	0.0	0.0	0.0
Senile and ill-defined	0.1	0.4	0.2	0.1	0.0
III. Injuries	1.5	1.4	0.8	1.1	0.8
Unintentional	0.7	0.7	0.7	0.7	0.4
Transport	0.3	0.5	0.4	0.4	0.2
Motor vehicle transport	0.3	0.4	0.4	0.4	0.2
Water transport	0.0	0.0	0.0	0.0	0.0
Poisoning	0.2	0.0	0.0	0.2	0.0
Falls	0.1	0.0	0.1	0.1	0.0
Fires	0.0	0.0	0.0	0.0	0.1
Drowning	0.0	0.0	0.0	0.0	0.0
Intentional	0.7	0.6	0.1	0.5	0.3
Suicide	0.6	0.6	0.1	0.5	0.3
Homicide	0.1	0.0	0.0	0.0	0.0
War	0.0	0.0	0.0	0.0	0.0
Undetermined	0.1	0.1	0.0	0.0	0.1
Total	7.1	7.3	6.0	7.3	8.8

(Next table section begins on the following page.)

Table A-3a (continued)—***Industrialized Market***

Cause	*Italy*	*Japan*	*Luxembourg*	*Malta*	*Netherlands*
I. Communicable and reproductive	0.1	0.2	0.3	0.3	0.1
Diarrhea	0.0	0.0	0.0	0.1	0.0
Tuberculosis	0.0	0.0	0.0	0.0	0.0
Malaria	0.0	0.0	0.0	0.0	0.0
Venereal diseases	0.0	0.0	0.0	0.0	0.0
Helminths	0.0	0.0	0.0	0.0	0.0
Respiratory infections	0.1	0.1	0.1	0.3	0.0
Maternal	0.0	0.0	0.0	0.0	0.0
II. Noncommunicable	5.9	4.6	7.1	6.1	6.3
Neoplasms	3.2	2.5	3.7	2.8	3.6
Esophagus	0.0	0.0	0.0	0.0	0.0
Stomach	0.2	0.6	0.1	0.1	0.1
Colon/rectum	0.2	0.3	0.4	0.2	0.3
Liver	0.0	0.1	0.0	0.0	0.0
Lung	0.2	0.2	0.3	0.0	0.4
Breast	0.9	0.3	1.2	0.8	1.2
Cervix	0.0	0.1	0.3	0.1	0.1
Lymphatic/hematopoietic	0.3	0.2	0.1	0.3	0.2
Lip, oral cavity, pharynx	0.0	0.0	0.0	0.1	0.0
Endocrine	0.2	0.1	0.1	0.2	0.2
Diabetes mellitus	0.2	0.1	0.0	0.2	0.1
Cardiovascular	1.4	1.3	1.9	2.0	1.5
Hypertensive disease	0.1	0.0	0.0	0.1	0.0
Ischemic heart disease	0.4	0.1	0.6	0.8	0.7

Cerebrovascular	0.5	0.6	0.6	0.4	0.4
Atherosclerosis	0.0	0.0	0.0	0.0	0.0
Respiratory	0.1	0.1	0.1	0.0	0.1
COPD	0.1	0.1	0.1	0.0	0.1
Digestive	0.5	0.2	0.9	0.4	0.2
Chronic liver disease/cirrhosis	0.4	0.1	0.7	0.2	0.1
Ulcers stomach/duodenum	0.0	0.0	0.0	0.0	0.0
Senile and ill-defined	0.1	0.0	0.0	0.1	0.3
III. Injuries	0.7	0.9	1.5	0.2	0.8
Unintentional	0.5	0.3	0.5	0.1	0.3
Transport	0.3	0.2	0.4	0.0	0.2
Motor vehicle transport	0.3	0.2	0.4	0.0	0.2
Water transport	0.0	0.0	0.0	0.0	0.0
Poisoning	0.0	0.0	0.0	0.0	0.0
Falls	0.1	0.0	0.0	0.0	0.0
Fires	0.0	0.0	0.0	0.0	0.0
Drowning	0.0	0.0	0.0	0.0	0.0
Intentional	0.2	0.6	0.8	0.0	0.5
Suicide	0.2	0.5	0.7	0.0	0.4
Homicide	0.0	0.0	0.0	0.0	0.0
War	0.0	0.0	0.0	0.0	0.0
Undetermined	0.0	0.0	0.2	0.0	0.0
Total	6.7	5.6	8.9	6.5	7.2

(Next table section begins on the following page.)

*Table A-3a (continued)—**Industrialized Market***

Cause	*New Zealand*	*Northern Ireland*	*Norway*	*Portugal*	*Scotland*
I. Communicable and reproductive	0.2	0.3	0.1	0.2	0.3
Diarrhea	0.0	0.0	0.0	0.0	0.0
Tuberculosis	0.0	0.0	0.0	0.0	0.0
Malaria	0.0	0.0	0.0	0.0	0.0
Venereal diseases	0.0	0.0	0.0	0.0	0.0
Helminths	0.0	0.0	0.0	0.0	0.0
Respiratory infections	0.1	0.2	0.1	0.1	0.2
Maternal	0.0	0.0	0.0	0.0	0.0
II. Noncommunicable	7.9	7.7	5.9	6.8	8.7
Neoplasms	4.0	4.2	3.4	2.9	4.3
Esophagus	0.0	0.1	0.0	0.0	0.1
Stomach	0.1	0.1	0.1	0.4	0.1
Colon/rectum	0.6	0.4	0.3	0.2	0.4
Liver	0.0	0.0	0.0	0.0	0.0
Lung	0.4	0.5	0.3	0.1	0.8
Breast	1.2	1.3	0.8	0.9	1.2
Cervix	0.2	0.2	0.2	0.1	0.2
Lymphatic/hematopoietic	0.3	0.3	0.2	0.2	0.3
Lip, oral cavity, pharynx	0.0	0.0	0.0	0.0	0.0
Endocrine	0.3	0.1	0.1	0.2	0.2
Diabetes mellitus	0.2	0.0	0.1	0.1	0.1
Cardiovascular	2.3	2.3	1.3	1.8	2.8
Hypertensive disease	0.1	0.1	0.0	0.0	0.0
Ischemic heart disease	1.2	1.2	0.7	0.4	1.6

Cerebrovascular	0.6	0.6	0.3	0.8	0.7
Atherosclerosis	0.0	0.0	0.0	0.0	0.0
Respiratory	0.7	0.3	0.2	0.2	0.4
COPD	0.6	0.3	0.2	0.1	0.3
Digestive	0.2	0.3	0.3	0.7	0.5
Chronic liver disease/cirrhosis	0.1	0.2	0.2	0.6	0.2
Ulcers stomach/duodenum	0.0	0.0	0.0	0.0	0.0
Senile and ill-defined	0.0	0.0	0.1	0.6	0.0
III. Injuries	1.3	1.0	0.9	1.1	0.9
Unintentional	0.8	0.7	0.4	0.6	0.4
Transport	0.6	0.3	0.2	0.4	0.2
Motor vehicle transport	0.6	0.3	0.2	0.4	0.2
Water transport	0.0	0.0	0.0	0.0	0.0
Poisoning	0.0	0.1	0.0	0.0	0.0
Falls	0.0	0.1	0.0	0.1	0.1
Fires	0.0	0.1	0.0	0.0	0.1
Drowning	0.0	0.0	0.0	0.0	0.0
Intentional	0.4	0.3	0.5	0.2	0.4
Suicide	0.4	0.2	0.5	0.2	0.3
Homicide	0.1	0.1	0.1	0.0	0.1
War	0.0	0.0	0.0	0.0	0.0
Undetermined	0.1	0.1	0.0	0.2	0.1
Total	9.4	9.1	6.9	8.1	9.9

(Next table section begins on the following page.)

*Table A-3a (continued)—**Industrialized Market***

Cause	Spain	Sweden	Switzerland	United States	West Germany
I. Communicable and reproductive	0.2	0.2	0.1	0.3	0.1
Diarrhea	0.0	0.0	0.0	0.0	0.0
Tuberculosis	0.0	0.0	0.0	0.0	0.0
Malaria	0.0	0.0	0.0	0.0	0.0
Venereal diseases	0.0	0.0	0.0	0.0	0.0
Helminths	0.0	0.0	0.0	0.0	0.0
Respiratory infections	0.1	0.1	0.0	0.1	0.0
Maternal	0.0	0.0	0.0	0.0	0.0
II. Noncommunicable	5.3	5.4	4.2	7.8	6.4
Neoplasms	2.7	3.2	2.6	3.7	3.4
Esophagus	0.0	0.0	0.0	0.0	0.0
Stomach	0.2	0.1	0.1	0.1	0.2
Colon/rectum	0.2	0.3	0.2	0.3	0.3
Liver	0.0	0.0	0.0	0.0	0.0
Lung	0.1	0.3	0.2	0.7	0.2
Breast	0.8	0.8	0.8	1.0	1.0
Cervix	0.1	0.2	0.1	0.2	0.2
Lymphatic/hematopoietic	0.2	0.3	0.2	0.3	0.2
Lip, oral cavity, pharynx	0.0	0.0	0.0	0.0	0.0
Endocrine	0.2	0.1	0.1	0.3	0.1
Diabetes mellitus	0.1	0.1	0.1	0.2	0.1
Cardiovascular	1.4	1.1	0.7	2.3	1.4
Hypertensive disease	0.0	0.0	0.1	0.1	0.1
Ischemic heart disease	0.3	0.4	0.2	1.0	0.5

Cerebrovascular	0.4	0.3	0.2	0.4	0.3
Atherosclerosis	0.0	0.0	0.0	0.0	0.0
Respiratory	0.2	0.2	0.1	0.3	0.2
COPD	0.1	0.1	0.1	0.2	0.1
Digestive	0.5	0.2	0.3	0.5	0.6
Chronic liver disease/cirrhosis	0.3	0.1	0.2	0.3	0.4
Ulcers stomach/duodenum	0.0	0.0	0.0	0.0	0.0
Senile and ill-defined	0.1	0.0	0.2	0.2	0.2
III. Injuries	0.7	1.2	1.1	1.3	0.9
Unintentional	0.5	0.4	0.5	0.8	0.4
Transport	0.3	0.3	0.3	0.5	0.3
Motor vehicle transport	0.3	0.2	0.2	0.5	0.3
Water transport	0.0	0.0	0.0	0.0	0.0
Poisoning	0.0	0.0	0.0	0.1	0.0
Falls	0.0	0.0	0.1	0.0	0.0
Fires	0.0	0.0	0.0	0.0	0.0
Drowning	0.0	0.0	0.0	0.0	0.0
Intentional	0.2	0.6	0.5	0.5	0.5
Suicide	0.1	0.5	0.5	0.3	0.5
Homicide	0.0	0.1	0.1	0.2	0.1
War	0.0	0.0	0.0	0.0	0.0
Undetermined	0.0	0.2	0.1	0.0	0.0
Total	6.1	6.7	5.4	9.4	7.5

(Next table section begins on the following page.)

*Table A-3a (continued)—**Industrialized Nonmarket***

Cause	*Bulgaria*	*Czecho-slovakia*	*Hungary*	*Poland*	*Romania*	*Yugoslavia*
I. Communicable and reproductive	0.5	0.3	0.2	0.3	0.7	0.3
Diarrhea	0.0	0.0	0.0	0.0	0.0	0.0
Tuberculosis	0.0	0.0	0.0	0.0	0.1	0.1
Malaria	0.0	0.0	0.0	0.0	0.0	0.0
Venereal diseases	0.0	0.0	0.0	0.0	0.0	0.0
Helminths	0.0	0.0	0.0	0.0	0.0	0.0
Respiratory infections	0.3	0.2	0.1	0.1	0.3	0.1
Maternal	0.0	0.0	0.0	0.0	0.3	0.0
II. Noncommunicable	8.0	8.7	10.8	9.1	9.5	8.5
Neoplasms	3.2	4.0	4.3	3.9	3.4	3.2
Esophagus	0.0	0.0	0.0	0.0	0.0	0.0
Stomach	0.3	0.2	0.2	0.2	0.2	0.2
Colon/rectum	0.3	0.4	0.4	0.3	0.2	0.3
Liver	0.1	0.0	0.1	0.1	0.0	0.0
Lung	0.2	0.3	0.5	0.3	0.2	0.3
Breast	0.7	0.8	1.0	0.7	0.7	0.8
Cervix	0.2	0.3	0.4	0.4	0.5	0.2
Lymphatic/hematopoietic	0.2	0.3	0.3	0.2	0.2	0.2
Lip, oral cavity, pharynx	0.0	0.0	0.1	0.0	0.0	0.0
Endocrine	0.2	0.2	0.2	0.3	0.2	0.2
Diabetes mellitus	0.2	0.2	0.2	0.2	0.1	0.2
Cardiovascular	3.4	2.9	3.9	3.3	3.9	3.1
Hypertensive disease	0.2	0.1	0.2	0.3	0.6	0.2
Ischemic heart disease	0.7	1.2	1.4	0.9	0.9	0.8

Cerebrovascular	1.3	0.9	1.3	0.7	1.3	1.0
Atherosclerosis	0.1	0.1	0.1	0.3	0.1	0.0
Respiratory	0.1	0.2	0.3	0.2	0.4	0.2
COPD	0.1	0.2	0.2	0.2	0.3	0.1
Digestive	0.4	0.6	1.3	0.4	0.9	0.6
Chronic liver disease/cirrhosis	0.2	0.3	1.0	0.1	0.7	0.4
Ulcers stomach/duodenum	0.0	0.0	0.1	0.1	0.0	0.0
Senile and ill-defined	0.2	0.0	0.0	0.4	0.0	0.7
III. Injuries	1.0	1.0	1.8	1.0	1.2	1.1
Unintentional	0.6	0.6	0.7	0.6	1.2	0.6
Transport	0.3	0.2	0.3	0.3	1.2	0.3
Motor vehicle transport	0.3	0.2	0.3	0.2	0.0	0.3
Water transport	0.0	0.0	0.0	0.0	0.0	0.0
Poisoning	0.0	0.1	0.1	0.1	0.0	0.0
Falls	0.1	0.1	0.1	0.1	0.0	0.0
Fires	0.0	0.0	0.0	0.0	0.0	0.0
Drowning	0.0	0.0	0.0	0.0	0.0	0.0
Intentional	0.3	0.5	1.1	0.3	0.0	0.5
Suicide	0.3	0.4	1.0	0.3	0.0	0.4
Homicide	0.0	0.0	0.1	0.1	0.0	0.1
War	0.0	0.0	0.0	0.0	0.0	0.0
Undetermined	0.0	0.0	0.0	0.1	0.0	0.0
Total	9.5	10.1	12.8	10.4	11.5	9.8

Source: Authors' calculations.

*Table A-3b. Cause-Specific 45Q15 for Men in Countries with Complete Recent Vital Registration Data Classified According to Cause of Death—**Asia***

Cause	*Hong Kong*	*Singapore*	*Sri Lanka*
I. Communicable and reproductive	0.8	1.0	2.3
Diarrhea	0.0	0.0	0.7
Tuberculosis	0.2	0.3	0.6
Malaria	0.0	0.0	0.0
Venereal diseases	0.0	0.0	0.0
Helminths	0.0	0.0	0.0
Respiratory infections	0.4	0.5	0.4
II. Noncommunicable	10.1	13.1	13.9
Neoplasms	5.4	4.9	1.4
Esophagus	0.4	0.1	0.1
Stomach	0.3	0.5	0.1
Colon/rectum	0.3	0.4	0.0
Liver	1.2	0.2	0.0
Lung	1.3	1.4	0.1
Breast	0.0	0.0	0.0
Cervix	0.0	0.0	0.0
Lymphatic/hematopoietic	0.3	0.4	0.1
Lip, oral cavity, pharynx	0.8	0.8	0.2
Endocrine	0.1	0.4	0.3
Diabetes mellitus	0.1	0.4	0.3
Cardiovascular	2.4	5.7	5.0
Hypertensive disease	0.2	0.3	0.4
Ischemic heart disease	0.8	3.5	1.3

Cerebrovascular	0.9	1.2	0.6
Atherosclerosis	0.0	0.0	0.0
Respiratory	0.8	0.6	0.7
COPD	0.6	0.5	0.5
Digestive	0.8	0.7	1.1
Chronic liver disease/cirrhosis	0.4	0.5	0.4
Ulcers stomach/duodenum	0.1	0.1	0.0
Senile and ill-defined	0.1	0.1	3.4
III. Injuries	1.6	2.2	6.8
Unintentional	0.8	1.0	2.6
Transport	0.3	0.6	0.8
Motor vehicle transport	0.3	0.6	0.6
Water transport	0.0	0.0	0.0
Poisoning	0.0	0.0	0.2
Falls	0.2	0.1	0.3
Fires	0.0	0.0	0.0
Drowning	0.1	0.0	0.3
Intentional	0.6	0.7	3.5
Suicide	0.6	0.6	2.8
Homicide	0.1	0.1	0.7
War	0.0	0.0	0.0
Undetermined	0.1	0.4	0.6
Total	12.5	16.3	22.9

(Next table section begins on the following page.)

Table A-3b (continued)—**Latin America/Caribbean**

Cause	*Argentina*	*Bahamas*	*Barbados*	*Chile*	*Costa Rica*	*Cuba*
I. Communicable and reproductive	1.0	2.6	0.5	1.6	0.5	0.4
Diarrhea	0.0	0.0	0.0	0.0	0.0	0.0
Tuberculosis	0.3	0.6	0.0	0.5	0.2	0.0
Malaria	0.0	0.0	0.0	0.0	0.0	0.0
Venereal diseases	0.0	0.0	0.0	0.0	0.0	0.0
Helminths	0.0	0.0	0.0	0.0	0.0	0.0
Respiratory infections	0.2	1.4	0.4	0.8	0.1	0.3
II. Noncommunicable	15.6	15.3	9.8	11.8	9.0	9.8
Neoplasms	4.2	4.7	2.1	3.2	3.2	2.8
Esophagus	0.2	0.4	0.1	0.1	0.0	0.1
Stomach	0.3	0.9	0.2	0.8	0.9	0.2
Colon/rectum	0.3	0.3	0.0	0.1	0.1	0.2
Liver	0.1	0.0	0.1	0.1	0.1	0.0
Lung	1.3	0.8	0.5	0.5	0.3	0.9
Breast	0.0	0.0	0.0	0.0	0.0	0.0
Cervix	0.0	0.0	0.0	0.0	0.0	0.0
Lymphatic/hematopoietic	0.3	0.3	0.4	0.3	0.5	0.4
Lip, oral cavity, pharynx	0.2	0.3	0.4	0.1	0.1	0.1
Endocrine	0.3	1.3	1.0	0.3	0.4	0.3
Diabetes mellitus	0.3	0.8	0.7	0.3	0.3	0.3
Cardiovascular	7.3	4.9	4.7	3.1	2.8	4.9
Hypertensive disease	0.3	0.7	0.1	0.1	0.1	0.3
Ischemic heart disease	2.1	2.6	1.1	1.1	1.5	2.8

Cerebrovascular	1.7	0.9	1.7	1.1	0.5	1.2
Atherosclerosis	0.1	0.0	0.0	0.0	0.0	0.0
Respiratory	0.2	0.2	0.3	0.2	0.2	0.2
COPD	0.2	0.2	0.3	0.2	0.2	0.2
Digestive	1.5	2.2	0.2	3.1	1.1	0.6
Chronic liver disease/cirrhosis	0.7	1.7	0.1	2.6	0.8	0.2
Ulcers stomach/duodenum	0.0	0.0	0.0	0.1	0.1	0.1
Senile and ill-defined	0.7	0.5	0.3	0.8	0.1	0.1
III. Injuries	3.3	5.6	3.3	5.9	3.9	4.7
Unintentional	2.0	1.4	2.8	1.8	2.7	4.7
Transport	0.8	1.1	1.0	0.8	1.3	0.0
Motor vehicle transport	0.7	0.9	1.0	0.7	1.2	0.0
Water transport	0.0	0.0	0.0	0.0	0.0	0.0
Poisoning	0.0	0.0	0.1	0.0	0.2	0.0
Falls	0.1	0.1	0.2	0.2	0.3	0.0
Fires	0.1	0.1	0.0	0.1	0.0	0.0
Drowning	0.3	0.0	1.0	0.1	0.5	0.0
Intentional	1.0	1.6	0.4	0.8	1.1	0.0
Suicide	0.5	0.1	0.1	0.5	0.7	0.0
Homicide	0.5	1.5	0.3	0.3	0.4	0.0
War	0.0	0.1	0.0	0.0	0.0	0.0
Undetermined	0.3	2.6	0.0	3.2	0.1	0.0
Total	19.8	23.5	13.6	19.3	13.4	15.0

(Next table section begins on the following page.)

Table A-3b (continued)—***Latin America/Caribbean***

Cause	*Guyana*	*Martinique*	*Mexico*	*Panama*	*Puerto Rico*
I. Communicable and reproductive	1.5	0.7	2.2	1.1	1.1
Diarrhea	0.0	0.0	0.6	0.1	0.0
Tuberculosis	0.1	0.1	0.7	0.5	0.1
Malaria	0.0	0.0	0.0	0.0	0.0
Venereal diseases	0.0	0.0	0.0	0.0	0.0
Helminths	0.1	0.0	0.0	0.0	0.0
Respiratory infections	0.4	0.4	0.6	0.4	0.8
II. Noncommunicable	18.6	12.0	14.4	7.8	13.6
Neoplasms	1.3	3.2	1.6	2.0	3.0
Esophagus	0.0	0.3	0.0	0.0	0.3
Stomach	0.3	0.2	0.2	0.3	0.2
Colon/rectum	0.1	0.1	0.1	0.1	0.2
Liver	0.0	0.1	0.0	0.0	0.0
Lung	0.1	0.4	0.3	0.4	0.4
Breast	0.0	0.0	0.0	0.0	0.0
Cervix	0.0	0.0	0.0	0.0	0.0
Lymphatic/hematopoietic	0.2	0.1	0.2	0.2	0.4
Lip, oral cavity, pharynx	0.0	0.0	0.0	0.0	0.3
Endocrine	1.0	0.3	1.4	0.4	1.0
Diabetes mellitus	0.9	0.2	1.2	0.3	0.6
Cardiovascular	8.8	3.6	3.5	2.9	4.8
Hypertensive disease	0.6	0.3	0.1	0.3	0.7
Ischemic heart disease	2.4	0.1	1.3	1.2	2.2

Cerebrovascular	3.4	1.6	0.7	0.8	0.6
Atherosclerosis	0.0	0.1	0.0	0.0	0.1
Respiratory	0.1	0.1	0.2	0.2	0.2
COPD	0.1	0.1	0.2	0.2	0.2
Digestive	4.3	1.1	4.4	0.7	2.7
Chronic liver disease/cirrhosis	1.7	0.8	3.2	0.3	1.9
Ulcers stomach/duodenum	0.5	0.1	0.2	0.1	0.1
Senile and ill-defined	1.4	1.6	0.8	0.6	0.1
III. Injuries	4.1	4.4	8.8	4.4	5.8
Unintentional	2.0	2.3	6.1	3.0	2.6
Transport	0.9	1.7	2.1	1.8	1.6
Motor vehicle transport	0.0	1.7	2.0	1.6	1.5
Water transport	0.0	0.0	0.0	0.0	0.0
Poisoning	0.5	0.1	0.1	0.0	0.1
Falls	0.2	0.2	0.5	0.2	0.2
Fires	0.0	0.0	0.1	0.0	0.0
Drowning	0.0	0.1	0.5	0.5	0.3
Intentional	1.0	0.6	2.6	1.0	2.9
Suicide	0.1	0.2	0.2	0.4	0.8
Homicide	0.0	0.4	2.4	0.6	2.1
War	0.9	0.0	0.0	0.0	0.0
Undetermined	1.0	1.5	0.1	0.4	0.4
Total	24.2	17.1	25.3	13.4	20.6

(Next table section begins on the following page.)

Table A-3b (continued)—***Latin America/Caribbean***

Cause	*St. Vincent*	*Suriname*	*Trinidad*	*Uruguay*	*Venezuela*
I. Communicable and reproductive	1.9	2.3	1.2	0.6	1.4
Diarrhea	0.8	0.3	0.0	0.0	0.1
Tuberculosis	0.4	0.3	0.1	0.1	0.3
Malaria	0.0	0.0	0.0	0.0	0.0
Venereal diseases	0.0	0.0	0.0	0.0	0.0
Helminths	0.0	0.1	0.0	0.0	0.0
Respiratory infections	0.4	1.1	0.6	0.2	0.3
II. Noncommunicable	15.4	20.1	16.1	14.5	11.8
Neoplasms	3.8	1.9	1.9	5.0	2.4
Esophagus	0.0	0.0	0.1	0.2	0.1
Stomach	0.4	0.2	0.2	0.4	0.5
Colon/rectum	0.0	0.3	0.2	0.3	0.1
Liver	0.4	0.3	0.0	0.0	0.1
Lung	1.2	0.1	0.4	1.6	0.4
Breast	0.0	0.0	0.0	0.0	0.0
Cervix	0.0	0.0	0.0	0.0	0.0
Lymphatic/hematopoietic	0.6	0.3	0.3	0.4	0.3
Lip, oral cavity, pharynx	0.0	0.0	0.1	0.3	0.0
Endocrine	0.3	1.1	2.3	0.3	0.7
Diabetes mellitus	0.3	1.0	2.2	0.3	0.6
Cardiovascular	5.3	9.3	7.2	4.9	5.5
Hypertensive disease	1.1	0.6	0.6	0.2	0.4
Ischemic heart disease	2.3	5.3	4.0	2.0	3.0

Cerebrovascular	0.2	1.5	1.9	1.4	1.0
Atherosclerosis	0.0	0.0	0.0	0.1	0.0
Respiratory	0.5	0.6	0.4	0.2	0.2
COPD	0.5	0.6	0.4	0.2	0.2
Digestive	2.5	2.6	2.1	0.9	1.4
Chronic liver disease/cirrhosis	0.4	1.5	1.1	0.5	0.8
Ulcers stomach/duodenum	0.0	0.3	0.1	0.0	0.1
Senile and ill-defined	0.7	1.9	0.4	1.7	0.4
III. Injuries	4.9	9.1	4.8	3.3	6.8
Unintentional	1.5	4.7	3.3	2.5	4.7
Transport	0.6	2.1	1.4	0.7	3.0
Motor vehicle transport	0.6	2.1	1.4	0.7	2.9
Water transport	0.0	0.0	0.0	0.0	0.0
Poisoning	0.0	0.0	0.0	0.0	0.1
Falls	0.4	0.2	0.3	0.1	0.3
Fires	0.0	0.1	0.2	0.0	0.0
Drowning	0.4	1.1	0.6	0.4	0.4
Intentional	1.1	3.7	1.3	0.8	2.1
Suicide	0.0	3.0	0.8	0.5	0.5
Homicide	1.1	0.7	0.5	0.3	1.6
War	0.0	0.0	0.0	0.0	0.0
Undetermined	2.4	0.6	0.2	0.0	0.0
Total	22.2	31.5	22.1	18.3	20.0

(Next table section begins on the following page.)

Table A-3b (continued)—***Middle East/North Africa***

Cause	*Bahrain*	*Israel*	*Kuwait*	*Mauritius*	*Seychelles*
I. Communicable and reproductive	0.4	0.3	0.5	1.4	4.9
Diarrhea	0.0	0.0	0.0	0.1	0.0
Tuberculosis	0.0	0.0	0.1	0.1	0.0
Malaria	0.0	0.0	0.0	0.0	0.0
Venereal diseases	0.0	0.0	0.0	0.0	0.0
Helminths	0.0	0.0	0.0	0.0	0.0
Respiratory infections	0.3	0.2	0.3	0.7	2.1
II. Noncommunicable	12.4	10.5	8.9	21.7	20.9
Neoplasms	1.9	2.8	1.9	2.0	2.4
Esophagus	0.0	0.0	0.1	0.0	0.9
Stomach	0.1	0.2	0.1	0.2	0.0
Colon/rectum	0.0	0.2	0.1	0.1	0.0
Liver	0.1	0.0	0.0	0.0	0.0
Lung	0.7	0.7	0.4	0.4	0.4
Breast	0.0	0.0	0.0	0.0	0.0
Cervix	0.0	0.0	0.0	0.0	0.0
Lymphatic/hematopoietic	0.1	0.5	0.4	0.2	0.0
Lip, oral cavity, pharynx	0.0	0.0	0.1	0.1	0.2
Endocrine	0.6	0.2	0.2	1.7	0.0
Diabetes mellitus	0.5	0.2	0.2	1.6	0.0
Cardiovascular	7.0	4.5	5.6	10.8	12.7
Hypertensive disease	0.5	0.1	0.9	0.8	2.1
Ischemic heart disease	4.8	2.9	3.5	5.2	3.8

Cerebrovascular	0.2	0.5	0.3	2.7	3.3
Atherosclerosis	0.0	0.0	0.4	0.0	1.3
Respiratory	0.3	0.4	0.3	1.0	1.6
COPD	0.2	0.3	0.1	0.6	1.6
Digestive	0.5	0.6	0.5	3.0	2.6
Chronic liver disease/cirrhosis	0.2	0.4	0.2	1.6	0.7
Ulcers stomach/duodenum	0.0	0.0	0.0	0.4	0.8
Senile and ill-defined	1.8	1.1	0.1	0.6	0.6
III. Injuries	1.6	2.2	2.3	3.7	7.5
Unintentional	0.8	1.4	2.1	2.3	3.7
Transport	0.6	0.7	1.4	1.0	0.7
Motor vehicle transport	0.6	0.7	1.4	1.0	0.3
Water transport	0.0	0.0	0.0	0.0	0.0
Poisoning	0.0	0.0	0.0	0.0	0.0
Falls	0.0	0.1	0.1	0.2	0.0
Fires	0.0	0.0	0.0	0.3	0.0
Drowning	0.2	0.1	0.1	0.4	2.5
Intentional	0.8	0.7	0.1	1.4	1.8
Suicide	0.2	0.5	0.1	1.2	0.9
Homicide	0.0	0.2	0.0	0.2	0.9
War	0.0	0.0	0.0	0.0	0.0
Undetermined	0.0	0.1	0.1	0.1	2.0
Total	14.4	13.0	11.7	26.8	33.3

(Next table section begins on the following page.)

Table A-3b (continued)—***Industrialized Market***

Cause	*Australia*	*Austria*	*Belgium*	*Canada*	*Denmark*	*England*
I. Communicable and reproductive	0.2	0.3	0.3	0.2	0.3	0.2
Diarrhea	0.0	0.0	0.0	0.0	0.0	0.0
Tuberculosis	0.0	0.1	0.0	0.0	0.0	0.0
Malaria	0.0	0.0	0.0	0.0	0.0	0.0
Venereal diseases	0.0	0.0	0.0	0.0	0.0	0.0
Helminths	0.0	0.0	0.0	0.0	0.0	0.0
Respiratory infections	0.1	0.2	0.2	0.1	0.1	0.1
II. Noncommunicable	10.2	11.8	11.4	10.5	11.7	11.1
Neoplasms	3.6	4.2	4.4	3.9	4.0	3.8
Esophagus	0.1	0.1	0.2	0.1	0.1	0.2
Stomach	0.2	0.3	0.2	0.2	0.2	0.3
Colon/rectum	0.5	0.4	0.3	0.4	0.4	0.4
Liver	0.0	0.1	0.0	0.0	0.0	0.0
Lung	0.9	1.1	1.8	1.3	1.2	1.1
Breast	0.0	0.0	0.0	0.0	0.0	0.0
Cervix	0.0	0.0	0.0	0.0	0.0	0.0
Lymphatic/hematopoietic	0.4	0.3	0.3	0.4	0.4	0.4
Lip, oral cavity, pharynx	0.2	0.3	0.1	0.2	0.1	0.1
Endocrine	0.3	0.3	0.2	0.4	0.4	0.3
Diabetes mellitus	0.2	0.2	0.1	0.2	0.3	0.1
Cardiovascular	4.5	4.7	4.1	4.4	4.5	5.6
Hypertensive disease	0.0	0.2	0.1	0.0	0.1	0.1
Ischemic heart disease	3.3	2.7	2.3	3.2	3.2	4.4

Cerebrovascular	0.5	0.7	0.5	0.4	0.6	0.6
Atherosclerosis	0.0	0.0	0.2	0.0	0.2	0.0
Respiratory	0.4	0.3	0.6	0.3	0.4	0.4
COPD	0.4	0.2	0.4	0.2	0.3	0.4
Digestive	0.7	1.8	0.8	0.7	1.0	0.4
Chronic liver disease/cirrhosis	0.5	1.4	0.6	0.5	0.8	0.2
Ulcers stomach/duodenum	0.1	0.1	0.0	0.0	0.1	0.1
Senile and ill-defined	0.1	0.0	0.7	0.2	0.7	0.0
III. Injuries	3.3	4.7	3.9	3.6	3.8	2.0
Unintentional	2.1	2.7	2.3	2.1	1.7	1.1
Transport	1.5	1.6	1.6	1.3	1.0	0.7
Motor vehicle transport	1.3	1.4	1.6	1.1	0.9	0.6
Water transport	0.0	0.0	0.0	0.1	0.0	0.0
Poisoning	0.1	0.1	0.1	0.1	0.2	0.1
Falls	0.1	0.4	0.2	0.1	0.2	0.1
Fires	0.0	0.0	0.0	0.1	0.0	0.0
Drowning	0.1	0.1	0.1	0.1	0.0	0.0
Intentional	1.2	1.9	1.5	1.4	1.8	0.6
Suicide	1.0	1.9	1.3	1.2	1.7	0.6
Homicide	0.1	0.1	0.1	0.1	0.1	0.0
War	0.0	0.0	0.0	0.0	0.0	0.0
Undetermined	0.0	0.1	0.1	0.1	0.3	0.3
Total	13.7	16.8	15.5	14.3	15.8	13.3

(Next table section begins on the following page.)

*Table A-3b (continued)—**Industrialized Market***

Cause	*Finland*	*France*	*Greece*	*Iceland*	*Ireland*
I. Communicable and reproductive	0.4	0.3	0.2	0.1	0.4
Diarrhea	0.0	0.0	0.0	0.0	0.0
Tuberculosis	0.0	0.0	0.0	0.0	0.0
Malaria	0.0	0.0	0.0	0.0	0.0
Venereal diseases	0.0	0.0	0.0	0.0	0.0
Helminths	0.0	0.0	0.0	0.0	0.0
Respiratory infections	0.2	0.1	0.1	0.0	0.3
II. Noncommunicable	12.8	12.9	9.1	8.5	11.9
Neoplasms	3.1	5.7	3.5	3.0	3.9
Esophagus	0.0	0.5	0.0	0.0	0.2
Stomach	0.3	0.2	0.3	0.5	0.3
Colon/rectum	0.2	0.3	0.1	0.1	0.5
Liver	0.0	0.1	0.0	0.0	0.0
Lung	0.9	1.4	1.2	0.8	1.1
Breast	0.0	0.0	0.0	0.0	0.0
Cervix	0.0	0.0	0.0	0.0	0.0
Lymphatic/hematopoietic	0.4	0.4	0.3	0.3	0.4
Lip, oral cavity, pharynx	0.1	0.7	0.1	0.0	0.1
Endocrine	0.2	0.3	0.1	0.2	0.2
Diabetes mellitus	0.2	0.1	0.1	0.2	0.1
Cardiovascular	7.3	3.1	4.1	4.9	6.1
Hypertensive disease	0.1	0.1	0.0	0.1	0.1
Ischemic heart disease	5.1	1.4	2.2	3.4	4.7

Cerebrovascular	1.0	0.6	0.7	0.9	0.6
Atherosclerosis	0.2	0.0	0.0	0.0	0.0
Respiratory	0.3	0.3	0.3	0.0	0.6
COPD	0.3	0.2	0.1	0.0	0.5
Digestive	0.8	1.4	0.6	0.0	0.4
Chronic liver disease/cirrhosis	0.5	1.0	0.4	0.0	0.1
Ulcers stomach/duodenum	0.1	0.0	0.0	0.0	0.1
Senile and ill-defined	0.1	1.0	0.3	0.0	0.0
III. Injuries	5.8	4.4	2.7	3.5	2.6
Unintentional	2.9	2.6	2.4	2.5	1.7
Transport	1.1	1.5	1.5	1.4	1.0
Motor vehicle transport	0.8	1.4	1.5	0.7	0.9
Water transport	0.0	0.0	0.0	0.5	0.1
Poisoning	0.8	0.0	0.0	0.5	0.1
Falls	0.3	0.2	0.1	0.3	0.1
Fires	0.1	0.0	0.0	0.2	0.1
Drowning	0.2	0.1	0.2	0.0	0.2
Intentional	2.6	1.6	0.3	1.0	0.8
Suicide	2.3	1.5	0.3	0.9	0.7
Homicide	0.3	0.1	0.1	0.1	0.1
War	0.0	0.0	0.0	0.0	0.0
Undetermined	0.3	0.2	0.0	0.1	0.2
Total	19.0	17.6	12.0	12.1	14.9

(Next table section begins on the following page.)

Table A-3b (continued)—***Industrialized Market***

Cause	*Italy*	*Japan*	*Luxembourg*	*Malta*	*Netherlands*
I. Communicable and reproductive	0.2	0.4	0.1	0.2	0.1
Diarrhea	0.0	0.0	0.0	0.0	0.0
Tuberculosis	0.0	0.1	0.0	0.0	0.0
Malaria	0.0	0.0	0.0	0.0	0.0
Venereal diseases	0.0	0.0	0.0	0.0	0.0
Helminths	0.0	0.0	0.0	0.0	0.0
Respiratory infections	0.1	0.2	0.1	0.1	0.1
II. Noncommunicable	11.7	8.3	13.4	10.7	10.8
Neoplasms	5.0	3.8	5.2	3.5	4.1
Esophagus	0.2	0.2	0.1	0.0	0.1
Stomach	0.4	0.9	0.3	0.3	0.2
Colon/rectum	0.3	0.4	0.5	0.1	0.4
Liver	0.1	0.6	0.2	0.0	0.0
Lung	1.7	0.5	1.8	1.2	1.5
Breast	0.0	0.0	0.0	0.0	0.0
Cervix	0.0	0.0	0.0	0.0	0.0
Lymphatic/hematopoietic	0.4	0.3	0.5	0.3	0.4
Lip, oral cavity, pharynx	0.3	0.1	0.3	0.2	0.0
Endocrine	0.2	0.2	0.1	0.1	0.3
Diabetes mellitus	0.2	0.1	0.1	0.1	0.2
Cardiovascular	3.9	2.8	5.1	6.1	4.4
Hypertensive disease	0.1	0.0	0.1	0.0	0.1
Ischemic heart disease	2.1	0.5	2.8	3.2	3.0

Cerebrovascular	0.8	1.1	1.0	1.1	0.5
Atherosclerosis	0.0	0.0	0.1	0.2	0.0
Respiratory	0.4	0.2	0.6	0.3	0.2
COPD	0.2	0.1	0.4	0.1	0.2
Digestive	1.5	1.0	1.3	0.3	0.4
Chronic liver disease/cirrhosis	1.2	0.7	1.1	0.1	0.3
Ulcers stomach/duodenum	0.1	0.0	0.1	0.0	0.0
Senile and ill-defined	0.2	0.1	0.4	0.1	0.8
III. Injuries	2.6	2.7	4.3	1.3	1.8
Unintentional	1.9	1.3	2.7	1.2	1.0
Transport	1.2	0.8	1.8	0.5	0.7
Motor vehicle transport	1.1	0.7	1.8	0.5	0.7
Water transport	0.0	0.0	0.0	0.0	0.0
Poisoning	0.0	0.0	0.0	0.1	0.0
Falls	0.2	0.1	0.4	0.3	0.1
Fires	0.0	0.0	0.0	0.1	0.0
Drowning	0.1	0.1	0.1	0.0	0.0
Intentional	0.6	1.3	1.4	0.0	0.7
Suicide	0.5	1.3	1.3	0.0	0.7
Homicide	0.1	0.0	0.1	0.0	0.1
War	0.0	0.0	0.0	0.0	0.0
Undetermined	0.1	0.1	0.3	0.2	0.0
Total	14.5	11.5	17.9	12.2	12.7

(Next table section begins on the following page.)

*Table A-3b (continued)—**Industrialized Market***

Cause	*New Zealand*	*Northern Ireland*	*Norway*	*Portugal*	*Scotland*
I. Communicable and reproductive	0.3	0.3	0.1	0.5	0.4
Diarrhea	0.0	0.0	0.0	0.0	0.0
Tuberculosis	0.0	0.0	0.0	0.2	0.0
Malaria	0.0	0.0	0.0	0.0	0.0
Venereal diseases	0.0	0.0	0.0	0.0	0.0
Helminths	0.0	0.0	0.0	0.0	0.0
Respiratory infections	0.1	0.2	0.1	0.2	0.3
II. Noncommunicable	11.4	12.0	10.5	12.4	13.7
Neoplasms	3.9	4.0	3.2	3.8	4.4
Esophagus	0.1	0.1	0.1	0.2	0.2
Stomach	0.2	0.3	0.2	0.6	0.3
Colon/rectum	0.7	0.4	0.3	0.3	0.4
Liver	0.1	0.0	0.0	0.0	0.0
Lung	0.9	1.3	0.8	0.7	1.5
Breast	0.0	0.0	0.0	0.0	0.0
Cervix	0.0	0.0	0.0	0.0	0.0
Lymphatic/hematopoietic	0.4	0.4	0.4	0.3	0.3
Lip, oral cavity, pharynx	0.1	0.1	0.1	0.2	0.1
Endocrine	0.4	0.1	0.3	0.3	0.3
Diabetes mellitus	0.2	0.1	0.2	0.2	0.2
Cardiovascular	5.7	6.4	4.9	3.6	7.0
Hypertensive disease	0.1	0.1	0.1	0.0	0.1
Ischemic heart disease	4.3	5.0	3.6	1.6	5.6

Cerebrovascular	0.5	0.7	0.6	1.2	0.8
Atherosclerosis	0.0	0.0	0.0	0.0	0.0
Respiratory	0.5	0.5	0.2	0.5	0.5
COPD	0.4	0.4	0.2	0.3	0.5
Digestive	0.4	0.5	0.6	1.9	0.7
Chronic liver disease/cirrhosis	0.2	0.2	0.4	1.5	0.4
Ulcers stomach/duodenum	0.0	0.1	0.0	0.1	0.1
Senile and ill-defined	0.0	0.0	0.5	1.6	0.0
III. Injuries	4.1	3.1	3.3	4.7	2.8
Unintentional	2.9	1.8	2.0	3.1	1.6
Transport	2.1	1.1	1.1	2.2	0.8
Motor vehicle transport	1.8	1.0	0.6	2.1	0.7
Water transport	0.2	0.0	0.3	0.0	0.0
Poisoning	0.1	0.2	0.1	0.0	0.1
Falls	0.1	0.2	0.2	0.4	0.2
Fires	0.1	0.1	0.1	0.0	0.1
Drowning	0.2	0.1	0.1	0.1	0.1
Intentional	1.2	1.1	1.3	0.7	1.0
Suicide	1.0	0.4	1.2	0.6	0.8
Homicide	0.2	0.7	0.1	0.1	0.2
War	0.0	0.0	0.0	0.0	0.0
Undetermined	0.1	0.1	0.0	0.8	0.3
Total	15.7	15.4	14.0	17.7	16.9

(Next table section begins on the following page.)

Table A-3b (continued)—***Industrialized Market***

Cause	*Spain*	*Sweden*	*Switzerland*	*United States*	*West Germany*
I. Communicable and reproductive	0.4	0.4	0.4	0.7	0.2
Diarrhea	0.0	0.0	0.0	0.0	0.0
Tuberculosis	0.1	0.0	0.0	0.0	0.0
Malaria	0.0	0.0	0.0	0.0	0.0
Venereal diseases	0.0	0.0	0.0	0.0	0.0
Helminths	0.0	0.0	0.0	0.0	0.0
Respiratory infections	0.2	0.3	0.1	0.2	0.1
II. Noncommunicable	10.9	8.8	8.7	12.6	12.3
Neoplasms	4.2	2.7	3.7	4.0	4.4
Esophagus	0.2	0.1	0.1	0.1	0.2
Stomach	0.4	0.2	0.2	0.1	0.3
Colon/rectum	0.2	0.3	0.3	0.3	0.4
Liver	0.1	0.0	0.0	0.0	0.1
Lung	1.1	0.5	1.1	1.4	1.2
Breast	0.0	0.0	0.0	0.0	0.0
Cervix	0.0	0.0	0.0	0.0	0.0
Lymphatic/hematopoietic	0.3	0.3	0.4	0.4	0.3
Lip, oral cavity, pharynx	0.2	0.1	0.3	0.1	0.3
Endocrine	0.2	0.2	0.2	0.6	0.3
Diabetes mellitus	0.2	0.2	0.1	0.2	0.1
Cardiovascular	3.7	4.2	3.1	5.5	4.4
Hypertensive disease	0.0	0.0	0.1	0.2	0.1
Ischemic heart disease	1.7	3.0	1.8	3.3	2.6

Cerebrovascular	0.8	0.5	0.3	0.5	0.6
Atherosclerosis	0.0	0.2	0.1	0.0	0.0
Respiratory	0.5	0.2	0.2	0.4	0.3
COPD	0.3	0.2	0.2	0.3	0.3
Digestive	1.5	0.5	0.6	0.9	1.3
Chronic liver disease/cirrhosis	1.1	0.4	0.5	0.6	1.0
Ulcers stomach/duodenum	0.0	0.0	0.0	0.0	0.1
Senile and ill-defined	0.3	0.1	0.3	0.3	0.6
III. Injuries	2.9	3.4	3.9	4.4	2.7
Unintentional	2.2	1.5	2.1	2.5	1.4
Transport	1.3	0.8	1.2	1.6	0.9
Motor vehicle transport	1.2	0.7	1.0	1.4	0.9
Water transport	0.0	0.0	0.0	0.0	0.0
Poisoning	0.0	0.2	0.1	0.2	0.0
Falls	0.1	0.2	0.3	0.1	0.2
Fires	0.0	0.1	0.0	0.1	0.0
Drowning	0.1	0.1	0.1	0.1	0.0
Intentional	0.5	1.5	1.7	1.8	1.2
Suicide	0.4	1.3	1.7	1.0	1.2
Homicide	0.1	0.1	0.1	0.8	0.1
War	0.0	0.0	0.0	0.0	0.0
Undetermined	0.2	0.5	0.2	0.1	0.1
Total	14.2	12.6	13.0	17.7	15.2

(Next table section begins on the following page.)

Table A-3b *(continued)*—**Industrialized Nonmarket**

Cause	*Bulgaria*	*Czecho-slovakia*	*Hungary*	*Poland*	*Romania*	*Yugoslavia*
I. Communicable and reproductive	1.0	0.6	0.5	0.6	1.2	0.5
Diarrhea	0.0	0.0	0.0	0.0	0.0	0.0
Tuberculosis	0.1	0.1	0.2	0.2	0.4	0.2
Malaria	0.0	0.0	0.0	0.0	0.0	0.0
Venereal diseases	0.0	0.0	0.0	0.0	0.0	0.0
Helminths	0.0	0.0	0.0	0.0	0.0	0.0
Respiratory infections	0.7	0.5	0.2	0.3	0.7	0.2
II. Noncommunicable	15.7	18.2	21.2	19.1	16.4	15.5
Neoplasms	4.6	6.3	6.6	5.7	4.3	4.6
Esophagus	0.1	0.1	0.3	0.2	0.1	0.1
Stomach	0.6	0.4	0.5	0.6	0.6	0.5
Colon/rectum	0.4	0.6	0.5	0.3	0.2	0.3
Liver	0.2	0.0	0.2	0.2	0.1	0.0
Lung	1.5	2.4	2.4	2.1	1.4	1.6
Breast	0.0	0.0	0.0	0.0	0.0	0.0
Cervix	0.0	0.0	0.0	0.0	0.0	0.0
Lymphatic/hematopoietic	0.3	0.4	0.4	0.3	0.3	0.3
Lip, oral cavity, pharynx	0.2	0.4	0.6	0.3	0.2	0.3
Endocrine	0.2	0.2	0.3	0.3	0.2	0.2
Diabetes mellitus	0.2	0.2	0.2	0.3	0.1	0.2
Cardiovascular	7.8	8.2	9.4	9.1	7.5	6.2
Hypertensive disease	0.4	0.2	0.3	0.4	0.7	0.2
Ischemic heart disease	3.2	5.0	5.3	4.5	2.9	2.8

Cerebrovascular	2.2	1.5	2.1	1.1	1.7	1.4
Atherosclerosis	0.2	0.3	0.3	0.9	0.2	0.1
Respiratory	0.5	0.6	0.7	0.5	1.1	0.4
COPD	0.3	0.5	0.6	0.4	0.8	0.3
Digestive	1.4	1.8	3.1	1.0	2.1	1.5
Chronic liver disease/cirrhosis	0.9	1.1	2.5	0.5	1.4	1.0
Ulcers stomach/duodenum	0.1	0.2	0.2	0.2	0.2	0.1
Senile and ill-defined	0.4	0.1	0.0	1.5	0.0	1.5
III. Injuries	4.1	4.2	6.3	5.3	4.8	4.0
Unintentional	3.0	2.5	3.1	3.4	4.8	2.6
Transport	1.1	1.0	1.4	1.5	4.8	1.3
Motor vehicle transport	0.9	0.7	1.1	1.1	0.0	1.2
Water transport	0.0	0.0	0.0	0.0	0.0	0.0
Poisoning	0.3	0.2	0.2	0.7	0.0	0.1
Falls	0.4	0.4	0.5	0.3	0.0	0.2
Fires	0.1	0.1	0.1	0.1	0.0	0.0
Drowning	0.3	0.2	0.3	0.2	0.0	0.2
Intentional	1.1	1.5	3.2	1.4	0.0	1.3
Suicide	0.9	1.4	3.1	1.3	0.0	1.1
Homicide	0.2	0.1	0.1	0.1	0.0	0.1
War	0.0	0.0	0.0	0.0	0.0	0.0
Undetermined	0.0	0.1	0.0	0.5	0.0	0.1
Total	20.7	23.0	28.1	25.0	22.4	20.0

Source: Authors' calculations.

Table A-4. Sample Distributions of the 1982 Census and the 1988 Disease Surveillance Points in China by Type of Area

	1982 census		*1988 DSP*	
Area	*Number*	*Percentage*	*Number*	*Percentage*
City	138,369,692	13.9	5,849,904	59.8
Large city	63,058,543	6.3	5,355,784	54.7
Middle city	41,745,767	4.2	221,739	2.3
Small city	33,565,382	3.4	272,381	2.8
Rural	859,433,218	86.1	3,934,986	40.2
The richest	215,100,808	21.6	1,806,661	18.5
The rich	323,833,424	32.5	1,484,904	15.2
The poor	288,691,715	28.9	643,421	6.5
The poorest	31,807,271	3.2		
Total	997,802,910	100.0	9,784,890	100.0

Source: Authors' calculations.